ARGUMENT AS DIALOGUE

A Concise Guide

GARY GOSHGARIAN
Northeastern University

KATHLEEN KRUEGER

Longman

Boston   Columbus   Indianapolis   New York   San Francisco   Upper Saddle River
Amsterdam   Cape Town   Dubai   London   Madrid   Milan   Munich   Paris   Montreal   Toronto
Delhi   Mexico City   Sao Paulo   Sydney   Hong Kong   Seoul   Singapore   Taipei   Tokyo

Executive Editor: Suzanne Phelps Chambers
Development Editor: Anne Leung
Senior Marketing Manager: Sandra McGuire
Production Manager: Stacey Kulig
Project Coordination, Text Design, and Electronic Page Makeup: PreMediaGlobal
Cover Design Manager: Wendy Ann Fredericks
Cover Designer: Nancy Sacks
Cover Image: © Exactostoc/SuperStock
Photo Researcher: Rebecca Karamehmedovic
Senior Manufacturing Buyer: Roy Pickering
Printer and Binder: Edwards Brothers
Cover Printer: Lehigh Phoenix Color

For permission to use copyrighted material, grateful acknowledgment is made to the copyright holders on p. 293, which are hereby made part of this copyright page.

Library of Congress Cataloging-in-Publication Data

Goshgarian, Gary.
Argument as dialogue : a concise guide / Gary Goshgarian, Kathleen Krueger.
   p. cm.
  Includes index.
  ISBN-13: 978-0-205-01912-0
  ISBN-10: 0-205-01912-9
  1. Persuasion (Rhetoric) 2. English language—Rhetoric. 3. College readers. I. Krueger, Kathleen.
II. Title.
  PE1431.G6 2010
  808'.0427—dc22

                      2010046857

1 2 3 4 5 6 7 8 9 10—DOC—14 13 12 11 —

Longman
is an imprint of

www.pearsonhighered.com   ISBN-13: 978-0-205-01912-0
                                  ISBN-10:   0-205-01912-9

Contents

Preface

As the title suggests, *Argument as Dialogue: A Concise Guide* is a guide to writing argumentative papers. It focuses on promoting meaningful discussion, that is, the effective exchange of opinions and ideas. As the title indicates, we move away from traditional models of confrontation and dispute and, instead, promote ways to create dialogue by examining different points of view with an open mind. This exploration of multiple perspectives on an issue helps students reach informed positions and develop their own compelling cases.

While dialogue and consensus are encouraged, we realize that not all arguments can be resolved to everyone's satisfaction. However, understanding the principles of persuasive writing and the techniques of argument provides students with the tools to engage productively in negotiation. And although students may not always reach a consensus of opinion, they will be able to discuss diverse issues in a thoughtful and productive way.

About this Book

This book consists of nine rhetorical chapters that explain the strategies of reading and writing arguments and that are designed to stimulate critical thinking, reading, and writing, and to introduce students to research skills. With over two dozen sample arguments (both professional and student) on contemporary issues spread throughout the chapters, *Argument as Dialogue* explores how issues are argued while emphasizing the actual process of persuasive writing—from brainstorming exercises to shaping the final product. Each of the nine chapters focuses on a particular facet or principle of persuasive writing, including a visuals chapter that addresses how visuals can act as arguments in and of themselves, or as auxiliary support for written arguments.

Chapter 1 offers an overview of argumentation, clarifies key terminology, and introduces the processes of debate, dialogue, and deliberation. Chapter 2 focuses on critical reading, presenting a series of activities designed to help students evaluate arguments and recognize their primary components. An extensive section on testing arguments for logical fallacies ends the chapter. Chapter 3 discusses how to begin writing arguments. It helps students find worthwhile and interesting topics to write about by demonstrating techniques for brainstorming, limiting topics, and formulating claims. Chapter 4 examines the presence of audience, encouraging students to think about the different kinds of readers they may have to address. This chapter suggests ways to evaluate readers' concerns and strategies to reach different audiences.

Chapter 5 focuses on the organization of the argument essay by analyzing two basic types of arguments—position and proposal. Outlining is reviewed as a tool to ensure effective organization. Chapter 6 considers the importance of evidence. We demonstrate that the effectiveness of a writer's argument largely depends on how well the writer uses evidence—facts, testimony, statistics, and observations—to support his or her ideas. Chapter 7 introduces the socially constructed Toulmin model of logic as a way of testing the premises of the writer's argument.

Chapter 8 explores the principles of visual argument in art, advertisements, editorial cartoons, photographs, and ancillary graphics such as charts and tables. Focusing on developing visual literacy skills, the chapter shows students how to apply the tools of critical analysis to the many visual arguments they encounter every day. Finally, Chapter 9 discusses research strategies, including locating and evaluating print and electronic sources, note-taking, and drafting and revising argument essays. The Documentation Guide provides documentation formats and two annotated and fully documented sample student papers for both MLA and APA styles, each incorporating visual devices.

Study Apparatus

The study apparatus of the book is designed to help students thoughtfully consider the issues, their own opinions on these issues, and how they might engage in meaningful dialogue. Following each essay are study questions aimed at encouraging critical thinking about the writing strategies of the author as well as writing assignments to help students synthesize the information they have read and their own opinions. Some questions include suggestions for using the Internet to explore a topic more fully and to aid research.

Supplements

PEARSON
mycomplab ▐

The only online application to integrate a writing environment with proven resources for grammar, writing, and research. MyCompLab gives students help at their fingertips as they draft and revise. Instructors have access to a variety of assessment tools including commenting capabilities, diagnostics and, study plans, and an e-portfolio. Created after years of extensive research and in partnership with faculty and students across the country. MyCompLab offers a seamless and flexible teaching and learning environment built specifically for writers.

Instructor's Manual

Argument as Dialogue: A Concise Guide comes with an Instructor's Manual to assist and guide instructors as they teach each chapter. The manual provides answers to the study questions that follow the readings in the textbook.

Dialogues: An Argument Rhetoric and Reader

A full rhetoric-reader edition of this book, now in its 7th edition, is published by Pearson under the title, *Dialogues: An Argument Rhetoric and Reader.* It contains this guide plus nine thematically organized chapters of argument essays.

Acknowledgments

Many people behind the scenes deserve much acknowledgment and gratitude. It would be impossible to thank all of them, but there are some for whose help we are particularly grateful. First, we would like to thank those instructors who reviewed drafts of this book and who supplied helpful comments and suggestions: Marcia Allen, University of Maryland University College; Désiré Baloubi, Shaw University; Candace Boeck, San Diego State University; Cathy Brostrand, Mt. San Jacinto College; Gert Coleman, Middlesex County College; William Donati, University of Nevada, Las Vegas; Kurt Harris, Southern Utah University; Tom Hemmeter, Arcadia University; Debra Johanyak, University of Akron; James M. Lang, Assumption College; Glenda Mora, Gavilan College; Joan Naake, Montgomery College; Phyllis Pae, Lakeland Community College; Robert Stafford, Cuyamaca College; and Jule Wallis, Wayne State University.

We would also like to thank Katharine Goodfellow for her invaluable suggestions and assistance.

Finally, our thanks to the people at Longman Publishers, especially our editor, Suzanne Phelps-Chambers, her ever-efficient editorial assistant, Laney Whitt, and Anne Leung, our development editor. We are very appreciative of their fine help.

Gary Goshgarian
Kathleen Krueger

Understanding Persuasion: Thinking Like a Negotiator

Think of all the times in the course of a week when someone tries to convince you of something. You listen to the radio on the way to school or work and are relentlessly bombarded by advertisements urging you to buy vitamins, watch a particular television show, or eat at the new Mexican restaurant in town. You open a newspaper and read about the latest proposals to lower the drinking age, raise the age for retirement, and provide tax relief for the poor. The phone rings and the caller tries to sell you a newspaper subscription or to convince you to vote for candidate X. There's a knock on your bedroom door and your sister wants to borrow a CD and the keys to your car. Whether the issue is as small as a CD or as important as taxes, everywhere you turn you find yourself called on to make a decision and to exercise a choice.

If you think about all these instances, you'll discover that each decision you finally do make is heavily influenced by the ability of others to persuade you. People who have mastered the art of argument are able to influence the thoughts and actions of others. Your ability to understand how argument works and how to use it effectively will help you become aware of the ways in which you are influenced by others, as well as become more persuasive yourself. Anyone can learn to argue effectively by learning the techniques needed to create successful arguments.

This book is designed to help you achieve two goals: (1) to think critically about the power of other people's arguments and (2) to become persuasive in your own arguments.

Argument

Broadly speaking, *persuasion* means influencing someone to do something. It can take many forms: fast-paced glittering ads, high-flying promises from salespeople, emotional appeals from charity groups—even physical threats. What will concern us in this book is *argument*—the form of persuasion that relies on reasoning and logical thought to convince people. While glitter, promises, emotional appeals, and even veiled threats may work, the real power of argument comes from the arguer's ability to convince others through language.

Because this is a book about writing, we will concentrate on the aspects of persuasion that most apply in writing, as opposed to those that work best in other forms (advertisements or oral appeals, for instance). Although written arguments can be passionate, emotional, or even hurtful, a good one demonstrates a firm foundation of clear thinking, logical development, and solid supporting evidence to persuade a reader that the view expressed is worth hearing. The ultimate goal might be to convince readers to change their thinking on an issue, but that does not always happen. A more realistic goal might be to have your listeners seriously consider your point of view and to win their respect through the logic and skill of your argument.

Most of what you write in college and beyond will attempt to persuade someone that what you have to say is worthy of consideration, whether it's a paper stating your views on immigration laws, an analysis of "madness" in *King Lear,* a letter to the editor of your school newspaper regarding women's varsity basketball, or a lab report on the solubility of salt. The same demands of persuasion and argument will carry into your professional life. Such writing might take the form of business reports, memos to colleagues, progress reports on students, medical evaluations, results of a technical study, proposals, maybe even a sales speech. In searching for a job or career, you might have to sell yourself in letters of inquiry.

The success or failure of those attempts will strongly depend on how well you argue your case. Therefore, it's important that as a college student you learn the skills of writing persuasive arguments. Even if you never write another argument, you will read, hear, and make them the rest of your life.

What Makes an Argument?

Arguments, in a sense, underlie nearly all forms of writing. Whenever you express ideas, you are attempting to persuade somebody to agree with you. However, not every matter can be formally argued. Nor are some things worth the effort. So, before we go on to discuss the different strategies, we should make clear which subjects do and do not lend themselves to argument.

Facts Are Not Arguable

Because facts are readily verifiable, they can't be argued. Of course, people might dispute a fact. For instance, you might disagree with a friend's claim that Thomas Jefferson was the second president of the United States. But to settle your dispute, all you have to do is consult an encyclopedia. What makes a fact a fact and, thus, inarguable, is that it has only one answer. It occurs in time and space and cannot be disputed. A fact either *is* or *is not* something. Thomas Jefferson was the third president of the United States, not the second. John Adams was the second. Those are facts. So are the following statements:

■ The distance between Boston and New York City is 214 miles.
■ Martin Luther King, Jr.'s birthday is now celebrated in all 50 states.
■ I got a 91 on my math test.
■ The Washington Monument is 555 feet high.
■ The Japanese smoke more cigarettes per capita than any other people on earth.
■ My dog Fred died a year ago.
■ Canada borders the United States to the north.

All that is required to prove or disprove any of these statements is to check with some authority for the right answer. Sometimes facts are not easily verifiable. Consider for instance, "Yesterday, 1,212,031 babies were born in the world" or "More people have black hair than any other color." These statements may be true, but it would be a daunting, if not impossible, challenge to prove them. And what would be the point?

Opinions Based on Personal Taste or Preference Are Not Arguable

Differing opinions are the basis of all argument. However, you must be careful to distinguish between opinions based on personal taste and opinions based on judgments. Someone who asks your "opinion" about which color shoes to buy is simply seeking your color preference—black versus brown, say. If someone asks your "opinion" of a certain movie, the matter could be more complicated.

Beyond whether or not you liked it, what might be sought is your aesthetic evaluation of the film: a judgment about the quality of acting, directing, cinematography, set design—all measured by critical standards you've developed over years of movie-going. Should you be asked your "opinion" of voluntary euthanasia, your response would probably focus on moral and ethical questions: Is the quality of life more important than the duration of life? What, if any, circumstances justify the taking of a life? Who should make so weighty a decision—the patient, the patient's family, the attending physician, a health team?

The word *opinion* is commonly used to mean different things. As just illustrated, depending on the context, opinion can refer to personal preference, a reaction to or analysis of something, or an evaluation, belief, or judgment, all of which are different. In this text, we categorize all these different possibilities as either opinions of taste or opinions of judgment.

Opinions of taste come down to personal preferences, based on subjective and, ultimately, unverifiable judgments. Each of the following statements is an opinion of taste:

- George looks good in blue.
- Pizza is my favorite food.
- Brian May of the group Queen is the greatest living rock guitarist.
- Video games are a waste of time.

Each of these statements is inarguable. Let's consider the first: "George looks good in blue." Is it a fact? Not really, since there is no objective way to measure its validity. You might like George in blue, whereas someone else might prefer him in red. Is the statement then debatable? No. Even if someone retorts, "George does *not* look good in blue," what would be the basis of argument but personal preference? And where would the counterargument go? Nowhere.

Even if a particular preference were backed by strong feelings, it would not be worth debating, nor might you sway someone to your opinion. For instance, let's say you make the statement that you never eat hamburger. You offer the following as reasons:

1. You're turned off by the sight of ground-up red meat.
2. When the meat is cooked, its smell disgusts you.
3. Hamburgers remind you of the terrible argument that broke out at a family barbecue some years ago.
4. You once got very sick after eating meatloaf.
5. You think beef cattle are the dirtiest of farm animals.

Even with all these "reasons" to support your point of view, you have not constructed an argument that goes beyond your own personal preference. In fact, the "reasons" you cite are themselves grounded in personal preferences. They amount to explanations rather than an argument. The same is true of the statements about pizza, musicians, and video games.

Opinions Based on Judgments Are Arguable

An *opinion of judgment* is one that weighs the pros and cons of an issue and determines their relative worth. That "something" might be a book, a song, or a public issue, such as capital punishment. Such an opinion represents a position on an issue that is measured against standards other than those of personal taste—standards that are rooted in values and beliefs of our culture: what's true and false, right and wrong, good and bad, better and worse. Consequently, such an opinion is arguable.

In other words, personal opinions or personal preferences can be transformed into bona fide arguments. Let's return to the example of hamburger. Suppose you want to turn your own dislike for ground meat into a paper persuading others to give up eating beef. You can take several approaches to make a convincing argument. For one, you can take a health slant, arguing that vegetarians have lower mortality rates than people whose diets are high in animal fat and cholesterol or that the ingestion of all the hormones in beef increases the risk of cancer. You might even take an environmental approach, pointing out that the more beef we eat, the more we encourage the conversion of woodlands and rain forests into grazing land, thus destroying countless animals and their habitats. You can even take an ethical stand, arguing from an animal-rights point of view that intensive farming practices create inhumane treatment of animals—that is, crowding, force-feeding, and force-breeding. You might also argue that the killing of animals is morally wrong.

The point is that personal opinions can be starting points for viable arguments. But those opinions must be developed according to recognized standards of values and beliefs.

The Uses of Argument

Many arguments center on issues that are controversial. Controversial issues, by definition, create disagreement and debate because people hold opposing positions about them. And, most of the time, there are more than two sides. Depending on the issue, there may be multiple opinions and perspectives. Because these views are often strongly held, we tend to view argument only in the form of a *debate,* an encounter between two or more adversaries who battle with each other over who is right. The media does much to contribute to the way we picture argument, particularly in the area of politics.

Every four years or so, the image returns to our television screens. Two candidates, dark-suited and conservatively dressed, hands tightly gripping their respective podiums, face off for all of America to watch. Each argues passionately for his or her solution to war, the economy, environmental crises, poverty, educational failings, high taxes, and countless other problems. Each tries desperately to undermine the arguments of the opponent in an effort to capture the votes of those watching. It's a winner-take-all debate, and it's often the image we see in our minds when we think of argument.

Argument *is* a form of persuasion that seeks to convince others to do what the arguer wants. Argument allows us to present our views and the reasons behind those views clearly and strongly. Yet argument can serve more productive purposes than the above illustration. Although argument can be a debate between two or more opponents who will never see eye-to-eye, in the world outside presidential debates and television sound bites argument can also begin a *dialogue* between opposing sides. It can enable them to listen to each other's concerns and to respond in a thoughtful way. Rather than attempt to demolish their opponent's arguments, these negotiators can often arrive at positions that are more valuable because they try to reconcile conflicting viewpoints by understanding and dealing directly with their opponent's concerns. Through the practice of *debate, dialogue,* and *deliberation,* real change can happen. In this chapter, we explore these three essential elements of argument and explain how they will enable you to be more effective when you write to persuade others.

Debate

Think for a moment of all the associations the word *debate* suggests to you: winning, losing, taking sides, opposition, and competition. Debate is how we traditionally think of argument. It is a situation in which individuals or groups present their views as forcefully and persuasively as possible, often referring to their opponents' arguments only to attack or deride them. Practiced with just this goal in mind, debate can serve the purpose of presenting your position clearly in contrast to your opposition's, but it does little to resolve controversial issues. Focusing too much on the adversarial qualities of debate can prevent you from listening and considering other viewpoints. You can become so preoccupied with defeating opposing arguments that you fail to recognize the legitimacy of other opinions. This may lead you to ignore them as you fashion your own argument.

Consider the last time you debated an issue with someone. Perhaps it was an informal occasion in which you attempted to convince that person of your point of view. It may have been about an instructor or the best place to spend spring break or what movie to see. Your aim was to persuade the other person to "see it your way," and, if it was a typical debate, you were successful only if the other individual acquiesced. Debates are traditionally won or lost, and losers often feel frustrated and disappointed. Even more important, reasonable concerns on the losing side are often overlooked or not addressed. Debate does not provide a mechanism for compromise. It is not intended to provide a path toward common ground or a resolution in which all parties achieve a degree of success and positive change is made. Although some issues are so highly contentious that true consensus can never be achieved, an effective argument must acknowledge and respond to opposition in a thoughtful and productive manner.

But debate is an important way to develop your arguments because it allows you to explore their strengths and weaknesses. It can be a starting point for argument rather than a conclusion. Debate contains some of the essential elements of argument: Someone with a strong opinion tries to demonstrate the effectiveness of that view, hoping to persuade others to change positions or to take a particular course of action. When we debate, we have two objectives: to state our views clearly and persuasively and to distinguish our views from those of our opponents. Debate can help us develop our arguments because it encourages us to *formulate a claim, create reasons to support it,* and *anticipate opposition.*

Formulating Claims

The claim is the heart of your argument. Whether you hope to protest a decision, change your readers' minds, or motivate your audience to take action, somewhere in your argument must be the assertion you hope to prove. In an argument essay, this assertion or claim functions as the *thesis* of the paper, and it is vital to the argument. The claim states precisely what you believe. It is the *position* or opinion you want your readers to accept or the action you want them to take. Thus, it's very important to state your claim as clearly as possible. It will form the basis for the rest of your argument.

Claims often take the form of a single declarative statement. For example, a claim in an argument essay about homelessness might look like this:

> If we look further into the causes of homelessness, we will discover that in many cases it is not the homeless individual who is at fault but rather conditions that exist in our society that victimize certain individuals.

A claim for an essay about teen pregnancy might be stated even more simply:

> People who blame the rise in teenage pregnancies on the sexual references in popular music ignore several crucial realities.

Sometimes writers signal their claims by certain words: *therefore, consequently, the real question is, the point is, it follows that, my suggestion is.* Here's an example:

> Therefore, I believe that scientists can find other effective ways to test new medicines and surgical techniques other than relying on helpless laboratory animals.

Because some arguments make recommendations for solving problems, your claim might be framed as a conditional statement that indicates both the problem and a consequence. This can be accomplished with split phrases such as *either . . . or, neither . . . nor, if . . . then.* For example,

> If we continue to support a system of welfare that discourages its recipients from finding employment, the result will be a permanent class of unemployed citizens who lack the skills and incentives to participate in their own economic benefit.

Claims must have support to convince a reader, so they are often followed by "because" statements—that is, statements that justify a claim by explaining why something is true or recommended or beneficial:

> Outlawing assisted suicide is wrong because it deprives individuals of their basic human right to die with dignity.

Formulating your claim when you debate is a first step for three basic reasons:

1. It establishes the subject of your argument.
2. It solidifies your own stand or position about the issue.
3. It sets up a strategy on which your argument can be structured.

There are no hard-and-fast rules for the location of your claim. It can appear anywhere in your essay: as your opening sentence, in the middle, or as your conclusion. However, many writers state their claim early in the essay to let their readers know their position and to use it as a basis for all the supporting reasons that follow. In later chapters, we will look at strategies for arriving at a claim and ways to organize your reasons to support it effectively.

Creating Reasons

We have all seen a building under construction. Before the roof can be laid or the walls painted or the flooring installed, the support beams must be carefully placed and stabilized. Reasons are the support beams of an argument essay. Whether your claim will be considered correct, insightful, or reasonable will depend on the strength and persuasiveness of your reasons.

Reasons answer some basic questions about your claim:

1. Why do you believe your claim to be true?
2. On what information or assumptions do you base your claim?
3. What evidence can you supply to support your claim?
4. Do any authorities or experts concur with your claim?

You can derive reasons from personal experience, readings, and research. Your choices will depend on your claim and the information and evidence you need to make your reasons convincing. Let's use one of the examples from our discussion about claims to demonstrate what we mean:

> **Your Claim:** Outlawing assisted suicide is wrong because it deprives individuals of the basic human right to die with dignity.
>
> **Question 1:** Why do you believe your claim to be true?
>
> **Response:** When individuals are terminally ill, they suffer many indignities. They lose control of their bodily functions and must be dependent on others for care. A prolonged illness with no hope of recovery causes the individual and family members to suffer needlessly. When death is imminent, individuals should be given the right to decide when and how to end their lives.

Question 2: On what information or assumptions do you base your claim?

Response: I believe that no individual wants to suffer more than necessary. No one wants to lose his or her independence and have to rely on others. Everyone wants to be remembered as a whole human being, not as a dying invalid.

Question 3: What evidence can you supply to support your claim?

Response: This is based on personal examples and on readings about how terminal illness is dealt with in hospitals and clinics.

Question 4: Do any authorities or experts concur with your claim?

Response: Yes, many authorities in the field of medicine agree with my claim. I can use their statements and research to support it.

By examining the responses to the questions, you can see how reasons can be created to support your claim. The answer to the first question suggests several reasons why you might be opposed to outlawing assisted suicide: the indignities suffered by the terminally ill, unnecessary suffering, the right to control one's own fate. Question 2 explores your assumptions about what the terminally ill might experience and provides additional reasons to support your claim. The third and fourth questions suggest ways to support your claim through personal examples, references to ideas and examples found in readings related to your topic, and the support of experts in the field.

Credibility is an essential element in creating reasons. To be a successful debater, you must be believable; you must convince your audience that you are knowledgeable about your subject and that the facts, statistics, anecdotes, and whatever else you use to support your reasons are accurate and up-to-date. This means constructing your reasons through research and careful analysis of all the information available. For example, if you argue in an essay that there are better ways to run the U.S. Post Office, you will need to understand and explain how the current system operates. You can use the facts and statistics that you uncover in your research to analyze existing problems and to support your ideas for change. Being thoroughly informed helps you present and use your knowledge persuasively. Acquainting yourself with the necessary information will make you appear believable and competent. In later chapters, we will discuss how to formulate reasons to support your claim and how to evaluate evidence and use it effectively.

Another way to achieve credibility is to avoid logical fallacies, which will undermine the logic or persuasiveness of your argument. *Logical fallacies,* a term derived from the Latin *fallere,* meaning "to deceive," are unintentional errors in logic or deliberate attempts to mislead the reader by exaggerating evidence or using methods of argument that appeal to prejudice or bias. In Chapter 2, we will review the most common forms of logical fallacies so you can recognize them in the arguments of others and avoid them in your own writing.

Anticipating Opposition

Because debate anticipates opposition, you need to be certain that your reasons can withstand the challenges that are sure to come. Your goal as a successful debater is not only to present your reasons clearly and persuasively but to be prepared for the responses of people holding other views. For instance, in an essay on discrimination in women's collegiate sports, you may state that the operating budget of the women's varsity basketball team at your school is a fraction of that for the men's team. As evidence, you might point to the comparative lack of advertising, lower attendance at games, and lesser coverage than for the men's team. Unless you anticipate other perspectives on your issue, your argument could fall apart should someone suggest that women's basketball teams have lower budgets simply because they have smaller paying audiences. Not anticipating such a rebuttal would weaken your position. Had you been prepared, you could have acknowledged that opposing point and then responded to it by reasoning that the low budget is the cause of the problem, not the result of it. Putting more money into advertising and coverage could boost attendance and, thus, revenue.

In short, it is not enough simply to present your own reasons, no matter how effectively you support them. Unless you are familiar with opposing reasons, you leave yourself open to being undermined. To make your case as effective as possible, you must acknowledge and respond to the strongest reasons that challenge your own. To present only the weakest points of those who disagree with you or to do so in a poor light would likely backfire on your own credibility.

The following are strategies we recommend to help you become more aware of views that are different from your own and ways you might respond to them.

"Yes, but . . ." Exchanges

One way to be aware of the reasons on the other side is to research your topic carefully. After you've done some reading, a useful method to explore the way others might respond to your ideas is to engage in a "Yes, but . . . " exchange. Imagine you are face-to-face with someone holding a different position and, as you run down the list of your own reasons, his or her response is "Yes, but . . . [something]." What might that "something" be? Your task is first to acknowledge the validity of the other individual's viewpoint, and then to respond to that idea with reasons of your own. Consider, for instance, how a debate about affirmative action programs might proceed. You begin:

> Affirmative action programs discriminate against white males by denying them employment for which they are qualified.

From what you've heard and read, your opponent might respond this way:

> Yes, there are probably instances in which white males have lost employment opportunities because of affirmative action programs, but without these programs minority candidates would never be considered for some job openings regardless of their qualifications.

Another reason might be:

> Race and gender should not be considerations when hiring an applicant for a job.

From your readings, you may uncover this opposing reason:

> Yes, in an ideal society race and gender would never be factors for employers, but since we don't live in such a society, affirmative action programs ensure that race and gender don't become negative considerations when an individual applies for a job.

Imagining your debate in a "Yes, but . . . " exchange will help you work through a number of possibilities to strengthen your reasons in the light of opposition and to become more aware of other viewpoints.

Pro/Con Checklists

Another method to help you become more aware of opposing viewpoints is to create a pro/con checklist. Making such a checklist is useful for several reasons. First, it helps you solidify your own stand on the issue. It puts you in the position of having to formulate points on which to construct an argument. Second, by anticipating counterpoints you can better test the validity and strength of your points. By listing potential resistance you can determine the weak spots in your argument. Third, tabulating your own points will help you decide how to organize your reasons—which points to put at the beginning of your paper and which to put in the conclusion. Depending on the issue, you may decide for the sake of impact to begin with the strongest point and end with the weakest. This is the strategy of most advertisers—hitting the potential customer right off with the biggest sales pitch. Or you may decide to use a climactic effect by beginning with the weakest point and building to the strongest and most dramatic. Last, by ordering your key points you can create a potential framework for constructing your argument. Below is an example of a pro/con checklist.

Sample Pro/Con Checklist

CLAIM: Human cloning should be outlawed because it is unnecessary and unethical.

PRO	CON
Human cloning is unnecessary because we have better ways to treat infertility.	Current fertility treatments are very expensive and are often unsuccessful.
Because we have too many unwanted children in the world already, we should not create more.	People have a right to have their own children.
Cloning is an unnatural process.	It is no more unnatural than many of the ways we currently treat infertility.
Human cloning will devalue the uniqueness of each individual.	A clone will still be a unique and separate human being.

Moving from Debate to Dialogue

Debate is an important step in constructing an argument. It propels us to find a strong position and to argue that position as effectively as possible. But if we define argument as only debate, we limit the potential power of argument in our society. One common misconception is that all arguments are won or lost. This may be true in formalized debates, but in real life few arguments are decided so clearly; and when they are, the conflicting issues at the heart of the debate can persist and continue to create dissent among individuals and groups. The prolonged tensions and sometimes violent confrontations that surround the issue of abortion may be the outcome of a debate that supposedly was resolved by a Supreme Court decision, *Roe* v. *Wade,* but remains a continuing problem because the debate did not engender a dialogue in which conflicting sides listened to each other and reconsidered their views from a more informed perspective. Argument must do more than provide an opportunity to present one's views against those of an opponent. We need to use it as a vehicle to explore other views as well and to help us shape a process in which change can happen and endure.

Dialogue

Take another moment to consider words that come to mind when you think of *dialogue:* discussion, listening, interaction, and understanding. By definition, a dialogue includes more than one voice, and those voices are responsive to each other. When we have a dialogue with someone, we don't simply present our own views. We may disagree, but we take turns so that no one voice monopolizes the conversation. The object of a dialogue is not to win or lose; the object is to communicate our ideas and to listen to what the other person has to say in response.

For example, you may find a policy in a particular class regarding make-up tests unfair. Since your instructor seems to be a reasonable person, you visit her office to discuss your objections. Your dialogue might proceed like this:

You: Professor, your syllabus states that if a student misses a test, there are no make-ups. I think that this is unfair because if a student is genuinely ill or has an important conflict, the student will be penalized.

Professor: I can understand your concern, but I have that policy because some students use make-ups to gain extra time to study. And, by asking other students about the questions on the test, they gain an advantage over students who take the test when it's scheduled. I don't think that's fair.

You: I hadn't thought of that. That's a good reason, but I'm still worried that even if I have a legitimate excuse for missing a test, my grade in the course will suffer. What can I do if that happens?

Professor: Let me think about your problem. Perhaps there's a way that I can be fair to you and still not jeopardize the integrity of my exams.

You: What if a student provides a physician's note in case of illness or a few days' advance notice in case of a conflict? Would you be able to provide an alternative testing day if that should happen?

Professor: That might be a good way to deal with the problem, as long as the make-up could be scheduled soon after. I'm going to give this more thought before I decide. I appreciate your suggestions. Stop by tomorrow and we can come to an agreement.

This hypothetical dialogue works because each participant listens and responds to the ideas of the other. Each has an important stake in the issue, but both focus on finding constructive ways to deal with it rather than trying to prove that the other is wrong. As a result, a compromise can be reached, and each person will have made a contribution to the solution.

When we move from debate to dialogue, we move from an arbitrary stance to one that allows for change and modification. Dialogue requires that both sides of the debate do more than simply present and react to each other's views in an adversarial fashion; it demands that each side respond to the other's points by attempting to understand them and the concerns they express. Often it is difficult for those participating in a debate to take this important step. In such cases, it will be your task, as a student of argument, to create the dialogue between opposing sides that will enable you to recognize common concerns and, if possible, to achieve a middle ground.

Creating a dialogue between two arguments involves identifying the writers' claims and key reasons. This is a skill we discuss in Chapter 2, when we look at strategies for reading and analyzing argument essays.

Deliberation

Deliberate is a verb that we don't use very much and we probably don't practice enough. It means to consider our reasons for and against something carefully and fully before making up our minds. We often speak of a jury deliberating about its verdict. Jury members must methodically weigh all the evidence and testimony that have been presented and then reach a judgment. Deliberation is not a quick process. It takes time to become informed, to explore all the alternatives, and to feel comfortable with a decision.

Deliberation plays an important part in the process of developing arguments. *Debate* focuses our attention on opposition and the points on which we disagree. *Dialogue* creates an opportunity to listen to and explore the arguments that conflict with our own. Deliberation, the careful consideration of all that we have learned through debate and dialogue, enables us to reach our own informed position on the conflict. Because we have participated in both debate and dialogue, we have a more complete understanding of the opposing arguments, as well as the common ground they may share. We are able to take the concerns of all sides into account.

Deliberation does not always resolve an issue in a way that is pleasing to all sides. Some issues remain contentious and irreconcilable, so that the parties are unable to move beyond debate. And, just as a jury sometimes reaches a verdict that is not what either the defense or the prosecution desires, deliberation does not ensure that all concerns or arguments will be considered equally valid. However, deliberation does ensure that you have given the arguments of all sides careful attention. And, unlike a

Review: Basic Terminology

Argument Essay

An essay that attempts to convince or persuade others through reason, logic, and evidence to do what the writer wants or believe as the writer wishes.

Claim

The statement in your essay that expresses your position or stand on a particular issue. The claim states precisely what you believe. It is the viewpoint you want your readers to accept or the action you want them to take.

Reasons

The explanation or justification behind your claim. To be effective, reasons must be supported by evidence and examples.

Debate

The act of presenting your claim and reasons, and challenging and being challenged by someone who holds a different viewpoint. Debate often focuses on differences between opponents rather than shared concerns and values.

Dialogue

The act of listening and responding to those who hold viewpoints that are different from your own on a particular issue. The object of a dialogue is to find common ground by trying to understand other viewpoints while sharing your own. It is intended to reduce conflict rather than promote it.

Deliberation

The careful and informed consideration of all sides of an issue before reaching a conclusion or position on it. Deliberation can result in the resolution of a contentious issue.

jury, you have much broader parameters to determine your position. You do not have to decide *for* or *against* one side or the other. Your deliberations may result in an entirely new way of viewing a particular issue or solving a problem.

Consider, for example, a debate about whether a new football stadium should be built in a city experiencing economic problems, such as high unemployment and a failing public school system. One side of the debate may argue that a new stadium would result in additional jobs and revenue for the city from the influx of people who would come to watch the games. Another side may argue that the millions of dollars intended to subsidize a new stadium would be better spent creating job-training programs and promoting remedial education for school-children. Your deliberation would involve several steps:

1. Becoming informed about the issue by reading and researching the information available
2. Creating a dialogue by listening to the arguments of all sides in the debate and trying to understand the reasons behind their claims
3. Weighing all the arguments and information carefully
4. Determining your own position on the issue

Your position might agree with one side or the other, or it might propose an entirely different response to the situation—say, a smaller stadium with the extra funds available to the schools, or a delay in the construction of a stadium until the unemployment problem is solved, or an additional tax to fund both, and so on. It would then be your task to convince all sides of the value of your position.

Deliberation enables you to use argument productively. It allows you to consider all sides of a problem or issue and to use your own critical analysis to find a way to respond.

As you learn more about writing your own arguments, you'll find that debate, dialogue, and deliberation can help you identify different perspectives, search for shared concerns, and develop your own position on an issue.

Taking a "War of Words" Too Literally
Deborah Tannen

> The following essay provides important insights into the ways in which we often approach argument in our society. This article by Deborah Tannen is adapted from her book, *The Argument Culture: Moving from Debate to Dialogue,* which explores how U.S. culture promotes a warlike, adversarial approach to problem-solving. Tannen is a professor of linguistics at Georgetown University. She is the author of the bestsellers *You Just Don't Understand: Women and Men in Conversation* and *Talking from 9 to 5: Women and Men in the Workplace.* As you read Tannen's article, think about whether you have had experiences similar to those Tannen describes, when disagreements could have been settled more successfully through dialogue and thoughtful deliberation than through conflict.

1   I was waiting to go on a television talk show a few years ago for a discussion about how men and women communicate, when a man walked in wearing a shirt and tie and a floor-length skirt, the top of which was brushed by his waist-length red hair. He politely introduced himself and told me that he'd read and liked my book *You Just Don't Understand*, which had just been published. Then he added, "When I get out there, I'm going to attack you. But don't take it personally. That's why they invite me on, so that's what I'm going to do."

2   We went on the set and the show began. I had hardly managed to finish a sentence or two before the man threw his arms out in gestures of anger, and began shrieking—briefly hurling accusations at me, and then railing at length against women. The strangest thing about his hysterical outburst was how the studio audience reacted: They turned vicious—not attacking me (I hadn't said anything substantive yet) or him (who wants to tangle with someone who screams at you?) but the other guests: women who had come to talk about problems they had communicating with their spouses.

3   My antagonist was nothing more than a dependable provocateur, brought on to ensure a lively show. The incident has stayed with me not because it was typical of the talk shows I have appeared on—it wasn't, I'm happy to say—but because it exemplifies the ritual nature of much of the opposition that pervades our public dialogue.

4   Everywhere we turn, there is evidence that, in public discourse, we prize contentiousness and aggression more than cooperation and conciliation. Headlines blare about the Starr Wars, the Mommy Wars, the Baby Wars, the Mammography Wars; everything is posed in terms of battles and duels, winners and losers, conflicts and disputes. Biographies have metamorphosed into demonographies whose authors don't just portray their subjects warts and all, but set out to dig up as much dirt as possible, as if the story of a person's life is contained in the warts, only the warts, and nothing but the warts.

5   It's all part of what I call the argument culture, which rests on the assumption that opposition is the best way to get anything done: The best way to discuss an idea is to set up a debate. The best way to cover news is to find people who express the most extreme views and present them as "both sides." The best way to begin an essay is to attack someone. The best way to show you're really thoughtful is to criticize. The best way to settle disputes is to litigate them.

6   It is the automatic nature of this response that I am calling into question. This is not to say that passionate opposition and strong verbal attacks are never appropriate. In the words of Yugoslavian-born poet Charles Simic, "There are moments in life when true invective is called for, when it becomes an absolute necessity, out of a deep sense of justice, to denounce, mock, vituperate, lash out, in the strongest possible language." What I'm questioning is the ubiquity, the knee-jerk nature of approaching almost any issue, problem or public person in an adversarial way.

7   Smashing heads does not open minds. In this as in so many things, results are also causes, looping back and entrapping us. The pervasiveness of warlike formats and language grows out of, but also gives rise to, an ethic of aggression: We come to value aggressive tactics for their own sake—for the sake of argument. Compromise becomes a dirty word, and we often feel guilty if we are conciliatory rather than confrontational—even if we achieve the result we're seeking.

8   Here's one example. A woman called another talk show on which I was a guest. She told the following story: "I was in a place where a man was smoking, and there was a no-smoking sign. Instead of saying 'You aren't allowed to smoke in here. Put that out!' I said, 'I'm awfully sorry, but I have asthma, so your smoking makes it hard for me to breathe. Would you mind terribly not smoking?' When I said this, the man was extremely polite and solicitous, and he put his cigarette out, and I said, 'Oh, thank you, thank you!' as if he'd done a wonderful thing for me. Why did I do that?"

9   I think the woman expected me—the communications expert—to say she needs assertiveness training to confront smokers in a more aggressive manner. Instead, I told her that her approach was just fine. If she had tried to alter his behavior by reminding him of the rules, he might well have rebelled: "Who made you the enforcer? Mind your own business!" She had given the smoker a face-saving way of doing what she wanted, one that allowed him to feel chivalrous rather than chastised. This was kinder to him, but it was also kinder to herself, since it was more likely to lead to the result she desired.

10   Another caller disagreed with me, saying the first caller's style was "self-abasing." I persisted: There was nothing necessarily destructive about the way the woman handled the smoker. The mistake the second caller was making—a mistake many of us make—was to confuse ritual self-effacement with the literal kind. All human relations require us to find ways to get what we want from others without seeming to dominate them.

11   The opinions expressed by the two callers encapsulate the ethic of aggression that has us by our throats, particularly in public arenas such as politics and law. Issues are routinely approached by having two sides stake out opposing positions and do battle. This sometimes drives people to take positions that are more adversarial than they feel—and can get in the way of reaching a possible resolution. . . .

12   The same spirit drives the public discourse of politics and the press, which are increasingly being given over to ritual attacks . . . I once asked a reporter about the common journalistic practice of challenging interviewees by repeating criticism to them. She told me it was the hardest part of her job. "It makes me uncomfortable," she said. "I tell myself I'm someone else and force myself to do it." But, she said she had no trouble being combative if she felt someone was guilty of behavior she considered wrong. And that is the crucial difference between ritual fighting and literal fighting: opposition of the heart.

13   It is easy to find examples throughout history of journalistic attacks that make today's rhetoric seem tame. But in the past such vituperation was motivated by true political passion, in contrast with today's automatic, ritualized attacks—which seem to grow out of a belief that conflict is high-minded and good, a required and superior form of discourse.

14   The roots of our love for ritualized opposition lie in the educational system that we all pass through.

15   Here's a typical scene: The teacher sits at the head of the classroom, pleased with herself and her class. The students are engaged in a heated debate. The very noise level reassures the teacher that the students are participating. Learning is going on. The class is a success.

16   But look again, cautions Patricia Rosof, a high school history teacher who admits to having experienced just such a wave of satisfaction. On closer inspection, you notice that only a few students are participating in the debate; the majority of the class is sitting silently. And the students who are arguing are not addressing subtleties, nuances or complexities of the points they are making or disputing. They don't have that luxury because they want to win the argument—so they must go for the most dramatic

statements they can muster. They will not concede an opponent's point—even if they see its validity—because that would weaken their position.

17   This aggressive intellectual style is cultivated and rewarded in our colleges and universities. The standard way to write an academic paper is to position your work in opposition to someone else's. This creates a need to prove others wrong, which is quite different from reading something with an open mind and discovering that you disagree with it. Graduate students learn that they must disprove others' arguments in order to be original, make a contribution and demonstrate intellectual ability. The temptation is great to oversimplify at best, and at worst to distort or even misrepresent other positions, the better to refute them.

18   I caught a glimpse of this when I put the question to someone who I felt had misrepresented my own work: "Why do you need to make others wrong for you to be right?" Her response: "It's an argument!" Aha, I thought, that explains it. If you're having an argument, you use every tactic you can think of—including distorting what your opponent just said—in order to win.

19   Staging everything in terms of polarized opposition limits the information we get rather than broadening it.

20   For one thing, when a certain kind of interaction is the norm, those who feel comfortable with that type of interaction are drawn to participate, and those who do not feel comfortable with it recoil and go elsewhere. If public discourse included a broad range of types, we would be making room for individuals with different temperaments. But when opposition and fights overwhelmingly predominate, only those who enjoy verbal sparring are likely to take part. Those who cannot comfortably take part in oppositional discourse—or choose not to—are likely to opt out.

21   But perhaps the most dangerous harvest of the ethic of aggression and ritual fighting is—as with the audience response to the screaming man on the television talk show—an atmosphere of animosity that spreads like a fever. In extreme forms, it rears its head in road rage and workplace shooting sprees. In more common forms, it leads to what is being decried everywhere as a lack of civility. It erodes our sense of human connection to those in public life—and to the strangers who cross our paths and people our private lives.

QUESTIONS FOR DISCUSSION AND WRITING

1. Do you agree with Tannen's assertion that public discussions about controversial issues have been turned into "battles and duels" by the media? Why or why not? Look through current newspapers or magazines for evidence of this trend. Do other forms of media, such as television and radio, also encourage the same?

2. How has the "argument culture" affected our ability to resolve issues? Think of current controversies that have been negatively affected by the tendency of some to defend their own "turf" rather than listen and respond constructively to others with differing views?

3. Tannen cites a woman who called in to a talk show and questioned whether her conciliatory approach to a potential conflict was the best course of action (paragraphs 8 and 9). In your journal, discuss your own experiences confronting someone whose behavior you found unacceptable. What approaches proved successful for you? Do you agree with Tannen that the woman was wise to avoid conflict?

4. In your own experience, have you found that schools and teachers promote and reward students who engage in heated debate with other students, as Tannen contends in paragraphs 18 to 20? Do you think this strategy discourages students who are uncomfortable with this confrontational behavior? Have you found that a "winner-take-all" approach to argument is a productive way to solve disagreements? What problems can arise from this approach? Any benefits?

SAMPLE ARGUMENTS FOR ANALYSIS

Read the following two essays to find the basic components in writing arguments and to practice debate, dialogue, and deliberation. After you have read each essay carefully, respond to these questions about them:

1. Identify each writer's claim and restate it in your own words. What do you think is the writer's purpose in writing the essay?
2. What reasons does each writer use to support his claim? Make a list of the reasons you find in each essay. Are the reasons convincing?
3. Find examples of the ways each writer supports those reasons. How convincing is the evidence he presents? Is it pertinent? reliable? sufficient? Is it slanted or biased?
4. Does the writer acknowledge views about the subject that are different from his own? Where does he do this? What is the writer's attitude toward those who hold different views? Does he try to understand those views or does he respond only negatively toward them?
5. Using debate, dialogue, and deliberation, complete the following activities individually or in small groups:
   a. To become acquainted with opposing reasons, write a "yes, but . . ." exchange or a pro/con checklist.
   b. Using your checklist or exchange, create a dialogue between two or more opposing sides on the issue that attempts to find points of disagreement as well as common ground or shared concerns among them. Look for opportunities for each side to listen and respond constructively to the other.
   c. Deliberate. Review the reasons and examples from a number of perspectives. What reasons on either side do you find the most compelling? What concerns have particular merit? How can you balance the interests of all sides of the issue? Formulate a claim that takes into account what you have learned from listening and considering several perspectives and provide reasons to support it.

The Case Against Tipping

Michael Lewis

Many people have strong views about tipping. Some consider it an optional act of kindness to express appreciation for good service, an additional expense over what they have already paid. For others it is an essential part of their day's wages, and thus their income. The following essay by Michael Lewis explores this dichotomy. Lewis is a contributing editor at *Vanity Fair* and the author of several bestselling books including *Liar's Poker* (1990), *Moneyball: The Art of Winning an Unfair Game* (2004), and most recently, *Home Game: An Accidental Guide to Fatherhood* (2009).

As you read this article, which originally appeared in the *New York Times Magazine* in 1997 and was updated by the author for this book, think about your own attitudes toward the practice of tipping. What motivates a tip? If you have ever been on the receiving end, did you find that relying on others' generosity for your income left you vulnerable to their whims?

1   No lawful behavior in the marketplace is as disturbing to me as the growing appeals for gratuities. Every gentle consumer of cappuccinos will know what I'm getting at: Just as you hand your money over to the man behind the counter, you notice a plastic beggar's cup beside the cash register. "We Appreciate Your Tips," it reads in blue ink scrawled across the side with calculated indifference. The young man or woman behind the counter has performed no especially noteworthy service. He or she has merely handed you a $2 muffin and perhaps a ruinous cup of coffee and then rung them up on the register. Yet the plastic cup waits impatiently for an expression of your gratitude. A dollar bill or two juts suggestively over the rim—no doubt placed there by the person behind the counter. Who would tip someone a dollar or more for pouring them a cup of coffee? But you can never be sure. The greenbacks might have been placed there by people who are more generous than yourself. People whose hearts are not made of flint.

2   If you are like most people (or at any rate like me), you are of two minds about this plastic cup. On the one hand, you do grasp the notion that people who serve you are more likely to do it well and promptly if they believe they will be rewarded for it. The prospect of a tip is, in theory at least, an important incentive for the person working behind the counter of the coffee bar. Surely, you don't want to be one of those people who benefit from the certain hop to the worker's step that the prospect of a tip has arguably induced without paying your fair share of the cost. You do not wish to be thought of as not doing your share, you cheapskate.

3   And these feelings of guilt are only compounded by the niggling suspicion that the men who run the corporation that runs the coffee shops might be figuring on a certain level of tipping per hour when they decide how generous a wage they should extend to the folks toiling at the counters. That is, if you fail to tip the person getting you that coffee, you may be directing and even substantially affecting that person's level of income, especially in today's down economy.

4   That said, we are talking here about someone who has spent all of 40 seconds re-trieving for you a hot drink and a muffin. When you agreed to buy the drink and the muffin you did not take into account the plastic-cup shakedown. In short, you can't help but feel you are being had.

5   There in a nutshell is the first problem with tipping: the more discretion you have in the matter the more unpleasant it is. Tipping is an aristocratic conceit—"There you go, my good man, buy your starving family a loaf"—best left to an aristocratic age. The practicing democrat would rather be told what he owes right up front. Offensively rich people may delight in peeling off hundred-dollar bills and tossing them out to groveling servants. But no sane, well-adjusted human being cares to sit around and evaluate the performance of some beleaguered coffee vendor.

6   This admirable reticence means that, in our democratic age at least, gratuities are inexorably transformed into something else. On most occasions where they might be conferred—at restaurants, hotels and the like—tips are as good as obligatory. "Tipping is customary," reads the sign in the back of a New York City taxi, and if any-thing, that is an understatement. Once, a long time ago, I tried to penalize a cabdriver for bad service and he rolled alongside me for two crowded city blocks, shouting ob-scenities through his car window. A friend of mine who undertipped had the message drummed home more perfectly: a few seconds after she stepped out of the cab, the cab knocked her over. She suffered a fracture in her right leg. But it could have been worse. She could have been killed for . . . undertipping! (The driver claimed it was an accident. Sure it was.)

7   There, in a nutshell, is the second problem with tipping: the less discretion you have in the matter, the more useless it is as an economic incentive. Our natural and ad-mirable reluctance to enter into the spirit of the thing causes the thing to lose what-ever value it had in the first place. It is no accident that the rudest and most inept service people in America—New York City cabdrivers—are also those most likely to receive their full 15 percent. A tip that isn't a sure thing is socially awkward. But a tip that is a sure thing is no longer a tip really. It's more like a tax.

8   Once you understand the impossibility of tipping in our culture, the plastic cup on the coffee-bar counter can be seen for what it is: a custom in the making. How long can it be before the side of the coffee cup reads "Tipping Is Customary"? I called Starbucks to talk this over, and a pleasant spokeswoman told me that this chain of coffee bars, at least, has no such designs on American mores. The official Starbucks line on their Plexiglas container is that it wasn't their idea but that of their customers. "People were leaving loose change on the counter to show their gratitude," she said. "And so in 1990 it was decided to put a tasteful and discreet cup on the counter. It's a way for our customers to say thanks to our partners." (Partners are what Starbucks calls its employees.)

9   Perhaps. But you can be sure that our society will not long tolerate the uncertainty of the cup. People will demand to know what is expected of them, one way or the other. Either the dollar in the cup will become a routine that all civilized coffee buyers will endure. Or the tasteful and discreet cup will disappear altogether, in deference to the straightforward price hike.

10   A small matter, you might say. But if the person at the coffee-bar counter feels entitled to a tip for grabbing you a coffee and muffin, who won't eventually? I feel we are
creeping slowly toward a kind of baksheesh economy in which everyone expects to be
showered with coins simply for doing what they've already been paid to do. Let's band
together and ignore the cup. And who knows? Someday, we may live in a world where a
New York City cabdriver simply thanks you for paying what it says on the meter.

QUESTIONS FOR DISCUSSION AND WRITING

1. Do you think Lewis has had much experience in a job that relies on
   tips? What evidence can you find to demonstrate this?
2. Do you agree with Lewis? In your journal, respond to Lewis's ideas
   by exploring your own views on tipping. What experiences have you
   had that support your own view?

Women Soldiers Crucial to US Mission
Paula Broadwell

American fighting forces are engaged in brutal engagements in two countries, Iraq
and Afghanistan. We have all seen film footage of our military men and women
kiss their families goodbye as they prepare to deploy. We have also seen news
footage of the wars. Yet what we don't see on the evening news are women in fa-
tigues, women toting automatic weapons, women rushed from battle or from an
IED attack to medical facilities. It's almost always male soldiers. But what is the full
reality? Who are engaged in combat? Who are the targets of an IED? Yes, women
are serving, but their roles are barely visible. In this piece, West Point graduate Paula
Broadwell explains that while official policy prevents women from serving in combat, women are there. And she argues strongly that modern military policy should
be revised to reflect this reality. Broadwell is a research associate at Harvard
University's Center for Public Leadership and serves on the board of Women in
International Security. This article originally appeared on the op-ed page of the *Boston
Globe* on August 26, 2009.

1   Recent headlines about whether G.I. Jane should be serving in combat or combat
units—a violation of official policy—touched a nerve with women warriors.
2   A group called the Center for Military Readiness has been lobbying Congress to
restrict women's roles in war. But in fact, today's wars have already decided when and
where women are to be deployed. Instead of restricting women's opportunities, it is time
for Pentagon leadership to consider codifying the reality of the role of women in combat.
Defense Secretary Robert Gates should keep time with the beat of reality on the ground.
3   On today's battlefield, there is little differentiation between "front" and "rear" area
operations. Whether they are in "combat units" or not, women are on the front lines,

and they are invaluable. Period. By not acknowledging that in official policy, we diminish the sacrifices and contributions these women make every day.

4   Women have played an increasing role in recent wars, and the trend is likely to continue. Over 7,000 women served in Vietnam. In the first Persian Gulf War, 33,000 women deployed to the Gulf. Since Sept. 11, more than 220,000 of our total deployed forces have been women.

5   Even as the military fights wars in Iraq and Afghanistan, the class that entered West Point in 2008 contained more women than any other class since women first came to the academy in 1976. Higher-ranking women are also pursuing combat command experience for promotion opportunities. If we prohibit women from acquiring that experience, they will never earn the same status as their male counterparts—although they may be doing effectively the same jobs.

6   Putting those concerns aside, our thin-stretched military can ill afford to keep women out of combat zones. Excluding women from combat units—infantry, armor, special operations, and some artillery units—hurts those units, because there are simply not enough male soldiers to fill their forward support companies.

7   Stability operations, peacekeeping, and counterinsurgency are unequivocally the norm for today's military and tomorrow's. These operations require winning local populations' hearts and minds, and female soldiers are well equipped to engage with the half of the population that shares their gender. The generation of soldiers who grew up in this complex environment understands that having well-trained women helps accomplish the mission. Officially restricting such a key resource from the front lines is naive and counterproductive—as many of our closest allies have recognized.

8   Myriad examples of the unofficial policy illustrate women's increasingly important front-line role in the no-boundary combat zone. In some special operations units, women are essential for cover and approach missions—and can easily and should morph into the assault elements if appropriate. Marine Female Engagement Teams (FETs) in Afghanistan also reflect the changing nature of counterinsurgents. An all-female unit of 46 Marines, the FET is the military's latest innovation in its competition with the Taliban for the populace's loyalty. Afghan women are viewed as good intelligence sources, and more open to the basics of the military's hearts-and-minds effort—including hygiene, education, and an end to the violence.

9   Without a doubt, this is a complex question with a lot of attendant emotion. Assuming women can meet physical requirements, one of the remaining concerns centers on the potential for women to be disruptive to combat unit cohesion. Experience in Iraq and Afghanistan has proven otherwise. According to a member of the well-disciplined Special Forces, elite women have integrated smoothly into many operations without disruption.

10   Human sexuality will always present a challenge to organizational discipline. In an isolated combat unit, it could present challenges, and long-term infantry operations in isolated outposts could create a situation where issues of sex impede an organization's survival skills. But on forward-operating bases, managing sexual issues should be like managing routine personnel issues. Banning sex is futile and impossible; the best approach is to set rules regarding fraternization, maintain awareness of relationships within the command, and strictly and fairly discipline transgressors.

11   At this point, the question is not whether women should be serving in combat, but whether we have enough women at all for today's wars.

12   We are ready, and we are already there.

QUESTIONS FOR DISCUSSION AND WRITING

1. Have you served in the military or does a family member or close friend serve in the military? Prior to reading this essay, what was your opinion about women in combat? Was this based on personal experience? the experience of a friend or relative? your ideas about gender roles? or on arguments you've heard in the media? Did this essay change your thinking or challenge your ideas on the subject? How is your opinion the same or different than before reading this piece?

2. In your own words summarize the claim or the assertion that Broadwell makes in this piece. What prompted her to express her ideas about the role of women in the military?

3. List three arguments Broadwell makes supporting the role of women in combat. Then classify each piece of evidence whether it be statistics, personal experience, events in recent history or a personal judgment. Which argument did you find the most convincing? Which argument was the least convincing? Why?

4. Does what you know about Broadwell's background make her credible, neutral, or biased when it comes to arguing about women in combat? Explain.

5. Broadwell discusses the argument that women can be disruptive to combat unit cohesion. Does she acknowledge one or both sides of the issue? Does this strengthen or weaken her argument?

EXERCISES

1. Try to determine from the following list which subjects are arguable and which are not.
   a. Letter grades in all college courses should be replaced by pass/fail grades.
   b. Sororities and fraternities are responsible for binge drinking among college students.
   c. Lobster is my favorite seafood.
   d. Professor Greene is one of the best professors on campus.
   e. Children are better off if they are raised in a traditional nuclear family.
   f. Advertisements now often appear in commercial films using a strategy called product placement.
   g. Minorities make up only 10 percent of upper management positions in corporate America.
   h. The earth's population will be 7 billion by the year 2011.
   i. Juveniles who commit serious crimes should be sent to adult prisons.
   j. Last night's sunset over the mountains was spectacular.

    k. Advertisers often mislead the public about the benefits of their products.

    l. AIDS testing for health care workers should be mandatory.

  m. Bilingual education programs fail to help non-English-speaking children become part of mainstream society.

    n. Scenes of the nativity often displayed at Christmastime should not be allowed on public property.

    o. The tsunami that struck Asia in December of 2004 is the worst natural disaster in recorded history.

    p. Couples should have to get a license before having children.

    q. Given all the billions of galaxies and billions of stars in each galaxy, there must be life elsewhere.

    r. Secondhand smoke causes cancer.

2. In your argument notebook, create a pro/con checklist for the following topics. Make two columns: pro on one side, con on the other. If possible, team up with other students to brainstorm opposing points on each issue. Try to come up with five or six solid points and counterpoints.

    a. I think women are better listeners than men.

    b. If a juvenile is charged with a serious crime and his/her parents are found to be negligent, the parents should be charged with the crime as well.

    c. "Hard" sciences such as math are more difficult than "soft" sciences such as sociology.

    d. There should be a mandatory nationwide ban of cigarette smoking in all places of work including office buildings, restaurants, bars, and clubs.

    e. The university should reduce tuition for those students who maintained an A average during the previous year.

    f. ROTC should be made available to all students in U.S. colleges and universities.

    g. The majority of American people support prayer in school.

    h. Mandatory national ID cards would reduce the threat of terrorism in this country.

3. Use one of these topics to construct a dialogue in which the object is not to oppose the other side but to respond constructively to its concerns. As a first step, analyze the reasons provided by both sides and make a list of their concerns, noting whether any are shared. Then create a dialogue that might take place between the two.

4. Write about a recent experience in which you tried to convince someone of something. What reasons did you use to make your claim convincing? Which were most successful? What were the opposing reasons? How did you respond?

Reading Arguments: Thinking Like a Critic

We read for a variety of purposes. Sometimes it's to find information about when a particular event will take place, or to check on the progress of a political candidate, or to learn how to assemble a piece of furniture. Other times we read to be entertained by a favorite newspaper columnist, or to discover the secrets behind making a pot of really good chili. But if you've ever picked up a book, a magazine article, a newspaper editorial, or a piece of advertising and found yourself questioning the ideas and claims of the authors, then you've engaged in a special kind of reading called *critical reading*. When you look beyond the surface of words and thoughts to think about the ideas and their meaning and significance, you are reading critically.

Critical reading is active reading. It involves asking questions and not necessarily accepting the writer's statements at face value. Critical readers ask questions of authors such as these:

■ What do you mean by that phrase?
■ Can you support that statement?
■ How do you define that term?
■ Why is this observation important?
■ How did you arrive at that conclusion?
■ Do other experts agree with you?
■ Is this evidence up-to-date?

By asking such questions, you are weighing the writer's claims, asking for definitions, evaluating information, looking for proof, questioning assumptions, and making judgments. In short, you are actively engaged in thinking like a critic.

Why Read Critically?

When you read critically, you think critically. Instead of passively accepting what's written on a page, you separate yourself from the text and decide what is convincing to you and what is not. Critical reading is a process of discovery. You discover where an author stands on an issue, and you discover the strengths and weaknesses of an author's argument. The result is that you have a better understanding of the issue. By asking questions of the author, by analyzing where the author stands with respect to others' views on the issue, you become more knowledgeable about the issue and more able to develop your own informed viewpoint on the subject.

Critical reading not only sharpens your focus on an issue, it also heightens your ability to construct and evaluate your own arguments. That will lead you to become a better writer because critical reading is the first step to critical writing. Good writers look at the written word the way a carpenter looks at a house—they study the fine details and how those details connect to create the whole. It's the same with critical reading. The better you become at analyzing and reacting to another's written work, the better you are at analyzing and reacting to your own, by asking: Is it logical? Are my points clearly stated? Do my examples really support my ideas? Have I explained this term clearly? Is my conclusion persuasive? In other words, critical reading will help you use that same critical eye with your own writing, making you both a better reader and a better writer.

Additionally, as you sharpen your skills as a reader and a writer, you will also develop your critical skills as an interpreter of arguments embodied not in words but in visual images. As you will see in Chapter 8, argumentation is not limited to verbal presentation. Photographs, political cartoons, and advertisements, among others, express potent and persuasive arguments in visual imagery.

Even though you may already employ many of the strategies of critical reading, we'd like to offer some suggestions and techniques to make you an even better critical reader.

Preview the Reading

Even before you begin reading, you can look for clues that may reveal valuable information about the subject of the article, the writer's attitude about the subject, the audience the writer is addressing, and the purpose of the article. As a prereading strategy, try to answer the following questions:

1. *Who is the writer?* Information about the writer is sometimes provided in a short biographical note on the first or last page of the reading. The writer's age, education, current profession, and professional background can tell you about his or her experience and perspective on the subject. For instance, a physician who is writing about assisted suicide may have a very different attitude toward that subject than an individual who has a degree in divinity. A writer who has held a high-ranking position in a government agency or a political appointment will bring that experience to bear in a discussion of a political issue. A writer's background and professional training can provide knowledge and credibility; you may be more inclined to believe an expert in a field than someone with little or no experience. However, direct experience can also limit the writer's perspective. A review of this information before you read can help you better evaluate the writer as an authority.

2. *Where was the article originally published?* Often the publication in which the article originally appeared will indicate the writer's audience and purpose. Some publications, such as scholarly journals, are intended to be read by other professionals in a particular field. Writers for such a journal assume that readers are familiar with the terminology of that profession and possess a certain

level of education and experience. For example, an author writing about cancer research in a scholarly medical journal such as the *Journal of the American Medical Association (JAMA)* would assume a high degree of medical expertise on the part of the readers. An author writing about the same cancer research in *Newsweek* would provide a greatly simplified version with little medical terminology. Popular magazines you see at newsstands are designed to communicate to a larger, more general audience. Writers make an effort to explain difficult concepts in terms an inexperienced reader can understand. Knowing where the article was originally published will prepare you for the demands of the reading. It may also prepare you for the writer's point of view. Publications are usually designed for a specific audience. The *Wall Street Journal,* for example, has a readership largely comprising people interested in the economy, business, or investments. The articles in it reflect the concerns and interests of the business community. In contrast, an article appearing in *High Times,* a publication that endorses the use and legalization of marijuana, has a very different set of readers. By familiarizing yourself with the publication in which the article originally appeared, you can learn much about the writer's likely political and professional opinions, knowledge you can use to judge the credibility of his or her argument.

3. *When was the article originally published?* The date of publication can also provide background about what was happening when the article was published. It will indicate factors that might have influenced the writer and whether the evidence used in the reading is current or historical. For instance, an article written about the economy during a recession would be strongly influenced by factors of high unemployment and business failures. The writer's argument might not be as convincing during a period of growth and stability. Some readings are timeless in their consideration of basic truths about people and life; others can be challenged about whether their arguments still apply to current circumstances.

4. *What does the title reveal about the subject and the author's attitude toward it?* The title of an article often indicates both the subject of the article and the writer's attitude toward it. After you have identified the subject, look carefully at the words the writer has used to describe it. Are their connotations negative or positive? What other words do you associate with them? Does the title make reference to another written work or to a well-known slogan or familiar saying? Sometimes writers use their titles to suggest a parallel between their subject and a similar situation in recent times or a particular event in history. An article about the possibility of an annihilating nuclear attack in 2020 might be titled "Hiroshima in the Twenty-First Century." These choices are deliberate ways to inform readers about a writer's views and ideas on a subject. By considering the language in the title, you will be more aware of the writer's intent.

Let's try a preview of the first reading in this chapter. By carefully reading the introductory paragraph, you can learn the following information:

Preview Question 1: Who is the writer? As the introduction tells us, Henry Wechsler is the director of the College Alcohol Studies Program at the Harvard

School of Public Health. His professional title suggests that he is knowledge-able about alcohol use, particularly at the college level, because he directs a program that studies this area. You are about to read an essay, then, written by an expert in the field of alcohol research.

Preview Question 2: Where was the article originally published? By reading further in the paragraph, you find that the article was originally published in the *Boston Globe*. This is a widely circulated newspaper located in a major American city. The writer would expect the article to be read by a large cross-section of people with diverse economic and educational backgrounds. Because Boston is the city where Harvard and many other colleges are located, readers might have a special interest in issues that affect the college community.

Preview Question 3: When was the article originally published? The introduction tells you that the article first appeared on October 2, 1997. Although this was written some 13 years ago, the topic is still relevant to current concerns.

Preview Question 4: What does the title reveal about the subject and the author's attitude toward it? The title of the article, "Binge Drinking Must Be Stopped," suggests an emphatic and nonnegotiable attitude on the part of the author.

As you can see, your preview of the article has provided much valuable information that will help prepare you to begin the critical reading process.

Skim the Reading

Just as an athlete would never participate in a competitive event without first stretching his or her muscles and thoroughly warming up, you will find that successful critical reading is a process that benefits from a series of activities aimed at increasing your understanding of the writer's ideas. The first time through, you may wish to skim the reading to get a general idea of its subject and intent. Further readings should be slower and more thoughtful so that each reason presented can be analyzed and evaluated and each idea judged and considered. Now that you have previewed the material about the author, the original publication and date, and the title, you are ready to skim the reading to find its basic features.

When you skim a reading, you are trying to discover the topic and the claim. Start by reading the first one or two paragraphs and the last paragraph. If the reading is a relatively short newspaper article, such as the following sample essay, this may be enough to give you a general idea of the writer's topic and point of view. If the reading is longer and more complex, you will also need to examine the first sentence or two of each paragraph to get a better sense of the writer's ideas.

SAMPLE ARGUMENT FOR ANALYSIS

For practice, let's skim the first reading in this chapter. To organize your impressions from skimming the reading, it's a good idea to write down some of them in your journal.

Binge Drinking Must Be Stopped
Henry Wechsler

"Binge" drinking is a problem that plagues many colleges and universities across America. Fueled by an "alcohol culture," students will drink to excess at apartment parties or fraternity houses just off campus. But the disturbing fact is that thousands of them die each year as a result of alcohol abuse. And, as argued in the essay below, too many college administrators are apparently turning a blind eye to the problem. Dr. Henry Wechsler is a social psychologist with a long-term commitment to research on alcohol and drug abuse among young people. A lecturer in the Department of Society, Human Development and Health at the Harvard School of Public Health, he is the principal investigator of the College Alcohol Study. Since its inception in 1992, the study has surveyed over 50,000 students at 120 colleges in 40 states, producing dozens of publications that have focused national attention on college binge drinking and its harmful effects. Dr. Wechsler is the author of 18 books and monographs including most recently *Dying to Drink* (2003). This essay was originally published in the *Boston Globe* in 1997 and has been updated by the author for this edition of *Argument as Dialogue: A Concise Guide*.

1   A recent study conducted for the National Institute on Alcohol Abuse and Alcoholism estimated that over 1800 college students 18–24 years of age died from alcohol related injuries in the past year. We should be saddened and outraged by these tragic deaths of young men and women just starting to fulfill their life's promise.

2   These deaths are an extreme and unfortunate consequence of a style of drinking that is deeply entrenched and widespread in American colleges. Binge drinking is a reality of college life in America and perhaps the central focus of fraternity house life.

3   Since the Harvard School of Public Health study on college binge drinking was released in 1994, colleges have been deluged with reports on alcohol abuse. Even before our results became public, it was inconceivable that college administrators were unaware of the existence of alcohol problems at their institutions.

4   A quick ride in a security van on a Thursday, Friday, or Saturday night could provide all the information needed. A conversation with the chief of security could easily reveal where the binge drinking takes place and which students, fraternities, and alcohol outlets are violating college rules or local ordinances.

5   An incoming freshman learns during the first week of school where the alcohol and parties are and often has a binge drinking experience even before purchasing a textbook. If students can find it so easily, so can college administrators. It is not that complicated: Drunken parties are usually at certain fraternity houses and housing complexes just off campus. The beer that fuels these parties is bought in the liquor stores offering cut rate prices for large purchases. Heavy drinking also takes place in the many bars encircling most campuses where large quantities of alcohol are sold cheaply.

6   If we know so much about the problem, why is it that we have not been able to do much about it? First, because colleges, like problem drinkers, do not recognize that they have a problem. And those that do think that they have solved it through half-measures.

It has been there for so long that they have adapted to it. They are lulled into complacency as long as the problem does not seem to increase or a tragedy does not occur.

7   Second, the solutions that are offered are usually only partial: a lecture, an awareness day, a new regulation in the dorms. The root of the problem is seldom touched. The focus is on the students, and not on the suppliers and marketers of the alcohol. The supply of large quantities of cheap alcohol is viewed as outside the purview of college officials. "It's off campus" is a euphemism for "that's not my job." The bar or liquor store may be off campus, but it is controlled by licensing boards that city officials and colleges can substantially influence. The fraternity house may be off campus and not owned by the college, but it is affiliated with and depends on the college for its existence. Many colleges and universities simply wink at the activities of the fraternities and claim no responsibility.

8   Third, when new policies are established, they are often assumed to be in effect without proper verification. It is easy to say there is no drinking allowed in a dormitory or a fraternity, but enforcement is necessary to put the policy into effect. Legally, no alcohol can be sold to people under age 21, but 86 percent of college students drink.

9   We can no longer be shocked at what is happening on many college campuses and in many fraternities. This is no longer a time merely to form a committee to study the situation. It is time to act.

10   Action needs to be taken on many fronts: the college president's office, the fraternity and sorority system, the athletics department, community licensing boards, and foremost, those students who are sick of the drinking they see around them.

11   Parents who pay for college tuitions should demand a safe environment for their children. Binge drinking need not remain an integral part of college life. University presidents must make it their responsibility to produce change.

After skimming "Binge Drinking Must Be Stopped," you might record the following (we indicate in parentheses the paragraphs in which we found our ideas):

> Wechsler starts off with a reference to a study that reports on the large number of college student deaths as the result of alcohol-related injuries. He says we should be saddened and outraged by this. Then he suggests that binge drinking has become very common on college campuses, particularly in fraternities *(paragraphs 1 and 2).* Wechsler believes parents should insist that colleges provide a safe environment for their children by finding solutions for binge drinking. University presidents must take responsibility for solving this problem *(paragraph 11).*

By skimming the article, you now have some sense of what the reading will be about and the writer's position. Before beginning a closer reading of the text, you will want to take one additional step to prepare yourself to be an active and responsive reader: Consider your experience with the topic.

Consider Your Own Experience

Your next step in the reading process is to consider your own experience. Critical reading brings your own perspective, experience, education, and personal values to your reading. Sometimes you begin with very little knowledge about the subject of your reading. It may be a topic that you haven't given much thought or one that is unfamiliar and new. Other times you may start with some of your own ideas and opinions about the subject. By taking the time to consider what you know and how your own experiences and values relate to the author's ideas, you can add a dimension to your reading that enables you to question, analyze, and understand the writer's ideas more effectively. You will be a more active critical reader because you can respond to the writer's ideas with ideas of your own.

Before beginning a close reading, take the time to reflect on these questions:

■ What do I know about this subject?
■ What have I heard or read about it recently?
■ What attitudes or opinions do I have about the subject?

Exploring what you already know or think about a subject can have several benefits: You can use your knowledge to better understand the situation or issue described in the reading; you can compare your own experience with that of the writer; you can formulate questions to keep in mind as you read; and you can become more aware of your own opinions about the subject. For instance, you may be reading an article about the benefits of the proposed plan for improving your state's welfare system. If you have some knowledge about this proposal from reading news stories or hearing discussions about it, you will begin your reading with some understanding of the issue. If you have had actual experience with the welfare system or know of others' experiences, you can provide examples of your own to challenge or support those of the writer. If you have taken the time to consider questions you have about the proposed plan, you will be actively seeking answers as you read. And, by exploring your own views on the subject before you read, you will find that the ideas in the article will enrich, inform, and possibly change your opinion.

After previewing and skimming the reading, John, a freshman composition student, wrote the following reflection on the topic of binge drinking in his journal:

It would be hard to be a student at college and not notice the heavy drinking that goes on every weekend. Some people just can't have fun unless they drink too much. It's a fact of college life—for some people. And if you live in a small college community, sometimes that's all there is to do on Saturday night. I've seen some kids really ruin their lives with too much partying. They forget why they came to college in the first place—or maybe that is why they came. But not everybody drinks to excess. Most of us just like to get a little buzz and socialize and have fun. Most of us will go just so far and stop, but there's always a few who can't seem to stop until they pass out or puke their guts out on the sidewalk. Yeah, we've all been told the dangers of drinking too much, but some people aren't mature enough to see that they're hurting themselves. Binge drinking happens every weekend around here. It's not a pretty sight, but I'm not sure how the college president or anybody else could stop it. College students have always partied to relieve tension and to socialize. It's been going on for years. Why is college drinking suddenly such a big issue? And, if the drinking takes place outside of campus, how can the college stop it? If students want to get alcohol, even if they're underage, they'll find a way. Why should the college tell us whether we can drink or not?

John clearly has considerable experience with the topic and some strong opinions of his own. By considering them before he begins a close reading of the article, he is ready to explore and challenge the ideas he encounters in the reading.

Annotate the Reading

Annotating the text is the next stage of critical reading to help you become a thoughtful and careful reader. *Annotating* is responding to the ideas in the reading right on the pages of your text. (If you don't own the publication the essay appears in, make a photocopy.) There are many different ways to annotate a reading, but many readers use the following methods:

- ■ Highlight or underline passages that you consider significant.
- ■ Write questions in the margins that respond to the writer's ideas or that you wish to follow up with further investigation.
- ■ Circle words or phrases that need to be defined or made clearer.
- ■ Add comments or brief examples of your own that support or challenge the writer's.
- ■ Draw lines between related ideas.
- ■ Note the writer's use of transitions and qualifiers that subtly shade meaning.
- ■ Point out with arrows or asterisks particularly persuasive examples.
- ■ Mark difficult-to-understand sections of the text that need a closer look.

Annotation is a way to create an active dialogue between you and the writer by responding in writing to individual points in the reading. Your annotations become a personal record of your thoughts, questions, objections, comments, and agreements with the writer. Annotation can help you read like a critic because it makes you slow down and pay attention to each idea as you read. As an additional benefit, your written comments in the margin will serve as a reminder of your response to the ideas in the essay when you read it again. Figure 2.1 on pages 33–35 is an example of some of the ways you might annotate "Binge Drinking Must Be Stopped."

Binge Drinking Must Be Stopped

1   A recent study conducted for the National Institute on Alcohol Abuse and Alcoholism estimated that over 1800 college students 18–24 years of age died from alcohol related injuries in the past year. We should be saddened and outraged by these tragic deaths of young men and women just starting to fulfill their life's promise.

Does everyone at college drink?

2   These deaths are an extreme and unfortunate consequence of a style of drinking that is deeply entrenched and widespread in American colleges. Binge drinking is a reality of college life in America and perhaps the central focus of fraternity house life.

claim

3   Since the Harvard School of Public Health study on college
binge drinking was released in 1994, colleges have been deluged
with reports on alcohol abuse. Even before our results became
public, it was inconceivable that college administrators were
unaware of the existence of alcohol problems at their institutions.

find more info on this flooded

4   A quick ride in a security van on a Thursday, Friday, or
Saturday night could provide all the information needed. A conversation with the chief of security could easily reveal where the
binge drinking takes place and which students, fraternities, and
alcohol outlets are violating college rules or local ordinances.

Is this the job of a college administrator?

5   An incoming freshman learns during the first week of
school where the alcohol and parties are and often has a binge
drinking experience even before purchasing a textbook. If students can find it so easily, so can college administrators. It is not
that complicated: Drunken parties are usually at certain fraternity houses and housing complexes just off campus. The beer
that fuels these parties is bought in the liquor stores offering cut
rate prices for large purchases. Heavy drinking also takes place
in the many bars encircling most campuses where large quantities of alcohol are sold cheaply.

qualifier
How does he know this?

6   If we know so much about the problem, why is it that we
have not been able to do much about it? First, because colleges,
like problem drinkers, do not recognize that they have a problem. And those that do think that they have solved it through
half-measures. It has been there for so long that they have
adapted to it. They are lulled into complacency as long as the
problem does not seem to increase or a tragedy does not occur.

who is "we"?

Is this contradicted by the next ¶ ?

7   Second, the solutions that are offered are usually only partial: a
lecture, an awareness day, a new regulation in the dorms. The root
of the problem is seldom touched. The focus is on the students, and
not on the suppliers and marketers of the alcohol. The supply of
large quantities of cheap alcohol is viewed as outside the purview of
college officials. "It's off campus" is a euphemism for "that's not
my job." The bar or liquor store may be off campus, but it is controlled by licensing boards that city officials and colleges can substantially influence. The fraternity house may be off campus and not
owned by the college, but it is affiliated with and depends on the
college for its existence. Many colleges and universities simply
wink at the activities of the fraternities and claim no responsibility.

Don't colleges try to do something about binge drinking?

Agreed. These don't change behaviour much.

less offensive substitute word

What does he mean?

8   Third, when new policies are established, they are often
assumed to be in effect without proper verification. It is easy to
say there is no drinking allowed in a dormitory or a fraternity,
but enforcement is necessary to put the policy into effect.
Legally, no alcohol can be sold to people under age 21, but
86 percent of college students drink.

Impressive statistic

9   We can no longer be shocked at what is happening on many
college campuses and in many fraternities. This is no longer a
time merely to form a committee to study the situation. It is time
to act.

Who is "we"? Has it changed?

10   Action needs to be taken on many fronts: the college president's office, the fraternity and sorority system, the athletics
department, community licensing boards, and foremost, those
students who are sick of the drinking they see around them.

His solution. What should they do?

11   Parents who pay for college tuitions should demand a safe
environment for their children. Binge drinking need not remain
an integral part of college life. University presidents must make
it their responsibility to produce change.

Who is responsible? Don't the drinkers have some responsibility?

essential   *Are college students "children"?*

Figure 2.1

Summarize the Reading

Before you can begin to analyze and evaluate what you read, it's important to understand clearly what the writer is saying. *Summarizing* is a type of writing used to capture the essential meaning of a reading by focusing only on the writer's main points.
When you summarize, you "tell back," in a straightforward way, the writer's main
ideas. Although summaries can vary in length depending on the length of the original
reading, all summaries share these qualities:

■ **A summary is considerably shorter than the original.**   Because a summary
is concerned only with the writer's main ideas, supporting details and examples
are usually omitted. The length of a summary will vary depending on your purpose and the length and content of the original.

■ **A summary is written in your own words.**   Although it may be necessary to
use certain of the writer's words for which there are no substitutes, a summary is
written in your own words. If you find it necessary to include a short phrase from
the original, then quotation marks must be used to set it off. (In Chapter 9, we
discuss ways to use summary in a researched argument paper and the need to
document the ideas in your summary with a citation.)

■ **A summary is objective.**   When you summarize, your job is to "tell back" the
writer's main ideas with no comments or personal opinions of your own. Of course,
once you have completed your summary, you are free to respond to it in any way
you wish.

■ **A summary is accurate.**   It's a good idea to reread several times before you
attempt to summarize a reading because it's important that you truly understand
what the writer means. Sometimes it takes many tries to capture that exact meaning.

■ **A summary is thorough.**   Even though a summary is, as we've explained,
much shorter than the original, a good summary contains each of the writer's
main points.

Summarizing is an important step in critical reading because you need to understand a writer's ideas thoroughly before you can explain them, in writing, to others. Don't be discouraged when you first try to summarize a reading. Over time and with practice you will feel more comfortable writing summaries.

A good method to begin summarizing a reading is to write a one-sentence summary of the ideas in each paragraph. (Brief paragraphs that elaborate the same point can be summarized together.) By considering each paragraph separately, you will be sure to cover all the main ideas in the reading and be able to see at a glance how the ideas in the essay are connected to each other and how the writer has chosen to sequence them.

Let's go back to the essay "Binge Drinking Must Be Stopped" and try a one-sentence summary of each paragraph (we combine short paragraphs that are about the same idea):

Paragraphs 1: According to a recent study, some 1800 college students 18–24 years of age died from alcohol related injuries this past year—a tragic reality.

Paragraph 2: Colleges should be aware of the problem of excessive drinking among their students because studies have been released about it.

Paragraph 3: By speaking with law enforcement professionals in their own communities, colleges could become aware of where alcohol laws are being broken.

Paragraph 4: Freshmen learn where to find alcohol when they first arrive on campus: fraternities, student housing, and bars close to campus.

Paragraph 5: Colleges aren't doing anything about the problem because they have accepted it and don't want to admit it exists.

Paragraph 6: Because the cause of the problem is the availability of alcohol off campus, colleges don't think it is their responsibility to act even though they could exercise a strong influence over the places that sell alcohol to students.

Paragraph 7: Colleges don't check to see whether their own alcohol policies are being enforced.

Paragraphs 8 and 9: Rather than just talk about this problem, we need to do something about it at many different levels within the college and the community.

Paragraph 10: College presidents need to take responsibility for reducing the practice of excessive drinking at their colleges to provide a safe place for students.

Your one-sentence summary of each paragraph should reveal the essential parts of the essay: the claim and the main reasons the writer uses to support the claim. Once you have identified these important elements, you are ready to begin your summary. It might look something like this (note that we've added the name of the writer and the title of the article):

In his essay "Binge Drinking Must Be Stopped," Henry Wechsler expresses his concern about the common practice of excessive drinking on college campuses. He suggests that colleges are failing in their responsibility to deal with this problem adequately. Although colleges should be informed about the problem, they won't acknowledge its seriousness. Because it doesn't happen on their campuses, they don't feel that it is their responsibility. Wechsler thinks that colleges could exercise their influence off campus in ways that would help to solve the problem. And, even when colleges do have alcohol policies to restrict drinking, they don't check to see if their policies are being enforced. The problem of binge drinking needs to be dealt with now at many different levels within the college and the community. Wechsler thinks that college presidents need to take responsibility for dealing with binge drinking so that it is no longer an important part of college life.

In looking over this summary, you'll notice that we begin with a general sentence that presents the writer's topic and claim. Then, after reviewing our one-sentence paragraph summaries, we have chosen the writer's main reasons to include in the rest of our paragraph. We have tried to eliminate any ideas that are repeated in more than one paragraph, so we can focus on only the major points.

Summarizing a reading means taking all the separate ideas the writer presents, deciding which ones are important, and weaving them together to create a whole. Our next step in the critical reading process is to consider the ways in which the writer has presented those ideas.

Analyze and Evaluate the Reading

To *analyze* something means to break it down into its separate parts, examine those parts closely, and evaluate their significance and how they work together as a whole. You already began this process when you summarized the main idea in each paragraph of your reading. But analysis goes beyond identifying the ideas in the essay. When we analyze, we consider how each part of the essay functions. We are discovering and evaluating the assumptions and intentions of the writer, which lie below the surface of the writing and which we consider separately from the meaning of the essay itself. Analysis helps us consider how successfully and effectively the writer has argued.

Although there is no set formula for analyzing an argument, we can offer some specific questions you should explore when reading an essay that is meant to persuade you:

- What are the writer's assumptions? What does the writer take for granted about the readers' values, beliefs, or knowledge? What does the writer assume about the subject of the essay or the facts involved?
- What kind of audience is the writer addressing?
- What are the writer's purpose and intention?
- How well does the writer accomplish those purposes?
- What kinds of evidence has the writer used—personal experience or scientific data or outside authorities?
- How convincing is the evidence presented? Is it relevant? Is it reliable? Is it specific enough? Is it sufficient? Is it slanted or dated?
- Does the writer's logic seem reasonable?
- Did the writer address opposing views?
- Is the writer persuasive?

For the sake of illustration, let's apply these questions to our reading:

■ *What are the writer's assumptions?*
The writer assumes that the estimated number of alcohol-related student deaths indicates a widespread problem of binge drinking on college campuses. He thinks that colleges have a responsibility to control the behavior of their students. He assumes that college students will continue to binge drink without any such controls.

■ *What kind of audience is the writer addressing?*
He seems to be addressing college administrators, parents of college students, and readers who have a special interest in college life.

■ *What are the writer's purpose and intention?*
He wants to make his readers aware that a problem exists and that colleges are not effectively dealing with it.

■ *How well does the writer accomplish this purpose?*
He makes a strong argument that colleges refuse to acknowledge that there's a problem.

■ *What kinds of evidence has the writer used?*
He refers to a recent study for the National Institute on Alcohol Abuse and Alcoholism as well as others by the Harvard School of Public Health, and he uses examples of student hangouts that he has heard about but not experienced personally. He seems familiar with college programs on alcohol awareness. He implies that he consulted with the campus security chief for some of his information.

■ *How convincing is the evidence?*
Wechsler mentions a scientific study in paragraph 1 with figures and then again in paragraph 3; but he does not offer much in the way of details concerning the second study. While Wechsler could provide more solid evidence that the problem is widespread, his examples of places where students can find alcohol seem convincing.

■ *Does the writer's logic seem reasonable?*
Wechsler effectively links the evidence he presents to his claim that excessive drinking on college campuses is being ignored by college administrators.

■ *Did the writer address opposing views?*
No. We never hear how college administrators respond to this criticism. We also don't know if college students agree with the description of their behavior.

■ *Is the writer persuasive?*
The writer is persuasive if we assume that the problem is widespread and that colleges can have a major impact on students' behavior when they are not on campus.

Argue with the Reading

Asking questions and challenging assumptions are important ways to read critically. Although you may not feel qualified to pass judgment on a writer's views, especially if the writer is a professional or an expert on a particular subject, you should keep in mind that as a part of the writer's audience, you have every right to determine whether an argument is sound, logical, and convincing. Your questions about and objections to the writer's ideas will help you evaluate the effectiveness of his or her argument and form your own judgment about the issue.

You may wish to record some of these thoughts in your annotations in the margins of the text. However, a good strategy for beginning writers is to respond at greater length in a journal. You might start by jotting down any points in the essay that contradict your own experience or personal views. Note anything you are skeptical about. Write down any questions you have about the claims, reasons, or evidence. If some point or conclusion seems forced or unfounded, record it and briefly explain why. The more skeptical and questioning you are, the more closely you are reading the text and analyzing its ideas. In particular, be on the lookout for logical fallacies, those instances in which the writer—whether unintentionally or purposefully—distorts or exaggerates evidence or relies on faulty logic to make a point. We discuss these fallacies extensively later in this chapter.

Likewise, make note of the features of the text that impress you—powerful points, interesting wording, original insights, clever or amusing phrases or allusions, well-chosen references, or the general structure of the essay. If you have heard or read different views on the issue, you might wish to record them as well.

As an example, let's consider some questions, challenges, and features that might have impressed you in our sample essay:

- Wechsler claims that binge drinking is a common practice at colleges across America. Is that true? Does binge drinking take place at all colleges or only on certain campuses? Do all students engage in this practice, or is it more common among certain age groups, gender, fraternity members as opposed to nonmembers, residential students? Do college students drink more than noncollege students in the same age group?
- The statistic about the number of student deaths (paragraph 1) and percentage of college students who drink (paragraph 8) is convincing.
- Colleges exist to educate students. Are they responsible for monitoring students' behavior when they are not attending classes or socializing off campus? Is it realistic to expect colleges to do this?
- Are colleges really denying that the problem exists? Don't they have counseling services to help students with drinking problems? What else can they do?
- Wechsler's points about the influence that colleges have in their communities (paragraph 7) are persuasive.
- Mentioning the concerns of students who don't drink and the parents of college students is a clever strategy Wechsler uses to expand his audience and pressure colleges to act.

Create a Debate and Dialogue Between Two or More Readings

Few of us would expect to be experts on tennis or golf after watching one match or tournament. We know that it takes time and effort to really begin to understand even the fundamentals of a sport. Reading a single article on a particular subject is the first step in becoming educated about the issues at stake, but a single essay provides us with only one perspective on that subject. As we continue to read about the subject, each new article will offer a new perspective and new evidence to support that view. The more we read, the more complex and thorough our knowledge about the subject becomes. Creating a dialogue between two or more readings is the next step in the process of critical reading.

When you annotate a reading in the earlier stages of critical reading, you begin a dialogue between yourself and the writer. When you create a dialogue between two or more readings, you go one step further: You look at the ideas you find in them to see how they compare and contrast with each other, how they are interrelated, and how the information from one reading informs you as you read the next. By creating a dialogue between the ideas you encounter in several readings, you will be able to consider multiple viewpoints about the same subject.

SAMPLE ARGUMENT FOR ANALYSIS

Begin reading this second selection on binge drinking by following the steps we've outlined in this chapter:

1. Preview the information about the author, where the article first appeared, the date of publication, and the title.
2. Skim the reading to discover the writer's topic and claim.
3. Consider your own experience, values, and knowledge about the subject.
4. Annotate the reading.
5. Summarize the essay.
6. Analyze and evaluate the effectiveness of the reading.
7. Argue with the reading.

Stop Babysitting College Students
Froma Harrop

> Froma Harrop presents another viewpoint on the subject of binge drinking and college students in the following essay, which appeared in the *Tampa Tribune.* Harrop, an editorial writer and columnist for the *Providence Journal,* argues that college students should be the ones held responsible for their behavior, not businesses and educational institutions.

1   Anyone suspicious that the American university experience has become a four-year extension of childhood need look no farther than the colleges' latest response to the binge-drinking "problem." Now, in a grown-up world, college administrators would tell students who down four or five stiff drinks in a row that they are jerks.

2   If they commit violent acts as a result, the police get called. If they drive after drinking, they go to the slammer. If they die from alcohol poisoning, they have nothing but their own stupidity to blame.

3   But if they can drink responsibly, then let them have a good time.

4   Forget about hearing any such counsel, for that would turn students into self-directing adults. Better to blame the problem on all-purpose "cultural attitudes" and "societal pressures" abetted by the villainous alcohol industry.

5   Thus, demands grow for better policing of off-campus liquor outlets. That is, turn local businesses into babysitters. There are calls to ban sponsorship of college events by companies selling alcohol or the marketing of such beverages on campus. That is, protect their charges from evil influences and trample on free speech. (What should colleges do with the frequent references in Western literature to the glories of drink? Rabelais, for example, said, "There are more old drunkards than old physicians.")

6   One former college official has suggested that universities stop serving champagne at parents' weekend brunches or at fundraising events. Remove the bad example for the sake of the children. (Somehow it is hard to believe that a college with any sense of self-preservation would insist that its big-check writers remain cold sober.)

7   The truth is, most Americans can drink without a problem. Careful use of alcohol relaxes and warms the drinker with a sense of well-being. Winston Churchill and Franklin Roosevelt saved Western civilization without ever missing a cocktail hour. Students have long enjoyed their own drinking traditions. Brahms' Academic Overture, the stately piece heard over and over again at college commencements, took its melody from a student drinking song.

8   Where is there a campus drinking crisis, anyway? Six college students have supposedly died this year from excessive drinking. These cases are lamentable, but many more college students died from sports-related injuries or car accidents.

9   An even more interesting question is: How many noncollege people in their late teens or early 20s have died from alcohol poisoning? Take note that no one is memorizing this particular statistic—even though the majority of high school students do not go on to college. That number is not etched on our national worry list for the following strange reason: Our society considers the 19-year-old who has a job an adult, while universities see the 19-year-old pre-law student as a child. Working people who cause trouble because they drink are punished. College students are given others to blame.

10   College administrators should know that, from a purely practical point of view, playing hide-the-bottle does no good when dealing with an alcoholic. Indeed, anyone who has hung around Alcoholics Anonymous or Al-Anon can immediately identify such behavior as "enabling." Rather than allow the problem drinker to sink into the

mire of his addiction until he can no longer stand it and takes steps to straighten out, the enabler tries to save him. Rest assured that students interested in getting smashed for the night will find the booze.

11   Let us end here with yet another proposition: that binge drinking is more about binge than drinking. It would seem that someone who gulps five glasses of Jim Beam in five minutes is not looking for a pleasant high. Binge drinking is a stunt that has more in common with diving off bridges or swallowing goldfish than the quest for inebriation.

12   What any increase in binge drinking probably indicates is that the students really don't know how to drink. Binging may just be the latest evidence of decline in our nation's table arts. Instead of savoring wine and spirits in the course of a civilized meal, young people are administering them. The colleges' response is to put condoms on bottles.

Construct a Debate

Now that you have a good understanding of Froma Harrop's views on college students' binge drinking, you are ready to consider the ideas in both the essays you read. Our first step will be to consider the differences between these two writers by constructing a debate. From your summaries of the readings, select the main ideas that seem directly opposed to each other. To highlight those differences, create two columns, one for each writer. Here are a few of the ideas Wechsler and Harrop debate in their essays:

Wechsler	*Harrop*
Binge drinking is a major problem on college campuses: A student has died.	Binge drinking is not a major problem on campuses: Few students have died.
Colleges have a responsibility to take action about this problem.	Students are responsible for their own drinking.
Colleges should prevent off-campus suppliers of alcohol from selling it to college students.	Colleges should not "police" off-campus suppliers of alcohol.
Colleges should provide a safe environment for students.	College students are adults and should take care of themselves.
Binge drinking continues because colleges aren't treating it as an important problem.	Binge drinking happens because some college students haven't learned to drink responsibly.

These are just a sampling of the many ideas that might be debated by these writers. You should be able to come up with several more.

By considering differences, you can see at a glance the ways in which these writers oppose each other. Your next step is to find the ideas they have in common. This may take more searching, but it's an important step in creating a dialogue between them. To get you started, we'll list a few of the ideas we found. See if you can come up with a few more:

1. Both writers acknowledge that drinking takes place on college campuses.
2. Both writers indicate that binge drinking can be a problem and that students have died as a result.
3. Both writers agree that colleges are aware that binge drinking takes place off campus.

Now that you have found both differences and common ideas, you are ready to create a dialogue. When you create a dialogue between two readings, you find ways for the writers to speak to each other that recognize their differences and points of agreement.

Your dialogue will reveal how the ideas in both readings interrelate. Let's try to create a dialogue using some of the ideas we found:

Wechsler: Binge drinking is a serious problem on college campuses. It's an activity that has become commonplace.

Harrop: I agree that college students engage in binge drinking, but six deaths this year don't necessarily indicate that this is a crisis.

Wechsler: Just because more students haven't died doesn't mean that it isn't a dangerous activity and should be ignored. Colleges need to take steps to ensure that more students aren't harmed by this common practice.

Harrop: It's unfortunate that students have died, but why should we think it is the college's responsibility to police student drinking? College students are adults and should suffer the consequences of their behavior. It's their choice whether to drink and how much.

Wechsler: Colleges are responsible for their students. They need to find ways to prevent students from getting alcohol. They are responsible to the parents who pay the tuition and to the other students who have to tolerate excessive drinking among their peers.

Harrop: Practically speaking, colleges can't prevent students from drinking. Students who want to drink will find a way because they are adults with drinking problems, not children in need of supervision.

Complete this dialogue by finding additional ways in which the writers' ideas speak to each other.

As you can see, the dialogue helps us explore the readings in far greater depth than if we had read both essays in isolation. Each writer's ideas help us to evaluate the ideas of the other. By interrelating them in a dialogue, we can better appreciate how the perspective of each writer changes the way similar facts and information are interpreted. For instance, Henry Wechsler is outraged by the estimated 1800 alcohol-related student deaths. In contrast, Froma Harrop does not find the deaths of six college students from excessive drinking an alarming statistic when she compares it with the number of college students who have died from other accidental causes. It is up to us as readers to decide which writer's interpretation is more persuasive.

SAMPLE ARGUMENTS FOR ANALYSIS

To practice creating your own dialogue between readings, read the following two letters to the editor, which appeared in two newspapers before and after Henry Wechsler's article. Read them critically, going through the steps we outlined in this chapter, and add them to the dialogue already created between Wechsler and Harrop. We think you'll find that your understanding of the issue will increase and that you'll feel more confident about forming your own position on the question of college binge drinking.

Letter from the *Washington Post*

To the Editor:

1   When we saw the headline "Party Hardly" and the revolting picture of four bare-chested, probably underage fraternity brothers guzzling cheap beer, we thought, "Finally! Your paper is tackling an issue that affects every college student." Much to our chagrin, however, the article wasted two pages of newsprint glorifying drunkenness and poor study habits.

2   Perhaps you need to be aware of some ugly facts before your next article on college drinking: One out of every four student deaths is related to alcohol use (research shows that as many as 360,000 of the nation's 12 million undergraduates will die as a result of alcohol abuse); alcohol is a factor in 66 percent of student suicides and 60 percent of all sexually transmitted diseases; studies show that between 33 percent and 59 percent of drinking college students drive while intoxicated at least once a year (with as many as 30 percent driving impaired three to 10 times per year); and alcohol consumption was a factor in at least half of the cases of a study of college women who had been raped by an acquaintance.

3   Alcohol affects not only those who drink it: Those students who do not drink are affected by their classmates or roommates who do. Students at schools with high levels of binge drinking are three times more likely to be pushed, hit or sexually assaulted than are students at schools with less drinking. Students who live with people who drink heavily often are kept awake by obnoxious behavior or the sound of their roommates vomiting in the trash can.

4   The shame does not lie solely with your paper, however. *The Princeton Review,* which ranks "party schools" based on how much students use alcohol and drugs, how few hours students study every day and the popularity of fraternities and sororities, should focus on what most feel is the real purpose of a college education: to learn—not to learn how to party.

Kathryn Stewart
Corina Sole

Letter from the *Times-Picayune*

To the Editor:

1   The entire nation is justifiably concerned about recent tragic deaths caused by alcohol abuse on our college campuses. College students everywhere know where to procure alcohol and where to consume it without being "hassled."

2   Public dialogue asks if institutions are doing enough to control the situation. Unfortunately, it must be stated that colleges and universities are doing all they can.

3   A typical university fosters an alcohol awareness program, provides the services of a substance abuse coordinator, disciplines students for infractions and provides an atmosphere in which young people can grow responsibly.

4   There is more that must be done. Parents at one time held their sons and daughters accountable for the company they kept. A student who deliberately associates with a group known for its excesses, or who joins an organization suspended or expelled by the institution, is choosing bad company. Peer pressure does the rest.

5   The courts restrict the ability of colleges to discipline students for off-campus behavior unless the activity in question has a fairly direct relationship with institutional mission.

6   They require due process, including confrontation by witnesses, for any disciplinary action. Peer pressures in the college-age group are so strong that testimony of witnesses is frequently difficult to obtain.

7   Until we return to a system in which colleges can function, at least in part, in loco parentis (in place of the parent), other agencies of society will have to step in.

8   To be fully effective, a college would need the ability to impose severe sanctions, including dismissal, on the base of reasonable proof of misbehavior or association with bad elements. Advocates of unrestrained constitutional rights will have difficulty with this, but the student enters a contractual relationship with a college to pursue an education.

9   The educators, not the legal system, should do the educating. Colleges exist to form good citizens, conscious of their own rights and the rights of others. Colleges and universities should be evaluated on the basis of the results of their educational work.

James C. Carter, S.J.
Chancellor,
Loyola University,
New Orleans

Deliberate About the Readings

As we explained in Chapter 1, deliberation is a way to arrive at your own position on a particular issue. You can't begin deliberation until you have really listened to and reflected on the complexities each issue involves. Once you have engaged in all the steps in the process of critical reading, you are ready to deliberate.

In your deliberation, first consider each of the writer's claims and main points. Then, thinking like a critic, find a way to respond that defines your own position on the issue. Using the four readings in this chapter, a deliberation in your journal about college binge drinking might look like this:

All the writers see binge drinking as a problem, although they differ about where they place the blame and how they plan to solve the problem. Wechsler thinks that binge drinking among college students occurs because colleges are indifferent to it and refuse to recognize its seriousness. He urges colleges to use their influence and power to prevent students from obtaining alcohol. He doesn't seem to think that the students who engage in binge drinking have a lot of control over their behavior. Carter, Sole, and Stewart all agree with Wechsler about the seriousness of the problem; however, they disagree about where to place the blame. Carter thinks that colleges are doing all they can and should be given more legal power to discipline students who binge drink. Sole and Stewart suggest that the media is to blame by endorsing values that encourage students to drink and party rather than concentrate on their studies. Only Harrop places the blame squarely on the shoulders of the binge drinkers themselves. She feels strongly that students need to be treated as adults with drinking problems and suffer the consequences of their actions.

After reading these writings, I am convinced that binge drinking is a problem worthy of our attention. The statistics that Wechsler, Stewart, and Sole cite are convincing and impressive. I also know from my own experience that many students drink excessively, and I think that six deaths are too many for us to ignore. I also think that binge drinking is a problem that affects the entire college community, not just the drinkers, as Stewart and Sole point out. However, I tend to agree with Harrop that students must be held responsible for their own actions. I disagree with Carter that schools should act like parents. College is about becoming an adult in all areas of our lives, not just academics.

Any solution to the problem of binge drinking needs to include the students who abuse alcohol. Unless those students also see their drinking habits as a problem, nothing the college or legal system can impose will affect their behavior. Perhaps a combination of actions, including broader and stronger efforts to educate students about alcohol abuse, greater enforcement and harsher penalties for underage drinking by the legal system, and efforts by colleges to restrict alcohol availability in the community and on the campus, would make a significant dent in this problem.

Now try writing your own deliberation, in which you consider the points you find most important in each reading, to arrive at your own position on the issue of binge drinking.

Look for Logical Fallacies

When you read the arguments of others, you need to pay attention to the writer's strategies, assertions, and logic to decide if the argument is reasonable. Like the cross-examining attorney in a court case, you must examine the logical connections between

Preview: Logical Fallacies

- Ad hominem argument
- Ad misericordiam argument
- Ad populum argument
- Bandwagon appeal
- Begging the question
- Circular reasoning
- Dicto simpliciter
- False analogy
- False dilemma
- Faulty use of authority
- Hasty generalization
- Non sequitur
- Post hoc, ergo propter hoc
- Red herring
- Slippery slope
- Stacking the deck
- Straw man

the claim, the reasons, and the evidence to reveal the strengths and weaknesses of the writer's argument.

Sometimes writers make errors in logic. Such errors are called **logical fallacies**, a term derived from the Latin *fallere,* meaning "to deceive." Used unintentionally, these fallacies deceive writers into feeling that their arguments are more persuasive than they are. Even though an argument may be well developed and contain convincing evidence, a fallacy creates a flaw in the logic of an argument, thereby weakening its structure and persuasiveness.

Not all logical fallacies are unintentional. Sometimes a fallacy is deliberately employed—for example, when the writer's goal has more to do with persuading than with arriving at the truth. Every day we are confronted with fallacies in media commercials and advertisements. Likewise, every election year the airwaves are full of candidates' bloated claims and pronouncements rife with logical fallacies of all kinds.

Recognizing logical fallacies when they occur in a reading is an important step in assessing the effectiveness of the writer's argument. This final section of our chapter will acquaint you with some of the most common logical fallacies.

Ad Hominem Argument

From the Latin "to the man," the **ad hominem** argument is a personal attack on an opponent rather than on the opponent's views. Certainly the integrity of an opponent may be important to readers. Nonetheless, writers are usually more persuasive and credible when they focus on issues rather than character flaws. If, for instance, you are reading a paper against the use of animals in medical research and the writer refers to the opposition as "cold-hearted scientists only interested in fame and fortune," you might question whether the writer objects to the scientists' views or to their personal prosperity. Name-calling and character assassination should make you suspicious of the writer's real motives or balanced judgment. Personal criticisms, even if true, can be overemphasized and, therefore, undercut the writer's credibility.

However, there may be cases in which an ad hominem argument is a legitimate rhetorical tool. When the special interests or associations of an individual or group appear to have a direct impact on their position on an issue, it is fair to raise questions about their lack of objectivity on that basis. For example, the organizer of a petition to build a state-supported recycling center may seem reasonably suspect if it is revealed that he owns the land on which the proposed recycling center would be built. While the property owner may be motivated by sincere environmental concerns, the direct relationship between his position and his personal life makes this fair game for a challenge.

Examples of Ad Hominem Arguments

- How could Tom accuse her of being careless? He's such a slob.
- Of course he doesn't see anything wrong with violent movies. The guy's a warmonger.
- We cannot expect Ms. Lucas to know what it means to feel oppressed; she is the president of a large bank.

Ad Misericordiam Argument

Its name also derived from Latin, the **ad misericordiam** argument is the appeal "to pity." This appeal to our emotions need not be fallacious or faulty. A writer, having argued several solid points logically, may make an emotional appeal for extra support. Your local Humane Society, for instance, might ask you to donate money so it can expand its facilities for abandoned animals. To convince you, the society might point out how, over the last few years, the number of strays and unwanted pets has tripled. And because of budget constraints, the society has been forced to appeal to the public. It may claim that a donation of $25 would house and feed a stray animal for a month. Any amount you give, they explain, will ultimately aid the construction of a new pet "dormitory" wing. To bolster the appeal, the Humane Society literature might then describe how the adorable puppy and kitten in the enclosed photo will have to be put to death unless the overcrowding of the society's facilities is relieved by donations such as yours.

When an argument is based solely on the exploitation of the reader's pity, however, the issue gets lost. There's an old joke about a man who murdered his parents and appealed to the court for leniency because he was an orphan. It's funny because it ludicrously illustrates how pity has nothing to do with murder. Let's take a more realistic example. If you were a lawyer whose client was charged with bank embezzlement, you would not get very far basing your defense solely on the fact that the defendant was abused as a child. Yes, you may touch the hearts of the jurors, even move them to pity. Yet that would not exonerate your client. The abuse the defendant suffered as a child, as woeful as it is, has nothing to do with his or her crime as an adult. Any intelligent prosecutor would point out the attempt to manipulate the court with a sob story while distracting it from more important factors such as justice.

Examples of Ad Misericordiam Arguments

■ It makes no difference if he was guilty of Nazi war crimes. The man is 85 years old and in frail health, so he should not be made to stand trial.
■ Paula is 14 years old and lives on welfare with her mother; she suffers serious depression and functions like a child half her age. She should not be sent to adult court, where she will be tried for armed robbery, so she can spend her formative years behind bars.

Ad Populum Argument

From the Latin "to the people," an **ad populum** argument is just that—an argument aimed at appealing to the supposed prejudices and emotions of the masses. Writers attempt to manipulate readers by using emotional and provocative language to add appeal to their claims. The problem with the ad populum argument, however, is that such language sometimes functions as a smoke screen hiding the lack of ideas in the argument. You'll find examples of this fallacy on the editorial pages of your local newspaper—for example, the letter from parents raising a furor because they don't want their child or the children of their friends and neighbors taught by teachers with foreign accents; or the columnist who makes the ad populum case against capital punishment by inflating the number of innocent people wrongfully executed by the state; or the writer who argues that if gays and lesbians are allowed to serve in the military, our national defense will be jeopardized by "sex maniacs."

Examples of Ad Populum Arguments

■ High school students don't learn anything these days. Today's teachers are academically underprepared.
■ If you want to see the crime rate drop, tell Hollywood to stop making movies that glorify violence.
■ Doctors oppose health reform because it will reduce their large incomes.

Bandwagon Appeal

This familiar strategy makes the claim that everybody is doing this and thinking that. If we don't want to be left out, we had better get on the **bandwagon** and do and think the same things. The basic appeal in this argument is that of belonging to the group, behaving like the majority. It plays on our fears of being different, of being excluded. Of course, the appeal is fallacious inasmuch as we are asked to "get with it" without weighing the evidence of what is being promoted: "Smart shoppers shop at Sears"; "America reads Danielle Steel."

Examples of Bandwagon Appeals

- Everybody's going to the System of a Down concert.
- Nobody will go along with that proposal.
- The majority of the American people want a constitutional amendment outlawing flag burning.

Begging the Question

Similar to circular reasoning, **begging the question** passes off as true an assumption that needs to be proven. For instance, to say that the defendant is innocent because he passed a polygraph test begs the question: Does passing a polygraph test mean somebody is innocent? Sometimes the begged question is itself loaded in a bigger question: "Are you ever going to act like you are equal and pay for one of our dates?" The begged question here is whether paying the costs of a date is a measure of sexual equality.

Examples of Begging the Question

- That foolish law should be repealed.
- She is compassionate because she's a woman.
- If you haven't written short stories, you shouldn't be criticizing them.

Circular Reasoning

Circular reasoning is another common fallacy into which many writers fall. In it, the conclusion of a deductive argument is hidden in the premise of that argument. Thus, the argument goes around in a circle. For instance: "Steroids are dangerous because they ruin your health." This translates: Steroids are dangerous because they are dangerous. Sometimes the circularity gets camouflaged in a tangle of words: "The high cost of living in today's America is a direct consequence of the exorbitant prices manufacturers and retailers are placing on their products and services." Cut away the excess, and this translates: The high cost of living is due to the high cost of living. Repetition of key terms or ideas is not evidence. Nor does it prove anything. Instead of simply restating your premise, find solid evidence to support it.

Examples of Circular Reasoning

- People who are happy with their work are cheerful because they enjoy what they're doing.
- Smoking is bad for you because it ruins your health.
- Bank robbers should be punished because they broke the law.

Dicto Simpliciter

The fallacy known as **dicto simpliciter** comes from the Latin *dicto simpliciter ad dictum secundum quid,* which roughly translates as "from a general truth to a specific case regardless of the qualifications of the latter." In its briefer form, it means "spoken simply" and refers to a sweeping generalization that doesn't always apply. A dicto simpliciter argument makes the logical fallacy of exploiting an overly simplistic or unqualified "rule of thumb" while disregarding exceptions to that rule. For example, it's generally understood that birds fly. We know that at the local zoo Kiki the kiwi is a bird and is housed in the aviary. But to conclude that because she's a bird Kiki can therefore fly is fallacious reasoning. And the reason is that the kiwi bird is an exception—one of the few types of birds that are flightless.

Examples of Dicto Simpliciter Arguments

- If torture can save the lives of those who would be killed by terrorists, then the government should employ torture as a preemptive measure of protection.
- Exercise is good for people. Now that Bob is out of the hospital, he should get back to the treadmill.
- Guns kill. So we cannot allow the average citizen to possess a weapon.

Here's another more familiar matter where dicto simpliciter arguments might be heard. It is generally accepted that men are physically stronger than women. However, it would be a fallacious claim that women shouldn't be allowed in military combat since they aren't strong enough to carry weapons. This statement is a logical fallacy since it does not account for the exceptions to the rule—women who are stronger than the average. In other words, this argument exploits a stereotype.

False Analogy

An analogy compares two things that are alike in one or more ways. In any form of writing, analogies are very useful, as they expand meaning and demonstrate imagination. In arguments, they can be wonderful tools for persuasion. Unfortunately, they can also lead the writer astray and make his or her argument vulnerable to attack.

The problem with **false analogies** arises when the two things compared do not match up feature for feature, and ideas being compared do not logically connect or are pressed beyond legitimacy. The result is a false analogy. For instance, a candidate for a high-powered job may ask to be employed because of his extraordinary heroics during the Iraq War. He may even claim that being a CEO is like fighting a battle: He needs to be brave, tough in mind and body, and willing to take and deal out punishment. Although the argument might sound appealing, running a company involves more than combat skills. Certainly it is important for a corporate executive to be strong and tough-minded. However, an office full of five-star generals might not be expert at dealing with economic recession or product liability. The fallacy is an imperfect analogy: Business and soldiering overlap minimally.

A sound analogy will clarify a difficult or unfamiliar concept by comparing it with something easily understood or familiar.

Examples of False Analogy

- The Ship of State is about to wreck on the rocks of recession; we need a new pilot.
- This whole gun control issue is polarizing the nation the way slavery did people living above and below the Mason-Dixon line. Do we want another Civil War?
- Letting emerging nations have nuclear weapons is like giving loaded guns to children.

False Dilemma

A **false dilemma** involves the simplification of complex issues into an either/or choice. For example, "Either we legalize abortion or we send young women to back-alley butchers," "Love America or leave it," "Either we keep gun ownership legal or only criminals will have guns." Such sloganizing ultimatums, although full of dramatic impact, unfortunately appeal to people's ignorance and prejudices.

Examples of False Dilemma

- English should be the official language of the United States, and anybody who doesn't like it can leave.
- Movies today are full of either violence or sex.
- Either we put warning labels on records and compact discs, or we'll see more and more teenage girls having babies.

Faulty Use of Authority

The **faulty use of authority** occurs when someone who is an expert in one area is used as an authority for another unrelated area. For instance, the opinions of a four-star general about the use of force against an uncooperative foreign tyrant carry great weight in a discussion of U.S. foreign policy options. However, the opinions of that same individual about the Supreme Court's ruling on the question of assisted suicide are less compelling. His military expertise does not guarantee that his views on euthanasia are particularly valuable.

Advertisers frequently resort to the faulty use of authority to promote their products. Celebrities are asked to endorse products they may have no special knowledge about or any interest in aside from the sizable check they will receive for their services. Another example occurs when well-known popular figures rely on their achievements in one area to lend credibility to their views in another. For instance, the late Benjamin Spock, famous for his work on child development, became a spokesperson for the nuclear disarmament movement. Because of his reputation, people were willing to listen more closely to his views than to others who were less well known, yet his expertise in child-rearing gave him no more authority in this area than any other well-educated person. While Dr. Spock may, indeed, have been knowledgeable about nuclear arms, his expertise in that area would have to be demonstrated before he could be used as an effective authority on the subject.

Examples of Faulty Use of Authority

- You should buy these vitamins because Larry King recommended them on television last night.
- The American Bar Association states that secondhand smoke is a serious cancer threat to nonsmokers.
- Americans shouldn't find hunting objectionable because one of our most popular presidents, Theodore Roosevelt, was an avid hunter.

Hasty Generalization

As the name indicates, the **hasty generalization** occurs when a writer arrives at a conclusion based on too little evidence. It's one of the most frequently found fallacies. If the local newspaper's restaurant critic is served underdone chicken at Buster's Diner during her first and only visit, she would be making a hasty generalization to conclude that Buster's serves terrible food. Although this may be true, one visit is not enough to draw that conclusion. If, however, after three visits she is still dissatisfied with the food, she is entitled to warn her readers about eating at Buster's.

Hasty generalizations can also occur when the writer relies on evidence that is not factual or substantiated. A generalization can only be as sound as its supporting evidence. Writers should provide multiple and credible examples to support their points. Be wary of sweeping, uncritical statements and words such as *always, all, none, never, only,* and *most.* Note whether the writer qualifies the claim with words that are limiting, such as *many, some, often,* and *seldom.*

Examples of Hasty Generalizations

- That shopping mall is unsafe because there was a robbery there two weeks ago.
- I'm failing organic chemistry because the teaching assistant doesn't speak English well.
- This book was written by a Stanford professor, so it must be good.

Non Sequitur

From the Latin for "does not follow," a **non sequitur** draws a conclusion that does not follow logically from the premise. For instance, suppose you heard a classmate make the following claim: "Ms. Marshall is such a good teacher; it's hard to believe she wears such ugly clothes." The statement would be fallacious because the ability to teach has nothing to do with taste in clothing. Some of the worst teachers might be the best dressers. Although you might want to believe a good teacher would be a good dresser, there is no reason to think so. Writers must establish a clear connection between the premise and the conclusion. And unless one is made through well-reasoned explanations, readers will not accept the cause-and-effect relationship.

Political campaigns are notorious for non sequiturs: "Candidate Jones will be a great senator because she's been married for twenty years." Or, "Don't vote for Candidate Jones because she is rich and lives in an expensive neighborhood." Whether the voters decide to vote for Candidate Jones should not depend on the length of her marriage or the neighborhood in which she lives—neither qualifies her for or disqualifies her from public office. The non sequiturs attempt to suggest a relationship between her ability to be a successful senator and unrelated facts about her life.

Examples of Non Sequitur

- Mr. Thompson has such bad breath that it's a wonder he sings so well.
- She's so pretty; she must not be smart.
- I supported his candidacy for president because his campaign was so efficiently run.

Post Hoc, Ergo Propter Hoc

The Latin **post hoc, ergo propter hoc** is translated as "after this, therefore because of this." A post hoc, ergo propter hoc argument is one that establishes a questionable cause-and-effect relationship between events. In other words, because event *Y* follows event *X*, event *X* causes event *Y*. For instance, you would be making a post hoc argument if you claimed, "Every time my brother Bill accompanies me to Jacobs Field, the Cleveland Indians lose." The reasoning here is fallacious because we all know that although the Indians lose whenever Bill joins you at Jacobs Field, his presence does not cause the team to lose. Experience tells us that there simply is no link between the two events. The only explanation is coincidence.

Our conversations are littered with these dubious claims: "Every time I plan a pool party, it rains"; "Whenever I drive to Chicago, I get a flat tire"; "Every movie that Harry recommends turns out to be a dud." What they underscore is our pessimism or dismay, rather than any belief in the truth of such statements.

It's not surprising that post hoc reasoning is often found in arguments made by people prone to superstition—people looking for big, simple explanations. You would be committing such a fallacy if, for instance, you claimed that you got a C on your math test because a black cat crossed your path that morning or because you broke a mirror the night before. Post hoc fallacies are also practiced by those bent on proving conspiracies. Following the assassination of President Kennedy in 1963, there was considerable effort by some to link the deaths of many people involved in the investigation to a government cover-up, even though the evidence was scanty. Today, we hear Democrats protest that America goes to war every time Republicans are in office and Republicans protest that America gets poorer when Democrats are in office.

Examples of Post Hoc, Ergo Propter Hoc Arguments

■ Just two weeks after they raised the speed limit, three people were killed on that road.
■ I saw Ralph in the courthouse; he must have been arrested.
■ It's no wonder the crime rate has shot up. The state legislature voted to lower the drinking age.

You might also have heard people argue that since the women's liberation movement, the number of latchkey children has risen sharply. The claim essentially says that the women's movement is directly responsible for the rise in working mothers over the last 30 years. While it is true that the women's movement has made it more acceptable for mothers to return to the workforce, the prime reason is particular to the individual. For some, it is simple economics; for others, personal fulfillment; for others still, a combination of the two. The feminist movement is one among many factors linked with women in the workforce and the consequent rise in latchkey children.

Red Herring

A **red herring**, as the name suggests, is evidence that is fallaciously used to distract the audience from the true issues of an argument. The term is derived from the practice of using the scent of a red herring to throw hunting dogs off the trail of their real prey.

In modern life, this fallacy is more often used to confuse the audience by providing irrelevant information or evidence. For instance, when the head coach of a major league team was accused of using team funds on personal expenses, he defended himself by pointing to the team's winning record under his leadership. While the team had undeniably performed well during this period, his response was irrelevant to the charges made against him. He had hoped to distract his accusers from the real issue, which involved his lack of honesty and abuse of power. A red herring may distract the audience momentarily, but once it is discovered, it indicates that the individual has little or no effective reasons or evidence to support his or her position.

Examples of Red Herrings

- Even though that hockey player was convicted of vehicular homicide, he shouldn't go to jail because he is such a great athlete.
- Susan didn't hire John for the job because his wife is always late for meetings.
- The teacher gave me an F in the course because she doesn't like me.

Slippery Slope

The **slippery slope** presumes one event will inevitably lead to a chain of other events that end in a catastrophe—as one slip on a mountaintop will cause a climber to tumble down and bring with him or her all those in tow. This domino-effect reasoning is fallacious because it depends more on presumption than hard evidence: "Censorship of obscene material will spell the end to freedom of the press"; "A ban on ethnic slurs will mean no more freedom of speech"; "If assault rifles are outlawed, handguns will be next." America's involvement in Vietnam was the result of a slippery slope argument: "If Vietnam falls to the Communists, all of Southeast Asia, and eventually India and its neighbors, will fall under the sway of communism." Even though Vietnam did fall, the result has not been the widespread rise of communism in the region; on the contrary, communism has fallen on hard times.

Examples of Slippery Slope Arguments

- Legalized abortion is a step toward creating an antilife society.
- A ban on ethnic slurs will mean no more freedom of speech.
- If we let them build those condos, the lake will end up polluted, the wildlife will die off, and the landscape will be scarred forever.

Stacking the Deck

When writers give only the evidence that supports their premise, while disregarding or withholding contrary evidence, they are **stacking the deck**. (Science students may know this as "data beautification," the habit of recording only those results that match what an experiment is expected to predict.) A meat-packing manufacturer may advertise that its all-beef hot dogs "now contain 10 percent less fat." Although that may sound like good news, what we are not being told is that the hot dogs still contain 30 percent fat.

This stacking-the-deck fallacy is common not only in advertising but also in debates of controversial matters. The faculty of a college, for instance, may petition for the firing of its president for failing to grant needed raises while an expensive new football stadium is being built. The complaint would not be fair, however, if the faculty ignored mentioning that the stadium funds were specifically earmarked for athletic improvement by a billionaire benefactor. Also, if the complaint left unrecognized the many accomplishments of the president, such as the successful capital campaign, the plans for a new library, and the influx of notable scholars, it would be an example of stacking the deck.

As you progress through the chapters in this book, you will find that thinking like a critic is the key to understanding and responding to arguments. It will make you a stronger reader and a more effective writer. In the next chapter, we explore ways that you can think like a writer to find and develop topics for your own argument essays.

Examples of Stacking the Deck

- Parents should realize that private schools simply encourage elitism in young people.
- We cannot take four more years of her in office, given the way she voted against the death penalty.
- Dickens's *Bleak House* is six hundred pages of boring prose.

Straw Man

A **straw man** literally refers to a straw-stuffed dummy in the shape of a man and dressed in clothes: a scarecrow, for instance, or an effigy for burning or target practice. Metaphorically, the term refers to something less than a real person, or a weak or ineffective substitute. As a rhetorical term, the straw man (or straw person) refers to a strategy of refuting another person's actual position by substituting an exaggerated or distorted version of that position. What makes it a fallacy is that the user declares the opponent's conclusion to be wrong because of flaws in another, lesser argument: The straw man user presents a fictitious or misrepresented version of the opponent's argument, and refutes that. In short, it's a setup of the opponent, a deliberate misstatement or overstatement of his or her position. And it is easier to refute somebody whose real ideas have been pushed to the extreme—reduced to a dismissible straw man.

It's no surprise that the straw man argument is a familiar strategy in politics, as candidates will attack opponents on positions often much weaker than their best arguments. Consider, for example, this statement: "Senator Jane Smith claims that we should not fund the superbomber program. Do we really want her to leave our country defenseless?" In reality, Smith may be opposed to the superbomber program for technical, economic, or even strategic reasons, or she may be in favor of an alternative defense system. However, like a red herring, the opponent tries to refute Senator Smith's position by attacking a position that Smith doesn't hold—that she wants to leave the country defenseless. In short, the arguer arrives at a conclusion that easily dismisses the "straw man" he has set up while disregarding Smith's real arguments.

Examples of Straw Man Arguments

- Home schooling is dangerous because it keeps kids isolated from society.
- Discrimination in hiring is *not* unfair. An employer has to discriminate between competent and incompetent, good and bad workers. Otherwise, we'd be hiring people least qualified for the job.
- People who are opposed to urbanization just want to go back to living in caves.

EXERCISES

1. In your journal, list examples of logical fallacies you find in essays, news articles, editorials, advertising, junk mail, and other persuasive materials that you confront on a daily basis. Based on the information you and other group members collect, draw some hypotheses about which fallacies are most prevalent today and why. If your instructor asks you to do so, convert those hypotheses into an outline of an argument essay for your campus newspaper.

2. Explain the faulty logic of the following statements. Of what fallacy (or fallacies) is each an example?
   a. When did you stop hiring other people to take your exams for you?
   b. He's too smart to play football; besides, he broke his leg ten years ago.
   c. If we don't stop the publication of this X-rated material now, it won't be long before our children will be reading it at school.
   d. Karen must be depressed; she wore dark clothes all weekend.
   e. How can you accuse me of being late? You're such a slowpoke.
   f. Rap music isn't music because it's just noise and words.
   g. He's at least 6 feet 6 inches tall, so he must be a terrific basketball player.
   h. WGBB is the most popular radio station on campus because it has more listeners than any other station.
   i. Indians living on reservations get the necessities of life at government expense, so they have no worries.
   j. Take Tummy Tops laxatives instead of Mellow Malt, because Tummy Tops contains calcium while Mellow Malt has aluminum and magnesium.
   k. Lite Cheese Popcorn contains 34 percent fewer calories!
   l. Any decent person will agree that Nazism has no place in modern society.

Finding Arguments: Thinking Like a Writer

When confronted with an issue we feel strongly about, most of us have no trouble offering an energetically delivered opinion. Yet when we are asked to *write* an argument, we feel paralyzed. To express our ideas in written form forces us to commit ourselves to some position or to endorse a particular action. We have to take a risk and make a public statement about what we think and feel and believe. Our written words can be scrutinized. That makes us vulnerable, and nobody likes to feel exposed.

It is helpful to think of writing an argument as one way to explore our ideas about a subject or issue. As such, writing can be a means of growth and discovery. Investigating new ideas can be intimidating, but it's also exciting. This chapter will demonstrate how writers begin the process of researching ideas to write about in argument essays. As novelist E. M. Forster explained, "How will I know what I think until I've seen what I've said?"

Exploration, of course, takes time. We are not recommending a writing process that begins an hour before a paper is due; rather, we are recommending what successful writers do: Take time to think your writing through. This means starting assignments early, working through all the stages, and allowing time to revise and polish your work before you submit it. Learning to write well is the same as learning to perform any other skilled activity. You have to practice your strokes or your scales to be a good tennis player or pianist; likewise, you have to practice your craft to be a good writer. As you gain more experience, some of the stages of the writing process will go more quickly for you on most projects. Even when you become a polished logician, however, you may find yourself writing about a topic that requires you to work out the assumptions in your argument slowly and painstakingly. That's okay. All writers do that.

The Writing Process

Many rhetorical theorists have tried to describe the writing process, but that's a little like describing snowflakes: Each one is different. Each person has a different way of writing, especially depending on the job. Think about it. You can dash off a note to your roommate in a second; if you're writing a job application letter, you'll probably take a great deal more time. If you have only 20 minutes to answer an essay question on a history exam, you'll get it done somehow; but give you an entire semester to write a term paper on the same subject, and you will probably spend several weeks (if not months) doing the job. The scope and length of the assignment dictate a different writing process.

What most people studying the writing process agree on is that almost everyone goes through four distinct stages when writing: prewriting, drafting, rewriting, and editing.

Prewriting

When something prompts you to write (your instructor gives you an assignment, your boss tells you to write a report, a letter requires an answer, you feel strongly about a controversy and want to write a letter to the editor), you spend time either mentally or physically preparing to respond. You may make notes, go to the library, interview someone, or just stare out the window. This is the *prewriting* stage in which you're letting the ideas you'll use begin to incubate, to take form. In this chapter, we provide strategies you can use to make this early stage of writing work for you.

Drafting

In the second stage, you begin, however haltingly, to put words to paper. Some people make an outline; others write a bare-bones rough draft in an attempt to get some ideas down on paper. Many people like to start by sketching out their conclusions so that they can see where their writing must take them. Others prefer the linear, start-with-the-introduction system that moves them through the task. The first goal in the drafting stage is to get the framework of the writing in place so you can start adding material to fill it out. At some point in the process you also take your potential readers into account in order to get some idea of their expectations and receptivity.

Rewriting

Once you have a rough draft framed, you're ready to do the hard work of writing: *rewriting*. At this stage, you may move parts of your paper around, or make a new outline, or add or cut material to fill in gaps or eliminate imbalances. You will have your readers much more clearly in mind because your goal is to persuade them; what you know about their background, experiences, and values will help you decide on a final shape for your paper, even if it means throwing away a lot of what went into the rough draft. (A bad paper that's finished is still a bad paper; that's why you need to allow time for flexibility. Writers who are pressed for time sometimes have to polish something that's not good and hope their readers will not notice, a technique that does not usually work.) All writing is rewriting. So at this stage, most good writers turn to other writers for feedback—a sense of what prospective readers will think of their writing. In a classroom, this is done by exchanging drafts with classmates or having conferences with your instructor.

Editing

To maximize your chance of persuading readers, your writing needs to be as readable as possible. That's why, after you've rewritten it, you need to work on your sentence structure so that words "flow" smoothly. Or you may need to change words here and there to heighten their impact. If others have read your paper and offered feedback, you may wish to act on some of their suggestions for improvement. You always need to edit and proofread what you've written so that careless errors don't distract your readers from getting the message you're trying to convey.

In a nutshell, that's the writing process. Now let's look at how you might exploit the features of that process when you start writing arguments.

Finding Topics to Argue

Every writer knows the experience of being blocked—of having a topic but not knowing what to say about it, or of having only one point to make about an issue. Even worse is having an assignment but no topic. To help generate ideas, writers need to tap both internal and external resources.

In Your Immediate Vicinity

The world around you is full of arguments; you just need to take a moment to see them. Look at the front page and editorial pages of your campus newspaper, for instance. What's going on? Look at billboards and bulletin boards. What are people having meetings about? What changes are coming up? Listen to the conversations of people on the bus, or waiting in line at the bookstore, or in the library. What's up? What have you been reading for a class that gets you thinking? You might want to know how a theory for the origin of the universe was derived, or what the results of a recent study of employment success for former welfare recipients were based on, or even why two experts in the field of early childhood learning draw different conclusions from the same evidence. The reading you do for your own enjoyment may also provide some interesting ideas. A science fiction novel may make you wonder about the plausibility of alien life. Reading a murder mystery may make you think about the value of forensic anthropology. Look through the magazines in your room, or at the ads on television, or at the junk mail that fills your mailbox. Even casually reading magazines and newspapers on a daily or weekly basis will turn up issues and controversies. What claims are people making? What are people asking you to do, or think, or wear, or look like, or support? These are sources of potential arguments; all you have to do is become aware of them. As Thoreau put it, "Only that day dawns to which we are awake."

In Your Larger Worlds

Don't limit yourself to campus. Often there are debates and discussions going on in your workplace, in your place of worship, on your block, in your town. You belong to a number of communities; each has its issues of interest, and in those issues you can find plenty to write about. And those environments aren't the only places you'll find sources for arguments; the world turns on proposals, positions, and controversies. It's almost impossible to turn on the radio or television today without seeing someone presenting an opinion. Your computer (or the one available on your campus) can connect you to a global community engaged in debate and dialogue on every issue imaginable. On the Internet, you can participate in a number of discussions about controversial issues through listservs, Usenet newsgroups, blogs, and chat rooms. Make a list of the issues that interest you. What are the headlines in the newspaper? What's Congress voting on? What are the hot spots around the globe (or in the larger universe)? Don't stick to the familiar; there is much experimental territory just waiting to be explored.

Keeping a Journal

You've probably noticed that we encourage recording ideas and observations in a journal, a technique used by many professional writers. The journal doesn't have to be fancy; the cheap supermarket variety works just as well as the $2,000 laptop. (If you're comfortable at a keyboard, a USB flash drive makes a great notebook and fits in your shirt pocket, too—although you might want to keep a backup copy.)

Writers use journals as portable file cabinets of ideas. In a journal, we record anything in language that interests us, not just materials for current projects. We may copy down a word or phrase or sentence we hear that we like, or photocopy and staple in a piece by a writer we admire, or even add things that infuriate or amuse us. A journal becomes a supermarket of ideas and strategies, but there's something very positive about the simple act of copying words. Somehow, physically writing or typing them makes them yours; you learn something about technique in doing the physical work of copying. (That's why we don't recommend making too many photocopies; you don't mentally store the information in the same way you do when you copy a passage yourself.)

For the novice argument writer, a journal is invaluable. You can use yours to include notes on possible topics; examples of good introductions and conclusions; catchy words, phrases, and titles; examples of logical fallacies—just about anything a writer might need. A journal is also particularly helpful for creating *dialogues,* the voices and opinions of others who may hold views that are different from your own on particular issues. By keeping a record or notes on what people have to say in newspapers, magazine articles, television talk shows, and casual conversation about various controversial issues, you'll have a ready resource to consult when you begin to deliberate about your position on a particular issue.

When you begin keeping the journal, set yourself a formal goal: for example, adding 100 words a day or writing five days out of the week. Then *stick to it*. Journals don't fill themselves. It takes discipline to keep a journal, and discipline is a characteristic of good writers. If you don't do the groundwork, your creativity won't break through. Throughout this text, we've scattered suggestions and exercises for using journals; if you want to master the power of argument fully, we encourage you to *do* the exercises. Don't just read them. Write!

Developing Argumentative Topics

Topics alone aren't arguments, and many inexperienced writers have trouble making the jump from subject to argument. For example, you may be interested in heavy metal music. That's a subject—a big one. What can you argue about it? You could ask yourself, "What are the facts about heavy metal? When did it start? How can it be defined? What differentiates it from the mainstream rock played on most commercial radio stations? How has it evolved over the last 40 years? Why are some groups played, it seems, once an hour, and others almost totally ignored?" You can ask functional questions, such as "Who were the most influential figures in heavy metal music? Is heavy metal as relevant as it had been?" You might ask aesthetic questions about the importance of melody or lyrics or harmony, or ethical questions such as whether the music industry should put parental advisory labels on albums. You could even consider moral questions such as whether heavy metal music videos encourage sexism or violence. In recognizing the multiple possibilities of issues, you may find you have more to say on a topic than you think.

Getting Started

Sometimes getting started can be the most difficult step in the writing process. Where do I begin? What should I include? What ideas will work best? How shall I organize it all? You may have a hundred ideas in your head about the topic or—even worse—none at all. When this happens, there are a number of tried-and-true techniques that professional writers use to redirect those anxious questions and concerns into productive writing. While you may not need to use all the strategies each time you begin to write, you'll find that trying out each one of them will help you discover what works best for you.

Brainstorming

Brainstorming can help you get your ideas on paper in an informal and unstructured way. When you brainstorm, you write down as many ideas as you can about your subject, usually in short phrases, questions, or single words. Don't worry about placing them in any special order or even about making complete sense. The one rule to observe while you're brainstorming is not to judge the ideas that pop into your head and spill out onto your paper. When you give yourself permission to write down anything that seems related to your subject, you'll be surprised at the number of ideas that will occur to you. By not rejecting anything, you'll find that one idea will naturally lead to another. Even an idea that you may throw out later can lead you to an idea that may be a real gem. And the more ideas you record in your brainstorm, the more choices you will have to consider later as you sift through this record of your thoughts and decide what is and is not useful.

After reading the essays in Chapter 2 of this book, John, our first-year composition student, decided to write his first paper on college binge drinking. The topic was in the news because a student at another college in his state had died as the result of excessive drinking at a fraternity party. John began his prewriting preparation by brainstorming about the subject. Here's what he came up with:

binge drinking	want to forget all about the week
drinking until you feel sick	makes us feel grown up
getting together with friends for a good time	nothing better to do on Saturday night
partying after a tough week at school	why does the college care?
so many bars, so little time	people can really hurt themselves
half the people underage	prevention—how?
whose responsibility is it?	part of the college experience
am I responsible for my friends?	ignore it—will it go away?
could I get arrested?	trying to act cool

nobody checks anyway

feeling terrible the next morning

smelling like a beer can

role of the college administration

rite of passage

impact of peer pressure

what starts as fun can lead to death

definition of an adult

do other cultures experience this?

why drink to excess?

As you can see, John had many different ideas about binge drinking, and the more he brainstormed, the more he discovered what they were. After looking over his brainstorm, John chose a few of the ideas that especially interested him to explore further.

John was lucky to have a subject before he began brainstorming. But what happens if you don't have a particular topic in mind or your instructor doesn't assign one? You may find it difficult to come up with a topic, and you're not alone. Students often comment that the hardest part of writing is deciding what to write about.

Finding Ideas Worth Writing About

Let's suppose you're not assigned a specific paper topic and are left on your own to come up with an issue worth arguing about. That can be daunting, of course. When asked where he gets the ideas for his stories, best-selling author Stephen King's joke response was "Utica"—as if there were an idea shop in that New York town. Other writers respond with the tongue-in-cheek claim that there's a post office box in, say, Madison, Wisconsin, where you can write for ideas, but to qualify you need to be published. The point is that ideas for fiction as well as nonfiction are all around us. You just have to know where to look.

Again, one of the most useful prewriting strategies for coming up with an idea is brainstorming—just as you might do if you had a topic to expand upon. Take out a piece of paper and jot down whatever comes to mind in response to these questions:

- What issues in print or TV news interest you?
- What issues make you angry?
- What problems in your dorm/on campus/in your town/in your country concern you?
- What political issue concerns you most?
- What aspects about the environment worry you?
- If you were a professor/dean/college president/mayor/governor/senator/president, what would be the first thing you'd do?
- What policies/practices/regulations/laws would you like to see changed?
- What do you talk about or argue over with friends or classmates?
- What ideas from books or articles have challenged your thinking?
- What books/movies/music/fashions/art do you like, and why?
- What television shows do you like/hate, and why?
- What personalities in politics/show business/the media/academia do you have strong feelings about?

Here's a quick brainstorming list one student developed:

Issues That Interest Me

1. The war on terrorism
2. Excessive salaries for athletes
3. People who protest movie violence but oppose bans on assault rifles
4. The benefits of stem cell research
5. Reality TV
6. Social messages in rap music
7. Environmentally unfriendly vehicles
8. Immigration policies
9. Bullying in cyberspace
10. Movies

Another strategy is to brainstorm these items with a group of classmates. Begin by choosing a subject in the day's news, then play free-association with it. Say the subject is *sports* and you begin saying the word. The next student then says the first word that comes to mind; then the next student responds with a new word, et cetera, et cetera. For instance: sports; baseball; St. Louis Cardinals; World Series; the latest player trades. And maybe eventually you and the group will generate ideas worth debating—the need for better coaching; salary caps; the use of steroids; team loyalty, or the lack thereof; the designated hitter rule.

Once you have brainstormed a list, organize the issues according to categories—for example, sports, politics, social issues, environment, the media, television, education, and so on. Then transfer the list to your journal. Now, whenever an assignment comes up, you'll have a database of ideas worth writing about.

Next try to focus these ideas by deciding the following:

- Which subjects do I know something about?
- Have I had personal experiences with any particular subject?
- How do I feel about the subject? (angry? glad? sad? neutral?)
- What is my stand on the subject? Should I defend it? argue against it? Do I feel strongly enough to make suggestions for changes?
- Would this be a subject I'd want to do more research on?
- Who would be my audience—friends? instructor? parents? And how much does he, she, or they know about the topic?

In subsequent chapters, we'll discuss how to frame an argument on a topic, the ways of approaching your audience, the kinds of evidence to present, and so forth. But at this point, we're simply interested in helping you come up with a checklist of arguable subjects worth writing about. Whatever you come up with in your checklist, each topic should have three basic things:

1. It should be interesting.
2. It should appeal to readers.
3. It should have a specific slant.

Clustering

Some writers find that visualizing their ideas on a page helps them explore their subject in new ways. Clustering[1] is a technique you can use to do that. It involves choosing a key word, phrase, or even a short sentence, and placing it in the center of a blank page with a circle around it. Next you try to think of ideas, words, or other short phrases that you can associate or relate to your key word or phrase. As you do, write them in the blank area surrounding the center and circle them and draw lines linking them to your center circled word or phrase. As you accumulate more and more clusters, the words and phrases within them will generate ideas on their own; these can be linked to the words that inspired them. When you have exhausted your cluster, you will have a complex network of ideas that should provide many ways to begin to explore your subject. By choosing any one or a combination of these words or ideas as a starting point, you can move to freewriting to find ways of developing these ideas further.

Figure 3.1 shows how John used clustering to find new ways of thinking about binge drinking, the topic he had chosen for his paper. When John examined his cluster, he found a map of the many ideas he might explore further:

■ Should colleges play the role of in loco parentis and regulate student drinking or is drinking a matter of personal responsibility?

Figure 3.1 Sample Cluster

---

[1]Clustering is a technique explored by Gabriele L. Rico in her book *Writing the Natural Way: Using Right Brain Techniques to Release Your Expressive Powers* (Los Angeles: J. P. Tarcher, 1983).

■ What role does peer pressure play in binge drinking?
■ Are print ads and television commercials for beer partly responsible for binge drinking among young people?
■ Is the extent of binge drinking on college campuses exaggerated or overstated?
■ If a student violates campus drinking rules, what should the consequences be?

John's cluster revealed the complexity of the issue and became a starting point for him to investigate the subject in greater depth.

Freewriting

The next step is freewriting, which goes one step beyond brainstorming and which helps get a focus on the subject while developing things to say about it. Instead of simply listing phrases, questions, and words related to your subject, freewriting involves writing freely, and without stopping, whatever thoughts and ideas you have about your subject, without worrying about sentence structure, spelling, or grammar. As in brainstorming, when you freewrite, it's important not to censor your ideas. Your aim is to discover what you know about your subject, and the best way you can do that is by giving your mind permission to go wherever it pleases. Freewriting isn't intended to be a finished part of your paper; instead, it's a way to generate the ideas and focus that you can use later as you begin to draft the paper itself.

Freewriting can begin with anything: your topic, a particularly interesting idea you've read about, or an experience that you can connect with your subject. If you have used brainstorming or clustering before freewriting, these activities can provide you with a key word or phrase to get you started. For instance, John found a good idea from his brainstorm to begin his freewriting:

Getting together with friends for a good time. That's what everyone looks forward to every weekend. Put away the books, get out of the dorm, and party. Four, five, sometimes more drinks. Feeling no pain. Binge drinking just seems to happen. It isn't something you plan to do. When you're having a good time, you don't think about how terrible you're going to feel the next day or about all the stupid things you're doing. It's easy to get alcohol in town. Nobody ever checks for proof, and if they do you just go to another place down the street. It's so easy to get a phony ID anyway. And the crowds are so large, no one looks carefully. If college students want to drink, who's to say they can't? We're old enough to vote, die for our country, sign a contract. Why not drinking? And how are you ever going to learn to drink if you don't do it? College students drink for lots of reasons. Why? Well, it gets them in a party mood. It's fun. It makes us feel like adults. It's so cool. Everyone does it. There's nothing wrong with drinking, but is it a problem if you drink too much? Every weekend. They let it get out of control. Drunk driving, alcohol poisoning, stupid accidents. Binge drinking is drinking gone overboard. You can get in a car accident and end up killing or maiming yourself, another person. Even a friend. Then how would I feel? That's all I can think of right now.

John used his freewriting to think on paper. While he didn't come up with any conclusions about how he felt about binge drinking, he did produce a number of ideas that he explored later, when he worked on the first draft of his paper:

- College students binge drink for many reasons.
- Binge drinking can be a problem.
- Drinking is related to feeling adult.
- Binge drinking is not a planned behavior, but it can get to be a habit.

One of the best reasons for using freewriting before you begin the first draft of your paper is to avoid the most intimidating sight a writer can see: a blank page. Unfortunately, sometimes that blank page is the result of a blank mind and undue concern about how your writing and ideas will appear to others. When you freewrite, you write for yourself alone. It is a way to make your ideas flow. Freewriting generates ideas that will help you begin to think about your subject before worrying about polishing your writing for an audience.

Asking Questions

Once you have a subject in mind, a good strategy for generating ideas is to make a list of questions you have about the subject. Your questions can cover areas in which you need more information, as well as questions you might like to answer as you think and write about your topic. For instance, John tried this strategy for his topic of college binge drinking and came up with the following questions:

Why do college students binge drink?

How many college students actually binge drink?

Is binge drinking a result of peer pressure?

Do students binge drink to show they are adults?

Do most college students find binge drinking acceptable?

Is binge drinking strictly a college student activity or do other age and economic groups do this as well?

Do college students stop binge drinking once they leave college?

Who should be responsible for binge drinking? the drinkers? the college? the law?

Why do college administrations feel that they must respond to the problem of drinking if it's off campus?

Do colleges have a legal responsibility to protect their students?

Are the alcohol prevention programs on campus effective?

How often does binge drinking result in fatal accidents?

It's easy to see how one question can lead to another. By choosing one question or several related ones, John had real direction for exploring his topic and focusing his paper as he began his research and his first draft.

Engaging in Dialogue with Others

Talking to other people is a great source of ideas. None of the techniques we've discussed so far have to be solitary activities. By sharing your ideas and listening to the responses of others, you will find a wealth of new ideas and perspectives. In fact, you'll be engaging in the kind of *dialogue* we discussed in Chapter 1. You can do this in a number of ways: either participate in small peer groups in your class or in larger class discussions; speak individually with your instructor; seek out members of your community, on campus or outside your school; share ideas with others electronically through Internet chat rooms, e-mail, or listservs; or talk with family and friends. As Larry King and other talk show hosts prove every day, people love to talk. So, take advantage of it—and take notes.

Refining Topics

Once you have found—through the strategies we've discussed—subjects that strike you as interesting, you have to begin narrowing down your topic to a manageable size. The next step, then, is to look over your list and reduce it to those topics that are legitimately arguable. (See Chapter 1 for a refresher.)

Reducing Your Options

Your first step is to determine whether your subject is manageable. You don't want a subject that is too broad or unwieldy or that requires prohibitive amounts of research. For example, you would not want to argue that "welfare needs to be reformed." You could write a book about that if you had time to do all the research. To write a short paper, you have to narrow your subject. "The only people who should be eligible for welfare support should be disabled people and mothers of preschool children" is a manageable reduction of your first idea, and one that you can handle in an average-length paper (see Figure 3.2). The more narrow your topic, the more you restrict your research and tighten the focus of your argument.

Avoiding Overspecialized Topics

However, don't pick a topic that requires extensive specialized knowledge, such as how to reduce the trade deficit or the problems inherent in thermonuclear fusion. The issue you choose should be one you know a little something about and, to keep you interested, about which you have strong convictions. Also, it should be an

Figure 3.2 "Reducing Your Options" Diagram

issue you are willing to spend a reasonable amount of time exploring on your own online, in interviews, or perhaps in the library. Aside from writing a convincing argument, a parallel goal of any project you research is to become better informed and more appreciative of the complexity of the issue. Therefore, select a topic on which you wish to be well informed and that you are willing to investigate and reflect on.

Formulating a Working Claim

Once you have decided on your topic and used some of the strategies we've discussed, you are ready to create a working claim. As we explained in Chapter 1, the claim is the heart of your essay. It functions as a thesis statement. It states what you believe or what action you'd like your readers to take. In Chapter 1, we provided examples of the different ways you can state your claim. However, at this early stage of your writing, it would be difficult to create a claim that would be perfect for the paper you have yet to research and write. It's too early in the game to commit yourself. After all, your research may yield some surprising results, and you want to be open to all sides of the issue. At best, you can create a working claim—that is, a statement of your opinion or position on your topic that you can use temporarily to help you focus and organize your paper and limit your research.

After John, our first-year composition student, considered his subject of binge drinking by brainstorming, clustering, freewriting, asking questions about the topic, and engaging in dialogue with others, he realized what an enormous and complex topic it was and that he needed to narrow it. He began by asking questions about binge drinking. How prevalent is binge drinking? Who should be responsible for the regulation of student drinking? Are students themselves solely responsible? Should a college or university act in loco parentis? What are the consequences of ignoring the problem of binge drinking? What is the role of peer pressure in binge drinking? How can binge drinking be discouraged or controlled? What role does advertising play? Can binge drinking be fatal?

As John thought about the answers to these questions, he began to narrow the focus of his broad topic to one that he could explore in a paper of reasonable length. He decided that he would focus only on the issue of how to control or eliminate binge drinking on college campuses.

John's next step was to formulate a *working claim* for his paper on binge drinking. When he sat down to create his working claim, he examined and reflected on his topic and decided on the following *working claim*:

> Binge drinking is a serious problem on college campuses, and if we continue to ignore it or treat it as normal and acceptable student behavior, no one will ever find an effective way to eliminate it.

By creating a working claim early in his writing process, John benefited in a number of ways. He clearly took a position about his topic and expressed his point of view. While he had the opportunity to change his viewpoint as he thought further about his topic, his working claim served as a baseline. John's working claim also helped him organize the reasons he needed to support his position.

Let's take a look at John's working claim to see how it is organized. His claim can be divided into three parts:

1. Binge drinking is a problem on college campuses.
2. It is ignored or simply accepted as normal student behavior.
3. No one has yet found an effective way to solve this problem.

All these statements are arguable because, as we discussed in Chapter 1, they are based on judgment and interpretation, not on indisputable facts or personal opinion. As he developed his paper, John needed to decide on reasons to effectively convince his readers that these three parts of his working claim are true.

In addition, John's working claim helped him decide what he needed to investigate further. As John researched and became more knowledgeable about his topic, he revised his working claim to better reflect what he had learned. But at this stage of his paper, his working claim provided him with several specific areas that he needed to investigate in order to argue persuasively about them:

1. Is binge drinking really a problem on college campuses? How significant is it?
2. How is binge drinking ignored and by whom?
3. Is binge drinking regarded as normal student behavior and by whom?
4. What has been done to eliminate binge drinking?
5. What are some ways this problem can be dealt with?

In Chapter 9, we look at a number of ways available to John to research his topic. By using the questions suggested by his working claim as a guide, John had plenty of avenues to explore.

Thinking like a writer will help you make the jump from simply having an opinion on a subject to finding ways to express that opinion in an argument essay. In the next chapter, we look at the way in which audience influences and affects the choices we make about what to include in an argument essay and how to present our arguments.

SAMPLE STUDENT ARGUMENT FOR ANALYSIS

Stephanie Bower, a student majoring in English Literature, was interested in the subject of television news reporting. She realized what a complicated and multifaceted topic it is and that she needed to focus on a particular aspect of broadcast news. She began refining her topic by asking questions about TV news reporting. What does the viewing audience expect of television news? What is the responsibility of news broadcast? Are the when, where, why, what, and how enough? What are the qualities of a newscast that satisfy my expectations for good news coverage? Which news programming do I find inadequate? What differences exist between national and local news coverage? What is the state of reporting on my local news channels? What are the strengths and weaknesses of those channels? What role does advertising play in a broadcast? How can local television news be improved? What are critics of the television news industry saying about the caliber of local news? What would I discover if I were to examine the quality of local news on a minute-by-minute basis? What recommendations could be made to improve the news?

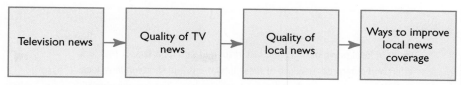

Figure 3.3 Stephanie's "Reducing Options" Diagram

As Stephanie thought about the answers, she realized that although each question poses an interesting issue to explore, she had to narrow the topic to one that she could cover in a paper of reasonable length. She thought back to some recent local news stories that had interested her, discovering to her dismay how complicated social issues had been pressed into just a few seconds. Worse, she was stunned to discover that extended coverage was given to a story about an abandoned dog. Reflecting on this, Stephanie realized she had material for a specific topic: local news—what was wrong with it, and how it might be improved. The box diagram in Figure 3.3 reflects her thought process as she narrowed down her topic.

Her working claim, then, both limited the range of her topic and very clearly expressed her point of view about it:

Local television news is known for its bare-bones coverage and journalistic mediocrity. Now, competing with the convenience of Internet news sources and the far more in-depth coverage available in newspapers, local television news must reconsider its responsibilities and its approach.

Bower 1

Stephanie Bower
Professor Van Zandt
English 111
4 December 2009

What's the Rush?
Speed Yields Mediocrity in Local Television News

1   Down to the second, time is a factor in television. Though national television news has outlets for lengthy reports and analysis in hour-long news magazines like *Dateline* and panel discussions like *Meet the Press*, local news is rendered almost exclusively in a "short story" format. Most local TV news stories are just twenty or thirty seconds long. These stories succeed in stating the basic facts, but they simply do not have time to do more. Though television newscasts operate in minutes and seconds, the brevity of local news stories is not just a natural feature of the medium. Rather, these stories are often the

Bower 2

result of local news stations that lack resources and reporters, or that lack effort and enterprise. Because of these limitations and shortcomings, local television news has developed a reputation for journalistic mediocrity. With dozens of quality online news sources available for consumption at your convenience, local television news faces more competition than ever. Local newscasts must reconsider their responsibilities and their approach. Otherwise, mediocrity will result in obsolescence.

2   Local television news is still a popular source of information about public affairs. People want news that is relevant to their specific communities—stories about local schools, ballot issues, town elections, and art events, the restaurant scene, historic sites, zoning issues, and known personalities. Local stations have the potential to reach large regional audiences looking for coverage of the stories affecting their towns and cities. Yet local news is known for its focus on sensational crime coverage and "soft" news, which focuses on human interest stories, sports, and entertainment. Increased cable news viewership and the rise of the Internet as a news source have caused some decline in local news viewership, making the business that much more competitive (Belt and Just). News directors may feel pressure "to produce the cheapest type of news that they think will draw and hold viewers—namely, low effort stories featuring crime, lifestyle, and entertainment" (Belt and Just 195). Yet these kinds of stories offer little real informational value to viewers. Not all news stories demand a great deal of time and depth, but many stories require more than the twenty or thirty seconds they are allotted during a local newscast. A news story that runs for one minute and thirty seconds can tell viewers the who, what, when, where, and how of a story, but it cannot delve into an analysis of a situation or its contextual significance.

3   Why don't more stations air high quality, in-depth local news coverage? The answer seems to come down to money. In the world of corporate-owned and advertiser-dependent media, it becomes unclear whether local journalism outlets are impartial civic informers or cogs in the machinery of big business. During sweeps weeks, local stations engage in a high-stakes war to see who wins the important time slots. Stations suddenly run in-depth "Special Reports," such as a 2008 special investigation on WHDH-TV, Boston's NBC affiliate station, into how much taxpayer money was being wasted because of lights left on overnight in state buildings. But despite the success

Bower 3

of this story, many local market stations do not spend time or money on the equipment, resources, and manpower required to do investigative or in-depth reporting on a regular basis. Deborah Potter, executive director of NewsLab, cites severely understaffed local news teams as a primary cause of low-quality coverage. She says the majority of local station budgets are spent on equipment and anchor salaries, and there is simply not enough left over to pay for reporters and photographers to go out in the field. Potter says this shortage is the reason why there is "so little enterprise, so much cheap-to-cover crime, and so little depth on the air. Most television reporters have a simple mission every day: Get out there and scratch the surface" ("The Body Count").

4   Because there are not enough reporters working to fill the time with hard news, stations become dependent on news wires and video feeds. It is cheaper to pull video of President Obama travelling overseas from the satellite feeds than to send a photographer and reporter out in the field to cover a local story, and it is faster to rephrase a story taken from the news wires than to research and report on an original story. Stories taken from the news wires and satellite video feeds account for many of the "quick-hit" twenty- or twenty-five-second pieces aired during local newscasts. These stories may contain legitimate news, but they are typically not stories covering local news topics.

5   Health-related stories are popular with viewers and are frequently included in local news lineups. Yet the quick-hit format of the stories is particularly troublesome in this arena. Elizabeth Jensen writes that local newscasts frequently feature health information, but their reports are "brief, often lack necessary perspective . . . and occasionally contain 'egregious errors' with potentially serious consequences." Jensen cites a large study which showed that the median length of health stories in local newscasts was just thirty-three seconds, and of these only 27% included an interview with someone in the health profession. She writes that local news tends to cover the "sexy" stories—high profile diseases of the moment, such as West Nile virus, avian flu, and H1N1 ("swine flu")—far more often than the things that are more likely to affect people's health, like diabetes or heart disease. These are certainly topical news stories; however, the amount of coverage these stories receive coupled with a lack of time and depth may create unnecessary alarm.

6   On October 7, 2009, I examined the story line-ups for the local 5 p.m. newscast on WHDH-TV, Boston's NBC affiliate. Excluding commercials, the full

Bower 4

air-time available for this newscast was twenty-two minutes. Of this, one minute and twenty-five seconds was spent on graphics and teases for upcoming stories. Five minutes was given to weather, one minute and fifteen seconds was given to sports, and one minute was given to entertainment. Two minutes and fifteen seconds was spent on national news. Local news accounted for nine minutes of coverage. Of this, four minutes and fifty seconds was devoted to the lead story about a grisly murder in New Hampshire. Yet even the time given to this story—by far the longest piece of news coverage—was shorter than the total time devoted to weather. The other local news stories were between fifteen seconds and one minute and forty-five seconds long.

7   Local news stories can often do little more than highlight key facts and perhaps include a sound bite or two. For example, one of the local stories was about 100 firefighters who would be getting their jobs back because of state stimulus funds. The story was thirty seconds long—long enough to state the plain facts, but not long enough to provide context on the layoffs, how the decision was made to use state stimulus funds for their rehire, information on why this was a necessary use of funds, or even to add a human element by speaking to any of the rehired firefighters.

8   Stations often select stories that can be told quickly and that require little background or context. In the precious minutes the station has to cover the local news, they often spend two to five minutes on national or international news stories—stories that will be covered again during the station's national nightly newscast. Because it is a video-driven medium, television news will often fill precious chunks of time with stories because of a novelty video clip. For example, on September 25, 2009, WHDH devoted one minute and forty-five seconds of the newscast to a story about a moose wandering through a local neighborhood. They had a great video clip of the moose in someone's backyard—but this was one of the longest local stories in the half-hour newscast.

9   Local news occasionally devotes time to entertainment stories, particularly if the story benefits the affiliate station and its network. For example, WHDH devoted over a minute of its September 25 newscast to the September 26 premiere of *Saturday Night Live*, airing on WHDH's parent network NBC. This kind of promotional entertainment coverage benefits the network, but it draws even more time away from quality local news coverage.

Bower 5

10   Because of the time constraints imposed on television news, it can never provide the in-depth coverage available in newspapers or online news sites, despite the countless graphics and brandings promising "I-teams" and "in-depth coverage." Dane Claussen notes that "the entire transcript of a half-hour local television news broadcast will fit onto less than one page of a newspaper" ("Cognitive Dissonance"). Stephanie Ebbert, City Hall Bureau Chief at the *Boston Globe*, says that local TV news is best-suited for "quick-hit" news:

> For more sophisticated, involved coverage, the consumer really has to turn to either a lengthier discussion of an event on a TV news magazine, or to radio or print media, which devote more resources to individual stories. That's not to say it can't be done on TV; it simply often isn't. The very subtleties that make some stories interesting and newsworthy are often difficult to crystallize in a minute and a half or to make friendly to viewers who are believed to be so very impatient. (personal interview)

Ebbert questions the idea that modern Americans, with their busy lifestyles and MTV-influenced visual perceptions, cannot pay attention long enough to ingest longer, more sophisticated TV news stories.

11   Todd Belt and Marion Just conducted a five-year, in-depth study of fifty local markets to determine the relationship between what a local news station covers and its level of commercial success. Are viewers as turned off by stories on public affairs and issues as news directors fear? Do they need fast-paced, attention-grabbing stories, as the industry seems to believe? Their study suggests that this is not the case. Belt and Just found that "audiences preferred news stories that reflected journalistic enterprise—station initiated investigations or on the spot reporting instead of merely reporting the news from other sources (Belt and Just 202-04)" Stations that included this kind of reportage fared better financially overall. They write, "Journalistic enterprise is one of the factors that leads to larger audiences and, therefore, greater advertising. . . . Stations that practice low effort journalism risk getting trapped in a downward spiral of declining ratings" (Belt and Just 202-04). The findings suggest that news producers are incorrect in their stubborn belief that audiences prefer soft news and investigative journalism is not worth the cost or effort.

12   If more time were given to news, it would have to taken from coverage of something else. So what has to go? Stations could take the time back from

Bower 6

the promotional graphics that devour precious seconds with useless visuals, or they could have less repetition of stories in back-to-back newscasts. Another option is to take the time from the twenty-second "quick hit" wire stories, particularly those that cover national news. Of course these stories are news and they are of interest to viewers, but if viewers want the national news tidbits, then isn't national network news the place to find them?

13   Another possible solution is to take the time back from the "Coming up next!" news teases designed to lure viewers to stay through the commercial break. Deborah Potter says that many viewers are turned off by local news because "they're annoyed by the tricks and gimmicks stations use to try to make them watch." Local news stations often run one-and-a-half to two minutes of tease video per half-hour newscast. This time, in addition to the time spent on promotional station graphics, branding slogans and music, adds up to a significant amount of seconds and minutes that could be spent expanding on news stories. Teases may work, and it is valuable for busy viewers to know what is coming up in case a story may be of particular interest to them. But stations should not underestimate their audiences by assuming they need to be continually wooed into watching a half hour of news. The story is what the viewers really want. Teases have no journalistic value and take time away from reporters and their pieces.

14   Today's news consumer has tremendous options for where, when, and how to get the news. There are dozens of high quality news sources online, and younger people in particular are comfortable with and trust these sources. Local television news has to offer something unique—coverage that is community-based, high-quality, and relevant. Eric Klinenberg calls the Internet "the ideal medium for deepening coverage with interactive links to video, text, and graphics" (58). Yet most news organizations do not yet have a model for earning the kind of profits online that they earn through television advertising, and TV is still the flagship enterprise for local news.

15   Local news affiliates may not have the financial resources or tremendous market sizes of their parent networks, but they still provide the important service of informing communities about their local schools, citizens, governments, and breaking news. Surely, it must be frustrating for professional television journalists to abandon insightful analysis and instead package the facts into a minute and thirty seconds of lead, soundbite, and tag. Research indicates that viewers want in-depth local news stories that are relevant to their lives and their communities. The question is whether local news stations will risk altering standard formats to give reporters the space to tell these stories.

Bower 7

Works Cited

Belt, Todd L., and Marion R. Just. "The Local News Story: Is Quality a Choice?" *Political Communication* 25 (2008): 194-95. Print.

"The Body Count." *American Journalism Review* 24.6 (2002): 60. Print.

Bradley, Samuel D., et al. "Wait! Don't Turn That Dial! More Excitement to Come! The Effects of Story Length and Production Pacing in Local Television News. . . ." *Journal of Broadcasting & Electronic Media* (2005): 3-22. Print.

Claussen, Dane S. "Cognitive Dissonance, Media Illiteracy, and Public Opinion on the News." *American Behavioral Scientist* 48 (2004): 212. Print.

Ebbert, Stephanie. Personal interview. 12 Dec. 2004.

Jensen, Elizabeth. "Study Laments Anemic Reporting." *Television Week* 13 Mar. 2006: n. pag. Print.

Klinenberg, Eric. "Convergence: News Production in a Digital Age." *Annals of the American Academy of Political and Social Science* 597 (2005): 48-64. Print.

Potter, Deborah. "Stemming the Losses: How Can TV News Win Back Viewers?" *American Journalism Review* 22.10 (2000): 49. Print.

QUESTIONS FOR DISCUSSION AND WRITING

1. Where does Stephanie Bower state her claim? Do you agree with Stephanie's working claim here? Did you have a strong opinion about local TV news before you read Stephanie's piece? Did reading her paper change your mind, or reinforce your thinking?
2. Did Stephanie sufficiently narrow her topic? Is her evidence convincing? Considering that some of her evidence is from leading critics of the world of journalism, did she make their information accessible to you and relevant to her claim?
3. Examine two instances in which Stephanie cites quotations from experts in the field to develop her argument. Comment on the way she incorporated the quotations into the text. Was it done successfully or awkwardly?
4. What two factors, according to Stephanie, account for mediocrity in local news? Do you agree? disagree?
5. What are some of the brandings such as "I-Team" or "Storm Center" or "in-depth coverage" your local stations use? How do these brandings

affect you? Do they earn your respect, your curiosity, or even your disdain? Explain your reaction.

6. What suggestions does Stephanie offer to improve the quality of local TV news? Which suggestions do you think could be realistically implemented? Which are obstacles too great to control in your opinion?

7. In your journal, select a local TV newscast, one that is broadcast nightly at the same time. Watch it every day if you can, or at least three times. Like Stephanie, break down the content of the newscast recording the length of time in minutes and seconds of the story, the topic of the story, and the depth of the story. Evaluate the content.

8. How do you respond to Stephanie's question, "Is journalism an impartial civic informer or a big business?" To shape your answer, use some of the evidence Stephanie presented in her paper and find some of your own.

EXERCISES

1. Get together with a small group of students in your class and brainstorm possible topics for an argument essay concerning a controversial issue on your campus or in your community. Try to think of at least ten topics that are current and that most people in your group find interesting and arguable.

2. Make a visit to the periodicals section of your college library and look through current issues of periodicals and newspapers on the shelves to find out what issues and subjects are being debated in America and around the world. Find one or more topics that interest you and make copies of those articles for further reading and response in your journal.

3. Take some time to explore the Internet by doing a keyword search using a Web search engine. In your journal, describe the results of your search. How many different sites devoted to your topic did you locate? What did you find surprising about the comments and opinions expressed by the participants?

4. Engage in a dialogue with other students, family members, friends, or people in the community who might have some interest and opinions on a potential topic. In your journal, record and respond to their diverse views.

5. Choose a topic that you might wish to investigate for an argument essay and use some of the strategies suggested in this chapter to get started: brainstorm, cluster, freewrite, question.

6. Formulate a list of questions about your potential topic.

7. After you have followed some of the strategies for exploring your topic, formulate a working claim. In your journal, identify which parts of your claim will need to be supported by reasons in your essay. Which parts of your claim will need to be investigated further?

4

Addressing Audiences: Thinking Like a Reader

As we've discussed in previous chapters, the purpose of writing an argument is to prompt your listeners to consider seriously your point of view and, thus, win your listeners' respect through the logic and skill of your thinking. When used productively, argument is a way to resolve conflict and achieve common ground among adversaries. Thus, one of the primary ways to measure the success of your argument is to gauge how effectively it reaches and appeals to your audience. Knowing something about your audience will enable you to use your knowledge to make your arguments most effective.

Creating an argument would be a simple task if you could be guaranteed an audience of readers just like yourself. If everyone shared your cultural, educational, religious, and practical experiences, persuading them to accept your point of view would require very little effort. Clearly, however, this is not the case. A quick look around your classroom will reveal the many differences that make argument a challenging activity. Is everyone the same age? race? gender? ethnicity? Do you all listen to the same music? dress alike? live in the same neighborhood? vote for the same candidates? attend the same place of worship? Unless you attend a very unusual school, the answer to most of these questions will be a resounding "no." People are different; what interests you may bore the person behind you, whereas what puts you to sleep may inspire someone else to passionate activism. And what you see on the surface isn't the whole story about your classmates, either. That rough-looking guy who works as a mechanic may write poetry in his spare time; that conservatively dressed woman may spend her weekends touring the countryside on a motorcycle. It's too easy to make assumptions about people's values and beliefs just by looking at them. If you want to persuade these people, you're going to have to assess them very carefully.

Knowing your audience will help you determine almost every aspect of the presentation of your case:

- the kind of language you use;
- the writing style (casual or formal, humorous or serious, technical or philosophical);
- the particular slant you take (appealing to the reader's reason, emotions, ethics, or a combination of these);
- what emphasis to give the argument;
- the type of evidence you offer;
- the kinds of authorities you cite.

Also, this knowledge will let you better anticipate any objections to your position. In short, knowing your audience lets you adjust the shape of your argument the way you would refocus a camera after each photo you shoot.

If, for instance, you're writing for your economics professor, you would use technical vocabulary you would not use with your English professor. Likewise, in a newspaper article condemning alcohol abusers, you would have to keep in mind that some of your readers or their family members might be recovering alcoholics; they may take exception to your opinions. A travel piece for an upscale international magazine would need to have a completely different slant and voice than an article for the travel section of a small local newspaper.

Knowing your audience might make the difference between a convincing argument and a failing argument. Suppose, for instance, you decide to write an editorial for the student newspaper opposing a recently announced tuition hike. Chances are you would have a sympathetic audience in the student body because you share age, educational status, and interests. Most students do not like the idea of a higher tuition bill. That commonality might justify the blunt language and emotional slant of your appeal. It might even allow a few sarcastic comments directed at the administration. That same argument addressed to your school's board of trustees, however, would probably not win a round of applause. With them it would be wiser to adopt a more formal tone in painting a sympathetic picture of your financial strain; it's always smart to demonstrate an understanding of the opposition's needs, maybe even a compromise solution. In this case, your appeal to the trustees would be more credible if you acknowledged the university's plight while recommending alternative money-saving measures such as a new fund-raising program.

Or suppose you write an article with a religious thrust arguing against capital punishment. You argue that even in the case of confessed murderers, state execution is an immoral practice running counter to Christian doctrine; for supporting evidence you offer direct quotations from the New Testament. Were you to submit your article to a religious publication, your reliance on the authority of the scriptures would probably appeal to the editors. However, were you to submit that same article to the "My Turn" column for *Newsweek,* chances are it would be turned down, no matter how well written. The editors aren't necessarily an ungodly lot, but *Newsweek,* like most other large-circulation magazines, is published for an audience made up of people of every religious persuasion, as well as agnostics and atheists. *Newsweek* editors are not in the business of publishing material that excludes a large segment of its audience. Knowing your readers works in two ways: It helps you decide what materials to put into your argument, and it helps you decide where to publish your argument, whether it be on an electronic bulletin board, in a local paper, or on the op-ed page of the *Wall Street Journal.*

The Target Audience

The essays in this book come from a variety of publications, many of them magazines addressed to the "general" American readership. Others, however, come from publications directed to men or women, the political right or left, or from publications for people of particular ethnic, racial, and cultural identities. These were written for *target audiences.* When writers have a "target" audience in mind, particularly readers who share the same interests, opinions, and prejudices, they can take shortcuts with little risk of alienating anybody, because writers and readers have so many things in common. Consider the following excerpts concerning the use of animal testing in scientific research:

> Contrary to prevailing misperception, in vitro tests need not replace existing in vivo test procedures in order to be useful. They can contribute to chemical-safety evaluation right now. In vitro tests, for example, can be incorporated into the earliest stages of the risk-assessment process; they can be used to identify chemicals having the lowest probability of toxicity so that animals need be exposed only to less noxious chemicals.

It is clear from the technical terminology (e.g., *in vitro, in vivo, toxicity*), professional jargon *(test procedures, chemical-safety evaluation, risk-assessment process)*, and the formal, detached tone that the piece was intended for a scientifically educated readership. Not surprisingly, the article, "Alternatives to Animals in Toxicity Testing," was authored by two research scientists, Alan M. Goldberg and John M. Frazier, and published in *Scientific American* (August 1989). Contrast it with another approach to the topic:

> Almost 30 years ago, Queen had been a child herself, not quite two years old, living in Thailand under the care of her mother and another female elephant, the two who had tended to her needs every day since her birth. They taught her how to use her trunk, in work and play, and had given her a sense of family loyalty. But then Queen was captured, and her life was changed irrevocably by men with whips and guns. One man herded Queen by whipping and shouting at her while another shot her mother, who struggled after her baby until more bullets pulled her down forever.

What distinguishes this excerpt is the emotional appeal. This is not the kind of article you would find in *Scientific American* or most other scientific journals. Nor would you expect to see this kind of emotional appeal in a newsmagazine such as *Newsweek* or *Time,* or a general interest publication such as the Sunday magazine of many newspapers. The excerpt comes from an animal rights newsletter published by PETA, People for the Ethical Treatment of Animals. Given that particular audience, the writer safely assumes immediate audience sympathy with the plight of elephants. There is no need for the author to qualify or apologize for such sentimentalizing statements as "Queen had been a child herself" and "They taught her how to use her trunk, in work and play, and had given her a sense of family loyalty." In fact, given the context, the author is probably more interested in reminding readers of a shared cause rather than winning converts to the cause of animal rights.

Sometimes targeting a sympathetic audience is intended to move people to action—to get people to attend a rally or to contribute money to a cause or to vote for a particular political candidate. During the 2008 presidential campaign, fund-raising letters went out asking for donations to one particular candidate who pledged to fight the high cost of health care. In one of several Web logs ("blogs") supporting that candidate, the pharmaceutical industry was portrayed as a "greedy goliath" that was no different than "illegal drug cartels, extorting money from hapless consumers." As used in this blog, the strategy in appealing to a target audience is to streamline the issue into an "us-versus-them" conflict—in this case, the consumer as innocent victim and the manufacturers as bad guys. The blogger went on to argue that drug manufacturers inflate their prices astronomically, citing as evidence how company CEOs enjoy incomes in the tens of millions of dollars. "The pharmaceutical industry exists for the sole purpose of preying upon Americans who are sick, unhealthy, in discomfort and injured," said the blogger. "Their goal is to insure [sic] that only your symptoms are treated." Crackling with charged language, the blog invited voters to join the effort to change a system that exploited the taxpaying consumer and bloated company profits.

While pharmaceutical companies may indeed inflate the cost of their products, the campaign blog was a one-way argument, addressed to people already sympathetic to the cause. But the blog lacked perspectives from the other side. Nothing was said about the billions of dollars spent by pharmaceutical companies to develop and bring to market a new drug, or the fact that only a small percentage of drugs that reach the market ever turns a profit. Nor was there mention of the fact that the FDA is funded by the pharmaceutical companies and not taxpayer dollars, or the fact that the time frame for turning a profit is a limited number of years, after which patents expire, allowing the generic makers to market the same product at reduced costs. In short, the function of the campaign letters and blogs was not to plumb the depths of the issue and offer a balanced argument. On the contrary, most of the target audience was already sold on the cause. The basic intention was to convert conviction into money and votes. And the means was charged, motivational rhetoric.

The General Audience

Unless you're convinced that your readers are in total agreement with you or share your philosophical or professional interests, you may have some trouble picturing just whom you are persuading. It's tempting to say you're writing for a "general" audience; but, as we said at the beginning of this chapter, general audiences may include very different people with different backgrounds, expectations, and standards. Writing for such audiences, then, may put additional pressure on you.

In reality, of course, most of your college writing will be for your professors. This can be a little confusing because you may find yourself trying to determine just what audience your professor represents. You may even wonder why professors expect you to explain material with which they are familiar. You may feel that defining technical terms to your psychology instructor who covered them in class the week before, or summarizing a poem that you know your English professor can probably recite, is a waste of time. But they have a good reason: They assume the role of an uninformed audience to let you show how much *you* know.

Of course, if you are arguing controversial issues you may find yourself in the awkward position of trying to second-guess your instructor's stand on an issue. You may even be tempted to tone down your presentation so as not to risk offense and, thus, an undesirable grade. However, most instructors try not to let their biases affect their evaluation of a student's work. Their main concern is how well a student argues a position.

For some assignments, your instructor may specify an audience for you: members of the city council, the readers of the campus newspaper, Rush Limbaugh's radio listeners, and so on. But if no audience is specified, one of your earliest decisions about writing should be in choosing an audience. If you pick "readers of *The National Review*," for instance, you'll know you're writing for mostly male, conservative, middle-aged, middle-class whites; the expectations of these readers are very different than for readers of *Jet* or *Vibe*. If you are constrained to (or want the challenge of) writing for the so-called general audience, construct a mental picture of who those people are so you'll be able to shape your argument accordingly. Here are some of the characteristics we think you might include in your definition.

The "general" audience includes those people who read *Newsweek, Time,* and your local newspaper. That means people whose average age is about 35, whose educational level is high school plus two years of college, who make up the vast middle class of America, who politically stand in the middle of the road, and whose racial and ethnic origins span the world. You can assume that they read the daily newspaper and/or online news sites, watch the television news, and are generally informed about what is going on in the country. You can assume a good comprehension of language nuances and a sense of humor. They are people who recognize who Shakespeare was, though they may not be able to quote passages or name ten of his plays. Nor will they necessarily be experts in the latest theory of black holes or be able to explain how photo emulsions work. However, you can expect them to be open to technical explanations and willing to listen to arguments on birth control, gun control, weight control, and the issues of women and gays in the military. More importantly, you can look upon your audience as people willing to hear what you have to say.

Guidelines for Knowing Your Audience

Before sitting down to write, think about your audience. Ask yourself the following questions: Will I be addressing other college students, or people from another generation? Will my audience be of a particular political persuasion, or strongly identified with a specific cultural background? How might the age of my readers and their educational background influence the way they think about a given issue? On what criteria will they make their decisions about this issue? A good example of profiling your audience was evident in the 2008 presidential election. On the one hand, the Republicans gambled that "experience" was the chief criteria for voters. The Democrats, on the other hand, focused on a need for "change." As the election results showed, the Democrats had assessed their audience more accurately than did the Republicans.

As the example above illustrates, an effective argument essay takes into account the values, beliefs, interests, and experiences of its audience. If you simply choose to argue what you feel is important without regard to your audience, the only person you persuade may be yourself! An effective argument tries to establish common ground with the audience. While this may be difficult at times, recognizing what you have in common with your audience will enable you to argue most persuasively.

Audience Checklist

1. Who are the readers I will be addressing?
   a. What age group?
   b. Are they male, female, or both?
   c. What educational background?
   d. What socioeconomic status?
   e. What are their political, religious, occupational, or other affiliations?
   f. What values, assumptions, and prejudices do they have about life?
2. Where do my readers stand on the issue?
   a. Do they know anything about it?
   b. If so, how might they have learned about it?
   c. How do they interpret the issue?
   d. How does the issue affect them personally?
   e. Are they hostile to my stand on the issue?
3. How do I want my readers to view the issue?
   a. If they are hostile to my view, how can I persuade them to listen to me?
   b. If they are neutral, how can I persuade them to consider my viewpoint?
   c. If they are sympathetic to my views, what new light can I shed on the issue? How can I reinspire them to take action?
4. What do I have in common with my readers?
   a. What beliefs and values do we share?
   b. What concerns about the issue do we have in common?
   c. What common life experiences have we had?
   d. How can I make my readers aware of our connection?

Before you can do this, however, you will need to create a profile of your audience. You may find the audience checklist on page 84 helpful in assessing an audience. If you like visual prompts, write the answers to these questions on a card or a slip of paper that you can hang over your desk or display in a window on your computer screen while you're working on your argument. Looking at these questions and answers occasionally will remind you to direct your arguments on your particular audience.

Using Debate and Dialogue

Debate and dialogue, two of the methods of developing arguments discussed in Chapter 1, can also be used to sharpen your awareness of audience. For an example of how this can happen, let's revisit John, our first-year composition student who had decided to write his argument essay on the topic of binge drinking. After reading critically in his subject area (Chapter 2) and formulating a working claim

(Chapter 3), John turned his attention to the question of audience. He found that using debate and dialogue helped him answer some of the questions in the audience checklist and provided essential information about how his audience might respond to his ideas.

John decided that his audience would be a general one composed of people of all ages. He anticipated that most people in his audience would not endorse excessive drinking, but with such a diverse group of people he was unsure exactly what reasons would fuel their opposition and how strongly they would agree or disagree with his reasons. John found that using two strategies, first, a "Yes, but..." exchange and, second, an imaginary dialogue between different perspectives, helped to answer questions 2 and 3 on the audience checklist: Where do my readers stand on the issue? and How do I want my readers to view the issue? He used the answers to these questions to develop ways to engage his readers in the essay.

Working with classmates in small peer groups, John found that a "Yes, but . . ." exchange revealed specific points that his audience might use to oppose his reasons. For instance, John began with the following statement:

College administrators have a responsibility to deter binge drinking by their students.

He received several responses from his peer group:

Yes, college administrators have a responsibility to their students, but that responsibility should be limited to academic matters.

Yes, binge drinking by students should be a concern to college administrators, but college administrators shouldn't interfere with the private lives or habits of their students.

Yes, college administrators should try to deter binge drinking by students, but they will be ineffective unless they receive support from the community and parents.

Although each of John's classmates agreed that college administrators had a valid interest in student binge drinking, there was considerable disagreement over how far that interest should extend and how effective any action taken by administrators would be. The "Yes, but..." exchange gave John greater insight into the ways others might respond to his ideas. As he developed his argument, he was able to acknowledge and address such concerns by his potential audience.

In a similar fashion, John used dialogue to gain insight into question 4 on the audience checklist: What do I have in common with my readers? In particular, John wanted to discover any concerns and values he and his readers might share about binge drinking. To create a dialogue, John interviewed several of his classmates, his teachers, members of his family, and a few individuals from the community; he also read articles by health professionals concerned with alcohol abuse and young adults. His goal was to listen to a wide spectrum of views on the subject and to keep an open mind. He used his journal to record comments and his own impressions. What emerged from this dialogue were several areas of shared concerns: Most agreed that binge drinking was an unhealthy practice that should be discouraged, and while there were many different suggestions about the measures that should be taken to eliminate it, all agreed that the students who engaged in binge drinking must ultimately accept responsibility for ending it. No solution would work, all agreed, unless the drinkers themselves were willing to stop. John found this information helpful because he knew that his audience would be more willing to listen to his argument if he could identify these shared values and concerns.

By engaging in both debate and dialogue, John gained knowledge that enabled him to appeal to his audience more effectively.

Adapting to Your Readers' Attitudes

Writing for a general audience is a challenge because in that faceless mass are three kinds of readers you'll be addressing:

1. People who agree with you
2. People who are neutral—those who are unconvinced or uninformed on the issue
3. People who don't share your views, and who might be hostile to them

Each of these different subgroups will have different expectations of you and give you different obligations to meet if you are to present a convincing argument. Even readers sympathetic to your cause might not be familiar with specialized vocabulary, the latest developments around the issue, or some of the more subtle arguments from the opposition. Those hostile to your cause might be so committed to their own viewpoints that they might not take the time to discover that you share common concerns. And those neutral to the cause might simply need to be filled in on the issue and its background. If you're going to persuade your readers, you'll have to tailor your approach to suit their attitudes.

When addressing an audience, whether general or one of a particular persuasion, you must try to put yourself in its place. You must try to imagine the different needs and expectations these readers bring to your writing, always asking yourself what new information you can pass on and what new ways of viewing you can find for addressing the issue you're arguing. Depending on whether you anticipate a neutral, friendly, or unfriendly group of readers, let's look at some of the strategies you might use.

Addressing a Neutral Audience

Some writers think a neutral audience is the easiest to write for, but many others find this the most challenging group of readers. After all, they're *neutral*; you don't know which way they're leaning, or what may make them commit to your position. Your best role is the conveyor of knowledge: The information you bring, and the ways in which you present it, are the means by which you hope to persuade a neutral audience. Here are some of the ways to convey that information.

Fill in the Background

There are some issues about which few people are neutral: abortion, capital punishment, drug legalization, same-sex marriage, gun control. However, there are other issues about which some readers have not given a thought. For instance, if you're part of a farming community, your concern about preserving good farmland might make you feel concerned about unchecked industrial development in your area. To make a convincing case for readers from, say, Chicago or New York City, you first would have to explain the shortage of prime agricultural land. On the other hand, were you a writer from a large town, you might need to explain to readers from rural Vermont or Iowa why you think they should be concerned over mandatory recycling in large cities. In both cases, your task would be to provide your readers with the information they need to evaluate the issue by relating some of the history and background behind the controversy. All the while, you need to encourage them to weigh the evidence with an open mind.

Present a Balanced Picture

Part of educating a neutral audience about your position involves presenting a balanced picture of the issue by presenting multiple perspectives about the issue, not just one. Even though you are trying to help your readers understand why your position has value, you will be more persuasive if you treat *all* views fairly, including opposing views. You should clearly and accurately lay out the key arguments of all sides; then demonstrate why your position is superior. Your readers need to feel that you have looked at the total picture and reached your position after carefully weighing all views, a process you hope your readers will engage in as well. Let your readers make their decisions based on their own analysis of the information you have provided. Don't be guilty of stacking the deck, a logical fallacy we discussed in Chapter 2. Not representing the other sides at all, or representing them unfairly and inaccurately, can leave you open to criticisms of distortion, and it may make your readers feel that you're misleading them.

Personalize the Issues

One sure way of gaining readers' attention is to speak their language—that is, address their personal needs, hopes, and fears. (It's what skillful politicians do all the time on the campaign trail.) If you want to engage your readers' attention, demonstrate how the problem will affect them personally. On the matter of farmland, explain why if nothing is done to prevent its loss, the prices of corn and beans will triple over the next three years. On the recycling issue, explain how unrestricted trash dumping will mean that city dwellers will try to dump more trash in rural areas. However, although personalizing the issue is an effective way to make your readers aware of the importance of your issue, you should avoid creating an ad misericordiam argument. To be fully credible, you should be certain that the reasons and evidence you present to your readers are anchored in fact rather than emotion.

Show Respect

When you're an informed person talking about an issue to people with less knowledge than you, there's a dangerous tendency to speak down to them. Think how you feel when someone "talks down" to you. Do you like it? How persuasive do you think you can be if your readers think you're talking down to them? Don't condescend or patronize them. Try not to simplify a complex issue so much that it is reduced to a false dilemma: "If we don't increase school taxes immediately, our children will no longer receive a quality education." Don't assume that your audience is so ill informed that it cannot envision a middle ground between the two alternatives. On the contrary, treat your readers as people who want to know what you know about the issue and who want you to demonstrate to them clearly and accurately why you think they should agree with you. Invite them into the discussion, encouraging them with sound reasons and strong evidence to consider the merits of your side. Although your audience may not be as informed as you, they are willing to listen and deserve respect.

Addressing a Friendly Audience

Writing an argument for the already converted is much easier than writing for a neutral audience or one that is hostile. In a sense, half the battle is won because no minds have to be changed. You need not brace yourself for opposing views or refutations. Your role is simply to provide readers with new information and to renew enthusiasm for and commitment to your shared position. Nonetheless, we do have some suggestions for keeping your argument fair and balanced.

Avoid Appealing to Prejudices

One of the risks of addressing a sympathetic audience is appealing to prejudices rather than reasons and facts. Although it might be tempting to mock those who don't agree with you or to demean their views, don't. Stooping to that level only diminishes your own authority and undermines your credibility. Two of the logical fallacies we discussed in Chapter 2 address this problem. The first, an ad hominem argument, is a personal attack on those who disagree with your position. Unfortunately, this approach will reflect negatively on *you*. Use reason and hard evidence instead of insults and ridicule to underscore the weakness of other arguments while you make your readers aware of your mutual concerns. The second fallacy is an ad populum argument and involves using the presumed prejudices of your audience members to manipulate their responses to your argument. Once again, this approach will make you appear unreasonable and biased and may backfire if your audience does not share your prejudices. Instead, encourage your readers to respect different viewpoints, recognizing the merits of their arguments even though you ultimately disagree. It's simply a more reasonable approach, one that allows you and your readers to share informed agreement, and it will win the respect of friends and foes alike.

Offer New Information About the Issue

Even when your readers agree with you, they may need to have their memories refreshed regarding the history of the issue. In addition, you should provide readers with important new information on the issue. Such new developments might involve recent judicial decisions, newly enacted legislation, or new scientific data that could serve to strengthen your position and their agreement or require a reconsideration of your views. Unless you are absolutely up-to-date about the progress of your issue, you will appear to be either ill informed or deliberately withholding information, seriously undermining your credibility with your audience, even a friendly one. Your willingness to share and educate your audience will enhance the persuasiveness of your views.

Addressing an Unfriendly Audience

As difficult as it may be to accept, some readers will be totally at odds with your views, even hostile to them. Writing for such a readership, of course, is especially challenging—far more than for neutral readers. So how do you present your argument to people you have little chance of winning over?

The Rogerian Approach: Seek Common Ground and Show Empathy

One sure fire strategy in writing for an unfriendly audience is the so-called Rogerian approach—a strategy that evolved in the 1970s out of the writings of Carl Rogers. Considered one of the most influential American psychologists of the past century, Rogers made contributions to the fields of psychotherapy, counseling, education, and conflict resolution. In his humanistic approach to these fields, he stressed the importance of the individual and the need for empathy.

In the Rogerian approach to argumentation, your goal is to find ways to connect with your audience through empathy and common experiences rather than going on the attack or trying to persuade the other side that you are right and they are wrong. Your strategy is to validate your own point of view by making concessions to the other side, saying that you understand and respect the opinion of the opposition.

The classical approach to argument was laid out by the Greek philosopher, Aristotle, who said that one should appeal to an audience on the three basic levels: reason or logic (*logos*); emotions (*pathos*); and ethical and moral sense (*ethos*). What distinguishes the Rogerian argument from the classical is the stronger emphasis on the emotional and ethical appeals rather than strictly logical ones. In other words, the Rogerian approach—to unfriendly audiences in particular—is to build an emotional or psychological bridge, a common ground through empathy. While the Rogerian approach doesn't actually concede to the opposition or even agree with them, it does cite some of the opposition points as valid. In other words, the Rogerian argument shows respect for contrary views, even recognizing the logic of their argument. At the same time, the arguer states his or her own stance on the issue, thus preventing unnecessary conflict and a deadlock. And, if handled properly, instead of an "I win/you lose" outcome, both sides emerge as winners in the end.

For example, let's say that you are trying to persuade a group of senior citizens in your community to support a tax increase to fund local schools. After analyzing your audience, you conclude that many seniors are living on limited incomes and are more concerned about the financial burden of additional taxes than the school system—something that is no longer a priority in their lives. This factor alone might make them an unfriendly audience, one not easily receptive to your position. Thus a good strategy to begin your argument might be to let them know that you are well acquainted with the difficulties of living on limited means. You might even refer to relatives or friends who are in a similarly difficult financial position. By letting the members of your audience know that you empathize with and understand their hardships, they will be more willing to listen to you. And in this way you have established an emotional and psychological bond.

Next, you could remind your audience of the beliefs and values you have in common. While it is unlikely that senior citizens still have children attending school, they nonetheless may value education and understand its importance. You let them know that you share this value, one that underlies your support for additional public school funding. This, then, is your common ground. And your thesis is that a tax increase would ensure that today's kids receive same quality of education that existed when the seniors themselves had young children. A tax increase today might benefit their grandchildren.

In so recognizing the concerns of your readers as legitimate and worthy of attention, you demonstrate that you are aware of and respect their views. But this means learning what their concerns are. In our example, it would be wise first to read up on specific reasons why seniors would choose not to support a tax increase for public school programs. Perhaps there's an imbalance in how the tax revenues would be applied. Perhaps some senior programs need to be funded also. Perhaps the proposed tax hike is too high. By doing some research and addressing those concerns, you will make your audience aware that you understand its opposition. In the end, this may make your readers more receptive to your argument.

In summary, the Rogerian argument begins by establishing a common ground with an audience—beliefs, opinions, and common values. Showing respect, the writer demonstrates a good understanding of the audience's views. Then in the core of the argument, the writer objectively states his or her own position. Without sounding dismissive or superior, the writer explains how his or her position is valid while explaining how that differs form the audience's stand. Finally, the writer states the thesis, making some concessions while inviting the audience to give a little also. In the end, the author demonstrates how adopting his or her perspective to some degree benefits both sides.

Convey a Positive Attitude

Whether or not they know it, an unfriendly audience will benefit from seeing the issue from another side. In a Rogerian approach, try to view yourself as someone shedding a different light on the problem. View the opposition as people who are potentially interested in learning something new. Without being defensive, arrogant, or apologetic, make your claim, enumerate your reasons, and lay out the evidence for your readers to evaluate on their own. Regard them as intelligent people capable of drawing their own conclusions. You may not win converts, but you might at least lead some to recognize the merits of your opinions. You might even convince a few people to reconsider their views.

Review: Addressing Audiences

A Neutral Audience
■ Fill in the background
■ Present a balanced picture
■ Personalize the issues
■ Show respect for your readers

A Friendly Audience
■ Avoid appealing to prejudices
■ Offer new information about the issue

An Unfriendly Audience
■ Seek common ground
■ Show empathy
■ Convey a positive attitude
■ Remember the Golden Rule

To Improve Your Credibility with Your Audience, Avoid These Fallacies

Ad hominem argument	Leveling a personal attack against an opponent. A reliance on ad hominem arguments undercuts your credibility and may make you appear mean-spirited and desperate. Focus instead on the substance of an opponent's claim.
Ad misericordiam argument	Attempting to exploit the audience's emotions rather than appealing to logic and reason. Avoid using arguments that rely only on wrenching the reader's heart strings rather than logic and real evidence.
Ad populum argument	Appealing to the audience's presumed prejudices rather than proven facts. Even if you know the prejudices of your audience, such an appeal at best only persuades those already convinced. Rely on the force of logic and supporting evidence rather than bias and stereotyping.
Stacking the deck	Presenting only evidence that supports your points and withholding contrary evidence. Instead, acknowledge that conflicting evidence exists and respond to it.
False dilemma	Presenting an issue as an either-or choice and ignoring the possibility of a middle ground. Treat your audience as intelligent equals who are aware that at least several thoughtful alternatives are likely to exist.

Remember the Golden Rule

Even though they may not agree with you, treat the opposition with respect. Look upon them as reasonable people who just happen to disagree with you. Demonstrate your understanding of their side of the issue. Show that you have made the effort to research the opposition. Give credit where credit is due. If some of their counterpoints make sense, say so. In short, treat those from the other side and their views as you would want to be treated. You may just win a few converts.

SAMPLE ARGUMENTS FOR ANALYSIS

How a writer appeals to his or her audience can have a positive or a negative effect on the way the writer's message is received. The following three articles—two by professionals and one by a student—are all concerned with the deleterious effects of cigarette smoking. Each writer is concerned with the efficacy and/or legitimacy of various regulations on smoking and the resulting treatment of smokers. Under its powers to regulate tobacco, the Food and Drug Administration in 2009 banned candy and fruit-flavored cigarettes, but not mentholated cigarettes. In "Let's Ban All Flavors of Cigarettes," Derrick Z. Jackson questions why menthol, which makes up 30 percent of the $87 billion U.S. cigarette market, was not included in the ban. The next piece, "The Bogus 'Science' of Secondhand Smoke," attacks claims by anti-smoking lobbies that even the smallest quantities of secondhand smoke can set the cancer process in motion. No apologist for the smoking industry, scientist Gio Batta Gori challenges the so-called scientific evidence used to support this claim. And our student piece by Denise Cavallaro questions the decision-making apparatus of her relatives and contemporaries who smoke despite statistics and numbers that show what a deadly decision they are making. For the first essay, by Derrick Z. Jackson, we have used annotations to illustrate some of the strategies he uses to appeal to his audience and the assumptions he makes about them. As a class exercise, read each of these essays and then consider the following questions:

1. Locate the claim or thesis statement and summarize the main ideas in each essay.
2. What kind of audience is each writer addressing? neutral? friendly? hostile? What evidence can you find to support this?
3. Which writers attempt to present a balanced picture to the audience? Provide examples.
4. Do the writers convey a positive attitude toward the audience? Do any of the writers antagonize the audience? How is this done?
5. Have these writers committed any of the logical fallacies we've discussed? Where do these errors occur, and how would you correct them?
6. How well does each writer establish common ground with the audience?
7. What is the purpose of each essay? How effectively does each writer accomplish this purpose?

Let's Ban All Flavors of Cigarettes

Derrick Jackson

Derrick Z. Jackson is a journalist and regular columnist and associate editor for the *Boston Globe*. A graduate of the University of Wisconsin-Milwaukee and post-graduate journalism fellow at Harvard University, he is the recipient of various honorary degrees. He also teaches journalism courses at Simmons College in Boston. This article appeared in his column on September 30, 2009.

Let's Ban All Flavors of Cigarettes

1   It was a good first step by the Food and Drug Administration to ban candy- and fruit-flavored cigarettes this month under its new powers to regulate tobacco. The next and much bigger step is ending Menthol Madness.

2   As cancer-stick observers know, Big Tobacco really did not mind closing the candy store on cigarettes flavored like Hershey's or Life Savers. They were not even one percent of the market. Menthol is by far the most prominent cigarette flavoring of all. But it was exempted from an immediate ban in the smoking-prevention act signed by President Obama in June.

*charged language
Assumes reader
appreciates allusion
to Big Brother*

3   The reason is simple: Menthol cigarettes are nearly 30 percent of the $87 billion U.S. cigarette market. Menthol masks the harshness of smoking with its cooling effect and minty taste. The tobacco lobby and political allies bemoaned the impact of a menthol ban on jobs and government coffers. In 2007, tobacco sales generated $26 billion in state and federal tax revenues.

4   When Obama signed the prevention act, he proclaimed that the tobacco industry's "millions upon millions in lobbying and advertising" on its "lies" to deny the deadly effects of smoking have "finally failed."

*Assumes reader
shares cynicism
about tobacco
industry's motives
Though liberal
author? not
afraid to
criticize Obama
Assumes
politically savvy
reader*

5   That is a lie as long as the menthol exemption exists. The exemption means that government coffers remain more important than the coffins for the annual 443,000 lives lost to tobacco. The concern over tax revenues still overrides the $193 billion in annual health-related economic costs from smoking—a figure provided by the Centers for Disease Control.

6   The FDA can still ban menthol. Public health-minded politicians negotiated an explicit provision in the prevention act that commits the FDA to study menthol within one year. Any serious study should clearly result in a ban.

*Assumes reader
is comfortable
with medical
journals and
medical data*

7   Medical journal studies over the last four years have found that smokers of menthol cigarettes are significantly more likely to have difficulty quitting smoking and that tobacco

companies have deliberately manipulated menthol levels (as they did with nicotine) to lure younger smokers with "milder" taste. While menthol cigarettes are nearly 30 percent of the overall U.S. market, 44 percent of smokers ages 12 to 17 reported smoking menthol brands.

8   The menthol exemption also leaves dangling in political midair explosive charges of racism. Menthol cigarettes are vastly disproportionately popular among African-Americans, with 80 percent of black smokers preferring menthol. According to the government, 30 percent of all cancer deaths are tied to cigarette smoking and African-Americans are 21 percent more likely to have lung cancer than white Americans. Smoking is tied to heart disease and strokes, and African-American men are twice as likely as white men to have strokes.

uses facts and reason not emotion

9   This was enough for seven former US health secretaries to protest the exemption. One of them, Joseph Califano, told the *New York Times* that the exemption was "clearly putting black children in the back of the bus." This week, the American Legacy Foundation, established in the tobacco settlement with the states, urged the FDA to ban menthol along with the other flavors. "Literally many hundreds of tobacco industry documents conclusively establish that the tobacco industry has for decades systematically developed and marketed menthol products," the foundation said, " . . . to lure youth and younger tobacco users by masking the harsh flavor."

Assumes literate reader who recognizes these references

10   But with at least a year to go before possible banning, Big Tobacco is systematically hooking as many new smokers as possible. Martin Orlowsky, the CEO of Lorillard, which makes the top-selling menthol Newport, said this month, "We will continue to leverage the very strong brand equity position Newport has, particularly in key markets where the opportunity—that is, menthol opportunity—is greatest."

strong language

sketches opposition plans

11   As to where those "key markets" are, Reynolds American CEO Susan Ivey said in 2006, "If you look at the demographics of menthol, it is very urban. It has always had a strong African-American component. It's always had actually a strong Caucasian component. What has changed a lot in the last five years is a lot of additional Hispanic in that demographic. . . . we would see that menthol would have additional opportunity."

12   The FDA cannot close that window of opportunity too soon.

strong call to action

The Bogus 'Science' of Secondhand Smoke
Gio Batta Gori

Gio Batta Gori, an epidemiologist and toxicologist, is a spokesman and consultant for the tobacco industry. He is a former deputy director of the National Cancer Institute's Division of Cancer Cause and Prevention and the recipient of the U.S. Public Health Service Superior Service Award in 1976 for his efforts to define less hazardous cigarettes. This article appeared on washingtonpost.com, January 30, 2007.

1 Smoking cigarettes is a clear health risk, as most everyone knows. But lately, people have begun to worry about the health risks of secondhand smoke. Some policymakers and activists are even claiming that the government should crack down on secondhand smoke exposure, given what "the science" indicates about such exposure.

2 Last July, introducing his office's latest report on secondhand smoke, then-U.S. Surgeon General Richard Carmona asserted that "there is no risk-free level of secondhand smoke exposure," that "breathing secondhand smoke for even a short time can damage cells and set the cancer process in motion," and that children exposed to secondhand smoke will "eventually . . . develop cardiovascular disease and cancers over time."

3 Such claims are certainly alarming. But do the studies Carmona references support his claims, and are their findings as sound as he suggests?

4 Lung cancer and cardiovascular diseases develop at advancing ages. Estimating the risk of those diseases posed by secondhand smoke requires knowing the sum of momentary secondhand smoke doses that nonsmokers have internalized over their lifetimes. Such lifetime summations of instant doses are obviously impossible, because concentrations of secondhand smoke in the air, individual rates of inhalation, and metabolic transformations vary from moment to moment, year after year, location to location.

5 In an effort to circumvent this capital obstacle, all secondhand smoke studies have estimated risk using a misleading marker of "lifetime exposure." Yet, instant exposures also vary uncontrollably over time, so lifetime summations of exposure could not be, and were not, measured.

6 Typically, the studies asked 60–70 year-old self-declared nonsmokers to recall how many cigarettes, cigars, or pipes might have been smoked in their presence during their lifetimes, how thick the smoke might have been in the rooms, whether the windows were open, and similar vagaries. Obtained mostly during brief phone interviews, answers were then recorded as precise measures of lifetime individual exposures.

7 In reality, it is impossible to summarize accurately from momentary and vague recalls, and with an absurd expectation of precision, the total exposure to secondhand smoke over more than a half-century of a person's lifetime. No measure of cumulative lifetime secondhand smoke exposure was ever possible, so the epidemiologic studies estimated risk based not only on an improper marker of exposure, but also on exposure data that are illusory.

8   Adding confusion, people with lung cancer or cardiovascular disease are prone to amplify their recall of secondhand smoke exposure. Others will fib about being non-smokers and will contaminate the results. More than two dozen causes of lung cancer are reported in the professional literature, and over 200 for cardiovascular diseases; their likely intrusions have never been credibly measured and controlled in second-hand smoke studies. Thus, the claimed risks are doubly deceptive because of interfer-ences that could not be calculated and corrected.

9   In addition, results are not consistently reproducible. The majority of studies do not report a statistically significant change in risk from secondhand smoke exposure, some studies show an increase in risk, and, astoundingly, some show a reduction of risk.

10   Some prominent anti-smokers have been quietly forthcoming on what "the sci-ence" does and does not show. Asked to quantify secondhand smoke risks at a 2006 hearing at the UK House of Lords, Oxford epidemiologist Sir Richard Peto, a leader of the secondhand smoke crusade, replied, "I am sorry not to be more helpful; you want numbers and I could give you numbers . . . , but what does one make of them? . . . These hazards cannot be directly measured."

11   It has been fashionable to ignore the weakness of "the science" on secondhand smoke, perhaps in the belief that claiming "the science is settled" will lead to policies and public attitudes that will reduce the prevalence of smoking. But such a Faustian bargain is an ominous precedent in public health and political ethics. Consider how minimally such policies as smoking bans in bars and restaurants really reduce the prevalence of smoking, and yet how odious and socially unfair such prohibitions are.

12   By any sensible account, the anachronism of tobacco use should eventually van-ish in an advancing civilization. Why must we promote this process under the tyranny of deception?

13   Presumably, we are grown-up people, with a civilized sense of fair play, and ded-icated to disciplined and rational discourse. We are fortunate enough to live in a free country that is respectful of individual choices and rights, including the right to honest public policies. Still, while much is voiced about the merits of forceful advocacy, not enough is said about the fundamental requisite of advancing public health with sus-tainable evidence, rather than by dangerous, wanton conjectures.

14   A frank discussion is needed to restore straight thinking in the legitimate uses of "the science" of epidemiology—uses that go well beyond secondhand smoke issues. Today, health rights command high priority on many agendas, as they should. It is not admissible to presume that people expect those rights to be served less than truthfully.

Smoking: Offended by the Numbers
Danise Cavallaro

> Danise Cavallaro is a former English major, and it's clear from her word choice, tone, and the slant she takes that she is addressing her peers. As she mentions in her essay, many college students smoke, even if only at parties. In this essay, updated for this edition of *Argument as Dialogue: A Concise Guide*, Cavallaro wonders why anyone would ever want to smoke at all.

Cavallaro 1

Danise Cavallaro
Professor Mitrani
English 102
13 October 2009

Smoking: Offended by the Numbers

I majored in English because I hate mathematics and numbers. I hate these numbers too, but at least they are non-mathematically interesting: 11; 445; 1,200; 50,000.

- Eleven is the number of chemical compounds found in cigarettes that have been proven to cause cancer.
- Four hundred forty-five is the number of people per day who are diagnosed with smoking-related lung cancer.
- One thousand two hundred is the number of people who die every day from tobacco.
- Fifty thousand is the number of people who die every year from secondhand smoke-related diseases ("Facts").

I thought that I would defy the rules of journalism and write out those numbers in longhand because they seem awfully small on the page when I looked at them numerically. I thought if they looked bigger on the page, they might hold a little more meaning. They're even larger when they're not written in longhand. Yankee Stadium, filled, holds just over 52,000 people. That's roughly all the people who die from secondhand smoke per year, plus about five-and-a-half days' worth of the daily death toll from firsthand smoke. That's not even counting the nearly 5 million people worldwide who die each year from a smoking-related disease—which would be 96 sold-out Yankee Stadiums. Now go back to thinking about just one Yankee Stadium. If you were at a baseball game, who would you be there with? Your parents or your family? Your boyfriend or girlfriend, your best friends, your roommate from college? Don't forget about yourself. Now imagine each of them hooked up on an oxygen tank, struggling to do something as simple as breathe, unable to pull enough air into their lungs to cheer a run or a tag-out at home. They're living, still very much medically alive, but think of their quality of life: struggling to breathe, severely limited activity, and feigned happiness at most things.

In my now 28 years of being alive, I have never once felt the urge to light a cigarette. However, I have a lot of friends and family who have. I'm still struggling to understand what makes cigarettes appealing. Kissing my ex fresh after he squashed his cigarette underneath his heel tasted similar to what I'd

Cavallaro 2

imagine licking an ashtray would be like. My best friend lives in Manhattan, complains to no end about how expensive things are, but has no problem forking over $9-$11 for a pack of cigarettes. Her parents give her a hard time about it every time she's home; and she usually retorts with, "At least my cigarettes are safer than the unfiltered ones you rolled in the Army!" This argument in no way rationalizes her decisions, which contribute to raising the risks of her contracting lung cancer and emphysema. My uncle watched my grandfather slowly lose a two-year battle with lung cancer caused by working with asbestos and smoking unfiltered cigarettes for more than 40 years, but he would take smoke breaks while visiting him in the hospital. He still smokes today. It makes me sick.

4   With all this firsthand knowledge, such as the statistics I cited above, along with the deluge of widely available facts and help (Are we not living in the Information Age?) and as smart as these select people are, how could anyone not be motivated to quit by the numbers alone? The anti-smoking ad campaigns are not strong enough (though the chemical additives put into tobacco are very powerful), and, for whatever silly economic reason, cigarettes are marketed as cool. People still buy them even though they're a waste of money, and smoke them even though they carry a high mortality rate, all in the name of being able to exercise their rights as autonomous Americans.

5   I wonder if smokers still think in that hard-headed "never going to happen to me" American way when they're gasping for breath as they walk up the stairs. It's no secret that nicotine is an extremely addictive drug, and one of the hardest to give up. As with many things, if quitting were easy more people would do it. Mount Everest would be as popular as Disneyland if it were merely a hill.

6   To help lower those numbers in America, I propose a national anti-smoking campaign similar to "Scared Straight," a program for would-be juvenile offenders that worked well by showing exactly what the troubled youths would become if they kept to the path they were on. The popular anti-tobacco website, "thetruth.com," famous for its silently-shocking TV commercials depicting nonviolent boycotts of tobacco companies, is a good start. Certainly, more can be done. It starts with the youth of today.

7   Bring in a cancer-ravaged lung to a high school health class. Consider the postmortem donation as a gift to science—the science of staying alive. Black and white X-rays of lungs filled with shadowy malignant growths don't shock and revolt nearly as much as once-live flesh does, or ever will. While nicotine-yellowed teeth are becoming increasingly easier to whiten with

do-it-yourself kits, it's impossible to peek at the inside of your own lungs to see the damage that's been done. Please plaster huge pictures of cancer- or emphysema-ravaged lungs across billboards along I-95. The media must realize that not being politically correct and therefore not afraid to shock or offend, may actually save lives. Grossing out the populace could be a highly effective tool—statistics and numbers printed on paper hardly look menacing, but disintegrating lung tissue is guaranteed to shock.

8   Within the past few years, the media have broadcast more edgy anti-smoking campaigns. Television commercials depict people regrettably living with tobacco-related tracheotomies, amputations, and late-stage cancers. The folks they show are openly remorseful, are suffering and are acutely aware of the chosen circumstances that brought them to their current situation. Unfortunately, the commercials show victims who are middle-aged or older. Nine in ten tobacco users start before they reach their 18th birthday, so this portrayed demographic may not resonate with youth (kidshealth.org).

9   One of the many problems with adolescent smoking is that the more deadly side effects are not felt until many years after high school, when smoking is less of a faux-cool habit and more of a way of life. Asthma, while not to be scoffed at, is a condition that is treatable and seldom lethal. Lung cancer, the most common cause of cancer death among men and women, is not optimistically treatable and is highly lethal. However, lung cancer is also the most preventable. Therefore, I propose banning the depiction of smoking in movies and television geared towards young adults. Adolescents, an extremely malleable age group, are obviously influenced by the media and seek to imitate the clothing, hairstyles, music, and lifestyles portrayed by the media. Remove the idea that smoking is an acceptable way of life, and it will reduce the numbers of people for whom smoking will become a way of life. America needs to be more honest with this easily influenced age group.

10   I also propose making cigarettes more expensive, as teenagers are famous for being broke. The harder it is for youth (or anyone) to afford this deadly habit, the less likely that it could actually become a habit. Given that the current recession has caused a lot of Americans to rethink their necessities, perhaps a $12 or $15 pack of cigarettes would help adjust priorities.

11   The problem with all this is, again, the numbers. America was founded on tobacco fields, funded by the trade of dried tobacco leaf between England and the Native Americans. Even a giant cornerstone of our economy

Cavallaro 4

rests on cigarettes. The biggest tobacco companies in the world have branched out and now own major corporations that supply nearly everything consumable. In his book *Ashes to Ashes: America's Hundred-Year Cigarette War, the Public Health and the Unabashed Triumph of Philip Morris*, Richard Kluger details how Philip Morris not only dominated the cigarette industry but has managed through its acquisitions of other companies—from beer to frozen vegetables—in the 1980s to insulate itself from an attack on its tobacco engine. To take down Philip Morris would be to upset an economic juggernaut to which many other companies on the NASDAQ are inexorably linked. It would be catastrophic to this country's economy. The "economic downturn" beginning in 2008 was hailed as the closest this country has been to a full-out Depression since the 1930s, and removing just Philip Morris from our economy would no doubt send America to shambles. Let's look at another huge facet of our economy—health care. Wouldn't it be nice to save over $150 billion each year in health care costs directly attributable to smoking? What could be done with all those newfound numbers?

12   It may be quite impossible to financially overturn the tobacco companies while it appears that addicted individuals might keep their cigarette plants a-humming forever. For example, my aforementioned best friend has a pack-per-week habit, which increases during midterms, finals, and immediately following bad dates. One pack of cigarettes a week, at $10 a pack, amounts to $520 per year. That's a lot of money for a law school student with no job—most of a month's rent, half a year's worth of cell phone bills, and a lot of delicious dinners at a good restaurant. I know many people who smoke a pack a day, which amounts to over $3,000 a year, even if they buy cheaper brands. The numbers add up, and it can be a hard choice where to apply your numbers.

13   Be selfish, America. Keep your numbers to yourself.

Cavallaro 5

Works Cited

"Facts." American Legacy Foundation, 2009. Web. 22 Oct. 2009.

Izenberg, Neil, MD. "Smoking Stinks!" *Kindshealth.org*. N.d. Web. 1 Oct. 2009.

Kluger, Richard. *Ashes to Ashes: America's Hundred-Year Cigarette War, the Public Health and the Unabashed Triumph of Philip Morris*. New York: Knopf, 1996. Print.

Choosing Your Words

Whether addressing friends, foes, or the undecided, you must take care that your readers fully understand your case. In part, this is accomplished by choosing your words carefully and by accurately defining any technical, unfamiliar, foreign, or abstract terms. Here are a few specific tips to follow to inform your readers without turning them off.

Distinguishing Denotation and Connotation

Many words, even the most common, carry special suggestions or associations, **connotations,** that differ from the precise dictionary definitions, **denotations.** For example, if you looked up the word *house* in the dictionary, one of the synonyms you'd find is *shelter.* Yet if you told people you live in a shelter, they would think that you live in a facility for the homeless or some kind of animal sanctuary. That is because *shelter* implies a covering or structure that protects those within from the elements or from danger. In other words, the term is not neutral, as is the word *house.* Likewise, dictionary synonyms for *horse* include *steed* and *nag,* but the former implies an elegant and high-spirited riding animal, while the latter suggests one that is old and worn out.

The denotations of words may be the same, but their connotations will almost always differ. And the reason is that dictionary denotations are essentially neutral and emotion-free, while connotations are most often associated with attitudes or charged feelings that can influence readers' responses. Therefore, it is important to be aware of the shades of differences when choosing your words. Consider the different meanings the connotations of the bracketed choices lend these statements:

> By the time I got home I was _____ [sleepy, exhausted, weary, beat, dead].

> My boyfriend drives around in a red _____ [car, vehicle, buggy, clunker, jalopy].

> I could hear him _____ [shout, yell, bellow, scream, shriek].

Connotations can also be personal and, thus, powerful tools for shaping readers' responses to what you say. Consider the word *pig.* The dictionary definition, or denotation, would read something like this: "A domestic farm animal with a long, broad snout and a thick, fat body covered with coarse bristles." However, the connotation of *pig* is far more provocative, for it suggests someone who looks or acts like a pig; someone who is greedy or filthy; someone who is sexually immoral. (Most dictionaries list the connotations of words, although some connotations might only be found in a dictionary of slang—e.g., *The New Dictionary of American Slang,* edited by Robert L. Chapman, or *Slang!* by Paul Dickson.)

There is nothing wrong with using a word because of its connotations, but you must be aware that connotations will have an emotional impact on readers. You don't want to say something unplanned. You don't want to offend readers by using words loaded with unintentional associations. For instance, you wouldn't suggest to advertisers that they "should be more creative when hawking their products" unless you intended to insult them. Although the term *hawking* refers to selling, it is unflattering and misleading because it connotes somebody moving up and down the streets peddling goods by shouting. Linguistically, the word comes from the same root as the word *huckster,* which refers to an aggressive merchant known for haggling and questionable practices.

Connotatively loaded language can be used to create favorable as well as unfavorable reactions. If you are arguing against the use of animals in medical research, you will get a stronger response if you decry the sacrifice of "puppies and kittens" rather than the cooler, scientific, and less charged "laboratory animals."

You can understand why politicians, newspaper columnists, and anyone advocating a cause use connotative language. The loaded word is like a bullet for a writer making a strong argument. Consider the connotative impact of the italicized terms in the following excerpts taken from essays in this text:

> "When you agreed to buy the drink and the muffin you did not take into account the plastic-cup *shakedown.* (Michael Lewis, "The Case Against Tipping, page 19)

> The *menthol exemption* also leaves dangling in political *midair explosive charges* of racism. (Derrick Jackson, "Let's Ban All Flavors of Cigarettes," page 93)

> "The English language has been *hacked and torn apart* in the effort to promote equality, but the result is a disconnection from reality." (Shannon O'Neill, "Literature Hacked and Torn Apart: Censorship in Public Schools," page 279)

Each of the italicized words was selected not for its denotations but its negative connotations. In the first example, Michael Lewis could have simply said "take into account the plastic cup" or said "take into account the plastic tipping cup." Instead he added the word "shakedown" which implies a criminal act of intimidation or extortion on the part of the coffee establishment. Similarly, Derrick Jackson suggests that claims against "menthol exemption" may be "midair explosive charges" of racial discrimination, evoking powerful images of bombs (a punning use of "charges") going off in protest against the government's allowing the cigarettes industry to continue marketing potentially deadly menthol products to African-Americans.

Being Specific

To help readers better understand your argument, you need to use words that are precise enough to convey your exact meaning. If you simply say, "The weather last weekend was *terrible,*" your readers are left to come up with their own interpretations of what the weather was like. Was it hot and muggy? cold and rainy? overcast and very windy? some of each? Chances are your readers won't come up with the same weather conditions you had in mind. However, if you said, "Last weekend it rained day and night and never got above 40 degrees," readers will have a more precise idea of the weekend's weather. And you will have accomplished your purpose of saying just what you meant.

The terms *general* and *specific* are opposites just as *abstract* and *concrete* are opposites. General words do not name individual things but classes or groups of things: animals, trees, women. Specific words refer to individuals in a group: your pet canary, the oak tree outside your bedroom window, the point guard. Of course, general and specific are themselves relative terms. Depending on the context or your frame of reference, a word that is specific in one context may be general in another. For instance, there is no need to warn a vegetarian that a restaurant serves veal Oscar and beef Wellington when simply *meat* will do. In other words, there are degrees of specificity appropriate to the situation. The following list illustrates just such a sliding scale, moving downward from the more general to the more specific.

General	animal	person	book	clothing	food	machine
↓	feline	female	novel	footwear	seafood	vehicle
	cat	singer	American	shoes	fish	fighter jet
Specific	Daisy,	Mary	*The Great*	her Nikes	tuna	F-17
	my pet	J.Blige	*Gatsby*			

General words are useful in ordinary conversation when the people you're addressing understand your meaning and usually don't ask for clarification. The same is true in writing when you are addressing an audience familiar with your subject. In such instances, you can get away with occasional broad statements. For example, if you are running for class president, your campaign speeches would not require a great number of specifics as much as general statements of promise and principles:

> If elected, I intend to do what I can to ensure a comfortable classroom environment for each student at this college.

But when your audience is unfamiliar with your subject or when the context requires concrete details, generalities and abstract terms fall flat, leaving people wondering just exactly what you are trying to communicate. Let's say, for instance, you write a note to your dean explaining why you'd like to change the room where your English class meets. You wouldn't get very far on this appeal:

> Room 107 Richards is too small and uncomfortable for our class.

However, if you offer some specifics evoking a sense of the room's unpleasantness, you'd make a more persuasive case for changing the room:

> Room 107 Richards has 20 fixed seats for 27 students, leaving those who come in late to sit on windowsills or the floor. Worse still is the air quality. The radiators are fixed on high and the windows don't open. By the end of the hour, it must be 90 degrees in there, leaving everybody sweaty and wilted including Prof. Hazzard.

What distinguishes this paragraph is the use of concrete details: "20 fixed seats for 27 students"; latecomers forced to "sit on windowsills or on the floor"; radiators "fixed on high"; "the windows don't open"; "90 degrees"; and everybody was left "sweaty and wilted including Prof. Hazzard." But more than simply conjuring up a vivid impression of the room's shortcomings, these specifics add substance to your argument for a room change.

Concrete language is specific language—words that have definite meaning. Concrete language names persons, places, and things: *Barack Obama, Mary Shelley, New Zealand, Venice Boulevard, book, toothpaste*. Concrete terms conjure up vivid pictures in the minds of readers because they refer to particular things or qualities that can be perceived by the five senses—that is, they can be seen, smelled, tasted, felt, and heard. Abstract words, in contrast, refer to qualities that do not have a definitive concrete meaning. They denote intangible qualities that cannot be perceived directly by the senses but are inferred from the senses—*powerful, foolish, talented, responsible, worthy*. Abstract words also denote concepts and ideas—*patriotism, beauty, victory, sorrow*. Although abstract terms can be useful depending on the context, writing that relies heavily on abstractions will fail to communicate clear meaning. Notice in the pairs below how concrete and specific details convert vague statements into vivid ones:

Abstract	He was very nicely dressed.
Concrete	He wore a dark gray Armani suit, white pinstriped shirt, and red paisley tie.
Abstract	Jim felt uncomfortable at Jean's celebration party.
Concrete	Jim's envy of Jean's promotion made him feel guilty.
Abstract	That was an incredible accident.
Concrete	A trailer truck jackknifed in the fog, causing seven cars to plow into each other, killing two, injuring eight, and leaving debris for a quarter mile along Route 17.

Abstract language is also relative. It depends on circumstances and the experience of the person using them. A *cold* December morning to someone living in Florida might mean temperatures in the forties or fifties. To residents of North Dakota, *cold* would designate air at subzero temperatures. It all depends on one's point of view. A *fair trial* might mean one thing to the prosecutor of a case, yet something completely different to the defense attorney. Likewise, what might be *offensive* language to your grandmother would probably not faze an average college student.

When employing abstract language, you need to be aware that readers may not share your point of view. Consequently, you should be careful to clarify your terms or simply select concrete alternatives. Below is an excerpt from a student paper as it appeared in the first draft. As you can see, it is lacking in details and specifics and has a rather dull impact.

Vague: Last year my mother nearly died from medicine when she went to the hospital. The bad reaction sent her into a coma for weeks, requiring life-support systems around the clock. Thankfully, she came out of the coma and was released, but somebody should have at least asked what, if any, allergies she had.

Although the paragraph reads smoothly, it communicates very little of the dramatic crisis being described. Without specific details and concrete words, the reader misses both the trauma and the seriousness of the hospital staff's neglect, thus dulling the argument for stronger safeguards. What follows is the same paragraph revised with the intent of making it more concrete.

> **Revised:** Last year my mother nearly died from a codeine-based painkiller when she was rushed to the emergency room at Emerson Hospital. The severe allergic reaction sent her into a coma for six weeks, requiring daily blood transfusions, thrice weekly kidney dialysis, continuous intravenous medicines, a tracheotomy, and round-the-clock intensive care. Thankfully, she came out of the coma and was released, but the ER staff was negligent in not determining from her or her medical records that she was allergic to codeine.

Using Figurative Language

Words have their literal meaning, but they also can mean something beyond dictionary definitions, as we have seen. The sentence "Mrs. Jones is an angel" does not mean that Mrs. Jones is literally a supernatural winged creature, but a very kind and pleasant woman. What makes the literally impossible meaningful here is figurative language.

Figurative language (or a **figure of speech**) is comparative language. It is language that represents something in terms of something else—in figures, symbols, or likeness (Mrs. Jones and an angel). It functions to make the ordinary appear extraordinary and the unfamiliar appear familiar. It also adds richness and complexity to abstractions. Here, for instance, is a rather bland literal statement: "Yesterday it was 96 degrees and very humid." Here's that same sentence rendered in figurative language: "Yesterday the air was like warm glue." What this version does is equate yesterday's humid air to glue on a feature shared by each—stickiness. And the result is more interesting than the original statement.

The comparison of humid air to glue is linked by the words *like*. This example represents one of the most common figures of speech, the simile. Derived from the Latin *similis,* the term means similar. A simile makes an explicit comparison between dissimilar things (humid air and glue). It says that *A* is like *B* in one or more respects. The connectives used in similes are most often the words *like, as,* and *than:*

■ A school of minnows shot by me like pelting rain.
■ His arms are as big as hams.
■ They're meaner than junkyard dogs.

When the connectives *like, as,* or *than* are omitted, then we have another common figure of speech, the **metaphor.** The term is from the Greek *meta* (over) + *pherin* ("to carry or ferry") meaning to carry over meaning from one thing to another. Instead of saying that A is like B, a metaphor equates them—A *is* B. For example, Mrs. Jones and an angel are said to be one and the same, although we all know that literally the two are separate entities.

■ This calculus problem is a real pain in the neck.
■ The crime in this city is a cancer out of control.
■ The space shuttle was a flaming arrow in the sky.

Sometimes writers will carelessly combine metaphors that don't go with each other. Known as **mixed metaphors,** these often produce ludicrous results. For example:

■ The heat of his expression froze them in their tracks.
■ The experience left a bad taste in her eyes.
■ The arm of the law has two strikes against it.

When a metaphor has lost its figurative value, it is called a **dead metaphor**: the *mouth* of a river, the *eye* of a needle, the *face* of a clock. Originally these expressions functioned as figures of speech, but their usage has become so common in our language that many have become **clichés** ("golden opportunity," "dirt cheap," "a clinging vine"). More will be said about clichés below, but our best advice is to avoid them. Because they have lost their freshness, they're unimaginative and they dull your writing.

Another common figure of speech is **personification,** in which human or animal characteristics or qualities are attributed to inanimate things or ideas. We hear it all the time: Trees *bow* in the wind; fear *grips* the heart; high pressure areas *sit* on the northeast. Such language is effective in making abstract concepts concrete and vivid and possibly more interesting:

■ Graft and corruption walk hand in hand in this town.
■ The state's new tax law threatens to gobble up our savings.
■ Nature will give a sigh of relief the day they close down that factory.

As with other figures of speech, personification must be used appropriately and with restraint. If it's overdone, it ends up calling undue attention to itself while leaving readers baffled:

Drugs have slouched their way into our schoolyards and playgrounds, laughing up their sleeves at the law and whispering vicious lies to innocent children.

For the sake of sounding literary, drugs here are personified as pushers slouching, laughing, and whispering. But such an exaggeration runs the risk of being rejected by readers as pretentious. If this happens, the vital message may well be lost. One must also be careful not to take shortcuts. Like dead metaphors, many once-imaginative personifications have become clichés: "justice is blind," "virtue triumphed," "walking death." While such may be handy catch phrases, they are trite and would probably be dismissed by critical readers as lazy writing.

Another figure of speech worth mentioning is the **euphemism,** which is a polite way of saying something blunt or offensive. Instead of toilets, restaurants have *restrooms.* Instead of a salesperson, furniture stores send us *mattress technicians.* Instead of false teeth, people in advertising wear *dentures.* The problem with euphemisms is that they conceal the true meaning of something. The result can be a kind of double-talk—language inflated for the sake of deceiving the listener. Business and government are notorious for such practices. When workers are laid off, corporations talk about *restructuring* or *downsizing.* A few years ago, the federal government announced *a revenue enhancement* when it really meant that taxes were going up; likewise, the Environmental Protection Agency referred to acid rain as *poorly buffered precipitation*; and when the CIA ordered a *nondiscernible microbinoculator,* it got a poison dart. Not only are such concoctions pretentious, they are dishonest. Fancy-sounding language camouflages hard truths.

Fancy-sounding language also has no place in good writing. When euphemisms are overdone, the result is a lot of verbiage and little meaning. Consider the example below before the euphemisms and pretentious language are reduced:

> **Overdone:** In the event that gaming industry establishments be rendered legal, law enforcement official spokespersons have identified a potential crisis situation as the result of influence exerted by the regional career-offender cartel.

Readers may have to review this a few times before they understand what's being said. Even if they don't give up, a reader's job is not to rewrite your words. Writing with clarity and brevity shows respect for your audience. Here is the same paragraph with its pretentious wordiness and euphemisms edited down:

> **Revised:** Should casino gambling be legalized, police fear organized crime may take over.

Of course, not all euphemisms are double-talk concoctions. Some may be necessary to avoid sounding insensitive or causing pain. To show respect in a sympathy card to bereaved survivors, it might be more appropriate to use the expression *passed away* instead of the blunt *died*. Recently, terms such as *handicapped* or *cripple* have given way to less derogatory replacements such as *a person with disabilities*. Likewise, we hear *a person with AIDS* instead of *AIDS victim*, which reduces the person to a disease or a label.

As with metaphors and personification, some euphemisms have passed into the language and become artifacts, making their usage potentially stale. People over age sixty-five are no longer "old" or "elderly," they're *senior citizens;* slums are *substandard housing;* the poor are *socially disadvantaged*. Although such euphemisms grew out of noble intentions, they tend to abstract reality. A Jules Feiffer cartoon from a few years ago captured the problem well. It showed a man talking to himself:

> I used to think I was poor. Then they told me I wasn't poor, I was needy. They told me it was self-defeating to think of myself as needy, I was deprived. Then they told me underprivileged was overused. I was disadvantaged. I still don't have a dime. But I have a great vocabulary.

Although euphemisms were created to take the bite off reality, they can also take the bite out of your writing if not used appropriately. As Feiffer implies, sometimes it's better to say it like it is; depending on the context, "poor" simply might have more bite than some sanitized cliché. Similarly, some old people resent being called "seniors" not just because the term is an overused label, but because it abstracts the condition of old age. Our advice regarding euphemisms is to know when they are appropriate and to use them sparingly. Good writing simply means knowing when the right expression will get the response you want.

Avoiding Clichés

A cliché (or trite expression) is a phrase that is old and overused to the point of being unoriginal and stale. At one time, clichés were fresh and potent; overuse has left them flat. In speech, we may resort to clichés for quick meaning. However, clichés can dull your writing and make you seem lazy for choosing a phrase on tap rather than trying to think of more original and colorful wording. Consider these familiar examples:

apple of his eye
bigger than both of us
climbing the walls
dead as a doornail
head over heels
last but not least
mind over matter
ripe old age
short but sweet
white as a ghost

The problem with clichés is that they fail to communicate anything unique. To say you were "climbing the walls," for example, is an expression that could fit a wide variety of contradictory meanings. Out of context, it could mean that you were in a state of high anxiety, anger, frustration, excitement, fear, happiness, or unhappiness. Even in context, the expression is dull. Furthermore, because such clichés are ready made and instantly handy, they blot out the exact detail you intended to convey to your reader.

Clichés are the refuge of writers who don't make the effort to come up with fresh and original expressions. To avoid them, we recommend being alert for any phrases you have heard many times before and coming up with fresh substitutes. Consider the brief paragraph below, which is full of clichés marked in italics, and its revision:

Trite: *In this day and age*, a university ought to be concerned with ensuring that its women students take courses that will strengthen their understanding of their own past achievements and future *hopes and dreams*. At the same time, any school *worth its salt* should be *ready and able* to provide *hands-on experience*, activities, and courses that reflect a commitment to diversity and inclusiveness. Education must *seize the opportunity* of leading us *onward and upward* so that we don't slide back to the male-only curriculum emphasis of the *days of old*.

Revised: A university today ought to be concerned with ensuring that its women students take courses that will strengthen their understanding of their own past achievements and future possibilities. At the same time, any decent school should provide experience, activities, and courses that reflect a commitment to diversity and inclusiveness. Education must lead us forward so that we don't revert to the male-only curriculum emphasis of the past.

Defining Technical Terms

Special or technical vocabulary that is not clear from the context can function as an instant roadblock to freely flowing communication between you and your readers—sympathetic to your views or not. You cannot expect a novice in political science to know the meaning of *hegemony* or a nonmedical person to know exactly what you mean by *nephrological necrosis.* To avoid alienating nonexpert readers, you'll have to define such uncommon terms.

You can do so without being obtrusive or disrupting the flow of your writing with "time-outs" here and there to define terms. Notice how smoothly Arthur Allen ("Prayer in Prison: Religion as Rehabilitation," page 175) slips a definition of *recidivism* into the following passage:

> In fact, the phenomenon is known as recidivism—that is, a convict re-offends after having been released from confinement. (Arthur Allen, "Prayer in Prison: Religion as Rehabilitation")

Clarifying Familiar Terms

Even some familiar terms can lead to misunderstanding because they are used in so many different ways with so many different meanings: *liberal, Native American, lifestyle, decent, active.* It all depends on who is using the word. For instance, to an environmentalist the expression *big business* might connote profit-hungry and sinister industrial conglomerates that pollute the elements; to a conservative, however, the phrase might mean the commercial and industrial establishment that drives our economy. Likewise, a *liberal* does not mean the same thing to a Democrat as it does to a Republican. Even if you're writing for a sympathetic audience, be as precise as you can about familiar terms. Remember the advice of novelist George Eliot: "We have all got to remain calm, and call things by the same names other people call them by."

Stipulating Definitions

For a word that doesn't have a fixed or standard meaning, writers often offer a *stipulative* definition that explains what they mean by the term. For instance, *Merriam-Webster's Dictionary* offers two basic and broad definitions of "literature": (1) "writings having excellence of form or expression and expressing ideas of permanent or universal interest"; (2) "the body of written works produced in a particular language, country, or age." But in her essay, "Literature Hacked and Torn Apart: Censorship in Public Schools" (page 276), Shannon O'Neill offers this stipulative definition of literature, stressing the function of fiction: "Literature is created in context, reflecting the fears and prejudices of the time." By stressing this historical function of fiction, she allows herself a defense of Mark Twain's use of the now-offensive racist term, "nigger," as a reflection of "the dialect and prejudice of the book's (*Huckleberry Finn*) period." She goes on to say that although we consider the "'n' word brutal and insulting" today, "without it, the book would be less effective in helping us understand our sad history of racism and tolerance for slavery." Even worse, excising the offensive terms would be revising not just literature but American history.

Sometimes an author will offer stipulative definitions for terms that are rare or used for the first time. This is done to communicate a new concept. In his essay, "Why They Kill Their Newborns" (page 187). Steven Pinker introduces the term "neonaticide" which he immediately defines as mothers who "kill their newborns or let them die."

Sometimes authors will take common words and invent a new term that stipulates a hybrid definition. One such example is "fingerprints" in the essay, "The Great Global Warming Swindle" (page 168). Here atmospheric scientist S. Fred Singer argues that there is no evidence that global warming is the byproduct of human activity but part of a natural cycle of climate change that has been going on for millennia. He writes, "computer models cannot account for the observed cooling of much of the past century (1940–75), nor for the observed *patterns* of warming—what we call the 'fingerprints.'" He argues that while the "fingerprints" indicate that the Antarctic is cooling, computer models predict just the opposite—a warming trend.

Stipulating your terms is like making a contract with your reader: You set down in black and white the important terms and their limits. The result is that you eliminate any misunderstanding and reduce your own vulnerability. And that can make the difference between a weak and a potent argument.

Avoiding Overdefinition

Where do you stop explaining and begin assuming your reader knows what you mean? What terms are "technical" or "specialized" or "important" enough to warrant definition? You certainly don't want to define terms unnecessarily or to oversimplify. In so doing, you run the risk of dulling the thrust of your claims while insulting the intelligence of your readers. Just how to strike a balance is a matter of good judgment about the needs and capabilities of your audience.

A good rule of thumb is to assume that your readers are almost as knowledgeable as you. This way, you minimize the risk of patronizing them. Another rule of thumb is the synonym test. If you can think of a word or short phrase that is an exact synonym for some specialized or important term in your argument, you probably don't need to define it. However, if you need a long phrase or sentence to paraphrase the term, you may want to work in a definition; it could be needed. And don't introduce your definitions with clauses like "As I'm sure you know" or "You don't need to be told that. . . . " If the audience didn't need to know it, you wouldn't be telling them, and if they do know what the terms mean, you may insult their intelligence with such condescending introductions.

Using Sarcasm and Humor Sparingly

Although we caution you against using sarcasm or humor too often, there are times when they can be very effective techniques of persuasion. Writers will often bring out their barbs for the sake of drawing blood from the opposition and snickers from the sympathetic. But artful sarcasm must be done with care. Too strong, and you run the risk of trivializing the issue or alienating your audience with a bad joke. Too vague or esoteric, and nobody will catch the joke. It's probably safest to use these touches when you are writing for a sympathetic audience; they're most likely to appreciate your wit. There is no rule of thumb here. Like any writer, you'll have to decide when to use these techniques and how to work them in artfully.

Review: To Choose Your Words Carefully...
■ Consider both denotative and connotative meanings.
■ Be as specific and concrete as your context requires.
■ Use figurative language to add richness and complexity.
■ Check figurative language for precision and clarity.
■ Be alert for clichés and unnecessary euphemisms.
■ Define technical terms that are not clear from the context.
■ Define familiar terms and terms with multiple meanings.

EXERCISES

1. Let's say you were assigned to write a position paper defending the construction of a nuclear power plant in your state. What special appeals would you make were you to address your paper to the governor? to residents living next to the site where the proposed plant is to be built? to prospective construction workers and general contractors? to local environmentalists?

2. Choose one of the following claims, then list in sentence form three reasons supporting the argument. When you've finished, list in sentence form three reasons in opposition to the claim:
   a. Snowboarders are a menace to skiers.
   b. To save lives, a 55-mile-per-hour speed limit should be enforced nationwide.
   c. Condoms should be advertised on television.
   d. Students with drug convictions should be denied federally subsidized student aid.

3. Let's assume you have made up your mind on gun control. Write a brief letter to the editor of your local newspaper stating your views on the issue. In your letter, fairly and accurately represent arguments of the opposition while pointing out any logical weaknesses, flaws, impracticalities, and other problems you see. What different emphasis would your letter have were it to appear in a gun owner's newsletter? in a pro-gun control newsletter?

4. Write a letter to your parents explaining why you need an extra hundred dollars of spending money this month.

5. Each of the sentences below will take on a different meaning depending on the connotations of the words in brackets. Explain how each choice colors the writer's attitude and the reader's reaction to the statement.
   a. Sally's style of dress is really [weird, exotic, unusual].
   b. If a factory is [polluting, stinking up, fouling] the air over your house, you have a right to sue.

    c. Anyone who thinks that such words have no effect is [unaware, ignorant, unconscious] of political history.

    d. The anti-immigration passion being stirred up in this country has become [popular, trendy, common].

    e. It was clear from the way she [stomped, marched, stepped] out of the room how she felt about the decision.

6. Identify the figures of speech used in the following sentences from essays in this book. In each example, note the two things being compared and explain why you think the comparisons are appropriate or not:

    a. "But such a Faustian bargain is an ominous precedent in public health and political ethics." (Gio Batta Gori, "The Bogus 'Science' of Secondary Smoke")

    b. "Biographies have metamorphosed into demonographies whose authors don't just portray their subjects' warts and all, but set out to dig up as much dirt as possible, as if the story of a person's life is contained in the warts, only the warts, and nothing but the warts." (Deborah Tannen, "Taking a 'War of Words' Too Literally")

    c. "Many colleges and universities simply wink at the activities of the fraternities and claim no responsibility." (Henry Wechsler, "Binge Drinking Must Be Stopped")

    d. "And so in 1990 it was decided to put a tasteful and discreet cup on the counter. It's a way for our customers to say thanks to our partners." (Michael Lewis, "The Case Against Tipping")

    e. "Natural selection cannot push the buttons of behavior directly; it affects our behavior by endowing us with emotions that coax us toward adaptive choices." (Steven Pinker, "Why They Kill Their Newborns")

    f. "As cancer-stick observers know Big Tobacco did not mind closing the candy store on cigarettes flavored like Hershey's or Life Savers." (Derrick Jackson, "Ban All Flavors of Cigarettes")

    g. "If unchecked, we could find ourselves in a time when it's acceptable for books, like 'witches,' to be burned." (Shannon O'Neill, "Literature Hacked and Torn Apart: Censorship in Public Schools")

7. Rewrite the following paragraph to eliminate the clichés and trite expressions.

It is not that we don't care about what goes on up in space; it's that the vast majority of red-blooded Americans are hard put to see what these untold billions of dollars can do. While great strides have been made in space research, we ask ourselves: Is life any safer? Are material goods all the more abundant? Are we living to a ripe old age because of these vast expenditures? Beyond the shadow of a doubt, the answer is a resounding no. Those in Congress with a vested interest need to be brought back to reality, for the nation's pressing problems of crime, homelessness, and unemployment are right here on Mother Earth. Nothing is sacred including the budget for NASA, which should follow the footsteps of other programs and be slashed across the board. Yes, that will be a rude awakening to some who will have to bite the bullet, but there are just so many tax dollars to go around. And in the total scheme of things, wasting it on exploring the depths of outer space is not the way it should be.

Shaping Arguments: Thinking Like an Architect

Just as there is no best way to build a house, there is no best way to structure an argument. Some essays take an inductive approach. Such an essay begins with a specific circumstance and then presents reasons and evidence in support of or in opposition to that circumstance. Other essays adopt a deductive approach, which begin with an idea or philosophical principle, move to a specific circumstance, then conclude with why that circumstance is right and should be maintained, or wrong and should be changed. Some essays express their conclusions in the opening paragraphs. Others build up to them in the last paragraph. Still others make use of narrative in part or as a whole—that is, a story or series of episodes or anecdotes structured on a time line. The effect is to dramatize the criteria of the author's argument rather than to argue them explicitly from point to point. As an architect designing a blueprint will tell you, the structure of a building depends on the site, the construction crew, and the prospective owners. Arguments are the same. Depending on your topic, your goals, and your readers, you'll write very different kinds of arguments.

Although no two arguments look alike, every argument has three basic structural parts: a beginning, a middle, and an end. This isn't a simplistic definition. As in architecture, each part of a structure is there for a purpose; leave out one of the parts, and the whole collapses. So let's look at those parts and the jobs they do.

Components of an Argument

What follows is an organizational pattern for argument papers—a pattern to which, with some variations, most of the essays in this book conform. We offer it to help you plan your own argument papers. Although this model provides the structure, framework, and components of most arguments, it is not a formula written in stone. You should not feel bound to follow it every time you construct an argument. In fact, you might find it more effective to move blocks of writing around or to omit material. For instance, on issues unfamiliar to your readers, it might make sense to begin with background information so the context of your discussion will be understood. With familiar issues, it might be more persuasive to open with responses to opposing views. On especially controversial topics, you might wish to reserve your responses for the main body of the paper. Or, for dramatic effect, you might decide to save your responses until the very end, thereby emphasizing your consideration of other perspectives. As a writer, you're free to modify this model any way you like; or you may want to try different models in different drafts of your paper to see which arrangement works best in each case. As with building houses, your choices in building arguments are numerous.

The Beginning

The beginning of your argument accomplishes, in a small space, three important goals:

■ It introduces you, the writer. Here your audience meets you—senses your tone, your attitude toward your subject, and the general style of the piece.
■ It appeals to your readers' reason, emotions, and/or sense of ethics. This can be done in a simple value statement, an anecdote, or some high-impact statistics intended to raise your readers' interest and concern.
■ It identifies the topic and indicates your stand.

Depending on the issue and the audience, the beginning of an argument can be several paragraphs in length. In most arguments, the beginning will end with a clear statement of the claim you are making—your thesis.

Although "Once upon a time ..." is probably the most remembered introduction, it's not always the most effective; more ingenuity on your part is needed to "hook" your readers. For example, in *The Village Voice,* columnist Nat Hentoff began a column calling for eliminating duplication in the U.S. military by saying that he had telephoned the Pentagon press office for a comment on the subject. "Oh," said the officer with whom he spoke, "You want the *other* press office." As Hentoff remarked, he could have ended the column at that point; instead, he went on to develop his idea, confident that this introductory example would make his readers sympathetic to his point.

Composing good beginnings requires hard work. That's why many writers keep a journal in which they copy the strategies of writers they admire; that's how we happened to have a copy of Hentoff's introduction. As beginning arguers, you may want to develop your own repertoire of start-up strategies by copying strategies you admire into your own argument journal.

The Middle

The middle portion of your argument is where you do the argumentative work: presenting your information, responding to other views, making your case. If you think of it in terms of building construction, here's where you pour a foundation and lay the framework; put in all the walls, floors, and systems; and have the building inspector examine your work. There are a number of substages.

Provide Background Information

Before you can begin presenting your reasons, you want to be sure that your audience has the information necessary to understand the issue. Background information should answer any of the following questions depending on your topic:

■ How significant is the issue? How many people are affected by it? Who are the people most affected?
■ What facts, statistics, or information do your readers need to know to follow your reasons?

- What terminology or key words need to be defined so your readers will understand your meaning?
- What factors have caused the problem or situation to develop?
- What will be the consequences if the situation is not corrected?

If handled correctly, this part of your essay can be the most persuasive and convincing because it lets your readers know why you are concerned and the reasons behind that concern. Moreover, it gives your readers the opportunity to share your concern. For example, in "Let's Ban All Flavors of Cigarettes," Derrick Z. Jackson begins his essay with the claim that the Food and Drug Administration's recent ban of fruit-flavored cigarettes is a good but negligible start toward prevention compared to a ban that would include mentholated cigarettes. He wonders cynically if the government is more interested in state and federal tax revenue. His statistics are grimly persuasive: fruit-flavored cigarettes represent less than 1 percent of the market compared to menthol which makes up 30 percent of the $87 billion market, generating over $25 billion in tax revenue.

Respond to Other Points of View

As we discussed in Chapter 4, it is important to let your audience know that you have seriously deliberated other points of view before reaching your own position. By doing this, you appear informed and open-minded. In this part of your essay, you should briefly review a number of viewpoints that are different from your own. If you've engaged in debate and dialogue, as we suggested in Chapter 1, you should be aware of opposing views and common concerns. Now is your opportunity to identify them and respond. You might even acknowledge the sincerity of those holding contrary views and cite the merits of their positions. Such acknowledgments help establish your authority as a writer. They will also help you define your own position more specifically for your readers by contrasting it with others.

Present Reasons in Support of Your Claim

The reasons supporting your claim comprise the heart of your essay and, therefore, its largest portion. Here you explain those reasons and present supporting evidence—facts, statistics, data, testimony of authorities, examples—to convince your readers to agree with your position or take a particular course of action. Depending on the issue, this part of your essay usually takes several paragraphs, with each reason clearly delineated for your readers.

Anticipate Possible Objections to Your Reasons

Even with a friendly audience, readers will have questions and concerns about your reasons. If you ignore these objections and leave them unanswered, you will weaken the effectiveness of your argument. Therefore, it is always wise to anticipate possible objections so you can respond to them in a constructive fashion that will strengthen and clarify your ideas. The kind of objections you anticipate, of course, will depend on your familiarity with your audience—their interests, values, beliefs, experiences, and so on. If you have carefully analyzed your audience, as suggested in Chapter 4, you will be more aware of the objections likely to surface in response to your reasons.

Review: The Structure of an Argument

The Beginning ...
- ■ Introduces you as a writer
- ■ States the problem
- ■ Establishes your position and appeal
- ■ Presents your claim (thesis)

The Middle ...
- ■ Provides background information
- ■ Responds to other points of view
- ■ Presents arguments supporting the claim
- ■ Anticipates possible objections

The End ...
- ■ Summarizes your position and implications
- ■ Invites readers to share your conclusion and/or take action

Raising objections and responding to them will once again demonstrate your awareness of alternative viewpoints. It will also give you an opportunity to strengthen your reasons and increase your credibility.

The End

The end is usually a short paragraph or two in which you conclude your argument. Essentially, your ending summarizes your argument by reaffirming your stand on the issue. It might also make an appeal to your readers to take action. Some writers include an anecdote, a passionate summation, or even a quiet but resonant sentence. Lincoln's "Gettysburg Address," for example, ends with the quiet "government of the people, by the people, and for the people," which is one of the most memorable phrases in American political history. Looking over the essays in this book, you will find that no two end quite alike. As a writer, you have many choices; experimentation is usually the best way to decide what will work for you. Many writers copy effective conclusions into their journals so they can refresh their memories when writing their own arguments.

SAMPLE ARGUMENT FOR ANALYSIS

To illustrate this three-part argument structure, we have included two sample argument essays for you to read. The first is "Indian Bones" by Clara Spotted Elk, a consultant for Native American interests. Although it is quite brief, the essay, published in the *New York Times*, contains all the essential components of an argument essay. It is followed by an analysis of its key structural features.

Indian Bones
Clara Spotted Elk

1 Millions of American Indians lived in this country when Columbus first landed on our shores. After the western expansion, only about 250,000 Indians survived. What happened to the remains of those people who were decimated by the advance of the white man? Many are gathering dust in American museums.

2 In 1985, I and some Northern Cheyenne chiefs visited the attic of the Smithsonian's Natural History Museum in Washington to review the inventory of their Cheyenne collection. After a chance inquiry, a curator pulled out a drawer in one of the scores of cabinets that line the attic. There were the jumbled bones of an Indian. "A Kiowa," he said.

3 Subsequently, we found that 18,500 Indian remains—some consisting of a handful of bones, but mostly full skeletons—are unceremoniously stored in the Smithsonian's nooks and crannies. Other museums, individuals and federal agencies such as the National Park Service also collect the bones of Indian warriors, women, and children. Some are on display as roadside tourist attractions. It is estimated that another 600,000 Indian remains are secreted away in locations across the country.

4 The museum community and forensic scientists vigorously defend these grisly collections. With few exceptions, they refuse to return remains to the tribes that wish to rebury them, even when grave robbing has been documented. They want to maintain adequate numbers of "specimens" for analysis and say they are dedicated to "the permanent curation of Indian skeletal remains."

5 Indian people are tired of being "specimens." The Northern Cheyenne word for ourselves is "tsistsistas"—human beings. Like people the world over, one of our greatest responsibilities is the proper care of the dead.

6 We are outraged that our religious views are not accepted by the scientific community and that the graves of our ancestors are desecrated. Many tribes are willing to accommodate some degree of study for a limited period of time—provided that it would help Indian people or mankind in general. But how many "specimens" are needed? We will not accept grave robbing and the continued hoarding of our ancestors' remains.

7 Would this nefarious collecting be tolerated if it were discovered that it affected other ethnic groups? (Incidentally, the Smithsonian also collects skeletons of blacks.) What would happen if the Smithsonian had 18,500 Holocaust victims in the attic? There would be a tremendous outcry in this country. Why is there no outcry about the Indian collection?

8 Indians are not exotic creatures for study. We are human beings who practice living religions. Our religion should be placed not only on a par with science when it comes to determining the disposition of our ancestors but on a par with every other religion practiced in this country.

9 To that end, Sen. Daniel K. Inouye will soon reintroduce the "Bones Bill" to aid Indians in retrieving the remains of their ancestors from museums. As in the past, the

"Bones Bill" will most likely be staunchly resisted by the collectors of Indian skeletons—armed with slick lobbyists, lots of money and cloaked in the mystique of science.
10   Scientists have attempted to defuse this issue by characterizing their opponents as radical Indians, out of touch with the culture and with little appreciation of science. Armed only with a moral obligation to our ancestors, the Indians who support the bill have few resources and little money.
11   But, in my view, the issue should concern all Americans—for it raises very disturbing questions. American Indians want only to reclaim and rebury their dead. Is this too much to ask?

Analyzing the Structure

Now let's examine this essay according to the organizational features discussed so far.

The Beginning

Paragraph 1 clearly introduces the nature of the problem: The remains of the Indians "decimated by the advance of the white man" have wrongfully ended up "gathering dust in American museums." It isn't until paragraph 6 that Spotted Elk spells out her position: "We are outraged that our religious views are not accepted by the scientific community and that the graves of our ancestors are desecrated." (Because this essay was written for newspaper publication, the paragraphs are shorter than they might be in a formal essay; you may not want to delay your thesis until the sixth paragraph in a longer essay.) Notice, too, that in the introduction the author's persona begins to assert itself in the brief and pointed summation of the American Indians' fate. When Spotted Elk mentions the staggering decline in the population of her ancestors, we sense a note of controlled but righteous anger in her voice. Citation of the gruesome facts of history also appeals to the reader's ethical sense by prompting reflection on the Indians' demise.

The Middle

- **Background Information**   Paragraphs 2 and 3 establish the context of the author's complaint. Paragraph 2 is personal testimony to the problem—how she and other Native Americans viewed unceremonious "jumbled bones" in the museum drawer and were stunned by the representative insensitivity of their host curator, who treated the human remains as if they were fossils. Paragraph 3 projects the problem to progressively larger contexts and magnitudes—from the single Kiowa in a drawer to the 18,500 in the Smithsonian at large; from that institution's collection to the estimated 600,000 remains in other museums, federal agencies and institutions, and "roadside tourist attractions." The broader scope of the problem is underscored here.
- **Response to Other Points of View**   In paragraph 4, Spotted Elk tersely sums up the opposing position of the "museum community and forensic scientists": ". . . they refuse to return remains to the tribes." She also states their reasoning: "They want to maintain adequate numbers of 'specimens' for analysis and say they are dedicated to the 'permanent curation of Indian skeletal remains.'"

■ **Reasons in Support of the Claim**   Paragraphs 5 through 9 constitute the heart of Spotted Elk's argument. Here she most forcefully argues her objections and offers her reasons with supporting details: Indians resent being treated as specimens and want to bury their dead as do other religious people (paragraphs 5 and 6). She follows with a concession that many Indians would accommodate some degree of anthropological study for a period of time, but do not approve of the huge permanent collections that now fill museums.

In paragraph 7, the author continues to support her claim that American Indians have been discriminated against with regard to the disposition of ancestral remains. She writes that there would be a public outcry if the remains of other ethnic groups such as Holocaust victims were hoarded. Her proposal for change appears in paragraph 8: "Our religion should be placed not only on a par with science when it comes to determining the disposition of our ancestors but on a par with every other religion practiced in this country." This is the logical consequence of the problem she has addressed to this point. That proposal logically leads into paragraph 9, where she mentions efforts by Senator Daniel Inouye to see the "Bones Bill" passed into law. Throughout, Spotted Elk uses emotional words and phrases—*grisly, unceremoniously, slick lobbyists, cloaked in mystique*—to reinforce her points.

■ **Anticipation of Possible Objections**   In paragraph 10, the author addresses objections of the opposition, in this case those "[s]cientists [who] have attempted to defuse this issue by characterizing their opponents as radical Indians, out of touch with the culture and with little appreciation of science." She refutes all three charges (of being "radical," as well as out of touch with Indian culture and science) with the phrase "[a]rmed only with a moral obligation to our ancestors"—a phrase that reaffirms her strong connection with her culture. On the contrary, it is science that is out of touch with the "living religion" of Native Americans.

The End

The final paragraph brings closure to the argument. Briefly the author reaffirms her argument that Native Americans "want only to reclaim and rebury their dead." The question that makes up the final line of the essay is more than rhetorical, for it reminds us of the point introduced back in paragraph 5—that American Indians are no different than any other religious people with regard to the disposition of their ancestors. A powerful question brings the essay's conclusion into sharp focus.

As we stated in the beginning of this chapter, there is no best structure for an argument essay. As you develop your own essay, you may find it more effective to move certain structural features to locations that serve your purposes better. For instance, you may find that background information is more persuasive when you include it as support for a particular reason rather than provide it prior to your reasons. Possible objections might be raised along with each reason instead of saved for later. Ron Karpati's essay, "I Am the Enemy," provides a good example of a different approach to structuring an argument essay. Read the essay to see if you can pick out the structural elements he included and how he organized them. Following the essay, we've provided a brief analysis of its organization.

I Am the Enemy
Ron Karpati

> Ron Karpati, a pediatrician and medical researcher of childhood illnesses, defends
> the use of animals in medical research. This article first appeared in *Newsweek's*
> "My Turn" column.

1   I am the enemy! One of those vilified, inhumane physician-scientists involved in animal research. How strange, for I have never thought of myself as an evil person. I became a pediatrician because of my love for children and my desire to keep them healthy. During medical school and residency, however, I saw many children die of leukemia, prematurity and traumatic injury—circumstances against which medicine has made tremendous progress, but still has far to go. More important, I also saw children, alive and healthy, thanks to advances in medical science such as infant respirators, potent antibiotics, new surgical techniques and the entire field of organ transplantation. My desire to tip the scales in favor of the healthy, happy children drew me to medical research.

2   My accusers claim that I inflict torture on animals for the sole purpose of career advancement. My experiments supposedly have no relevance to medicine and are easily replaced by computer simulation. Meanwhile, an apathetic public barely watches, convinced that the issue has no significance, and publicity-conscious politicians increasingly give way to the demands of the activists.

3   We in medical research have also been unconscionably apathetic. We have allowed the most extreme animal-rights protesters to seize the initiative and frame the issue as one of "animal fraud." We have been complacent in our belief that a knowledgeable public would sense the importance of animal research to the public health. Perhaps we have been mistaken in not responding to the emotional tone of the argument created by those sad posters of animals by waving equally sad posters of children dying of leukemia or cystic fibrosis.

4   Much is made of the pain inflicted on these animals in the name of medical science. The animal-rights activists contend that this is evidence of our malevolent and sadistic nature. A more reasonable argument, however, can be advanced in our defense. Life is often cruel, both to animals and human beings. Teenagers get thrown from the back of a pickup truck and suffer severe head injuries. Toddlers, barely able to walk, find themselves at the bottom of a swimming pool while a parent checks the mail. Physicians hoping to alleviate the pain and suffering these tragedies cause have but three choices: create an animal model of the injury or disease and use that model to understand the process and test new therapies; experiment on human beings—some experiments will succeed, most will fail—or finally, leave medical knowledge static, hoping that accidental discoveries will lead us to the advances.

5   Some animal-rights activists would suggest a fourth choice, claiming that computer models can simulate animal experiments, thus making the actual experiments

unnecessary. Computers can simulate, reasonably well, the effects of well-understood principles on complex systems, as in the application of the laws of physics to airplane and automobile design. However, when the principles themselves are in question, as is the case with the complex biological systems under study, computer modeling alone is of little value.

6   One of the terrifying effects of the effort to restrict the use of animals in medical research is that the impact will not be felt for years and decades: drugs that might have been discovered will not be; surgical techniques that might have been developed will not be, and fundamental biological processes that might have been understood will remain mysteries. There is the danger that politically expedient solutions will be found to placate a vocal minority, while the consequences of these decisions will not be apparent until long after the decisions are made and the decision making forgotten.

7   Fortunately, most of us enjoy good health, and the trauma of watching one's child die has become a rare experience. Yet our good fortune should not make us unappreciative of the health we enjoy or the advances that make it possible. Vaccines, antibiotics, insulin and drugs to treat heart disease, hypertension and stroke are all based on animal research. Most complex surgical procedures, such as coronary-artery bypass and organ transplantation, are initially developed in animals. Presently undergoing animal studies are techniques to insert genes in humans in order to replace the defective ones found to be the cause of so much disease. These studies will effectively end if animal research is severely restricted.

8   In America today, death has become an event isolated from our daily existence— out of the sight and thoughts of most of us. As a doctor who has watched many children die, and their parents grieve, I am particularly angered by people capable of so much compassion for a dog or a cat, but with seemingly so little for a dying human being. These people seem so insulated from the reality of human life and death and what it means.

9   Make no mistake, however: I am not advocating the needlessly cruel treatment of animals. To the extent that the animal-rights movement has made us more aware of the needs of these animals, and made us search harder for suitable alternatives, they have made a significant contribution. But if the more radical members of this movement are successful in limiting further research, their efforts will bring about a tragedy that will cost many lives. The real question is whether an apathetic majority can be aroused to protect its future against a vocal, but misdirected, minority.

Analyzing the Structure

The Beginning

In paragraph 1, Karpati introduces himself as a scientist and a pediatrician with a personal and professional interest in his topic. While his first sentence proclaims, "I am the enemy," Karpati almost immediately lets his readers know that he is only an enemy to those who oppose his work; he describes himself as a caring doctor who wishes to help children stay healthy. His second sentence informs the reader that his topic will be the use of animals as research subjects; in the next sentences, he strongly implies that advances in medicine are the results of research using animals. His claim, stated in paragraph 3, is that such research is important to public health. By using the example of ill or injured children who might benefit from this work, Karpati makes a strong emotional appeal to his readers.

The Middle
Background Information
This information appears in several places in the essay. Paragraph 1 includes a list of advances in medicine that have come about, the reader assumes, through animal research. Later, in paragraph 7, Karpati lists specific drugs and surgical procedures that have resulted from using animals as research subjects. However, Karpati seems more interested in informing readers how he, a scientist who uses animals to conduct his research, is characterized negatively by animal-rights supporters.

Response to Other Points of View
Because Karpati's essay is largely a defense of his position, he focuses heavily on the views of those who oppose him. In paragraph 2, he briefly summarizes the accusations of animal-rights supporters. In paragraph 3, he suggests that these objections are voiced by extremists. He also says that he is aware of the reasons why others wish to eliminate animal research. In paragraph 4, he acknowledges that "pain [is] inflicted on these animals in the name of medical science." He agrees with the opposition that "life is often cruel"; yet his examples imply that human suffering is more compelling to physicians than is the suffering of animals. In paragraph 9, he refers back to this point and lauds the animal-rights movement in making researchers more sensitive to the issue of animal suffering.

Reasons in Support of the Claim
In paragraphs 4 through 8, Karpati presents his reasons to support his claim that medical research using animals should be continued for the benefit of human health. In paragraphs 4 and 5, he explains that the alternatives to animal research—experimenting on human subjects, relying on accidental discoveries, or using computer simulation—are not satisfactory. In paragraph 6, he warns that the impact of restricting animal research will have a far-reaching and negative impact on medical science. Paragraph 7 cites how animal research has contributed to the healthy lives that most of his readers take for granted. Finally, in paragraph 8, he reasserts the importance of human life over the well-being of animals.

Possible Objections to Reasons
Karpati includes several objections to his reasons. For instance, in paragraphs 4 and 5, he anticipates that his readers might wonder why humans and computers can't be substituted for animals in research. He responds that experiments on humans will largely fail and computer simulations cannot duplicate complex biological processes.

The End
In the last paragraph, Karpati summarizes his main point: The efforts of radical members of the animal-rights movement to limit the use of animals in research "will bring

about a tragedy that will cost many lives." He makes a strong appeal to his readers to take action to prevent just that from happening.

Blueprints for Arguments

Our analysis of Karpati's essay gives some idea of its general organization, but it does not reflect subdivisions or how the various parts are logically connected. That can be done by making an outline. Think of an outline as a blueprint of the argument you're building: It reveals structure and framework but leaves out the materials that cover the frame.

Opinions differ as to the value of making outlines before writing an essay. Some writers need to make formal outlines to organize their thoughts. Others simply scratch down a few key ideas. Still others write essays spontaneously without any preliminary writing. For the beginning writer, an outline is a valuable aid because it demonstrates at a glance how the various parts of an essay are connected, whether the organization is logical and complete, whether the evidence is sequenced properly, and whether there are any omissions or lack of proportion. Your outline need not be elaborate. You might simply jot down your key reasons in a hierarchy from strongest to weakest:

Introduction

Reason 1

Reason 2

Reason 3

Reason 4

Conclusion

This blueprint might be useful if you want to capture your readers' attention immediately with your most powerful appeal. Or you might use a reverse hierarchy, beginning with your weakest argument and proceeding to your strongest, in order to achieve a climactic effect. The outline will help you build your case.

You might prefer, as do some writers, to construct an outline after, rather than before, writing a rough draft. This lets you create a draft without restricting the free flow of ideas and helps you rewrite by determining where you need to fill in, cut out, or reorganize. You may discover where your line of reasoning is not logical; you may also reconsider whether you should arrange your reasons from the most important to the least or vice versa in order to create a more persuasive effect. Ultimately, outlining after the first draft can prove useful in producing subsequent drafts and a polished final effort. Outlines are also useful when evaluating somebody else's writing. Reducing the argument of the opposition to the bare bones exposes holes in the reasoning process, scanty evidence, and logical fallacies.

The Formal Outline

Some instructors like students to submit *formal outlines* with their papers to show that they have checked their structure carefully. This kind of outlining has several rules to follow:

- ■ Identify main ideas with capital Roman numerals.
- ■ Identify subsections of main ideas with capital letters, indented one set of spaces from the main ideas.

■ Identify support for subsections with Arabic numerals indented two sets of spaces from the main ideas.

■ Identify the parts of the support with lowercase Roman numerals, indented three sets of spaces from the main ideas.

■ Identify further subdivisions with lowercase letters and then italic numbers, each indented one set of spaces to the right of the previous subdivision.

■ Make sure all items have at least two points; it's considered improper informal outlining to have only one point under any subdivision.

To demonstrate what a formal outline can look like, we have outlined Clara Spotted Elk's essay, "Indian Bones":

I. Hoarding of Indian remains
   A. At Smithsonian
      1. Single Kiowa at Smithsonian
      2. 18,500 others
   B. In other locations
II. Authorities' defense of collections
   A. Refusal to return grave-robbed remains
   B. Maintenance of "specimens"
III. Indians' response
   A. Outrage
      1. Desire to be seen as humans
      2. Desire to have religion accepted by science
      3. Nonacceptance of desecration of graves
      4. Resentment of lack of outcry by public
   B. Accommodation
      1. Limitation in time
      2. Service to Indians and mankind
   C. Demand equality with other religions
IV. "Bones Bill" legislation
   A. Resistance from scientific community
      1. Slick lobbyists
      2. Money
      3. Scientific mystique
      4. Characterization of Indians
         i. Radicals
         ii. Out of touch with culture
         iii. Little appreciation of science
   B. Indian counter-resistance
      1. Few resources
      2. Little money
      3. Moral obligation to ancestors

Keep in mind that an outline should not force your writing to conform to a rigid pattern and, thus, turn your essay into something stilted and uninspired. Follow the model as a map, taking detours when necessary or inspired.

Two Basic Types of Arguments

Consider the following claims for arguments:

1. Watching television helps to eliminate some traditional family rituals.
2. Pornography poses a threat to women.
3. The rising sea level is a real threat to our way of life.
4. Bilingual education programs fail to help non-English-speaking children become part of mainstream society.
5. Hate crime legislation is intended to allow certain people to have more protection under the law than others.
6. Cigarette advertising should be banned from billboards everywhere.
7. Wall Street should be more tightly regulated.
8. Americans by law should be required to vote.
9. The Ten Commandments ought to be posted in public places, schools, and government offices.
10. Pass/fail grades have to be eliminated across the board if academic standards are to be maintained.

Looking over these statements, you might notice some patterns. The verbs in the first five are all in the present tense: *helps, poses, is, fail, is intended to*. However, each of the last five statements includes "should" words: *should, should not, ought to be, have to be*. These **obligation verbs** are found in almost all claims proposing solutions to a problem. What distinguishes the first group from the second is more than the form of the verb. The first five claims are statements of the writer's stand on a controversial issue. The second group are proposals for what *should* be. Of course, not every kind of argument will fit our classification scheme. However, essentially every argument in this book—and the ones you'll most likely write and read in your careers—falls into one of these two categories or a combination of each, for often a writer states his or her position on an issue, then follows it with proposals for changes. Later in this chapter, we will discuss proposals. For the moment, let's take a look at position arguments.

Position Arguments

A *position argument* scrutinizes one side of a controversial issue. In such an argument, the writer not only establishes his or her stand but also argues vigorously in defense of it. Position arguments are less likely to point to a solution to a problem. Instead, they are philosophical in nature—the kinds of arguments on which political and social principles are founded, laws are written, and business and government policies are established. Position papers also tend to address themselves to the ethical and moral aspects of a controversy. If, for instance, you were opposed to the university's policy of mandatory testing for the AIDS virus, you might write a position paper protesting your school's infringement of individual rights and invasion of privacy.

As indicated by the present tense of the verbs in the first five claims, the position argument deals with the status quo—the way things are, the current state of affairs. Such an argument reminds the audience that something *currently* is good or bad, better or worse, right or wrong. Like all arguments, they tend to be aimed at changing the audience's feelings about an issue—abortion, animal research, health care, off-shore oil drilling, illegal immigration, the death penalty, and so on. That is why many position papers tend to direct their appeals to the reader's sense of ethics rather than to reason.

By contrast, proposal arguments identify a problem and recommend a solution. That's why their claims contain verbs that *obligate* the readers to take some action. In this sense, they are practical rather than philosophical. For instance, if you were concerned about the spread of AIDS among college students, you might write a paper proposing that condom machines be installed in all dormitories. When you offer a proposal, you're trying to affect the future.

Features to Look for in Position Arguments

What follows are some key features of position arguments. As a checklist, they can help you evaluate someone's stand on an issue and help guide you in writing your own position papers.

The writer deals with a controversial issue. The best kind of position paper is one that focuses on a debatable issue, one in which there is clear disagreement: the war on terrorism, abortion, capital punishment, gay marriage, health care, euthanasia, civil liberties, gun control, separation of church and state, censorship, sex in advertising, freedom of speech, homelessness, gun control. These are issues about which people have many different perspectives.

The writer clearly states a position. Readers should not be confused about where an author stands on an issue. Although the actual issue may be complex, the claim should be stated emphatically and straightforwardly. Don't waffle: "Using the death penalty in some situations and with some rights of appeal probably doesn't do much to lower crime anyway"; far better is an emphatic "Capital punishment is no deterrent to crime." In formulating your claim, be certain that your word choice is not ambiguous. Otherwise the argument will be muddled and, ultimately, unconvincing.

The writer recognizes other positions and potential objections. For every argument there are bound to be numerous other perspectives. Such is the nature of controversy. As a writer representing a position, you cannot assume that your readers are fully aware of or understand all the disagreement surrounding the issue. Nor can you make a persuasive case without anticipating challenges. So, in your argument, spell out accurately and fairly the main points of the opposition and objections that might arise. We offer six reasons for doing this:

1. *You reduce your own vulnerability.* You don't want to appear ill-informed or naive on an issue. Therefore, it makes sense to acknowledge opposing points of view to show how well you've investigated the topic and how sensitive you are to it. Suppose, for instance, you are writing a paper arguing that "anyone who commits suicide is insane." To avoid criticism, you would have to be prepared to answer objections that fully rational people with terminal illnesses often choose to take their own lives so as to avoid a painful demise and curtail the suffering of loved

ones. Even if you strongly disagree, recognizing views from the other side demonstrates that you are a person of responsibility and tolerance—two qualities for which most writers of argument strive.

2. *You distinguish your own position.* By citing opposing views, you distinguish your own position from that of others. This not only helps clarify the differences but also lays out the specific points of the opposition to be refuted or discredited. Some writers do this at the outset of their arguments. Consider, for instance, how Ron Karpati sums up the views of the opposition in the opening paragraphs of his essay "I Am the Enemy." (Page 120)

3. *You can respond to opposing views.* A good response can challenge an opponent's ideas and examine the basis for the disagreement—whether personal, ideological, or moral. For instance, when Michael Kelley, in "Arguing for Infanticide" (page 195), responds to Steven Pinker's "Why They Kill Their Newborns" (page 187), he points out that Pinker's very logical argument for neonaticide ignores the moral and ethical values of our society regarding the relationship between mothers and their children. Kelley does not suggest that Pinker's reasons are incorrect; instead he challenges the basis for Pinker's argument.

4. *You might also challenge an opponent's logic, demonstrating where the reasoning suffers from flaws in logic.* For instance, the argument that Ms. Shazadi must be a wonderful mother because she's a great office manager does not logically follow. While some qualities of a good manager might bear on successful motherhood, not all do. In fact, it can be argued that the very qualities that make a good manager—leadership, drive, ruthlessness, determination—might damage a parent-child relationship. This logical fallacy, called a false analogy, erroneously suggests that the two situations are comparable when they are not.

5. *You might challenge the evidence supporting an argument.* If possible, try to point out unreliable, unrealistic, or irrelevant evidence offered by the opposition; question the truth of counterarguments; or point to distortions. The realtor who boasts oceanside property is vulnerable to challenge if the house in question is actually half a mile from the beach. Look for instances of stacking the deck. For example, a writer might argue that supporting the building of a new sports complex will benefit the community by providing new jobs. However, if she fails to mention that workers at the old sports facility will then lose their jobs, she is misleading the audience about the benefits of this change. Challenge the evidence by looking for hasty generalizations. For example, a business degree from State U. may indeed guarantee a well-paying job after graduation, but the writer will need more than a few personal anecdotes to convince the reader that this is the case.

6. *You can gain strength through concessions.* Admitting weaknesses in your own stand shows that you are realistic, that you don't suffer from an inflated view of the virtues of your position. It also lends credibility to your argument while helping you project yourself as fair-minded. A successful example of this strategy is Ron Karpati's acknowledgment in paragraph 9 of "I Am the Enemy" (page 121) that the animal-rights movement has sensitized scientists to the needs of animals.

The writer offers a well-reasoned argument to support the position. A position paper must do more than simply state your stand on an issue. It must try to persuade readers to accept your position as credible and convince them to adjust their thinking about the issue. Toward those ends, you should make every effort to demonstrate the best reasons for your beliefs and support the positions you hold. That means presenting honest and logically sound arguments.

Persuaders use three kinds of appeal: to *reason,* to *emotions,* and to readers' sense of *ethics.* You may have heard these described as the appeals of *logos, pathos,* and *ethos.* Although it is difficult to separate the emotional and ethical components from a logical argument, the persuasive powers of a position argument may mean the proper combination of these three appeals. Not all arguments will cover all three appeals. Some will target logic alone and offer as support statistics and facts. Others centering around moral, religious, or personal values will appeal to a reader's emotions as well as reason. Arguments based on emotion aim to reinforce and inspire followers to stand by their convictions. However, relying too heavily on an emotional appeal can result in an ad misericordiam argument, one that attempts to exploit the readers' pity. The most successful arguments are those that use multiple strategies to appeal to readers' hearts and minds.

When the issue centers on right-or-wrong or good-or-bad issues, position arguments make their appeals to the audience's ethical sense. In such papers, your strategy has two intentions: one, to convince the reader that you are a person of goodwill and moral character—thus enhancing your credibility—and, two, to suggest that any decent and moral readers will share your position.

The writer's supporting evidence is convincing. A position paper does not end with an incontrovertible proof such as the demonstration of a scientific law or mathematical theorem. No amount of logic can prove conclusively that your functional judgment is right or wrong; if that were the case, there would be few arguments. It is also impossible to prove that your aesthetic judgments are superior to another's or that a particular song, movie, or book is better than another. But your arguments have a greater chance of being persuasive if you can present convincing evidence that your argument is valid.

We'll say more about evidence in Chapter 6, but for now remember that a strong argument needs convincing evidence: facts, figures, personal observations, testimony of outside authorities, and specific examples. In general, the more facts supporting a position, the more reason there is for the reader to accept that position as valid. The same is true when refuting another position. An author needs to give reasons and hard evidence to disprove or discredit an opponent's stand.

The writer projects a reasonable persona. Whenever we read an argument, we cannot help but be aware of the person behind the words. Whether it's in the choice of expressions, the tenacity of opinion, the kinds of examples, the force of the argument, the nature of the appeal, or the humor or sarcasm, we hear the author's voice and form an impression of the person. That impression, which is projected by the voice and tone of the writing, is the writer's *persona.*

Persona is communicated in a variety of ways: diction or the choice of words (formal, colloquial, slang, jargon, charged terms); the sentence style (long or short, simple

Checklist for Writing a Position Argument

Have you:
- chosen a controversial issue?
- clearly stated a position?
- recognized other positions and possible objections?
- developed a well-reasoned argument?
- provided convincing supporting evidence?
- projected a reasonable persona?

or complex); and the kinds of evidence offered (from cool scientific data to inflammatory examples). As in face-to-face debates, a full range of feelings can be projected by the tone of a written argument: anger, irony, jest, sarcasm, seriousness.

Persona is the vital bond linking the writer to the reader. In fact, the success or failure of an argument might be measured by the extent to which the reader accepts the persona. If you like the voice you hear, then you have already begun to identify with the writer and are more likely to share in the writer's assumptions and opinions. If, however, that persona strikes you as harsh, distant, or arrogant, you might have difficulty subscribing to the argument even if it makes logical sense.

A good position argument projects a reasonable persona, one that is sincere and willing to consider opposing views. Steer clear of ad hominem arguments, which make personal attacks on those with whom you disagree rather than on their views. Although readers may not be convinced enough to change their stand or behavior, a writer with a reasonable persona can at least capture their respect and consideration. Remember, the success of your argument will largely depend on your audience's willingness to listen.

A word of warning. Not every persona has to be reasonable or pleasant, although for a beginner this works best. If an arrogant persona is fortified by wit and intelligence, readers may find it stimulating, even charming. A persona—whether outrageous, humorous, or sarcastic—can be successful if executed with style and assurance. Some of the best arguments in Part Two of this book have biting edges.

When you read an argument with a memorable persona, jot down in your argument journal the details of how the writer created it; that way, you can turn back to this information when you're trying to create personas for the arguments you write.

SAMPLE POSITION ARGUMENT FOR ANALYSIS

Below is an example of a position argument whose title suggests the issue and the author's stand on it: "Is Anything Private Anymore?" In a digital world where highly personal information appears in a multitude of databases and where security cameras are everywhere, the author wonders if privacy still exists. Written by Sean Flynn, this essay first appeared in *Parade* magazine in September 2007.

"Is Anything Private Anymore?"
Sean Flynn

1   Kevin Bankston was a closet smoker who hid his habit by sneaking cigarettes outside his San Francisco office. He expected anonymity on a big city street. But in 2005, an online mapping service that provided ground-level photographs captured him smoking—and made the image available to anyone on the Internet. This year, Google's Street View project caught him again.

2   Coincidence? Absolutely. Yet Bankston's twice-documented smoking highlights a wider phenomenon: Privacy is a withering commodity for all of us.

3   What you buy, where you go, whom you call, the Web sites you visit, the e-mails you send—all of that information can be monitored and logged. "When you're out in public, it's becoming a near certainty that your image will be captured," says (the newly nonsmoking) Bankston.

4   Should you care? I've interviewed numerous people on all sides of the privacy debate to find out just how wary we should be.

5   One thing is clear: In today's world, maintaining a cocoon of privacy simply isn't practical. Need a mortgage or a car loan? A legitimate lender is going to verify a wealth of private information, including your name and address, date of birth, Social Security number and credit history. We all make daily trade-offs for convenience and thrift: Electronic tollbooths mean you don't have to wait in the cash-only lane, but your travel habits will be tracked. The Piggly Wiggly discount card saves you $206 on your annual grocery bill, but it counts how many doughnuts and six-packs you buy. MySpace posts make it easy to keep in touch with friends, but your comments live on.

6   So how do you live in a digital world and still maintain a semblance of privacy? Experts say it's crucial to recognize that those bits of data are permanent—a trail of electronic crumbs that is never swept away, available to anyone with the skills and inclination to sniff it out.

7   Privacy may not feel like much of an issue for those in their teens and 20s. They've grown up chronicling their lives on popular social networking sites like MySpace or Facebook for easy retrieval by friends and strangers alike. But some young people don't realize that what was funny to college buddies might not amuse a law-firm recruiter. Employers regularly research job applicants on the Internet. Some colleges are helping students prepare: Duke University hosts seminars on how to clean up a Facebook account. "You learn why posting pictures of you riding the mechanical bull at Shooters is a bad idea," says Sarah Ball, a senior whose own page is secure and clean.

8   Amy Polumbo, 22, restricted her page on Facebook to 100 or so people who knew her password. "It was a way for me to keep in touch with friends all over the country," she says. But after she was crowned Miss New Jersey in June, someone downloaded pictures of her and threatened blackmail. She thwarted the attempt by releasing the photos herself (they're quite innocent) but suffered weeks of embarrassment.

9   "I know how easy it is for someone to take advantage of you on the Internet," says Polumbo. "The Web is a place where people can destroy your reputation if you're not careful."

10   In fact, all kinds of transgressions now are easily retrievable. An employee at a New York City bank watched his reputation shrink when his colleagues pulled up an article from a small-town newspaper about his drunk-driving arrest two years earlier. Divorce lawyers have been issuing subpoenas for electronic tollbooth records to use in custody cases. (You say you're home at 6 p.m. to have dinner with the kids, but Fast Lane says you're getting off the Massachusetts Turnpike at 7 p.m.) Abbe L. Ross, a divorce lawyer in Boston, finds a gold mine in computers: financial data, e-mails, what Web sites a soon-to-be-ex spouse looks at and for how long. "I love to look through hard drives," she says.

11   Details about you already are stashed in enormous databases. Unless you pay cash for everything, data brokers almost certainly have compiled a profile of you that will be bought and sold dozens of times to marketers and direct-mail firms. "There's almost nothing they can't find out about you," says Jack Dunning, who worked in the junk-mail business for 35 years. Right now, there are roughly 50,000 such lists for sale in a $4 billion a year industry. Now junk mail is going digital: Companies can use personal profiles and records from Internet search engines to tailor advertising—both what you see and precisely when you see it—to individual consumers.

12   And new databases are being created all the time. Most of the major proposals for health-care reform, for example, include compiling medical records into easily and widely accessible digital files. In July, the FBI requested $5 million to pay the major phone companies to maintain logs of your calls—information the Feds can't legally stockpile themselves but might find useful later.

13   Surveillance cameras are increasingly ubiquitous in our post-9/11 world. Indeed, New York City plans to ring the financial district with them, as central London did several years ago.

14   Of course, there are upsides. London's network of cameras helped capture failed car bombers in June. And streamlined electronic medical records would make health care safer and more efficient.

15   Still, most experts say we need to be vigilant about the increasing encroachments on our privacy.

16   The ability to collect information and images has outpaced the security available to protect them. Since January 2005, nearly 160 million personal records have been stolen or inadvertently posted online.

17   And even if information stays secure, the big question remains: Who should be allowed to access these databases? The FBI might find evidence against a few bad guys in millions of phone records, but the government could track all of your calls too. (President Bush has acknowledged that the National Security Agency tapped phone calls, though whose and how many is unknown.)

18   Even more disturbing: All of those data files can be linked and cross-referenced. At the 2001 Super Bowl in Tampa, fans were scanned with cameras linked to facial-recognition software in a hunt for suspected terrorists. Some privacy advocates worry that police could videotape anti-war marches and create a library of digital faces or start mining Web pages for personal information.

19   Kevin Bankston was only caught smoking, but he's worried about larger implications: "The issue isn't whether you have anything to hide," he says. "The issue is whether the lack of privacy would give the government an inordinate amount of power over the populace. This is about maintaining the privacy necessary for us to flourish as a free society."

Analysis of Sample Position Argument

The writer deals with a controversial issue. Most people assume that personal privacy is an inherent right. But is that a realistic expectation in today's world? Few people realize that almost every electronic transaction, whether a bank deposit or store purchase, leaves a permanent digital record. Nor do they realize that every phone call, e-mail, grocery store purchase, or Facebook entry becomes part of huge data systems accessible to others. Controversy arises because such personal information can be used by businesses to track spending habits and, thus, target customers. Also controversial is how the government can keep tabs on its citizenry. That issue is even more controversial since some forms of surveillance—at airports, on highways, and in commercial and financial areas—are considered essential in the fight against terrorism. Of course, to many people, such surveillance constitutes an infringement on individual privacy and, thus, a diminishing of civil liberties. In his essay, Flynn clearly addresses the controversy that in our digital world it may be impossible to protect personal information.

The writer clearly states a position. The title of Flynn's essay implies the author's stand: that personal privacy no longer exists. He begins with the anecdote of a closet smoker who thought that cigarette breaks outside his office gave him anonymity. But an "online mapping service . . . captured him smoking—and made the image available to anyone on the Internet." He concludes this anecdote with a blunt generalization, "Privacy is a withering commodity for all of us" (paragraph 2)—a clear statement of his position. Flynn reiterates his position following other examples of privacy violations—e.g., his statement regarding the ready availability of telephone and health records: "Still, most experts say we need to be vigilant about the increasing encroachments on our privacy" (paragraph 15). And in paragraph 16: "The ability to collect information and images has outpaced the security available to protect them." Clearly, he has surveyed the many ways privacy is compromised and concludes that it is rapidly eroding.

The writer recognizes other positions and possible objections. Flynn creates a balanced essay by citing other points of view. At the end of paragraph 5, for example, he cites the consumer perks built into some everyday transactions: "We all make daily trade-offs for convenience and thrift: Electronic tollbooths mean you don't have to wait in the cash-only lane, but your travel habits will be tracked. The Piggly Wiggly discount card saved you $206 on your annual grocery bill, but it counts how many doughnuts and six-packs you buy. MySpace posts make it easy to keep in touch with friends, but your comments live on." Later, when discussing terrorism, he acknowledges "upsides": "London's network of cameras helped capture failed car bombers in June" (paragraph 14). And referring to "easily and widely accessible" health care files, he concedes, "streamlined electronic medical records would make health care safer and more efficient."

As the author explores the topic, his tone remains matter-of-fact and objective. His most emotionally potent comment comes at his conclusion when he refers back to the young smoker. Here his tone approaches a warning regarding surveillance in public places: "Kevin Bankston was only caught smoking. . . . This is about maintaining the privacy necessary for us to flourish as a free society."

The writer offers well-developed reasons to support the position. Flynn offers concrete, concise, and convincing evidence to support his position that personal privacy is greatly compromised today. He describes virulent threats and documents these with examples to which the general public can relate. One of his claims is that in today's world of commerce, it is almost impossible to maintain personal privacy—that nearly every transaction is recorded electronically and leaves a permanent trail available to anyone skilled "to sniff it out" (paragraph 6). And he gets specific: "Need a mortgage or a car loan? A legitimate lender is going to verify a wealth of private information, including your name and address, date of birth, Social Security number and credit history" (paragraph 5). Later, he argues that because of the enormous databases, "Companies can use personal profiles and records from Internet search engines to tailor advertising—both what you see and precisely when you see it—to individual consumers" (paragraph 11). For support, Flynn quotes an authority in the field of direct-mail and marketing: "'There's almost nothing they can't find out about you,' says Jack Dunning, who worked in the junk-mail business for 35 years."

Another threat Flynn names are the social networking sites that make personal information available to everyone, including potential employers as well as thieves and sexual predators. He supports his position with reference to students who naively chronicle their lives on MySpace or Facebook. Young people may not know that "employers regularly research job applicants on the Internet," Flynn writes. What may amuse college pals "might not amuse a law-firm recruiter" (paragraph 7). He further supports his position with more anecdotal evidence, a reference to the newly crowned Miss New Jersey, whose Facebook page contained photographs that were used as blackmail. Flynn even quotes her directly: "'The Web is a place where people can destroy your reputation if you're not careful'" (paragraph 9).

Another argument Flynn makes supporting his claim of a diminishing privacy is the ubiquitous use of surveillance cameras in public places. In paragraph 18, he offers the powerful example of the 2001 Super Bowl where "fans were scanned with cameras linked to facial-recognition software in a hunt for suspected terrorists." Flynn's logical concern is that "police could videotape anti-war marches and create a library of digital faces or start mining Web pages for personal information." Building on all his specific concerns, Flynn concludes with larger implications: that the increased lack of privacy could "'give the government an inordinate amount of power over the populace.'"

The writer's supporting evidence is convincing. Flynn's evidence is very convincing. He supports his position in a variety of ways, using anecdotes that the average person can identify with—references to smoker Kevin Bankston or young people using Facebook. He makes use of expert opinion, quoting, for instance, Jack Dunning, who worked for 35 years in the direct-mail business. Throughout the piece, he also cites numerous examples of our compromised privacy.

The writer projects a reasonable persona. Flynn's tone is reasonable and balanced, as his purpose is to alert the general public to the ways personal data is part of public or available records. His tone is friendly as his intention is not to alarm but to enhance awareness so that people can take sensible precautions. Thus, he gives numerous examples but does not inflate them or create a sense of panic.

Proposal Arguments

Position arguments examine existing conditions. *Proposal arguments,* however, look to the future. They make recommendations for changes to the status quo—namely, policy, practice, or attitude. Essentially, what every proposal writer says is this: "Here is the problem, and this is what I think should be done about it." The hoped-for result is a new course of action or way of thinking.

Proposals are the most common kind of argument. We hear them all the time: "There ought to be a law against that"; "The government should do something about these conditions." We're always making proposals of some kind: "Van should work out more"; "You ought to see that movie"; "We should recycle more of our trash." As pointed out earlier in this chapter, because proposals are aimed at correcting problems, they almost always make their claims in obligation verbs such as *ought to, needs to be,* and *must.*

Sometimes proposal arguments take up local problems and make practical recommendations for immediate solutions. For instance, to reduce the long lines at the photocopy machines in your campus library, you might propose that the school invest in more copiers and station them throughout the building. Proposal arguments also seek to correct or improve conditions with more far-reaching consequences. If, for example, too many of your classmates smoke, you might write a proposal to your school's administration to remove all cigarette machines from campus buildings or to limit smoking areas on campus.

Still other proposals address perennial social issues in an effort to change public behavior and government policy. A group of physicians might recommend that marijuana be legalized for medical use. An organization of concerned parents might ask the federal government to ban toys that contain toxic or flammable materials. Everyone has ideas about things that should be changed; proposals are the means we use to make those changes happen.

Features to Look for in Proposal Arguments

Proposals have two basic functions: (1) They inform readers that there is a problem; (2) they make recommendations about how to correct those problems. To help you sharpen your own critical ability to build and analyze proposal arguments, we offer some guidelines.

The writer states the problem clearly. Because a proposal argument seeks to change the reader's mind and/or behavior, you first must demonstrate that a problem exists. You do this for several reasons. Your audience may not be aware that the problem exists or they may have forgotten it or think that it has already been solved. Sympathetic audiences may need to be reinspired to take action. It is crucial, therefore, that proposals clearly define the problem and the undesirable or dangerous consequences if matters are not corrected.

For both uninformed and sympathetic audiences, writers often try to demonstrate how the problem personally affects the reader. An argument for greater measures against shoplifting can be more convincing when you illustrate how petty thefts inevitably lead to higher prices. A paper proposing the elimination of pesticides might interest the everyday gardener by demonstrating how carcinogenic chemicals can contaminate local drinking water. To make the problem even more convincing, the claim should be supported by solid evidence—statistics, historical data, examples, testimony of witnesses and experts, maybe even personal experience.

The writer clearly proposes how to solve the problem. After defining the problem clearly, you need to tell your readers how to solve it. This is the heart of the proposal, the writer's plan of action. Besides a detailed explanation of what should be done and how, the proposal should supply reliable supporting evidence for the plan: testimony of others, ideas from authorities, statistics from studies.

The writer argues convincingly that this proposal will solve the problem. Perhaps the first question readers ask is "How will this solution solve the problem?" Writers usually address this question by identifying the forces behind the problem and demonstrating how their plan will counter those forces. Suppose, for instance, you propose putting condom machines in all college dorms as a means of combating the spread of AIDS. To build a convincing case, you would have to summon evidence documenting how condoms significantly reduce the spread of AIDS. To make the connection between the problem and your solution even stronger, you might go on to explain how readily available machines leave students little excuse for unsafe sex. Students cannot complain that they jeopardized their health because they couldn't make it to a drugstore.

The writer convincingly explains how the solution will work. Generally readers next ask how the plan will be put into action. Writers usually answer by detailing how their plan will work. They emphasize their plan's advantages and how efficiently (or cheaply, safely, conveniently) it can be carried out. For the condom machine proposal, that might mean explaining how and where the machines will be installed and how students can be encouraged to use them. You might cite advantages of your proposal, such as the easy installation of the machines and the low price of the contents.

The writer anticipates objections to the proposed solution. Writers expect disagreement and objections to proposal arguments: Proposals are aimed at changing the status quo, and many people are opposed to or are fearful of change. If you want to persuade readers, especially hostile ones, you must show that you respect their sides of the argument too. Most proposal writers anticipate audience response to fortify their case and establish credibility. (See Chapter 4 for more discussion of audience response.)

The writer explains why this solution is better than the alternatives. Although you may believe that your solution to the problem is best, you cannot expect readers automatically to share that sentiment. Nor can you expect readers not to wonder about other solutions. Good proposal writers investigate other solutions

Checklist for Writing a Proposal Argument

Have you:
- stated the problem clearly?
- proposed a solution clearly?
- explained why the solution will work?
- demonstrated how the solution will work?
- addressed possible objections?
- shown why the solution is better than alternatives?
- projected a reasonable persona?

that have been tried to solve this problem so they can weigh alternative possibilities and attempt to demonstrate the superiority of their plan and the disadvantages of others. If you are knowledgeable about ways the problem has been dealt with in the past, you might be able to show how your plan combines the best features of other, less successful solutions. For instance, in the condom machine proposal you might explain to your readers that universities have attempted to make students more aware that unsafe sex promotes the spread of AIDS; however, without the easy availability of condom machines, students are more likely to continue to engage in unsafe sex. The promotion of AIDS awareness and the presence of condom machines might significantly reduce that problem.

The writer projects a reasonable persona. As in position arguments, your persona is an important factor in proposals, for it conveys your attitude toward the subject and the audience. Because a proposal is intended to win readers to your side, the best strategy is to project a persona that is fair-minded. Even if you dislike somebody else's views on an issue, projecting a reasonable and knowledgeable tone will have a more persuasive effect than a tone of belligerence.

If you are arguing for condom machines in dormitories, you would be wise to recognize that some people might object to the proposal because availability might be interpreted as encouragement of sexual behavior. So as not to offend or antagonize such readers, adopting a serious, straightforward tone might be the best mode of presenting the case.

SAMPLE PROPOSAL ARGUMENT FOR ANALYSIS

The following argument was written by Amanda Collins, a first-year English composition student, whose assignment was to write a proposal argument. In her paper, she argues for the implementation of foreign language teaching in American elementary schools, focusing in particular on her own home town of East Bridgewater, Massachusetts. Read her essay and respond to the questions that follow. Note that she used research to support her ideas and documentation to acknowledge her sources. The style of documentation used in this paper is MLA, which we discuss in detail in the Documentation Guide.

Amanda Collins
Professor Ingram
ENG 1350
15 December 2009

Bring East Bridgewater Elementary
into the World

Introduction

According to a survey of ten European countries and Russia, the average age of students beginning foreign language instruction is eight (Bergentoft 13). In Sweden, ninety-nine percent of the students in primary school study English. One hundred percent of the students study English in secondary schools (Bergentoft 19). However, "across the United States, only about one in three elementary schools offers its students the opportunity to gain some measure of skill in another language" (Met 37). The United States falls drastically short of the standards being set by the rest of the world.

The Commonwealth of Massachusetts is no exception. According to a report from the Center for Applied Linguistics (CAL), only forty-four schools across the state offer foreign language programs in primary school (Branaman, Rhodes, and Holmes). Schools not offering foreign language study leave their students at a disadvantage. Foreign language needs to be considered as vital to a child's education as are math, science and reading. Parents would not be happy if their children began math or English studies in high school. So why shouldn't parents be outraged that second languages do not hold much significance in the Massachusetts curriculum? (Brown 166). East Bridgewater must take steps to change this and open Central Elementary School to foreign language learning.

The world is changing as are the skills one needs to succeed. Globalization brings us together. People around the world are connected to each other more than ever before, whether through international communication, travel, or commerce. In a world today that is constantly crossing borders "there is a need for linguistically and culturally competent Americans" (Brown 165). And learning languages is one way to reach such competency. America's students need to be prepared for entrance into this ever-merging world where they will compete with their international peers who are fluent in two or three languages. It is time to adopt a plan like those proven successful elsewhere in America and abroad. It's time to give East Bridgewater's students an advantage. In order to do this, East Bridgewater must live up to the school system's motto, "There is no better place to learn," and mandate foreign language education in the elementary curriculum for every child.

Collins 2

4   Although the Massachusetts Department of Education adopted a curriculum framework in August 1999 that includes foreign language in the requirements for elementary schools, it is still a recommendation, not yet a requirement (Massachusetts Dept. of Educ.). Massachusetts's new Curriculum Framework for World Languages states that "students should graduate from high school able to read, write, and converse in a world language in order to participate in the multilingual, interdependent communities of the twenty-first century . . . to develop proficiency, this framework recommends a sequence of language learning that starts in kindergarten and continues through grade twelve and beyond . . . the World Languages discipline is about making connections" (Massachusetts Dept. of Educ.). The framework places the same value on learning a foreign language as is placed on mathematics, reading and science. Despite the framework's passing, foreign language is not mandated in the elementary curriculum. There is a real need not only to finalize the benefits that students gain by learning languages at an early age, but also to work toward advancing our schools' curricula to include Foreign Language in Elementary School (FLES).

Why Should Children Learn Foreign Languages?

5   Language is an important aspect of the education of students of all ages. It is becoming more important for citizens to be well versed in a language other than their own. The United States was basically a self-sufficient and self-contained country before the World Wars. "Rapid and widespread political, economic, and military changes after World War II gave rise to issues that were global in scope, and many people became aware of the impact that events outside U.S. borders had on domestic affairs" (Smith 38). The United States was learning just how fundamental foreign languages are.

6   One reason is that transcontinental communications have become essential to everyday life in the world. With so much cross-cultural interaction, we must prepare American children to grow into adults capable of interacting with other cultures. The future of the United States depends on continued and constant communication with countries that speak languages other than our own. There are only about 45 other countries outside the United States where English is spoken. So, in order to maintain the status that this country now enjoys, we must train American children to comprehend changes in the global community. Students must learn foreign languages.

7   In 1999 a study titled *Exploring the Economics of Language* found that "multilingual societies have a competitive advantage over monolingual societies in international trade" (Met 36). The study went on to point out

that businesses that had people with the proper language skills to negotiate and carry out commerce with foreign enterprises were at a distinct advantage over those that lacked such talent. So it stands to reason that giving America's students the opportunity to learn a foreign language increases their chances of succeeding in the business world. Likewise, the country benefits because successful businesses on the world level only help the American economy. As Andrew Smith asserts, there is a need to "prepare our students to meet the challenges of our increasingly, sometimes dangerously, interconnected world. It is not likely that the United States will exert global leadership for long with a citizenry that is globally deaf, dumb, and blind" (41).

8   Besides the business industry, other jobs require expertise in a second language. The State Department, the Central Intelligence Agency, and the National Security Agency are among more than 70 government agencies that require proficiency in foreign languages (Met 36). The non-profit service industries need employees to interact with other cultures and speak other languages. The Red Cross, for example, not only aids victims in the United States but throughout the world. Additionally, the Internet and other electronic communications, though originally English-based, are becoming more linguistically diverse, making proficiency in other languages indispensable. Again, we must not deprive students of the opportunity to advance in such career paths; we must provide them language training to make possible career success.

Other Benefits to Learning a Language Early

9   While most people have the ability to learn a foreign language at any age, there are benefits to starting that process when students are young (Lipton 1115). In 1959 neurologist Wilder Penfield claimed that the brain was best able to learn a foreign language before the age of ten. Later research by scientists Chugani and Phelps resulted in the same conclusion: the ideal time to begin studying a foreign language is before puberty (Lipton 1114). Thompson et al. discovered in the year 2000 that the area of the brain associated with language learning grew the most rapidly from age six to thirteen and then slowed. Another researcher suggested that children learning a language before the age of twelve will develop a more authentic accent (Lipton 1114). So this scientific evidence makes a strong case that foreign language learning must begin at a young age. But there are other studies that make the case even stronger.

Collins 4

10   In 1987, a Connecticut test of twenty-six thousand students revealed that children who began foreign language education before grade four did significantly better on speaking, listening, reading, writing and cultural understanding tests than students who started language learning in seventh grade or after (Brown 165). This and other similar studies initiated further investigation into the academic benefits of early foreign language learning.

11   Numerous studies have been conducted to evaluate the ways in which learning a language will enhance the simultaneous learning of other subjects. "Learning [foreign] languages . . . provides a unique conduit to higher-order thinking skills. From the early stages of learning, students move from a representational knowledge base to comparison, synthesis, and hypothesis, all elements of higher-order thinking skills" (Brown 167). Students can gain better understanding of the grammar of their native language when they study the grammar of a foreign tongue, and students who can speak another language can develop stronger reading skills (Met 38). On the national level, there is a call for improved literacy, which is why it is important for parents and educators to recognize how FLES helps students learn to read and write (Bruce 608). FLES students scored higher on the 1985 Basic Skills Language Arts Test than non-FLES students. Foreign language study has helped improve standardized test scores in mathematics and reading for students from a variety of backgrounds. Bilingualism also improves "cognitive functioning, such as metalinguistic skills and divergent thinking" (Met 38). It has even been suggested that students gain more creativity. Foreign language study helps students become more academically successful overall.

12   Additionally, because the world is full of many cultures, studying a foreign language helps prepare students for the cultural understanding that is necessary for the acceptance of such diversity. Brown states, "no other subject matter in the elementary school prepares students for the realization that there are other languages and cultures beyond their own" (167). This in turn aids in teaching students geography, history, and social studies because they will have something to build on, knowing that the United States is not the only country of consequence. Researchers Carpenter and Torney found that younger students studying languages are more open to other cultures and develop more positive attitudes toward foreign cultures and languages (Lipton 1114). From brain functions to academics to character development, learning foreign languages in elementary school is proven to be profitable.

Collins 5

Optimal Solution for East Bridgewater

13   There is no doubt that East Bridgewater must adopt some version of a FLES program. Based on the current circumstances at the Central Elementary School, I recommend that the East Bridgewater School Committee adopt a Sequential FLES program in which students study a language no more than thirty minutes per session up to five times a week.

14   As for the specific language, that decision can be left up to the School Committee. However, it is suggested that only one language be taught for the first year, or at least until the program is underway and running smoothly. And it makes sense to recommend Spanish since that language is used more often than other foreign languages in the United States.

15   Language instruction should take place at least three times a week for thirty minutes. Each school day is six hours long, minus time for lunch and recess. In order to arrange for the addition of a language program, the length of other lessons per day would have to be shortened slightly, but never by more than ten minutes each. This should not be a problem. Foreign languages are as equally important to a child's education as math, reading or science, and, therefore, would advance students' education in the long run. Since it has been proven that the study of a second language enhances students' performances in other subjects, the amount of time shaved from each subject's session would be more than made up for in the students' overall success.

16   To fund this undertaking, East Bridgewater should apply to the Federal Language Assistance Program (FLAP). As of the year 2000, Springfield and Medford were the only two towns to receive FLAP grants. Funds are also available through Goals 2000: Educate America Act of 1994. Under the Improving America's Schools Act of 1994, Title VII grants are given out for foreign language assistance. In the year 2001, the Massachusetts Board of Education received two, and Newton, Malden, Medford, Salem, and Springfield Public Schools each received a grant. East Bridgewater has the opportunity to apply for all of these grants.

17   Meetings should be scheduled with parents to discuss the importance of foreign language education. Brochures outlining fundraising activities should be distributed. The costs of the meetings and printed materials would be minimal, and they would be more than paid for with the benefits of the program. When parents and communities join together, fundraisers can bring in large revenues. East Bridgewater can hold benefits similar to the concert and art auction held by parents in Athens, Georgia. These grants and locally raised money can also help defray the cost of adding teachers to the staff and carrying out the proper training.

Collins 6

Books and other teaching materials can be purchased from grant funds as
well. There really is no shortage of money available. Once a town or district
realizes the advantages of foreign language learning and expresses a desire to
include it in their elementary school, the government and private agencies
could offer funds to help get those programs underway.

18

Teaching foreign language to students is a necessity. Linguistic and
national borders are becoming a thing of the past as the result of globalization.
It is a school's responsibility and a student's right to have every opportunity
afforded them to become globally aware and literate citizens. East
Bridgewater's School Committee shares that responsibility as educators of this
country's future leaders. Now is the time to act and close the gap on the foreign
language deficiency that exists in East Bridgewater's Central Elementary School.

Collins 7

Works Cited

Bergentoft, Rune. "Foreign Language Instruction: A Comparative Perspective."
 Annals of the American Academy of Political and Social Science 532
 (1994): 8-34. Print.

Branaman, Lucinaa, Nancy Rhodes, and Annette Holmes. "National Directory of
 Early Foreign Language Programs." Center for Applied Linguistics. CAL,
 1999. Web. 4 Dec. 2004.

Brown, Christine L. "Elementary School Foreign Language Programs in the
 United States." *Annals of the American Academy of Political and Social
 Science* 532 (1994): 164-76. Print.

Bruce, Anita. "Encouraging the Growth of Foreign Language Study." *Modern
 Language Journal* 86 (2002): 605-09. Print.

Caccavale, Therese. "Holliston Public Schools Foreign Language." Teacher Web,
 16 Oct. 2009. Web. 7 Dec. 2009.

Lambert, Richard D. "Problems and Processes in U.S. Foreign Language
 Planning." *Annals of the American Academy of Political and Social
 Science* 532 (1994): 47-58. Print.

Collins 8

Lipton, Gladys C. "The FLES Advantage: FLES Programs in the Third
     Millennium." *French Review* 74 (2001): 1113-24. Print.
Massachusetts Dept. of Educ. "World Languages Curriculum Framework."
     Massachusetts Dept. of Educ., Jan. 1996. Web. 1 Dec. 2009.
Met, Myriam. "Why Language Learning Matters." *Educational Leadership* 59
     (2001): 36-40. Print.
Smith, Andrew F. "How Global Is the Curriculum?" *Educational Leadership* 60
     (2002): 38-41. Print.

QUESTIONS FOR ANALYSIS AND DISCUSSION

Briefly summarize the main points of Amanda Collins's essay. Then answer the following questions about the essay to see how it fulfills our guidelines for a proposal argument:

1. Where does Collins identify the problem? Explain how she demonstrates that the problem is significant. Does she explain how today's young students can be affected? Where does she do this?
2. What solution does Collins propose? Where is it stated?
3. Does Collins explain how her solution will work? Where does she do this? Does she provide enough detail to understand how it will work?
4. Has Collins anticipated objections to her solution? in which paragraphs? How does she respond to the objection?
5. Does Collins seem aware of other attempts to solve the problem? Where does she refer to them?
6. What attitude about her subject does Collins convey to her readers? Does she seem reasonable and balanced? Where exactly?

Analyzing the Structure
The Beginning

Amanda Collins has already divided her paper into four parts: "Introduction," "Why Should Children Learn Foreign Language?" "Other Benefits to Learning a Language Early," and "Optimal Solution for East Bridgewater." Her "Introduction" constitutes the beginning of the essay. The middle includes those paragraphs grouped under her next two parts ("Why Should Children Learn Foreign Languages?" and "Other Benefits to Learning a Language Early"). The end corresponds to those paragraphs under "Optimal Solution for East Bridgewater."

In paragraph 1, Amanda introduces the problem: compared to several foreign countries, only about a third of American elementary schools offer foreign language teaching. And this creates a disadvantage not only for children who are preparing for a global world but for America. Then in paragraph 2, she tightens her focus to the state of Massachusetts, which, characteristic of the rest of the country, offers a paltry response: only 44 schools statewide offer foreign language programs at the primary level. She concludes that paragraph with a point-blank proposal that "East Bridgewater must take steps to change this and open Central Elementary School to foreign language learning."

We get a sense of Amanda from these introductory paragraphs. We hear both concern and sincerity in her tone. We also are clear on her positions. Equating foreign language learning with math and writing, she projects a sense of urgency if American young people are to grow up to function successfully in a world that is linguistically and culturally interconnected and competitive. She appeals to both reason and emotion when she states: "It is time to adopt a plan like those proven successful elsewhere in America and abroad. It's time to give East Bridgewater's students an advantage." She also appeals to a sense of ethics, reminding authorities of their responsibility and duty to live up to the school system's motto, "There is no better place to learn." And she concludes this part of the argument insisting that East Bridgewater mandate that foreign language be taught at Central Elementary so students can begin to share in the benefits to come.

The Middle
The next eight paragraphs Amanda has divided into two sections: "Why Should Children Learn Foreign Languages?" and "Other Benefits to Learning a Language Early." These represent the middle of Amanda's essays, where she makes her case, where she does the real arguing for her proposal.

Background Information Paragraphs 1, 2, and 4 set the context for Amanda's complaint and the basis for her proposal. In paragraph 1, she says how America "falls drastically short of the standards being set by the rest of the world." In the next paragraph she says that Massachusetts is characteristic of the larger problem with only 44 schools statewide—a small percentage—offering foreign language programs at the primary level. Paragraph 4 focuses on how despite an adopted curriculum that includes a foreign language requirement in Massachusetts schools, it has still not been mandated, leaving East Bridgewater students deprived.

Reasons in Support of the Claim Paragraphs 5 through 12 make up the heart of Amanda's essay. Here she supports her claim that it's important for children to learn foreign languages. And she offers several reasons. One key point is the competition in international business that American students will eventually face in the multilingual world of commerce. As evidence, she cites a source (paragraph 6) that claims how only 45 countries besides the United States speak English, implying that most of the rest of the 160 or so countries do not. So in a majority of the world's nations, commerce is conducted in foreign tongues.

She also refers to a study that supports her claim that "monolingual societies" are at a distinct disadvantage over those where other languages are spoken. She summons the support of Andrew Smith (paragraph 7) who also sees a need to prepare our children for an increasing global economy and culture. In the next paragraph, she points out that besides business, other careers require expertise in a second language—e.g., nonprofit organizations as well as some 70 government agencies, including the CIA, that require proficiency in foreign languages. She concludes that with the Internet and other electronic communications, once English-based, the world is becoming more linguistically diverse, making proficiency in other languages indispensable. Again, she argues, we must not deprive students the opportunity to advance in such career paths.

In paragraphs 9 through 12, Amanda offers other benefits to early language learning besides career success, thus bolstering her claim. Because children best learn foreign languages at a young age, she argues they will develop more authentic accents. Second, foreign language learning also helps children perform better in speaking, writing, and even mathematics. For support, she cites numerous studies, allowing her to conclude: "From brain functions, to academics, to character development, learning foreign languages in elementary school is proven to be profitable."

Response to Other Points of View Although Amanda cites no specific opposing views, she implies that America may be slow to develop language programs at the primary level because of a general apathy and/or the belief that speaking English is good enough. She hints at this when she mentions America's pre-World Wars sense of self-sufficiency and self-containment. And even though Americans had learned "how fundamental foreign languages" were following World War II, vigorous implementation, especially on the primary school level, has been lacking.

Anticipates Possible Objections to Reasons Amanda indirectly anticipates opposition to early language training: that if people need to learn a foreign language for their careers they can take courses as adults. With considerable supporting evidence, she argues that the earlier children learn foreign languages the better. And she cites scientific studies that confirm how young children absorb foreign languages faster and more efficiently than adolescents or adults.

The End

The final five paragraphs constitute the end of Amanda's argument. Here she returns to the problem in East Bridgewater and offers specific proposals on implementing foreign language training in Central Elementary. She recommends a program of half-hour sessions three to five times a week; she suggests Spanish since it is the second most-spoken language in America; she suggests various means of funding the program; and she recommends that parents get involved. She concludes with reaffirmations of her argument that it is important for young students to learn foreign languages and that it is a school's responsibility to provide students that opportunity. Her final sentence rounds out her argument and nicely returns to the home front: "Now is the time to act and close the gap on the foreign language deficiency that exists in East Bridgewater's Central Elementary School."

Narrative Arguments

Sometimes position and proposal arguments do not take on the familiar shapes as just discussed. Sometimes the author's position on an issue is implied rather than straightforwardly stated. Sometimes instead of a well-reasoned argument bound by a hierarchy of supporting details, the evidence is incorporated in a dramatic illustration of the issue. So is the author's stand. What we're talking about is argument in the form of a *narrative*.

Instead of spelling out the claims and making explicit points, the narrative argument relies on a scene, a series of episodes, or a story to advocate a change of behavior or way of thinking. Whether true or hypothetical, a narrative may serve as the body of an argument or it may be used at the beginning as a springboard to the central claim and discussion. Either way, a narrative can be a powerful strategy for winning the sympathy of an audience by describing experiences that evoke emotional responses. Below is an argument aimed at getting people to protest a governmental proposal to remove grizzly bears from list of animals protected by the Endangered Species Act. It begins with a student's personal narrative, an account that is emotionally appealing and that leads into an explicit appeal.

> We'd been hiking for three hours east of Yellowstone's Slough Creek when our guide motioned us to stop. "Bears," he whispered. We heard a piercing sound— more like a wailing cry than a roar. We cut through some sage and over a rise when we saw a grizzly bear mother and two yearling cubs. From about a hundred yards we watched in hushed fascination as the adorable cubs romped and wrestled in the grass while the mother watched from a short distance. They were seemingly unaware of our presence and continued to cavort, one cub trying to engage the mother in play by nudging her with his nose. This went on for several minutes until the mother made a sound and stood erect, sniffing the air. She must have sensed danger because she bellowed for the cubs to follow. In a moment they tumbled down a ravine and out of sight.

> To see that mother grizzly and her young at such close range was not just a rare experience but an eye-opener. It was a reminder that these magnificent, elusive creatures are in a constant struggle to survive. They reproduce only every three years and spend at least that time rearing their cubs. They are vulnerable to hunters, traffic, and male grizzlies which will kill their own cubs in order to render nursing mothers fertile again. While their numbers have increased over the past decades, these bears are threatened once again.

> The current administration has recently proposed taking grizzlies off the Endangered Species list, thus stripping them of the kind of protection from hunters that could push them to the edge of extinction once again. We must do everything in our power to make people aware of the continuing struggle to save these iconic vestiges of frontier America.

The appeal here makes a case for protecting the grizzlies by re-creating an encounter with a mother bear and her cubs, thus invoking in the reader identification with the author's sympathy for the creatures. Even if the reader has never encountered grizzly bears in the wild, the narrative at least evokes in readers yearnings for such.

To anyone who has ever visited a zoo or seen wildlife movies, the description of the cubs at play has a strong emotional appeal.

While this strategy—the use of a story—differs from the standard position and proposal argument, the narrative argument still has three basic parts—a beginning, middle and end—and, here, a paragraph for each. The first is the actual narrative, the "story" in which the author invites the reader to partake in the experience. Here we read the author's observations of the animals "cavorting"; the final sentence concludes with the animals' sensing danger and eventually departing. In essence, this opening paragraph is the author's invitation to share in the emotional experience of the encounter. The second paragraph shifts to an appreciation of that experience and an evaluation of the vulnerability of the animals. Here the author reminds us that these "magnificent" creatures are threatened by a variety of forces, and the author names specifics—hunters, vehicular traffic, and other grizzlies. The third paragraph states the specific problem that could further endanger the animals—the then-current administration's proposal to remove them from the Endangered Species list. And it concludes with a proposal for people who care to "do everything in ...[their] power to make people aware of the continuing struggle to save" the grizzlies.

A narrative can also constitute other peoples' experiences as in the third-person account below of a teenager's death by drug overdose. Like the above first-person narrative, the Web log entry that follows is constructed on a time line, moving from the deeper to the more recent past.

> Megan B. started smoking marijuana and drinking alcohol at the age of thirteen. But when those didn't work for her she decided she needed to step it up a level. So by fourteen she began using cocaine as well as taking prescription drugs including Ritalin, Xanax, and Percocet. There was no need to go to a doctor for prescriptions. Friends got them from their parents' medicine cabinets. Like so many kids, she regarded prescription drugs as "safer" than other drugs. She figured that since people took them legally all the time, she'd be fine with them. By the time she was sixteen, she had graduated to heroin, sniffing it with friends to calm herself and get sleep. The stuff was easy to get and only a few dollars a bag. But then her heroin use started spiraling out of control. She missed curfews. She missed school; she didn't come home nights, saying she was staying at friends' homes. When her parents asked if she was taking drugs, she, of course, lied. For some time they believed her. Then two months before her seventeenth birthday, she died from an overdose. Her parents had missed the warning signs—the erratic behavior, her bouts of depression, restlessness, angry denials—discounting them as teenage rebelliousness. By the time they tried to intervene, to get professional help, Megan was dead.

What makes this narrative so effective is its objective tone, its matter-of-fact chronicling of Megan B.'s sad demise. Nowhere in the passage does the author take on an admonishing or threatening tone; nor does she cite a lot of dry statistics about drugs and young people's deaths. Instead, the author creates a growing sense of inevitability that climaxes in the stark final announcement, "By the time they tried to intervene, to get professional help, Megan was dead." The Internet has hundreds of websites with narratives of the accidental deaths of drug victims. Likewise, there are dedicated sites with stories of deaths due to drunk driving, guns, house poisons, suicide, and other tragedies.

Features to Look for in Narrative Arguments

For a narrative argument to be successful, it should tell a story that clearly dramatizes a controversial issue. It should also meet some of the following basic criteria, which we offer as a checklist to evaluate your own or other writers' narratives.

The writer's narrative illustrates a controversial issue. Like either a position or proposal argument, the narrative should tell a story that dramatizes an experience or series of experiences relevant to a controversial issue.

The narrative is a scene, a series of episodes, or a story that advocates a change of behavior or way of thinking. A narrative is more than just the citation of personal evidence—yours or someone else's—in support of your stand on an issue. It is a running account of events, usually arranged in chronological order, that illustrate someone's experience with aspects of the issue being debated. Even if your audience is aware of the problem and may even be sympathetic, framing your argument as a narrative has the potential to invite the reader to identify personally with the character or characters in the discourse and, as a result, move them to action. A paper proposing stricter laws against drunk drivers, for instance, might be especially persuasive if it is cast as a real-life account of someone who experienced injury in an automobile accident caused by a drunk driver.

The narrative should be credible. Whether your narrative is based on your own personal experience or someone else's, it should have credibility if it is going to win the sympathy of an audience. If because of inaccuracies, contradictions, or unbelievable exaggeration the story strains for validity, your narrative will lose its power to persuade.

The narrative should be representative. No matter how credible, your narrative should be *representative* of the issue. Say, for instance, you were stopped for exceeding the speed limit by 30 miles per hour in a town you passed through infrequently. In your narrative, you describe how the police officer not only reprimanded you but also put you under arrest, escorting you to the police station where you were put in a jail cell overnight. No matter how harrowing that narrative may be, no matter how unpleasant the police reaction was, your case would be weak if you argued that the town's police force was out of control and should be investigated by the district attorney's office. Unless you had other evidence that police overreaction was standard in that town, your narrative would not be symptomatic of a real problem. In contrast, the tragic story of Megan B. whose drug abuse was not dealt with in time is representative of hundreds of young people who annually fall victim to drug overdoses.

The narrative must avoid sentimentality. Opening an argument with a strong narrative has the potential of snagging the readers' attention and sympathy from the start. But you should be careful not to let your appeal become too emotional or sink into melodrama, otherwise your argument will lose sympathy. Choose your words and present facts and details carefully. Avoid words and expressions that are emotionally too loaded, too forceful.

SAMPLE NARRATIVE ARGUMENT

Narratives can have a greater impact on readers than other kinds of arguments because narratives appeal to values and emotions common to most people and, thus, have more persuasive power than cool logic and dry statistics. What follows is an appeal for people to be open-minded about physician-assisted suicide. It's an argument that is fashioned on a narrative and, thus, structured on a time line—and one that is particularly poignant since much of it chronicles the author's grappling with his own terminal medical condition. Jerry Fensterman is the former director of development for Fenway Community Health in Boston, Massachusetts. This article appeared as a guest editorial in the *Boston Globe* on January 31, 2006, a few months before his death.

I See Why Others Choose to Die

Jerry Fensterman

1   The U.S. Supreme Court's recent decision to let stand Oregon's law permitting physician-assisted suicide is sure to fuel an ongoing national debate. Issues of life and death are deeply felt and inspire great passions. It would be wonderful, and unusual, if all those joining the fray would do so with the humility and gravity the matter deserves.

2   I am approaching 50, recently remarried, and the father of a terrific 13-year-old young man. By every measure I enjoy a wonderful life. Or at least I did until April 2004, when I was diagnosed with kidney cancer. Surgery was my only hope to prevent its spread and save my life. The discovery of a new lump in December 2004 after two surgeries signaled that metastasis was underway. My death sentence had been pronounced.

3   Life may be the most intense addiction on earth. From the moment I first heard the words "you have cancer" and again when I was told that it was spreading out of control, I recognized my addiction to life almost at the cellular level. I have tried since then, as I did before, to live life to the fullest. I also committed myself to doing everything within my power to extend my life.

4   Toward that end I am participating in my third clinical trial in a year. I have gained some small benefit from it. I am, however, one of the first people with my cancer to try this drug. Its median benefit seems to be only on the order of three months. So my expectations are modest. The side effects of these drugs are significant, as are the symptoms of the cancer's gallop through my body. All things considered, I believe I have earned my merit badge for "doing all one can in the face of death to stay alive."

5   That the experience has changed me is obvious. I have a few scars, have lost 50 pounds, and my hair is thinner. I rely on oxygen nearly all the time, can no longer perform the job I loved, and have difficulty eating. More profoundly, my universe has contracted. Simply leaving home has become an enormous task, and travel is essentially out of the question. I can no longer run, swim, golf, ski, and play with my son. I haven't yet learned how to set goals or make plans for a future that probably consists of weeks or months, not years. I am also nearing a point where I will not be able to take care of my most basic needs.

6   Mine has been a long, difficult, and certain march to death. Thus, I have had ample time to reflect on my life, get my affairs in order, say everything I want to the people I love, and seek rapprochement with friends I have hurt or lost touch with. The bad news is that my pain and suffering have been drawn out, the rewarding aspects of life have inexorably shrunk, and I have watched my condition place an increasingly great physical and emotional burden on the people closest to me. While they have cared for me with great love and selflessness, I cannot abide how my illness has caused them hardship, in some cases dominating their lives and delaying their healing.

7   Perhaps the biggest and most profound change I have undergone is that my addiction to life has been "cured." I've kicked the habit! I now know how a feeling, loving, rational person could choose death over life, could choose to relieve his suffering as well as that of his loved ones a few months earlier than would happen naturally.

8   I am not a religious person, but I consider myself and believe I have proved throughout my life to be a deeply moral person. Personally I would not now choose physician-assisted suicide if it were available. I do not know if I ever would. Yet now, I understand in a manner that I never could have before why an enlightened society should, with thoughtful safeguards, allow the incurably ill to choose a merciful death.

9   The Supreme Court's ruling will inflame the debate over physician-assisted suicide. Besides adding my voice to this debate, I ask you to carefully search your soul before locking into any position. If you oppose physician-assisted suicide, first try to walk a mile in the shoes of those to whom you would deny this choice. For as surely as I'm now wearing them, they could one day just as easily be on your feet or those of someone you care deeply about.

Analysis of Sample Narrative Argument

Unlike the Megan B. and grizzly bear examples, Fensterman does not begin with a story and conclude with his claim. Instead, he opens with an acknowledgment of the U.S. Supreme Court's ruling to let stand the law permitting physician-assisted suicide. He then follows with seven paragraphs that personalize his coming to terms with his "death sentence." These paragraphs constitute the body of the piece and, like most narratives, the contents are structured on a time line. In this case, the narrative begins in April 2004 when the author was diagnosed with kidney cancer and then relates events occurring in the next year and a half. In his final two paragraphs, he refers back to the controversy, saying that he would not choose physician-assisted suicide at this time and does not know if he ever would. But he has learned through his own experience of terminal illness why the option should be available.

Analyzing the Structure

The Beginning

Paragraph 1 constitutes the beginning of Fensterman's narrative argument—where he names the controversy, which his following narrative dramatizes. Here he specifically cites the U.S. Supreme Court's recent ruling "to let stand Oregon's law permitting physician-assisted suicide." Acknowledging how this will only fuel the ongoing national debate, he asks, because the issue is a matter of life and death, that people enter it "with the humility and gravity the matter deserves," thus anticipating his own personal story.

The Middle

Paragraphs 2 through 7 constitute Fensterman's personal narrative of his "death sentence." He immediately identifies himself as a 50-year-old recently remarried man and a father who "enjoys a wonderful life" and who clearly has a lot to live for. But in April 2004, he was diagnosed with cancer of the kidney. Over the next five paragraphs (3–7), he chronicles the events of the next two years. In December 2004, a new lump was discovered following two surgeries, signaling the cancer had spread. That "death sentence" announcement made Fensterman recognize his "addiction to life almost at the cellular level" (paragraph 3). As he says, since then he has dedicated himself to prolonging his life including participating in another clinical trial. But the benefits were short-lived and the side effects were significant—scars, weight loss, thinning of his hair. Worse, his universe "was contracted." He could no longer work, travel, "run, swim, golf, ski, and play" with his son. In paragraphs 6 and 7, as he approaches death, he says that he is reflecting on his life, getting his affairs in order, and contacting family members and friends. But what pains him the most is how his condition has become "an increasingly great physical and emotional burden on the people" to whom he is closest. And this hardship is what he "cannot abide" (paragraph 6). He concludes that he has become "cured" of his "addiction to life." As a result, he says he now understands "how a feeling, loving, rational person could choose death over life, could choose to relieve his suffering as well as that of his loved ones a few months earlier than would happen naturally" (paragraph 7).

The End

The final two paragraphs (8 and 9) make up the end of Fensterman's piece. Here he returns to the present tense and to his request for open-mindedness. Even after all the anguish he has undergone and the hardship no doubt assumed by his loved ones, Fensterman surprisingly announces that he "would not now choose physician-assisted suicide if it were available." That statement makes even stronger his appeal that "an enlightened society . . . allow the incurably ill to choose a merciful death." At the end of paragraph 9, he shifts to a powerful personal appeal, asking those who might be opposed to physician-assisted suicide to "walk a mile in the shoes of those to whom you would deny this choice." And he concludes with a reminder that he is wearing shoes that could one day "be on your feet or those of someone you care deeply about."

Analyzing the Narrative Features

The writer's narrative dramatizes a controversial issue. In the opening paragraph of Fensterman's piece, he cites the topic he will ultimately be addressing through his narrative argument, namely, the recent U.S. Supreme Court's decision to let stand Oregon's law permitting physician-assisted suicide. But his focus is a plea for open-minded debate, informed by an appreciation of the experience of a person suffering with a terminal illness. He recognizes that the passage of this law will provoke debate about the rightness or wrongness of physician-assisted suicide. But he wants to argue that one should be acutely aware of the feelings and circumstances of patients suffering a terminal illness before denying them the right to end their lives through physician-assisted suicide.

The writer's narration is credible. Fensterman's narrative is highly credible. In paragraph 2, he forthrightly identifies himself and his plight: "I am approaching 50, recently remarried, and the father of a terrific 13-year-old young man. By every measure I enjoy a wonderful life. Or at least I did until April 2004, when I was diagnosed with kidney cancer." He is an ordinary man, leading an ordinary life, and grateful for ordinary things. However, like everyone else's, his life is fragile, and it nearly crashed down around him when he was diagnosed with cancer. This is a situation everyone can identify with and one everyone secretly fears. At the same time, anyone who knows of the ravages of cancer or knows someone who has suffered from it can identify intensely with the piece.

The writer's narrative is representative of the issue. Fensterman's narrative could not be more representative of the issue. His reflection on the various stages of cancer diagnosis and treatment represent what so many people go through. In paragraph 3, he says that he recognizes that "Life may be the most intense addiction on earth. From the moment I first heard the words 'you have cancer' and again when I was told that it was spreading out of control, I recognized my addiction to life almost at the cellular level." He acknowledges the physical toll the disease takes: "I have a few scars, have lost 50 pounds, and my hair is thinner. I rely on oxygen nearly all the time, can no longer perform the tasks I love. . . . Simply leaving home has become an enormous task" (paragraph 5). The specific details reflect what many cancer victims feel. He also acknowledges the burden of his illness on those he loves: "While they have cared for me with great love and selflessness, I cannot abide how my illness has caused them hardship, in some cases dominating their lives and delaying their healing" (paragraph 6). Such a painful sentiment can be widely shared.

The writer's narrative avoids sentimentality. A subject such as imminent death is difficult to discuss without being emotional. Yet Fensterman manages to do just that while avoiding sentimentality. He is straightforward in his description of his own physical and emotional suffering. And in the proclamation that concludes the various stages he has gone through he dispassionately states, "Perhaps the biggest

Checklist for Writing a Narrative Argument

- Does your narrative dramatize a controversial issue?
- Is your narrative credible?
- Is your narrative representative of the issue?
- Does your narrative avoid sentimentality?
- Does your narrative advocate a change of behavior or a way of thinking?

and most profound change I have undergone is that my addiction to life has been 'cured.' I've kicked the habit" (paragraph 7).

The writer's narrative advocates a change of behavior or a way of thinking. Clearly, Fensterman has used the story of his personal struggle with cancer to influence the debate over the appropriateness of physician-assisted suicide. Every aspect of his narrative does that—from the diagnosis of the disease (paragraph 2), to his awareness of the toll cancer treatment is taking on his body and on the family and friends he loves (paragraphs 4, 5, and 6), to his realization that "I now know how a feeling, loving, rational person could choose death over life, could choose to relieve his suffering as well as that of his loved ones a few months earlier than would happen naturally." Although he admits that he personally would not choose physician-assisted suicide, the entire point of his narrative is to illustrate that in the face of terminal suffering a person should have a choice. As he so powerfully concludes, "If you oppose physician-assisted suicide, first try to walk a mile in the shoes of those whom you would deny this choice. For as surely as I'm now wearing them, they could one day just as easily be on your feet or those of someone you care about deeply" (paragraph 9).

EXERCISES

1. Look online or in current issues of a local or national newspaper for essays about controversial issues. Make a list in your journal of the strategies different writers use to begin their arguments. Bring your examples to class and work in a group to share your findings. Photocopy your examples so that each member has a "catalogue" of good introductions to consider.

2. Repeat exercise 1, but this time collect examples of conclusions from argument essays. Your goal here is to compile a catalogue of endings to consult.

3. Construct a formal outline for one of the essays other than "Indian Bones" in this chapter. Compare it with another student's. If there are places where your outlines differ, analyze how your readings are different.

4. Go back to the examples you found for exercise 1. Divide the essays you and the members of your group found into position and proposal arguments.

5. In your journal, respond to the ideas in Amanda Collins's, Sean Flynn's, or Jerry Fensterman's essay. With which of their reasons do you agree? How would you refute any of their reasons? Make a pro/con checklist that lists their reasons and points you might use to debate them.

6. Through the Internet or your library resources, do some reading on either Karpati's or Fensterman's subject to find out how others view the issue. Create a dialogue among the various positions on the issue and explore their points of view to find common or shared concerns or values. With this knowledge, deliberate about how you stand on the issue.

7. If you were to write an argument essay of your own on either subject, how would you begin your essay? Experiment with a few introductions. Next, write a first draft.

8. Write a narrative argument on some debatable issue with which you have had personal experience.

Using Evidence: Thinking Like an Advocate

Because the United States is a democracy, a widespread conviction in our society holds that having opinions is our responsibility as citizens—a conviction supported by our fast-forward multimedia culture. You see opinions expressed on the nightly news every time a reporter sticks a microphone in the face of somebody on the street, or whenever Oprah Winfrey moves into the studio audience. It's the heart of talk radio and television programs. In newspapers and magazines, it comes in the form of "opinion polls" that tally up our positions on all sorts of weighty issues:

"Should the use of marijuana for medical purposes be legalized?"

"Is the economy this year in better shape than it was last year at this time?"

"Do you think that the American judicial system treats people equally whether they are rich or poor?"

"Is the U.S. government doing enough to prevent acts of domestic terrorism?"

"Do men and women have the same opportunities for promotions and raises in the workplace?"

"Should openly gay men and women be allowed to serve in the U.S. military?"

All this on-the-spot opinion-making encourages people to take an immediate stand on an issue, whether or not they have sufficient understanding and information about it. However, holding an opinion on a matter does not necessarily mean that you have investigated the issue or that you have carefully considered the views of others or that you have gathered enough information to support your position. If you want to make successful arguments, you need more than a gut reaction or simple reliance on yourself for the "truth."

This means thinking of yourself as an *advocate*—a prosecutor or defense attorney, if you like. You need a case to present to the jury of your readers, one that convinces them that your interpretation of an issue is plausible. Like an advocate, when you're constructing an argument you look for support to put before your readers: facts, statistics, people's experiences—in a word, *evidence.* The jury judges your argument both on the evidence you bring forth and on your interpretation of that evidence. So, like an advocate, to write successful arguments you need to understand and weigh the value of the *supporting evidence* for your case.

How Much Evidence Is Enough?

Like any advocate, you need to decide *how much* evidence to present to your readers. Your decision will vary from case to case, although with more practice you'll find it easier to make a judgment. Common sense is a good predictor: If the evidence is enough to persuade you, it's probably enough to persuade like-minded readers. Unsympathetic readers may need more proof. The more unexpected or unorthodox your claim, the more evidence you need to convince skeptical readers. It's often as much a case of the *right* evidence as it is the *right amount* of evidence. One fact or statistic, if it touches on your readers' most valued standards and principles, may be enough to swing an argument for a particular group. Here's where outlining (Chapter 5) can help; an outline helps you make sure you present evidence for every assertion you make.

It's easier to gather too much evidence and winnow out the least effective than to have too little and try to expand it. One of our instructors used to call this the "Cecil B. DeMille strategy," after the great Hollywood producer. DeMille's theory was that if audiences were impressed by five dancers, they would be overwhelmed by five hundred—but just to be sure, he'd hire a thousand. That's a good strategy to have when writing arguments; you can always use a sentence such as "Of the 116 explosions in GMC trucks with side-mounted fuel tanks, four cases are most frequently cited" and then go on to discuss those four. You've let your readers know that another 112 are on record so they can weigh this fact when considering the four you examine in particular. You may never need a thousand pieces of evidence—or dancers—in an argument, but there's no harm in thinking big!

Why Arguments Need Supporting Evidence

Evidence is composed of facts and their interpretations. As we said in Chapter 1, facts are pieces of information that can be verified—that is, statistics, examples, testimony, historical details. For instance, it is a fact that SAT verbal scores across the nation have gone up for the last ten years. One interpretation might be that students today are spending more time reading and less time watching television than students in the last decade. Another interpretation might be that secondary schools are putting more emphasis on language skills. A third might be that changes in the test or the prevalence of test-preparation courses has contributed to the higher scores.

In everyday conversation, we make claims without offering supporting evidence: "Poverty is the reason why there is so much crime"; "The president is doing a poor job handling the economy"; "Foreign cars are better than American cars." Although we may have good reasons to back up such statements, we're not often called upon to do so, at least not in casual conversation. In written arguments, however, presenting evidence is critical, and a failure to do so is glaring. Without supporting data and examples, an argument is hollow. It will bore the reader, fail to convince, and collapse under criticism. Moreover, you'll be in danger of making a hasty generalization by drawing a conclusion with too little evidence. Consider the following paragraph:

> Video games are a danger to the mental well-being of children. Some children play
> video games for hours on end, and the result is that their behavior and concentration

are greatly affected. Many of them display bad behavior. Others have difficulty doing other, more important things. Parents with young children should be stricter about what video games their children play and how long they play them.

Chances are this paragraph has not convinced you that video games are a threat to children. The sample lacks the details that might persuade you. For instance, exactly what kind of bad behavior do children display? And what specific video games out of the hundreds on the market are the real culprits? How is concentration actually affected? What "more important things" does the author mean? And how many hours of video consumption need occur before signs of dangerous behavior begin to manifest themselves?

Consider how much sharper and more persuasive the following rewrite is with the addition of specific details, facts, and examples:

> Video games may be fun for children, but they can have detrimental effects on their behavior. They encourage violent behavior. A steady dose of some of the more violent games clearly results in more aggressive behavior. One study by the Department of Psychology at State University has shown that after two hours of "Urban Guerrilla," 60 percent of the 12 boys and 20 percent of the 12 girls tested began to mimic the street-fighting gestures—punching, kicking, karate-chopping each other. The study has also shown that such games negatively affect concentration. Even half an hour after their game playing had lapsed, the boys had difficulty settling down to read or draw. Since my parents restricted my little brother's game playing to weekends, he concentrates when completing his homework and has fewer fights with his best friend.

The statistics from the academic study, as well as the concrete case of the writer's own brother, give readers something substantial to consider. Presenting supporting evidence puts meat on the bones of your argument. (In Chapter 9, we will go into greater depth about how to gather research evidence, particularly from the library and the Internet.)

Forms of Evidence

We hope that when you begin to develop an argument, you utilize debate, dialogue, and deliberation, as we suggested in Chapter 1. As you do this, you need to expand and deepen your understanding of the issue by collecting useful evidence from both sides of the issue. Don't neglect this critical step: Remember, the bulk of your argument is composed of material supporting your claim.

Writers enlist four basic kinds of evidence to support their arguments: personal experience (theirs and others'), outside authorities, factual references and examples, and statistics. We'll examine each separately, but you'll probably want to use combinations of these kinds of evidence when building your arguments in order to convince a wide range of readers.

Personal Experience—Yours and Others'

The power of personal testimony cannot be underestimated. Think of the number of movies that have failed at the box office in spite of huge and expensive ad campaigns simply because word of mouth trashed it. Or, conversely, think of the number of times you've read a book on the recommendation of friends—or taken a certain course or shopped at a particular store. You might have chosen the college you're attending based on the recommendation of someone you know. Many people find the word-of-mouth judgments that make up personal testimony the most persuasive kind of evidence.

In written arguments, the personal testimony of other people is used to affirm facts and support your claim. Essentially, their experiences provide you with eyewitness accounts of events that are not available to you. Such accounts may prove crucial in winning over an audience. Suppose you are writing about the rising abuse of alcohol among college students. In addition to statistics and hard facts, your argument can gain strength from quoting the experience of a first-year student who nearly died one night from alcohol poisoning. Or, in an essay decrying discrimination against minorities in hiring, consider the authenticity provided by an interview of neighborhood residents who felt they were passed over for a job because of race or ethnic identity.

Your own eyewitness testimony can be a powerful tool of persuasion. Suppose, for example, that you are writing a paper in which you argue that the big teaching hospital in the city provides far better care and has a lower death rate than the small rural hospital in your town. The hard facts and statistics on the quality of care and comparative mortality rates you provide will certainly have a stark persuasiveness. But consider the dramatic impact on those figures were you to recount how your own trip to the rural emergency room nearly cost you your life because of understaffing or the lack of critical but expensive diagnostic equipment.

Personal observation is useful and valuable in arguments. However, you should be careful not to draw hasty generalizations from such testimony. The fact that you and three of your friends are staunchly in favor of replacing letter grades with a pass/fail system does not support the claim that the entire student body at your school is in favor of the conversion. You need a much greater sample. Likewise, the dislike most people in your class feel for a certain professor does not justify the claim that the university tenure system should be abolished. On such complex issues, you need more than personal testimony to make a case.

You also have to remember the "multiple-perspective" rule. As any police officer can tell you, there are as many versions of the "truth" of an incident as there are people who saw it. The people involved in a car accident see it one way (or more), yet witnesses in a car heading in the other direction may interpret events differently, as will people in an apartment six stories above the street on which the accident took place. Your job is to sort out the different testimonies and make sense of them. Personal experience—yours and that of people you know—is valuable. However, on major issues you need statistics and data, as well as the evidence provided by outside authorities. But before we turn to outside authorities here is an example of a position argument based on personal experience.

This position argument, based on personal experience, is written by Kari Peterson, an English major at the University of Hawaii in Honolulu. Here she argues for healthcare reform, using her own personal experience to make a convincing case for needed changes in coverage so that people of student age, like her, can get proper care without going into stifling debt.

Peterson 1

Kari Peterson
Professor Larson
English 101
1 December 2009

The Statistics Speak: A Real Person's
Argument for Universal Healthcare

The room's walls are antiseptic white. Everything is white—the cold tiles, the thin sheets, the drawn blinds on the only window in the small space. It's 2:35 in the morning or so the clock says. Time here feels fluid and neverending. My left arm throbs. No, it screams at me, echoing from the bicep through the shoulder and deep into my chest cavity. The catheter runs all the way to my heart like some strange alien. It hurts so badly that I wish it would just rip itself out in spectacular fashion as in movies. But this is a man-made alien, pumping me full of lifesaving antibiotics. These drugs have cruel tendencies also, making my stomach do repetitious back flips and my joints ache. I press the call button and beg for painkillers.

But the night nurse tells me she couldn't reach the physician. Later she asks if I know whether or not the morphine will be covered by my insurance carrier. I am ready to sell my soul at this point for relief. What's a few hundred dollars? The nurse asks, "Is Tylenol okay?" I try not to yell and tell her calmly no.

I am only twenty-two years old. I should be looking to the future, not prophesying its imminent end. That's hard to do when you're in a place where people so often go to die. This will be my reality for the next fourteen or more days. I may repeat it several times a year. Ironically, equally difficult is dealing with a hospitalization's aftermath of bureaucratic hassles and with a healthcare system unable or unwilling to offer the care I need.

I have Cystic Fibrosis. In the simplest of terms it is a congenital disease marked by recurring respiratory infection, pancreatic difficulties, a tendency towards the development of sinusitis and diabetes, and premature death. Unfortunately my condition is shared by 30,000 other Americans—most of whom are children and young adults because most CF patients do not survive into middle age. While I will always struggle with this disease, the healthcare system as it exists now is not sufficient or beneficial to me.

The United States is the only Western industrialized nation that has not implemented a universal healthcare system of some kind. On a per capita basis, United States citizens pay more than anyone else for healthcare. In terms of quality, the US is globally ranked an appalling 23rd in infant mortality and for overall healthcare 37th, according to the World Health Organization. So why is our healthcare so expensive and yet so abysmal in relative quality? Privatized insurance is one of the major culprits.

6   I currently rely on private insurance for my medical coverage under my parents' carrier as their dependent. I am able to do so as long as I maintain a full-time student status or until I turn 25. My 25th birthday present will be the sudden anxiety of potentially losing my health insurance. I will be able to attain insurance if I am hired by a company that offers benefits and if I survive the usual 90-day probationary period that most employers implement. Alternatively, I may also purchase private insurance. My circumstance is mired in caveats and catch 22s. Most 90-day probationary periods do not allow for sick leave, and I am likely to become ill in that 3-month window. I also may not be able to purchase private insurance because many providers have "pre-existing condition clauses" in their policies. These clauses are essentially a way of eliminating sick people from eating into company profits. Insurance carriers make more money if they don't have to render services and even more if they can jack up premiums simultaneously. Without health insurance, my medical costs are thousands of dollars per month even when I am "healthy." Every E.R. trip is a couple of thousand more, and hospital admissions can easily exceed twenty thousand when everything is totaled up. I would like for my parents to be able to keep our home.

7   Without insurance or an executive's income, I am left with one final option at my disposal. Assuming my health is poor enough to qualify, I can go on disability. It probably seems like such an obvious solution. From my vantage point, however, it looks like a bandage proposed as a remedy for a gunshot wound. To be eligible for disability, I would no longer be able to attend university or earn an annual income that exceeds $12,000 a year. My medications would be covered by Medicare, except for the two most critical for stabilizing my condition. Coincidentally, these are the two most expensive medications I take. Lastly there are emotional ramifications. No one wants to be labeled by the thing they hate most. No one wants to forget their life's ambitions. No one wants to be thought of as useless or worse. It's sad, but the prevailing attitude in America seems to be that somehow sick people are secondary citizens often deserving of their sad conditions.

8   The universal healthcare bill being proposed in the fall of 2009 would establish insurance legislation that prohibits "cherry picking"–i.e., the pre-existing condition clauses–as well as offer a public option to compete with the

Peterson 3

private sector. Universal healthcare does not mean that people would have to give up their current care if they are satisfied with it. In many ways, the bill functions as a simple means of breaking up the insurance monopoly. To compete with the government, insurance companies would have to lower premiums or simply offer high quality care. It will not put them out of business.

9   Finally, the ideology that is used as an arsenal against a universal healthcare system is so unequivocally un-American it must be addressed. The preamble to the United States Constitution states, "We the People of the United States, in Order to form a more perfect Union, establish Justice, insure domestic Tranquility, provide for the common defense, promote the general Welfare, and secure the Blessings of Liberty to ourselves and our Posterity."

10   Universal healthcare is not a handout to the undeserving. It is not unpatriotic. It is not unprecedented by the founding principles this nation holds true. It is, however, a matter of leveling the playing field and offering all persons equal opportunity to make the most of their destinies. It doesn't get any more American than that.

Peterson 4

Works Cited

"The World Health Organization's ranking of the world's health systems." 2007. Web. 2 Nov. 2009. <Theodora.http//www.geographic.org>

Outside Authorities

Think of the number of times you've heard statements such as these:

"Scientists have found that . . ."

"Scholars inform us that . . ."

"According to his biographer, President Lincoln decided that . . ."

What these statements have in common is the appeal to outside authorities—people recognized as experts in a given field, people who can speak knowledgeably about a subject. Because authoritative opinions are such powerful tools of persuasion, you hear them all the time in advertisements. Automobile manufacturers quote the opinions of professional race car drivers; the makers of toothpaste cite dentists' claims; famous basketball players push brand-name sneakers all the time. Similarly, a good trial lawyer will almost always rely on forensic experts or other such authorities to help sway a jury.

Outside authorities can provide convincing evidence to support your ideas. However, there are times when expert opinion can be used inappropriately. This faulty use of authority can undermine the effectiveness of your argument. For the most part, experts usually try to be objective and fair-minded when asked for opinions. But, an expert with a vested interest in an issue might slant the testimony in his or her favor. The dentist who has just purchased a huge number of shares in a new toothpaste company would not be an unbiased expert. You wouldn't turn for an unbiased opinion on lung cancer to scientists working for tobacco companies, or ask an employee facing the loss of his or her job to comment on the advisability of layoffs. When you cite authorities, you should be careful to note any possibility of bias so your readers can fairly weigh the contributions. (This is often done through *attribution*; see Chapter 9.) Knowing that Professor Brown's research will benefit from construction of the super-collider doesn't make her enthusiasm for its other potential benefits less credible, but it does help your readers see her contributions to your argument in their proper context.

You should also check the credentials of those experts you are citing as evidence. Certainly claims supported by the research of reliable authorities in the field can add to the validity of your argument. But research is often debated, and evidence often disputed. So you should evaluate the credentials of the expert or experts who conducted the studies—what organizations, institutions, and universities they are affiliated with; their educational background; the books and/or journals where they may have published their results. It would also be wise to familiarize yourself with the actual research to be certain that it looks like valid and convincing support for your argument.

Another faulty use of authority is the use of an expert to provide evidence in a subject area in which he or she possesses no expertise. If you are going to cite authorities, you must make sure that they are competent; they should have expertise in their fields. You wouldn't turn to a professional beekeeper for opinions on laser surgery any more than you would quote a civil engineer on macroeconomic theory. And yet, just that is done all the time in advertising. Although it makes better sense to ask a veterinarian for a professional opinion about what to feed your pet, advertisers hire known actors to push dog food (as well as yogurt and skin cream). Of course, in advertising, celebrity sells. But that's not the case in most written arguments. It would not impress a critical reader to cite Tom Cruise's views on the use of fetal tissue or the greenhouse effect. Again, think about the profile of your audience. Whose expertise would they respect on your topic? Those are the experts to cite.

Factual References and Examples

Facts do as much to inform as they do to persuade, as we mentioned in Chapter 1. If somebody wants to sell you something, they'll pour on the details. For instance, ask the used car salesperson about that black 2008 Ford Explorer in the lot and he or she will hold forth about what a "creampuff" it is: only 18,400 original miles, mint condition, five-speed transmission with overdrive, all-black leather interior, and loaded—AC, power brakes, cruise control, CD player, premium sound system, captain's chair, and so on. Or listen to how the cereal manufacturers inform you that their toasted Os now contain "all-natural oat bran, which has been found to prevent cancer."

Information is not always neutral. The very selection process implies intent. By offering specific facts or examples about your claim, you can make a persuasive argument.

The strategy in using facts and examples is to get readers so absorbed in the information that they nearly forget they are being persuaded to buy or do something. So common is this strategy in television ads that some have been given the name "infomercials"—ads that give the impression of being a documentary on the benefits of a product. For instance, you might be familiar with the margarine commercial narrated by a man who announces that at 33 years of age he had a heart attack. He then recounts the advice of his doctor for avoiding coronary disease, beginning with the need for exercise and climaxing with the warning about cutting down on cholesterol. Not until the very end of the ad does the narrator inform us that, taking advantage of his second chance, the speaker has switched to a particular brand of margarine, which, of course, is cholesterol free.

In less blatant form, this "informational" strategy can be found in newspaper columns and editorials, where authors give the impression that they are simply presenting the facts surrounding particular issues when in reality they may be attempting to persuade readers to see things their way. For instance, suppose in an apparently objective commentary a writer discusses how history is replete with people wrongfully executed for first-degree murder. Throughout the piece, the author cites several specific cases in which it was learned too late that the defendant had been framed or that the real killer had confessed. On the surface, the piece may appear to be simply presenting historical facts, but the more subtle intention may be to convince people that capital punishment is morally wrong. The old tagline from *Dragnet*, "Just the facts, ma'am," isn't quite the whole picture. How those facts are used is also part of their persuasive impact.

Often facts and examples are used to establish cause-and-effect relationships. It's very important, when both writing and reading arguments, to test the links the facts forge. While one event may indeed follow another, you can't automatically assume a causal relationship. This can result in a logical fallacy, in this case post hoc, ergo propter hoc. For instance, it may rain the day after every launch of the space shuttle, but does that prove that shuttle launches affect the weather in Florida? Similarly, we are all familiar with politicians who claim credit for improvements in the economy that have little to do with the legislation they have proposed. They hope to gain votes by having the public believe that there is a direct causal relationship between their actions and the economic improvement. Often this strategy backfires when opponents point out the lack of any actual connection.

Sometimes even experts disagree; one might see the rise in prostate cancer rates for vasectomy patients as reason to abolish the surgery; another might point to other contributing causes (diet, lack of exercise, hormonal imbalance). If you don't have the expertise to determine which of the conflicting experts is correct, you'll probably decide based on the *weight of the evidence*—whichever side has the most people or the most plausible reasons supporting it. This, in fact, is how most juries decide cases.

Statistics
People are impressed by numbers. Saying that 77 percent of the student body at your school supports a woman's right to choose is far more persuasive than saying that a lot of people on campus are pro-choice. **Statistics** have a special no-nonsense authority.

Batting averages, medical statistics, polling results (election and otherwise), economic indicators, the stock market index, unemployment figures, scientific ratings, FBI statistics, percentages, demographic data—they all are reported in numbers. If they're accurate, statistics are difficult to argue against, though a skillful manipulator can use them to mislead.

The demand for statistics has made market research a huge business in America. During an election year, weekly and daily results on voters' opinions of candidates are released from various news organizations and TV networks, as well as independent polling companies such as the Harris and Gallup organizations. Most of the brand-name products you buy, the TV shows and movies you watch, or the CDs you listen to were made available after somebody did test studies on sample populations to determine the potential success of these items. Those same statistics are then used in promotional ads. Think of the number of times you've heard claims such as these:

"Nine out of ten doctors recommend Zappo aspirin over any other brand."

"Our new Speed King copier turns out 24 percent more copies per minute."

"Sixty-eight percent of those polled approve of women in military combat roles."

Of course, these claims bear further examination. If you polled only ten doctors, nine of whom recommended Zappo, that's not a big enough sample to imply that 90 percent of *all* doctors do. To avoid drawing a hasty generalization from too small a sample, avoid using sweeping words such as *all, always, never,* or *none.* Either be straightforward about the statistics supporting your claim or limit your claim with qualifiers such as *some, many, often,* or *few.* As Mark Twain once observed, "There are lies, damned lies, and statistics."

Numbers don't lie, but they can be manipulated. Sometimes, to sway an audience, claim makers will cite figures that are inaccurate or dated, or they will intentionally misuse accurate figures to make a case. If, for instance, somebody claims that 139 students and professors protested the invitation of a certain controversial guest to your campus, it would be a distortion of the truth not to mention that another 1,500 attended the talk and gave the speaker a standing ovation. Providing only those numbers or statistics that support the writer's claim and ignoring or concealing figures that might indicate otherwise is one way of stacking the deck. While this practice might deceive—at least temporarily—an uninformed audience, the writer risks damaging his or her credibility once the true figures are revealed.

Be on guard for the misleading use of statistics, a technique used all too frequently in advertising. The manufacturer that claims its flaked corn cereal is 100 percent cholesterol free misleads the public because no breakfast cereal of any brand contains cholesterol (which is found only in animal fats). French fries prepared in pure vegetable oil are also cholesterol free, but that doesn't mean that they're the best food for your health. Manufacturers that use terms like *cholesterol-free, light,* and *low fat* are trying to get you to buy their products without really revealing the basis for their nutritional claims. Although it's tempting to use such crowd-pleasing statistics, it's a good idea to avoid them in your own arguments because they are deceptive. If your readers discover your deception, your chances of persuading them to accept your position or proposal become unlikely.

Different Interpretations of Evidence

As we already said, evidence consists of solid facts, scientific studies and data, historical analysis, statistics, quotations from accepted authorities, and pertinent examples, as well as personal narratives that your audience will find relevant and compelling.

But not all evidence is of equal worth or value; not all evidence makes an argument valid. And not all scientific facts have a single interpretation. This is why different people can look at the same scientific data and have completely different interpretations. Although they may not argue over facts or the data, they will strenuously debate the interpretations of facts. In fact, some of the most hotly contested issues in society and politics revolve around the interpretation of the evidence. And the reason that people disagree about interpretation is that people hold fundamental differences in underlying beliefs, values, and assumptions.

Different Definitions

People will disagree based on different definitions of terms and concepts. If your parents say to be home at a "reasonable" hour, does that mean 11 P.M. or 2 A.M.? What might be deemed "reasonable" to your parents may not be the same to you, especially if you showed up at 3 A.M. But if they specified to be home no later than 1 A.M., then you have precision, which means a 3 A.M. arrival would not be "reasonable."

The point is that arguments over the definition of a subjective term such as "reasonable" will never resolve the argument. The same is true when critics declare that this book or movie is the "best of the year." There will always be dissenters, even people who may think the selection or award winner was far worse than its competition. Criteria differ from person to person. For instance, what is "violent" to a 16-year-old video game fan is not the same as what is violent to an acknowledged pacifist. What is pornography to some is erotic art to others. In fact, for decades the U.S. Supreme Court could not come up with a clear definition of *pornography* in order to determine laws and regulations and eventually gave up, deciding that any regulation of such—with the exception of child pornography, which is prohibited under law—was an infringement on rights of free speech. Such avoidance by the courts essentially freed itself from the decades-long trap of word play.

The point is that language is relative; it is difficult for people to agree completely on the definition of any complex word. And adding to their complexity are the different connotations of words—connotations that signal different emotional reactions in an audience. Consider such charged words as "evil," "racist," "liberal," "Nazi," "religious extremist," even "terrorist." Often arguments are made in which such terms are employed beyond their dictionary definitions for the purpose of arousing strong reactions. With the proper audience, the effect can be powerful.

Different Interpretations of Tradition and Past Authority

It can be said that evidence sometimes lies in the eyes of the beholder. That is, what is evidence to some people may not be evidence to others. The reason is that writers often appeal to authority and traditions that for them have special weight. This is especially evident in arguments based on moral values and beliefs, such as those regarding the death penalty, euthanasia, abortion, same-sex marriages, immigration policies, and animal rights. Such appeals may be persuasive to those who believe in the authority of tradition, but not persuasive to others who don't share in those beliefs.

Sometimes people will claim that something is right because it has always been practiced. Consider, for instance, the following statements:

"When we were kids, we walked to school. So, you're not taking the car."

"Women have always taken their husband's last name in marriage, so why should we change now?"

"The ancient Greeks and Romans practiced euthanasia in order to end a patient's unnecessary suffering, so why shouldn't we?"

Each of these claims is a familiar appeal to tradition. Of course, such appeals raise the question that because something is an old practice does not necessarily mean it should be continued today. The logical fallacy is that behavior is never necessarily right simply because it has always been done.

Tradition is often used as evidence of a higher authority. But even such a fixed piece of evidence can actually be interpreted in different ways by different audiences as different sets of beliefs and assumptions may prevail. For instance, the dominant argument against gun control is the Second Amendment of the U.S. Constitution guarantee: "A well regulated militia, being necessary to the security of a free state, the right of the people to keep and bear arms, shall not be infringed." For the National Rifle Association and others, those words represent the highest legal authority in preserving and protecting the rights of law-abiding citizens to have guns in our American democracy. If your audience is highly traditional and interprets the Second Amendment straightforwardly, this is an argument to which they would be open. But another audience might reject that strict interpretation. That audience might not question people's right to bear arms but the interpretation of that amendment regarding the regulation of guns. While many people would agree that hunters, sportspeople, and collectors have the right to own guns, nearly everybody would argue that the Second Amendment does not give individuals the unlimited right to own any weapons they like. And that is where the debates become heated—on the question of just how much governmental restriction is too much. When tackling controversial issues, you must be aware of your audience's attitude toward your evidence.

Similarly, the First Amendment is often enlisted as the highest authority regarding an individual's right to free speech in America. But like gun control, that right is limited by the court's interpretation. In the eyes of the law, you cannot intentionally publish lies about a public figure, claiming, for instance, that a local politician sells illegal drugs on the side. Such a claim is libelous and an abridgment of your free-speech rights—and, of course, grounds for a lawsuit. Nor, in the eyes of the law, can you get away with crying "Fire!" in a crowded theater if there is no fire, because the ensuing panic could lead to injury.

While there are some restraints on the rights to free speech, the powerful First Amendment has been invoked to protect flag burning, nude dancing, Internet pornography, Nazi party parades, and Ku Klux Klan rants, to varying degrees of success. And although such claims may seem to undermine the guarantee by protecting dubious and malicious intentions, restriction of the principle could give way to even greater dangers—the tyrannical abuse by government. In several other free and democratic societies, censorship laws empower governments legally to prohibit certain kinds of speech that are protected by the U.S. Constitution.

Religious tradition is another powerful authority that is invoked in arguments about major social issues. References to Biblical or Koranic prohibitions are often presented as evidence against arguments in favor of certain public practices. For instance, consider same-sex marriages. Because of scriptural laws against homosexuality, many people argue that gay and lesbian couples should not be allowed to wed under the eyes of the law. The same is true regarding capital punishment. The Sixth Commandment from the Old Testament of the Bible says, "Thou shall not kill." For years, people opposed to legalized abortion have employed such "evidence." The same Sixth Commandment has also been referenced by others in opposition to capital punishment and euthanasia. But the problem with strict appeal to such authority for evidence is that, like tradition, interpretation of religious taboos can be ambiguous and contradictory. For instance, the Old Testament of the Bible also argues, "An eye for an eye, and a tooth for a tooth"—thus, "evidence" that can be enlisted in an argument in favor of the death penalty. Once again, familiarity with your audience should help you determine just the kind of authority and tradition you enlist as evidence. If, for instance, you knew you were addressing religiously conservative readers, summoning the moral import of the scriptures could be very persuasive on some of these public issues.

Different Interpretations of Scientific Data

As we said earlier, scientific data is a persuasive form of evidence. In fact, in most arguments scientific evidence is universally perceived as valid and acceptable. But not everybody interprets scientific evidence in the same way, nor do they draw the same conclusions. For example, one of the most talked about issues of our times is global warming. Over the last several decades, scientific data point to rising average temperatures of the earth's atmosphere and oceans. The data also cite the rise in carbon dioxide in the atmosphere, one of the components of the so-called "greenhouse gas." These are the hard facts. Many scientists have looked at the data and determined that there is a direct relationship—namely, that the rise in CO_2 has caused the rise in oceanic and atmospheric temperatures; they blame the effect on human consumption of fossil fuels. These scientists warn that unless something drastic is done, the world's weather will change for the worse for many populated areas, while polar caps will continue to melt and raise sea levels to catastrophic proportions, leading to global coastal flooding.

However, not everybody draws the same conclusion from the data. Not everybody blames the global warming phenomenon on human activity. Nor do they warn of catastrophic climate changes and serious effects on life. Nor do they offer the same political responses. In the following article, scientist Siegfried Frederick Singer responds to the alarms of many, including former vice president Al Gore, narrator of the Academy Award-winning movie, *An Inconvenient Truth*, and author of the book of the same title, and winner of the 2008 Nobel Peace Prize for his work on behalf of the environment.

The Great Global Warming Swindle

S. Fred Singer

Singer, an atmospheric physicist, is a research fellow at the Independent Institute, is Professor Emeritus of Environmental Sciences at the University of Virginia, and is a former founding director of the U.S. Weather Satellite Service. He is author of *Hot Talk, Cold Science: Global Warming's Unfinished Debate* (The Independent Institute, 1997). This article appeared on May 22, 2007, in the *San Francisco Examiner.*

1   Al Gore's *An Inconvenient Truth* has met its match: a devastating documentary recently shown on British television, which has now been viewed by millions of people on the Internet. Despite its flamboyant title, *The Great Global Warming Swindle* is based on sound science and interviews with real climate scientists, including me. *An Inconvenient Truth*, on the other hand, is mostly an emotional presentation from a single politician.

2   The scientific arguments presented in *The Great Global Warming Swindle* can be stated quite briefly:

3   1. There is *no* proof that the current warming is caused by the rise of greenhouse gases from human activity. Ice core records from the past 650,000 years show that temperature increases have *preceded—not resulted from*—increases in CO_2 by hundreds of years, suggesting that the warming of the oceans is an important *source* of the rise in atmospheric CO_2. As the dominant greenhouse gas, water vapor is far, far more important than CO_2. Dire predictions of future warming are based almost entirely on computer climate models, yet these models do not accurately understand the role of water vapor—and, in any case, water vapor is not within our control. Plus, computer models cannot account for the observed cooling of much of the past century (1940–75), nor for the observed *patterns* of warming—what we call the "fingerprints." For example, the Antarctic is cooling while models predict warming. And where the models call for the middle atmosphere to warm faster than the surface, the observations show the exact opposite.

4   The best evidence supporting natural causes of temperature fluctuations are the changes in cloudiness, which correspond strongly with regular variations in solar activity. The current warming is likely part of a natural cycle of climate warming and cooling that's been traced back almost a million years. It accounts for the Medieval Warm Period around 1100 A.D., when the Vikings settled Greenland and grew crops, and the Little Ice Age, from about 1400 to 1850 A.D., which brought severe winters and cold summers to Europe, with failed harvests, starvation, disease, and general misery. Attempts have been made to claim that the current warming is "unusual" using spurious analysis of tree rings and other proxy data. Advocates have tried to deny the existence of these historic climate swings and claim that the current warming is "unusual" by using spurious analysis of tree rings and other proxy data, resulting in the famous "hockey–stick" temperature graph. The hockey-stick graph has now been thoroughly discredited.

5 2. If the cause of warming is mostly natural, then there is little we can do about it. We cannot control the inconstant sun, the likely origin of most climate variability. None of the schemes for greenhouse gas reduction currently bandied about will do any good; they are all irrelevant, useless, and wildly expensive:

- Control of CO_2 emissions, whether by rationing or elaborate cap-and-trade schemes
- Uneconomic "alternative" energy, such as ethanol and the impractical "hydrogen economy"
- Massive installations of wind turbines and solar collectors
- Proposed projects for the sequestration of CO_2 from smokestacks or even from the atmosphere

6 Ironically, *even if* CO_2 were responsible for the observed warming trend, all these schemes would be ineffective—unless we could persuade every nation, including China, to cut fuel use by 80 percent!

7 3. Finally, no one can show that a warmer climate would produce negative impacts overall. The much-feared rise in sea levels does not seem to depend on short-term temperature changes, as the rate of sea-level increases has been steady since the last ice age, 10,000 years ago. In fact, many economists argue that the opposite is more likely—that warming produces a net benefit, that it increases incomes and standards of living. Why do we assume that the present climate is the optimum? Surely, the chance of this must be vanishingly small, and the economic history of past climate warmings bear this out.

8 But the main message of *The Great Global Warming Swindle* is much broader. Why should we devote our scarce resources to what is essentially a non-problem, and ignore the real problems the world faces: hunger, disease, denial of human rights—not to mention the threats of terrorism and nuclear wars? And are we really prepared to deal with natural disasters; pandemics that can wipe out most of the human race, or even the impact of an asteroid, such as the one that wiped out the dinosaurs? Yet politicians and the elites throughout much of the world prefer to squander our limited resources to fashionable issues, rather than concentrate on real problems. Just consider the scary predictions emanating from supposedly responsible world figures: the chief scientist of Great Britain tells us that unless we insulate our houses and use more efficient light bulbs, the Antarctic will be the only habitable continent by 2100, with a few surviving breeding couples propagating the human race. Seriously!

9 I imagine that in the not-too-distant future all the hype will have died down, particularly if the climate should decide to cool—as it did during much of the past century; we should take note here that it has not warmed since 1998. Future generations will look back on the current madness and wonder what it was all about. They will have movies like *An Inconvenient Truth* and documentaries like *The Great Global Warming Swindle* to remind them.

Having read the Singer piece, you can see that the effectiveness of *The Great Global Warming Swindle* rests entirely on a challenge to the validity of the evidence used by those who claim that global warming is caused by greenhouse gases, or emissions due to the burning of fossil fuels. First, Singer discredits these arguments in a general sense, pointing out that they are based on emotion and fear, not on sound science. He then breaks his argument into three parts. In the first, Singer points out that 650,000 years of evidence point to the fact that temperature increases have preceded— not resulted from—increases in CO_2 by hundreds of years. He says scientific evidence shows that the warming of oceans accounts for the rise in atmospheric CO_2. Singer also questions the validity of computer models, the cornerstone of the evidence offered by the global-warming contingent. He points out that computer models do not take into account the role of warming oceans and their impact on water vapor. He notes the role of solar activity and explains how it accounts for the "Medieval Warm Period" around 1100 A.D. as well as the "Little Ice Age" beginning three hundred years later.

In his second argument, he points out that since global warming is natural, little can be done about it. Arguments to develop alternative fuels are expensive and a large drain on the economy. Finally, he says that the fight against global warming diverts resources that should be used to fight bigger issues such as terrorism, nuclear threats, disease, hunger, and human rights.

Regardless of your own stand on the global warming issue, Singer's essay is an effective example of how evidence is clearly and instructively presented. Refer back to it when you need a model for your own presentation of evidence.

Some Tips About Supporting Evidence

Because, as argument writers, you'll be using evidence on a routine basis, it will help you to develop a systematic approach to testing the evidence you want to use. Here are some questions to ask yourself about the evidence you enlist in an argument.

Do You Have a Sufficient Number of Examples to Support Your Claim?

You don't want to jump to conclusions based on too little evidence. Suppose you want to make the case that electric cars would be better for the environment than motor vehicles. If all you offer as evidence is the fact that electric vehicles don't pollute the air, your argument would be somewhat thin. Your argument would be much more convincing if you offered the following evidence: that in addition to zero emission at

Preview: To Evaluate Supporting Evidence, Ask ...

- Is the evidence sufficient?
- Is the evidence detailed enough?
- Is the evidence relevant?
- Does the evidence fit the claim?
- Is the evidence up-to-date and verifiable?
- Is the evidence appropriate for the audience?
- Is the evidence biased?
- Is the evidence balanced and fairly presented?

the tailpipe—which is good for the atmosphere—electric cars do not use engine fluids or internal combustion parts, all of which constitute wastes that contaminate our landfills and water supplies. Furthermore, because electric vehicles don't use gasoline or oil, the hazards associated with storage of such fluids are eliminated.

Likewise, you should avoid making hasty generalizations based on your own experience as evidence. For instance, if your Acme Airlines flight to Chattanooga was delayed last week, you shouldn't conclude that Acme Airlines always leaves late. However, were you to consult airline industry records to demonstrate that over the last six months 47 percent of the frequent flyers interviewed complained that Acme flights left late, you would have a persuasive case.

Is Your Evidence Detailed Enough?

The more specific the details, the more persuasive your argument. Instead of generalizations, cite figures, dates, and facts; instead of paraphrases, offer quotations from experts. Remember that your readers are subconsciously saying, "Show me! Prove it!" If you want to tell people how to bake bread, you wouldn't write, "Mix some flour with some yeast and water"; you'd say, "Dissolve one packet of yeast in 1 cup of warm water and let it sit for ten minutes. Then slowly mix in 3 cups of sifted whole wheat flour." Or, as in our electric car example above, instead of simply asserting that there would be none of the fluid or solid wastes associated with internal combustion vehicles, specify that in electric vehicles there would be no motor oil, engine coolants, transmission fluid or filters, spark plugs, ignition wires, and gaskets to end up in landfills. What your readers want are specifics—and that's what you should give them.

Is Your Evidence Relevant to the Claim You Make or Conclusion You Reach?

Select evidence based on how well it supports the point you are arguing, not on how interesting, novel, or humorous it is or how hard you had to work to find it. Recall that using evidence that is unrelated or irrelevant is a logical fallacy called a non sequitur. For instance, if you are arguing about whether John Lennon was the most influential songwriter in rock-and-roll history, you wouldn't mention that he had two sons or that he owned dairy cattle; those are facts, but they have nothing to do with the influence of his lyrics. Historian Barbara Tuchman relates that in writing *The Guns of August,* she discovered that the Kaiser bought his wife the same birthday present every year: 12 hats of his choosing, which he required her to wear. Tuchman tried to use this detail in Chapter 1, then in Chapter 2, and so on, but was finally obligated to relegate the detail to a stack of notecards marked "Unused." It just didn't fit, even though for her it summarized his stubborn selfishness. (She did work it into a later essay, which is why we know about it.) Learn her lesson: Irrelevant evidence distracts an audience and weakens an argument's persuasive power.

Does Your Conclusion (or Claim) Exceed the Evidence?

Don't make generalizations about entire groups when your evidence points to select members. Baseball may be the national pastime, but it would be unwise to claim that *all* Americans love baseball. Experience tells you that some Americans prefer football or basketball, while others don't like any sports. Claims that are out of proportion to the evidence can result in a fallacy called the **bandwagon appeal.** The bandwagon appeal suggests to the audience that they should agree with the writer because everyone else does, rather than because the writer has supplied compelling evidence to support the reasons and claim. This is a favorite strategy of advertisers, who work to convince us that we should buy a certain product because everyone else is doing so. While this strategy is in itself fallacious, these salespeople are often unable to produce adequate evidence to support their sweeping claims of nationwide popularity for their product.

Is Your Evidence Up-to-Date and Verifiable?

You want to be sure that the evidence you enlist isn't so dated or vague that it fails to support your claim. For instance, figures demonstrating an increase in the rate of teen pregnancy will not persuade your audience if the numbers are ten years old. Similarly, it wouldn't be accurate to say that Candidate Nakamura fails to support the American worker because 15 years ago he purchased a foreign car. His recent and current actions are far more relevant.

When you're citing evidence, your readers will expect you to be specific enough for them to verify what you say. A writer supporting animal rights may cite the example of rabbits whose eyes were burned by pharmacological testing, but such tests have been outlawed in the United States for many years. Another writer may point to medical research that appears to abuse its human subjects, but not name the researchers, the place where the testing took place, or the year in which it occurred. The readers have no way of verifying the claim and may become suspicious of the entire argument because the factual claims are so difficult to confirm.

Is Your Evidence Appropriate for Your Audience?

As discussed in Chapter 3, before you write, it is important to spend some time identifying the audience you will address in your argument. Knowing your audience helps you determine the slant of your argument as well as your language and voice. Likewise, it will influence the evidence you choose to present, the sources of information you use, and the kind of authorities or experts in the field you cite to support your point of view. And that evidence could help make the difference between a convincing argument and one that fails.

Imagine that you are writing an argument against the use of steroids by college students. If you are writing a paper for your biology professor and are discussing the damaging effect of steroids on the body, you would use highly technical evidence—evidence most likely from medical journals aimed at scientists and medical professionals or from your biology textbook. If, however, you are writing an article for your college newspaper, your audience would be your peers, young adults both male and female who may be experimenting or tempted to experiment with steroids. Your focus might be on issues of peer pressure to look good or to succeed in athletics. Therefore the evidence you select might include quotations from known health professionals published in psychology journals or specialized websites, or from newspaper articles addressing the impact of steroids on one's mental and emotional health. Such evidence would not be highly technical.

Let's take another example. Assume that you decided to write a paper arguing that healthier food should be served in your student cafeteria. If you were addressing your peers, the evidence you cite might come from general publications devoted to nutrition or you might quote one of the many health and diet gurus published widely today. Your evidence would be geared to convince your peers that a healthier diet would lead to healthier and trimmer bodies and possibly better frames of mind. In contrast, if your goal was to convince the university's trustees, your argument would focus on the obligation of the university to provide a healthy diet. You might argue that doing so not only enhances the well-being of the student body but also the reputation of the university. And this enhancement translates into more student applications for admission. To support these arguments you would use evidence based on your own personal experience as well as experiences of your peers. Additionally, evidence taken from publications geared to university administrators would be convincing.

Keep in mind that whether your audience is a peer group, a professor, or a college administrator, you must document your evidence—you must let your reader know where you got your support material. You must document the source of any idea you *summarize* or *paraphrase or quote* directly from. The most widely used forms of documentation used in colleges and universities are the Modern Language Association (MLA) style, used widely in the humanities, and the American Psychological Association (APA) style, used widely in the social sciences. These are explained in greater detail in Chapter 9, Researching Arguments.

Is Your Evidence Slanted?

Sometimes writers select evidence that supports their case while ignoring evidence that does not. Often referred to as stacking the deck, this practice makes for an unfair argument, and one that could be disastrous for the arguer. Even though some of your evidence has merit, your argument will be dismissed if your audience discovers that you slanted or suppressed evidence.

For example, suppose you heard a friend make the following statements: "If I were you, I'd avoid taking a course with Professor Gorman at all costs. He gives surprise quizzes, he assigns 50 pages a night, and he refuses to grade on a curve." Even if these reasons are true, that may not be the whole truth. Suppose you learned that Professor Gorman is, in fact, a very dynamic and talented teacher whose classes successfully stimulate the learning process. By holding back that information, your friend's argument is suspect.

Sometimes writers will take advantage of their readers' lack of information on a topic and offer evidence that really doesn't support their claims. Recently several newspapers reported that a study written up in the *Archives of Internal Medicine* proved that eating nuts prevents heart attacks. According to the study, some thirty thousand Seventh-Day Adventists were asked to rate the frequency with which they ate certain foods. Those claiming to eat nuts five or more times a week reported fewer heart attacks. What the newspapers failed to report was that most Seventh-Day Adventists are vegetarians, and that those who ate more nuts also ate fewer dairy products (which are high in cholesterol and saturated fat, both of which contribute to heart disease) and eggs (also high in cholesterol) than others in the study. Newspapers have failed to report that all the subsequent pro-nut publicity was distributed by a nut growers' association.[1]

It is to your benefit to present all relevant evidence so that you clearly weigh both sides of an issue. As we discussed in Chapter 4, you want to demonstrate to your readers that you have made an effort to consider other perspectives and that your conclusions are fair and balanced. Otherwise your argument might not be taken seriously. Let's return to the argument that electric cars are more beneficial to the environment than cars with internal combustion engines. Your key evidence is the fact that electric cars do not use petroleum products and various motor parts that contribute to the pollution of air, land, and waterways. If you left your argument at that, you would be guilty of suppressing an important concern regarding electric vehicles: the disposal of the great amounts of lead in the huge electric vehicles' lead-acid batteries and even the lighter lead-carbon alternatives. Failure to acknowledge that opposing point reduces your credibility as a writer. Readers would wonder either about your attempt at deception or about your ignorance. Either way, they would dismiss your argument.

A much better strategy would be to confront this concern and then try to overcome it. While acknowledging that lead is a dangerous pollutant, you could point out that more than 95 percent of battery lead is recycled. You could also point out that progress is being made to improve battery technology and create alternatives such as lithium ion batteries used in recent concept cars.[2] The result is a balanced presentation that makes your own case stronger.

In summary, using evidence means putting yourself in an advocate's place. You'll probably do this while building your argument, and certainly when you revise; then you should see yourself as an advocate for the other side and scrutinize your evidence as if you were going to challenge it in court. As a reader, you need to keep that Missouri "show me!" attitude in mind at all times. A little healthy skepticism will help you test the information you're asked to believe. The next chapter will help you do so.

SAMPLE ARGUMENT FOR ANALYSIS

The following is a paper written by a student, Arthur Allen. In it, Allen considers the high rate of recidivism in America—that is, convicts committing more crimes after they've been released from prison. In his paper, he argues that religion might be a better form of rehabilitation than just more harsh punishment. Read the essay carefully and take notes about it in your argument journal. Then, either individually or in your peer group, answer the questions that follow. Notice the style is MLA, which is discussed in the documentation guide.

---

[1]Mirkin, Gabe, and Diana Rich. *Fat Free Flavor Full*. Boston: Little, Brown, 1995, 51.
[2]Jim Motavalli, "Axion's New Lead-Carbon Batteries May Help Usher In Electric Cars," thedailygreen .com//living-green/blogs, April 14, 2009.

To Test Your Evidence for Logical Fallacies, Ask These Questions

Stacking the deck — Did I present evidence that only supports my point of view? Have I withheld evidence that might contradict it?

Non sequitur — Is my evidence related and relevant to the reasons or claim it is supporting?

Hasty generalization — Have I provided sufficient evidence to support my conclusions?

Dicto simpliciter — Does my evidence cover exceptions to any generalizations that I've made?

Red herring — Does all of my evidence pertain to the true issue? Have I tried to distract my audience's attention with irrelevant concerns?

Bandwagon appeal — Can my evidence stand on its own? Have I argued that my audience should support my ideas because they reflect a popular viewpoint?

Faulty use of authority — Are the authorities I cite actually experts in my subject area? Could my authorities be biased because of their background or their professional or political associations?

Allen 1

Arthur Allen
Professor Capobianco
English 097
2 March 2009

Prayer in Prison: Religion as Rehabilitation

Prisons don't work if the prisoners are released only to commit more crimes. Unfortunately, that happens all too frequently. In fact, the phenomenon is known as recidivism—that is, a convict re-offends after having been released from confinement. The challenge faced within prisons across America

Allen 2

is how best to minimize recidivism in order to ensure that the convicts do not commit more crimes. There are two main schools of thought regarding the prevention of recidivism: increasing the harshness of the punishment (most often by increasing time in prison) or offering convicts rehabilitation programs.

The Canadian crime-reduction research group Canada Safety Council found that "there is little evidence that harsh penalties are the best way to prevent further offences" ("Crime"). The council cites studies in Australia, Canada, and America, all pointing to this conclusion. In fact, the group finds that "long prison sentences without other remedial programs may actually increase the chances of re-offending after release" ("Crime"). However, a seemingly more effective method of reducing recidivism, while largely controversial, is rehabilitation, more often than not using a religious basis.

The obvious concern with religion-based rehabilitation is the perceived clash with the Constitution, which prohibits the government from making any "law respecting an establishment of religion or forbidding free exercise thereof" (O'Connor 531). There are no questions, however, about its effectiveness: In Texas, about 40% of parolees who do not participate in any form of rehabilitation program return to prison within three years; in the same amount of time, less than 5% of those who participated in a rehabilitation program were rearrested (Bradley). Other implementations of these types of programs have been comparably successful in Louisiana (Van Wel) as well as in Iowa, Kansas and Minnesota (Alter).

One of the major rehabilitation programs nationally is the Interchange Freedom Initiative (IFI) Program, a third-party rehabilitation program based on offering religion to inmates. Sam Dye, director of the Interchange program in Iowa, says,

> The only true lasting change that is worth anything is change that comes from the inside out, change from the heart. You can coerce a person, from the outside, to do what you want them to do; but once that external pressure is gone, typically people go back to act the way they did before. So if you really want to change a person, you have to get a hold of their heart. (Bradley)

This seems to make sense: The prisoner must be changed from the inside out in order to keep that prisoner from committing a future crime. That is to say, prisoners will not change simply because they have been told they were

Allen 3

wrong or because they were punished severely. Recidivism occurs when there is no change in the status quo of the life of the criminal. If a person is pushed to the point where he or she needs to sell drugs and rob stores in order to pay the bills, a harsh prison life will not change that situation.

However, the question surrounding rehabilitation programs is not about their effectiveness but about their constitutionality. Les Nester, a lawyer and critic of the IFI program, says, "the concerns would be that the state is actually promoting and advancing Christianity. If you look at the programming, it is very sectarian, very evangelical programming . . . . I think the IFI program is a brainwash tactic" (Neary). He argues that because the state government is promoting the use of rehabilitation programs that use Christianity as a way to rehabilitate criminals, the state is declaring affiliation with a specific religion. However, the IFI is not purely a Christian program. It incorporates many faiths, including Judaism and Islam, in its treatment of prisoners. One graduate of the program states, "I think Islam has everything to do with my growth and development and my transformation that I have accomplished, in the sense that Islam taught me for the first time what it is to take responsibility for my actions" (Neary).

The argument for inclusion of any religion rather then exclusion of all religions is summed up succinctly in an article by William Bennett, who "states, "The First Amendment does not require the government to be neutral on the subject of religion. It requires it to be neutral only on any one particular form of religion" (Bennett 54). In other words, while the government should not show favoritism toward one particular religion, it also does not have the obligation of pretending religion does not exist. Thus, this distinction allows the government to sponsor religious programs in the context of furthering the social good (reduction of crime) as long as it does not promote one religious program over another.

In another article, John Swomley argues that the government could not give funding to one religious group without giving funding to all religious groups; this argument then implies that the government could not provide any funding to religious rehabilitation programs in prisons if it did not give funding to all 300-plus religious groups (Swomley 62). This argument is backwards: The government is free to give money to any religious group it sees fit. It is prohibited, however, from denying one group funding in the same situation where it would grant another group that same funding. To say that the government is responsible for giving "all or

Allen 4

none" to religious groups would be like saying the government is required to either employ all races in government positions or employ none of them. If a religion-based rehabilitation program wants to operate, it should not be denied fund but should be funded equally as all other religion-based rehabilitation programs representing different faiths.

8 Furthermore, civil liberties groups have actually held back from suing the IFI program because it provides a number of unique services including a support community both for convicts in prison and for those who have been released. As one graduate of the IFI program puts it, "Now I have someone I can call, even in the middle of the night. And when I start feeling bad . . . who you gonna call? You call your brother, he uses drugs. You call your sister, she's using drugs. Mom's upset with you. Dad's gone. Whereas, with IFI, I was given a family." In other words, because it is a third-party nonprofit program, the IFI is not only able to reach prisoners in a way government officials can't by offering spiritual growth and continuity, but also it provides follow-through support after prison by offering a new family to which the convicts feel a sense of loyalty and responsibility (Bradley).

As an alternative to harsher punishments, rehabilitation is clearly superior. When prison is the necessary evil in a person's life, the harshness of it will make little difference. The change must truly come from the inside out. And faith-based rehabilitation programs have proven successful.

Allen 5

Works Cited

Alter, Alexandra. "Study Touts Faith-Based Prison Rehabilitation Program." The Pew Forum on Religion and Public Life. Pew Forum, 19 June 2003. Web. 28 Feb. 2009.

Bennett, William. "America's Indentity Is Rooted in Religion." *Religion in America: Opposing Viewpoints*. Ed. William Dudley et al. San Diego: Greenhaven p, 2001. Print.

Bradley, Barbra. *God Pods*. NPR News. Iowa, 2001. Radio.

"Crime, Punishment, Safety." *Canada Safety Council*. Canada Safety Council, 2009. Web. 27 Feb. 2009.

Neary, Lynn. *Sing Sing Studies*. NPR News, Washington DC. 1998. Radio.

O'Connor, Karen, and Larry J. Sabato. *American Government: Continuity and Change*. New York: Pearson Education, 2004. Print.

Swomley, John. "TK." Religion in America: Opposing Viewpoints. Ed. William Dudley et al. San Diego: Greenhaven P, 2001. Print.

Van Wel, Alex. "US Prison Rehabilitation through Faith." BBC News. BBC, 2 Oct. 2002. Web. 27 Feb. 2009.

QUESTIONS FOR ANALYSIS AND DISCUSSION

1. What claim (Chapter 1) is Allen arguing? What are the reasons for his claim? What do you think the pros and cons he listed in developing this argument might have been?

2. Who is Allen's target audience? What clues does he give you? What values and prejudices might the readership hold?

3. What different forms of evidence (personal, outside authorities, factual references, statistics) does Allen provide? Which form(s) of evidence does he rely on most?

4. Evaluate the supporting evidence that Allen provides. Is it relevant? Is it detailed enough? Does it seem dated and verifiable? Does his claim exceed his evidence? Does his evidence strike you as slanted? If you were his reader, would you be persuaded by his reasons? What changes (if any) in evidence would you recommend to help him make his argument more persuasive?

5. Use debate, dialogue, and deliberation to respond to Allen's essay in your journal. See Chapter 1 to review this process.
   a. Create a dialogue to help you understand and respond productively to Allen's ideas.
   b. Given what you've learned through debate and dialogue, write at least a page in which you deliberate about the conflicting issues that Allen raises in his essay. How does your understanding of Allen's position change or modify your own viewpoint? Is there a way to reconcile conflicting concerns about this subject?

Establishing Claims: Thinking Like a Skeptic

You have decided the issue you're going to argue. With the aid of debate and dialogue, you've sharpened your ideas and considered alternative perspectives and common concerns. You've thought about your audience and determined what you have in common, where you might agree, and where you might disagree. After deliberating, you have formulated a working claim, and you have gathered solid evidence to support it. Now it's time to establish the logical structure of your argument and decide how best to arrange this material to persuade your readers.

If you've ever tried handing in a paper made up of slapped-together evidence and first-draft organization, you've probably discovered a blueprint for disaster. Perhaps you didn't test your work, didn't revise it, or didn't think about how it would appeal to a reader. You assumed that because *you* understood how the parts fit together, your readers would as well. To help you detect and correct these problems, this chapter focuses on thinking like a *skeptic*—a skeptical building inspector, to be exact—because a skeptical attitude works best.

To construct a persuasive argument, one that has a chance of convincing your readers, you have to pay careful attention to the logical structure you are building. You can't take anything for granted; you have to question every step you take, every joist and joint. You have to ask yourself if you're using the right material for the right purpose, the right tool at the right time. In other words, you have to think like a building inspector examining a half-built two-story house—one whose builder is notoriously crafty at compromising quality. A healthy skepticism—and a logical system—help uncover flaws before they create a disaster.

The Toulmin Model

Stephen Toulmin, a British philosopher and logician, analyzed hundreds of arguments from various fields of politics and law.[1] He concluded that nearly every argument has certain patterns and parts. The best arguments, Toulmin found, are those addressed to a skeptical audience, one eager to question the reasoning where it seems faulty, to demand support for wobbly assumptions, and to raise opposing reasons.

The slightly retooled version of the Toulmin model we describe below encourages you to become a skeptical audience. It also gives you the tools to write persuasive arguments aimed to win over a skeptical reader. It provides useful everyday terms to

---

[1]Toulmin, Stephen. *The Uses of Argument.* Cambridge: Cambridge UP, 1958.

help you unearth, weigh, and, if necessary, fix an argument's logical structures. It lets you verify that the major premises in your argument or those of your opposition are clear and accurate, helps you determine whether repairs to your claims are needed and whether counterarguments are addressed. It shows you where supporting evidence may be needed and helps you avoid logical fallacies. And, since Toulmin's terms are designed to be broadly practical, they allow you to present your case to a wide variety of readers.

Toulmin's Terms

According to Toulmin, a fully developed argument has six parts. They are the *claim,* the *grounds,* the *warrant,* the *backing,* the *qualifiers,* and the *rebuttals.*

The Claim

The **claim** is the assertion you are trying to prove—the same term as discussed in Chapter 1. It is the position you take in your argument, often as a proposal with which you are asking your reader to agree. In a well-constructed argument, each part makes its ultimate claim, its conclusion, seem inevitable. For example, *you should stay home from school if you have the flu.* This sounds like a reasonable claim, but some people may challenge it. You need to explain why your audience should agree with you.

The Grounds

Just as every argument contains a claim, every claim needs supporting evidence. The **grounds** are the hard data—statistics, research studies, facts, and examples that bolster your claim and that your audience accepts without requiring further proof. Grounds are the "truth" on which you base your claim. For example, *The influenza virus is highly contagious. According to the Centers for Disease Control, every year, an average of 36,000 people die in the United States from complications connected to the flu.* While some readers may accept the grounds as enough proof to accept your claim, others will require more information. This is where the warrant comes in.

The Warrant

The claim is usually stated explicitly. However, underlying the claim are a number of assumptions and principles that are also critical to the success of your argument. These are the **warrants** that implicitly support your argument by connecting your claim to the grounds. They enable your audience to follow the reasoning in your argument. They explain why the hard evidence supports your claim. So the success of your argument depends on whether the audience accepts these often half-buried assumptions, commonly held values, legal or moral principles, laws of nature, commonsense knowledge, or shared beliefs. Warrants tend to be based on values shared by the population. They may be true or mere presumptions based on emotion, rather than hard facts. For example, *The flu is easily passed from person to person, and it is* *inconsiderate to make other people sick. The responsible thing to do is to stay home until you feel better.*

Let's look at a few more examples. We are all familiar with the advertiser that promises that its shampoo will eliminate dandruff. The basic **claim** here is that you should shampoo your hair with this manufacturer's product. And as **grounds** the manufacturer says that studies have shown that 60 percent of those people who use their shampoo no longer have dandruff. One underlying **warrant** here is that people don't want dandruff—a commonly held assumption that you share with your audience. Another is that we assume 60 percent to be a sufficient proportion to accept the claim. Because warrants are based on commonly held values or patterns of reasoning, they are not easily detected. Here's another example:

Claim: Cigarette smoking is harmful to your health.
Grounds: The U.S. Surgeon General has warned that cigarettes cause a number of diseases including cancer, heart trouble, and injury to fetuses in pregnant women.
Warrant: The Surgeon General is a medical authority we can trust.

At times, warrants can be a challenge to determine since they are often based on unstated but commonly held assumptions. And that is why it is important to find them. More on that below.

The Backing

Because your warrant is an assumption, you cannot be certain that it will always be accepted by your readers. So you must provide reasons to back it up. These reasons, called **backing,** indicate that the warrant is reliable in a particular argument, though it doesn't have to be true in all cases at all times. For example, *The flu can lead to other serious conditions such as pneumonia. In fact, over 200,000 people end up hospitalized because of flu-related complications. It is better to stay home when you have the flu, rather than risk getting even more sick and missing more time at work or school.* The backing provides additional support to the warrant by addressing other facets of the claim. In this case, the risk of complications.

The Qualifiers

Qualifiers provide a way to indicate when, why, and how your claim and warrant are reliable. They're words or phrases such as *often, probably, possibly, almost always;* verbs like *may* and *might, can* and *could;* or adjectives and adverbs that yoke your claim to some condition. The subtlest kind of qualifier is an adjective that acknowledges that your claim is true to a degree: *Complications from the flu often make it harder to go back to school. Usually it takes longer for you to feel better.* The qualifiers *often* and *harder* and *usually* imply that the statement is conditional and not absolute. They allow for exceptions.

You need to consider a few guidelines about using qualifiers; like antibiotics, they're too powerful to use unwisely. Using too few qualifiers can indicate that you're exaggerating your argument's validity. As we've mentioned in previous chapters, common fallacies, such as *hasty generalizations,* are often potentially valid arguments that go astray by not qualifying their claims enough, if at all. Using *no* qualifiers can result in a claim that is too general and sweeping. Although many students think a qualified claim is a weak claim, in fact, the qualified claim is often the most persuasive. Few truths are *completely* true; few claims are *always* right. A well-qualified claim, then, shows that the writer respects both the difficulty of the issue and the intelligence of the reader.

Nevertheless, qualifiers alone cannot substitute for reasoning your way to the tough, subtle distinctions on which the most persuasive arguments depend. An example could be "Innocent people have an inviolable right to life." It's wisely qualified with the word "innocent" since just saying "People have an inviolable right to life" wouldn't hold up. Hitler, after all, was human. Did he too have "an inviolable right to life"? But even *innocent* is not qualification enough. It raises too many tough, troubling questions. "Innocent" of what? "Innocent" by whose judgment, and why? What if killing a few innocent people were the only way to end a war that is killing *many* innocent people?

Using a lot of qualifiers, therefore, is no guarantee that your argument is carefully reasoned. In fact, strongly qualifying your argument's claim may be a sign that you doubt your argument's validity. But such doubt can itself be encouraging. Misusing or overusing qualifiers can indicate that your instinct of anxiety is right—that you've discovered better reasons to doubt your initial argument than to defend it. In fact, acknowledging the appeal of a flawed claim—and describing how you only discovered its flaws once you tried trumpeting its strengths—is an effective way of earning the reader's respect. It shows you to be an honest arguer capable of learning from errors—and thus worth learning *from.*

Deciding what to state and what to imply is a large part of writing any good argument. Just as a building's cross-beams don't have to be visible to be working, not everything important in an argument has to be stated. For example, if someone were to claim that winters in Minnesota are "mostly long and cold," we probably wouldn't stop the flow of argument to ask him to define the qualifier *mostly.* We'd instead keep the qualifier in mind, and let the Minnesotan's definition of "mostly" emerge, implied, from the rest of the story. Similarly, it's sometimes wise to leave your argument's qualifiers implied.

Still, it's often better to risk belaboring the obvious. To minimize the chances that your reader will misunderstand (or altogether miss) your meaning, qualify your claims as clearly and explicitly as possible. "Reading" the argument you're writing like a skeptical reader will help you decide which qualifiers are needed, where they are needed, and how explicitly they need to be stated.

The Rebuttals

Reading your argument skeptically also allows you to participate, answer, and even preempt rebuttals. **Rebuttals** represent the exceptions to the claim. There are many different kinds of rebuttals, and any persuasive argument ought to acknowledge and incorporate the most important ones. Rebuttals are like large-scale qualifiers. They acknowledge and explain the conditions or situations in which your claim would not be true—while still proving how your claim *is* true under other conditions. It's wise, then, to anticipate such rebuttals by regularly acknowledging all your argument's limits. This acknowledgment will prompt you to craft your claims more carefully. For example, look at the claim that you should stay home from school if you have the flu. One could argue that if you are coughing and sneezing, you *probably* will give the flu to people sitting around you. Then again, you might not. You might sit in the back of the room, away from other people. Or you could take medication that reduces your sneezing. A challenger might argue that while it is inconsiderate to expose classmates to the flu, if one has an exam that one thinks cannot be missed or face failure, it may be in one's personal best interest to go to class. You would need to persuasively convince your reader that your claim holds true despite these challenges. You might anticipate the challenge and write: *Rather than expose your classmates to dangerous strains of flu, such as H1N1, go to your student health service and request a letter explaining your absence. This will protect your classmates and allow you the time to get better so that you can focus on the test later.*

Let's look at another example. Say that a sportswriter argues that allowing big-market baseball teams to monopolize talent ruins competition by perpetuating dynasties. Your rebuttal might be to cite the overlooked grounds of ignored evidence—grounds that complicate, if not contradict, the writer's claim: "Then why have small-market teams won four of the last ten World Series?" Had the sportswriter anticipated and integrated this rebuttal, she could have improved the argument—from her warrant on up. Her argument could have taken into account this rebuttal in the form of more careful qualifications. "While the rule of money doesn't guarantee that the richer teams will always win the World Series, it does make it more difficult for hard-pressed teams to compete for available talent." This is now, of course, a less sweeping claim—and, therefore, more precise and persuasive.

Of course, no writer can anticipate their readers' every rebuttal, nor should the writer even try. But you should test your argument by trying to rebut it yourself or working with classmates in small groups. Then revise your arguments with those rebuttals in mind.

Review: Six Parts of an Argument

Claim	The assertion you are trying to prove
Grounds	The supporting evidence for the claim
Warrant	A generalization that explains why the evidence supports the claim
Backing	The reasons that show the warrant is reliable
Qualifiers	The words that show when, how, and why your claim is reliable
Rebuttal	The exceptions to the claim

Finding Warrants

Finding your warrants in order to explicate your argument can help you in several ways: You persuade your reader more effectively, detect flaws in your own argument, and identify the cause of otherwise confusing debates more quickly.

For example, let's say you want to argue the claim that all students in American schools should be taught in English rather than in the students' native or family languages. The grounds supporting this claim are results of research showing a high correlation between English fluency and socioeconomic success.

For your audience to accept the connection between your claim and your grounds, you and they must agree on several warrants that underlie it. (Remember that warrants are underlying assumptions or common knowledge.) The first might be the assumption that schools prepare students for socioeconomic success in U.S. society. Since one of the purposes of an education is to develop skills such as reading, writing, and thinking critically, skills that are considered basic requirements for success, most of your audience would likely accept this assumption. Therefore, it can be left implied and unstated.

The second warrant implied by your claim may not be as readily acceptable to your audience as the one above and will need to be explicitly supported in your essay: that our English language skills affect whether we are successful. The third warrant, implied by the second, is that individuals who are not fluent in English will not be successful members of society. These warrants will need considerable backing to show that they are reliable. How do English language skills enable individuals to attain socioeconomic success? How are individuals who lack fluency in English adversely affected? You will want to provide additional backing in the form of evidence, examples, and statistics to demonstrate that English language skills have a significant impact on an individual's chances for social and economic success.

Your fourth and final warrant is particularly important because it establishes a critical link between your claim that all students should be taught in English and the need for fluency to succeed. This warrant assumes nonnative speaking students will achieve greater fluency in English in the English-only classroom. You will need additional backing to prove this warrant, especially when you take into account possible rebuttals. For instance, what about students who enter U.S. schools with no English skills at all? How can they learn the required curriculum with no fluency in English? Will English-only classrooms fail to teach them language skills as well as subject matter? Will this approach alienate them from the American educational system and, thus, from success in our society? Making your responses to these rebuttals explicit will strengthen your argument.

Using Toulmin's approach to analyze your argument allows you to dig beneath the surface of your claim to find the underlying assumptions that form its foundation. It also allows your audience to see that even if they disagree with your claim, they may agree with many of the principles and assumptions that support it. Revealing this common ground, however hidden it lies, can provide opportunities to begin a dialogue that emerges from the recognition of shared values and beliefs. For instance, take the notoriously divisive issue of capital punishment. Those who support capital punishment say, in essence, "A human life is so precious that anyone who is guilty of depriving another of it should forfeit his or her own life." Those who oppose capital punishment say, in effect, "Human life is so precious that we have no right to deprive another of it no matter what the cause." By digging down to the warrants that underlie these positions, we may be surprised to find that the two sides have much in common: a respect for and appreciation of the value of human life. This discovery, of course, is no guarantee that we can reconcile dramatically opposing views on a particular issue. But the recognition of commonality might provide a first step toward increasing understanding—if not consensus—between opposing sides.

Digging deeply to excavate your warrants can also help you avoid two common logical fallacies: post hoc, ergo propter hoc and slippery slope arguments. A post hoc, ergo propter hoc fallacy occurs when the writer mistakenly draws a causal relationship between two or more events or situations that are unrelated or simply coincidental. Similarly, a slippery slope argument is based on an assumption that a particular outcome is inevitable if certain events happen or if a situation is allowed to continue. In both cases, the writer fails to identify and support the underlying warrants that would create a convincing logical link.

SAMPLE ARGUMENTS FOR ANALYSIS

Now let's turn to two sample arguments to see how our version of the Toulmin model can help you test your own arguments more effectively. The first piece, originally published in the *New York Times Magazine,* provides a very logical but highly provocative argument about a crime that always receives considerable media attention: infanticide. The second article appeared a few days later in the *New York Times.* And while these essays relate events that happened several years ago, the issue of infanticide is still a national problem. In fact, statistically, the U.S. ranks high on the list of countries whose inhabitants kill their babies. For infants under the age of 1 year, the American homicide rate is 11th in the world. The author of the first essay, Steven Pinker, wrote this piece while director of the Center for Cognitive Neuroscience at Massachusetts Institute of Technology. Pinker is currently the Johnstone Family Professor of Psychology in the Department of Psychology at Harvard University. He is the author of *How the Mind Works* (1997) and most recently *The Stuff of Thought* (2007). Following Pinker's essay is a point-by-point counterargument (page 196) by Michael Kelley.

To Avoid Errors in Logic, Check for These Logical Fallacies

Post hoc, ergo propter hoc	Be certain to demonstrate a cause-effect relationship between events by uncovering all warrants that underlie your claim.
Slippery slope argument	Make explicit the chain of events that link a situation to its possible outcome. Provide proof that this progression will inevitably occur.

Warrants

Notice the many layers of warrants that can underlie a single claim:

Claim	All students in American public schools should be taught in English-only classrooms.
Grounds	Research shows high correlation between English fluency and socioeconomic success in America.
Warrant	Schools prepare students for success in our society.
Warrant	Success in American society can be determined by our English language skills.
Warrant	Individuals who are not fluent in English will not succeed in our society.
Warrant	Teaching classes only in the English language will ensure that students will be fluent in English.

Why They Kill Their Newborns
Steven Pinker

1   Killing your baby. What could be more depraved? For a woman to destroy the fruit of her womb would seem like an ultimate violation of the natural order. But every year, hundreds of women commit neonaticide: They kill their newborns or let them die. Most neonaticides remain undiscovered, but every once in a while a janitor follows a trail of blood to a tiny body in a trash bin, or a woman faints and doctors find the remains of a placenta inside her.

2   Two cases have recently riveted the American public. Last November, Amy Grossberg and Brian Peterson, 18-year-old college sweethearts, delivered their baby in a motel room and, according to prosecutors, killed him and left his body in a dumpster. They will go on trial for murder next year and, if convicted, could be sentenced to death. In June, another 18-year-old, Melissa Drexler, arrived at her high-school prom, locked herself in a bathroom stall, gave birth to a boy and left him dead in a garbage can. Everyone knows what happened next: she touched herself up and returned to the dance floor. In September, a grand jury indicted her for murder.

3   How could they do it? Nothing melts the heart like a helpless baby. Even a biologist's cold calculations tell us that nurturing an offspring that carries our genes is the whole point of our existence. Neonaticide, many think, could be only a product of pathology. The psychiatrists uncover childhood trauma. The defense lawyers argue temporary psychosis. The pundits blame a throwaway society, permissive sex education and, of course, rock lyrics.

4   But it's hard to maintain that neonaticide is an illness when we learn that it has been practiced and accepted in most cultures throughout history. And that neonaticidal

women do not commonly show signs of psychopathology. In a classic 1970 study of statistics of child killing, a psychiatrist, Phillip Resnick, found that mothers who kill their *older* children are frequently psychotic, depressed or suicidal, but mothers who kill their newborns are usually not. (It was this difference that led Resnick to argue that the category infanticide be split into neonaticide, the killing of a baby on the day of its birth, and filicide, the killing of a child older than one day.)

5   Killing a baby is an immoral act, and we often express our outrage at the immoral by calling it a sickness. But normal human motives are not always moral, and neonaticide does not have to be a product of malfunctioning neural circuitry or a dysfunctional upbringing. We can try to understand what would lead a mother to kill her newborn, remembering that to understand is not necessarily to forgive.

6   Martin Daly and Margo Wilson, both psychologists, argue that a capacity for neonaticide is built into the biological design of our parental emotions. Mammals are extreme among animals in the amount of time, energy and food they invest in their young, and humans are extreme among mammals. Parental investment is a limited resource, and mammalian mothers must "decide" whether to allot it to their newborn or to their current and future offspring. If a newborn is sickly, or if its survival is not promising, they may cut their losses and favor the healthiest in the litter or try again later on.

7   In most cultures, neonaticide is a form of this triage. Until very recently in human evolutionary history, mothers nursed their children for two to four years before becoming fertile again. Many children died, especially in the perilous first year. Most women saw no more than two or three of their children survive to adulthood, and many did not see any survive. To become a grandmother, a woman had to make hard choices. In most societies documented by anthropologists, including those of hunter-gatherers (our best glimpse into our ancestors' way of life), a woman lets a newborn die when its prospects for survival to adulthood are poor. The forecast might be based on abnormal signs in the infant, or on bad circumstances for successful motherhood at the time—she might be burdened with older children, beset by war or famine or without a husband or social support. Moreover, she might be young enough to try again.

8   We are all descendants of women who made the difficult decisions that allowed them to become grandmothers in that unforgiving world, and we inherited that brain circuitry that led to those decisions. Daly and Wilson have shown that the statistics on neonaticide in contemporary North America parallel those in the anthropological literature. The women who sacrifice their offspring tend to be young, poor, unmarried and socially isolated.

9   Natural selection cannot push the buttons of behavior directly; it affects our behavior by endowing us with emotions that coax us toward adaptive choices. New mothers have always faced a choice between a definite tragedy now and the possibility of an even greater tragedy months or years later, and that choice is not to be taken lightly. Even today, the typical rumination of a depressed new mother—how will I cope with this burden?—is a legitimate concern. The emotional response called bonding is also far more complex than the popular view, in which a woman is imprinted with a lifelong attachment to her baby if they interact in a critical period immediately following the baby's birth. A new mother will first coolly assess the infant and her

current situation and only in the next few days begin to see it as a unique and wonderful individual. Her love will gradually deepen in ensuing years, in a trajectory that tracks the increasing biological value of a child (the chance that it will live to produce grand-children) as the child proceeds through the mine field of early development.

10   Even when a mother in a hunter-gatherer society hardens her heart to sacrifice a newborn, her heart has not turned to stone. Anthropologists who interview these women (or their relatives, since the event is often too painful for the woman to discuss) discover that the women see the death as an unavoidable tragedy, grieve at the time and remember the child with pain all their lives. Even the supposedly callous Melissa Drexler agonized over a name for her dead son and wept at his funeral. (Initial reports that, after giving birth, she requested a Metallica song from the deejay and danced with her boyfriend turned out to be false.)

11   Many cultural practices are designed to distance people's emotions from a new-born until its survival seems probable. Full personhood is often not automatically granted at birth, as we see in our rituals of christening and the Jewish bris. And yet the recent neonaticides will seem puzzling. These are middle-class girls whose babies would have been kept far from starvation by the girl's parents or by any of thousands of eager adoptive couples. But our emotions, fashioned by the slow hand of natural se-lection, respond to the signals of the long-vanished tribal environment in which we spent 99 percent of our evolutionary history. Being young and single are two bad omens for successful motherhood, and the girl who conceals her pregnancy and pro-crastinates over its consequences will soon be disquieted by a third omen. She will give birth in circumstances that are particularly unpromising for a human mother: alone.

12   In hunter gatherer societies, births are virtually always assisted because human anatomy makes birth (especially the first one) long, difficult and risky. Older women act as midwives, emotional supports and experienced appraisers who help decide whether the infant should live. Wenda Trevathan, an anthropologist and trained midwife, has studied pelvises of human fossils and concluded that childbirth has been physically tor-turous, and therefore probably assisted, for millions of years. Maternal feelings may be adapted to a world in which a promising newborn is heralded with waves of cooing and clucking and congratulating. Those reassuring signals are absent from a secret birth in a motel room or a bathroom stall.

13   So what is the mental state of a teenage mother who has kept her pregnancy se-cret? She is immature enough to have hoped that her pregnancy would go away by it-self, her maternal feelings have been set at zero and she suddenly realizes she is in big trouble.

14   Sometimes she continues to procrastinate. In September, 17-year-old Shanta Clark gave birth to a premature boy and kept him hidden in her bedroom closet, as if he were E.T., for 17 days. She fed him before and after she went to school until her mother discovered him. The weak cry of the preemie kept him from being discovered earlier. (In other cases, girls have panicked over the crying and, in stifling the cry, killed the baby.)

15   Most observers sense the desperation that drives a woman to neonaticide. Prosecutors sometimes don't prosecute; juries rarely convict; those found guilty almost

never go to jail. Barbara Kirwin, a forensic psychologist, reports that in nearly 300 cases of women charged with neonaticide in the United States and Britain, no woman spent more than a night in jail. In Europe, the laws of several countries prescribed less-severe penalties for neonaticide than for adult homicides. The fascination with the Grossberg-Peterson case comes from the unusual threat of the death penalty. Even those in favor of capital punishment might shudder at the thought of two reportedly nice kids being strapped to gurneys and put to death.

16   But our compassion hinges on the child, not just on the mother. Killers of older children, no matter how desperate, evoke little mercy. Susan Smith, the South Carolina woman who sent her two sons, 14 months and 3 years old, to watery deaths, is in jail, unmourned, serving a life sentence. The leniency shown to neonaticidal mothers forces us to think the unthinkable and ask if we, like many societies and like the mothers themselves, are not completely sure whether a neonate is a full person.

17   It seems obvious that we need a clear boundary to confer personhood on a human being and grant it a right to life. Otherwise, we approach a slippery slope that ends in the disposal of inconvenient people or in grotesque deliberations on the value of individual lives. But the endless abortion debate shows how hard it is to locate the boundary. Anti-abortionists draw the line at conception, but that implies we should shed tears every time an invisible conceptus fails to implant in the uterus—and, to carry the argument to its logical conclusion, that we should prosecute for murder anyone who uses an IUD. Those in favor of abortion draw the line at viability, but viability is a fuzzy gradient that depends on how great a risk of an impaired child the parents are willing to tolerate. The only thing both sides agree on is that the line must be drawn at some point before birth.

18   Neonaticide forces us to examine even that boundary. To a biologist, birth is as arbitrary a milestone as any other. Many mammals bear offspring that see and walk as soon as they hit the ground. But the incomplete 9-month-old human fetus must be evicted from the womb before its oversized head gets too big to fit through its mother's pelvis. The usual primate assembly process spills into the first years in the world. And that complicates our definition of personhood.

19   What makes a living being a person with a right not to be killed? Animal-rights extremists would seem to have the easiest argument to make: that all sentient beings have a right to life. But champions of that argument must conclude that delousing a child is akin to mass murder; the rest of us must look for an argument that draws a small circle. Perhaps only the members of our own species, Homo sapiens, have a right to life? But that is simply chauvinism; a person of one race could just as easily say that people of another race have no right to life.

20   No, the right to life must come, the moral philosophers say, from morally significant traits that we humans happen to possess. One such trait is having a unique sequence of experiences that defines us as individuals and connects us to other people. Other traits include an ability to reflect upon ourselves as a continuous locus of consciousness, to form and savor plans for the future, to dread death and to express the choice not to die. And there's the rub: our immature neonates don't possess these traits any more than mice do.

21   Several moral philosophers have concluded that neonates are not persons, and thus neonaticide should not be classified as murder. Michael Tooley has gone so far as to say that neonaticide ought to be permitted during an interval after birth. Most philosophers (to say nothing of nonphilosophers) recoil from that last step, but the very fact that there can be a debate about the personhood of neonates, but no debate about the personhood of older children, makes it clearer why we feel more sympathy for an Amy Grossberg than for a Susan Smith.

22   So how do you provide grounds for outlawing neonaticide? The facts don't make it easy. Some philosophers suggest that people intuitively see neonates as so similar to older babies that you couldn't allow neonaticide without coarsening the way people treat children and other people in general. Again, the facts say otherwise. Studies in both modern and hunter-gatherer societies have found that neonaticidal women don't kill anyone but their newborns, and when they give birth later under better conditions, they can be devoted, loving mothers.

23   The laws of biology were not kind to Amy Grossberg and Melissa Drexler, and they are not kind to us as we struggle to make moral sense of the teenagers' actions. One predicament is that our moral system needs a crisp inauguration of personhood, but the assembly process for Homo sapiens is gradual, piecemeal and uncertain. Another problem is that the emotional circuitry of mothers has evolved to cope with this uncertain process, so the baby killers turn out to be not moral monsters but nice, normal (and sometimes religious) young women. These are dilemmas we will probably never resolve, and any policy will leave us with uncomfortable cases. We will most likely muddle through, keeping birth as a conspicuous legal boundary but showing mercy to the anguished girls who feel they had no choice but to run afoul of it.

An Analysis Based on the Toulmin Model

Clearly Steven Pinker has taken a controversial stance on a disturbing social issue. In fact, in light of civilized society's attitudes toward the sacredness of the mother-infant bond, his position is one that many people might find shocking and repugnant. How could he propose that neonaticide, the murder of one's newborn infant, be viewed as an acceptable form of behavior, one that we have inherited from our evolutionary ancestors? As Pinker readily admits in the first three paragraphs, neonaticide seems alien to most of the values we as civilized people cherish. Nevertheless, Pinker argues that while it may be regarded as immoral, neonaticide is not necessarily the act of a mentally deranged woman, but rather a difficult decision guided by an instinct for survival handed down to a mother by generations of women before her. While he does not condone or endorse this practice, Pinker urges his readers to try to understand a context that might drive women to commit such an act.

No matter how repugnant an idea may be, it cannot be repudiated unless it is understood. Therefore it is important to be detached and put aside emotion when confronted with ideas that are unacceptable. Genocide, child slavery, and child prostitution, for example, are topics most people would rather avoid. But to understand the forces underlying these practices, and to eradicate them, one must be knowledgeable about them.

This might require digesting material that is disturbing and contrary to all the values held by a civilized society.

So, while your first reaction to Pinker's ideas may be to dismiss them as outrageous and unworthy of serious consideration, a close analysis of his argument using the Toulmin method may demonstrate how carefully Pinker has crafted his argument to challenge many of our assumptions about human behavior and, in particular, motherhood.

Claims and Grounds

Pinker presents the first part of his claim in paragraph 4 of his essay: Neonaticide is not an abnormal behavior but one that has been practiced "in most cultures throughout history." This statement seems to contradict the popular notion of neonaticide. Because our society regards neonaticide as an immoral act, many people likely assume that it is a rare occurrence. However, Pinker anticipates this assumption in paragraph 1 by reminding us that neonaticide *does* occur in our own society. It is, he claims, more common than we realize, since most murders of newborn babies go undetected. Only "every once in a while" do we discover that this act has taken place because some physical evidence is found. While Pinker offers no grounds for his assertion that "every year, hundreds of women commit neonaticide," his audience's familiarity with newspaper accounts of newborns abandoned in dumpsters and public restrooms lends credibility to his statement. This point is important because it establishes a link between contemporary women's behavior and the practices of our "long-vanished tribal environment."

Pinker develops this idea further in paragraphs 6 through 8 by suggesting that this behavior has been programmed into our "biological design" through human evolutionary development. He provides the grounds to support this part of his claim by citing two scholarly sources: Philip Resnick's study of child-killing statistics, which indicates that women who kill their newborn babies are typically not mentally ill, and research by Martin Daly and Margo Wilson that suggests neonaticide may be an intrinsic part of our "biological design," a necessity for human beings with limited resources to invest in their offspring. Relying on these grounds, Pinker goes on to argue in paragraph 9 that neonaticide is an "adaptive choice," one that is preferable to nurturing an infant whose continued survival is in doubt because of either the physical condition of the child or environmental difficulties for the mother.

So far, then, we have found two of the essential parts of the Toulmin model in Pinker's essay:

Claim	Neonaticide is not a pathologic behavior but can be, rather, the result of evolutionary development.
Grounds	Various anthropological studies indicate that neonaticide is a common and accepted practice in many contemporary societies; studies by psychologists argue that neonaticide is a normal part of our parenting emotions; research by psychologists demonstrates that women who commit neonaticide are not mentally ill.

Warrants, Backing, and Rebuttals

Now let's move on to Pinker's warrants, which work to support his claim. Pinker never directly states, yet he strongly implies as a *warrant,* that "biology is destiny." It is clear from his claim and the grounds used to support it that Pinker believes the biological impulses of a new mother who commits neonaticide may overwhelm her civilized sense of what is morally or even emotionally right. Human beings, according to Pinker, are at the mercy of their neurological programming. Pinker offers *backing* for this *warrant* in paragraph 10 when he relates interviews by anthropologists with women who have killed their newborn babies and who appear to grieve sincerely for their children, regarding their actions as "an unavoidable tragedy." These women, according to Pinker, were compelled to make a difficult choice, which each did in spite of her maternal feelings toward the newborn. Pinker reinforces this point later in the essay when he states in paragraph 23 that "the laws of biology were not kind to Amy Grossberg and Melissa Drexler," two young women who killed their infants just after birth. Pinker strongly implies that biological forces were at work when these women made their decisions.

Pinker's warrant provides plenty of opportunity for *rebuttal* because even if the reader accepts the idea that human beings, despite the teachings of civilized society, are still subject to the dictates of more primitive and instinctive urges, Pinker asserts that the urge to kill one's baby is stronger than, say, the maternal instinct to nurture that infant. We have all heard of situations in which a mother has risked or sacrificed her own life to save that of her child. Why, we might ask, wouldn't this emotion dominate the behavior of a new mother? Pinker acknowledges this rebuttal in paragraph 11 when he points out that the neonaticides we read about in newspapers are often committed by middle-class girls who have the resources to support a child or the option to give the baby up for adoption.

Pinker responds to this rebuttal in two ways: First, he reiterates his claim that the internal forces of our evolutionary background are stronger than the individual's own sense of right and wrong. These young women are responding to the "signals of the long-vanished tribal environment in which we spent 99 percent of our evolutionary history." Moreover, Pinker goes on to suggest, neonaticide is triggered by environmental and social factors, specifically the age, marital status, and isolation of the new mother, that work to suppress more positive maternal responses. As he explains in paragraph 12, maternal feelings are more likely to emerge in an atmosphere of "cooing and clucking and congratulating" than in a "motel room or bathroom stall."

Pinker goes on to support his argument with several additional layers of warrants: If human behavior is controlled by deeply ingrained biological forces, then we can't be held legally responsible for these actions. In other words, while we may deeply deplore the act of neonaticide, we cannot fault these women for acting on an impulse they may not completely understand or feel able to control. In paragraph 15, Pinker provides backing for this claim by observing that few women in the United States are actually incarcerated for this crime and several European countries treat neonaticide less severely than other forms of homicide. Thus, although the killing of one's baby generates strong moral outrage in our society, we treat it less severely than most other offenses in the same category.

Logically, then, the next question must be "Why is this the case?" When older children are murdered by their mothers, as in Pinker's example of Susan Smith in paragraph 16, we waste little sympathy on the plight of the mother. We can agree with Pinker that "our compassion hinges on the child." Why do we react, according to Pinker, in a very different way to the death of a newborn? Pinker has very carefully brought us to his next warrant, which even he admits is the "unthinkable": Our reaction to the killing of a newborn and the killing of an older child is different because a newborn is not yet a "full person."

Pinker provides backing for his warrant in paragraphs 18 through 20. In paragraph 18, he points out a fact most readers would agree with: Unlike other mammals, human babies are helpless at birth. They are "incomplete." It will take an infant several years to achieve the level of physical development that some mammals enjoy at birth. Thus, a newborn baby cannot claim its rights as a person based on its physical completeness. Then, Pinker asks, on what basis can a newborn be seen as possessing "a right not to be killed"? By what traits do we define a person with a right to life? In paragraph 20, Pinker calls on the *backing* of "moral philosophers" who describe the traits human beings must possess to be considered fully human. Pinker concludes that newborn babies "don't possess these traits any more than mice do."

Anticipating that most readers will have a strong negative response to these ideas, Pinker acknowledges several rebuttals to this warrant. In paragraph 17, he recognizes that neither side of the abortion debate would agree with his assertion that birth should not be a marker to determine when a human being is given a right to life. To anti-abortionists, who maintain that "personhood" begins at conception, Pinker responds that if we adopt this viewpoint, the destruction of any fertilized human egg would be considered murder. To those in favor of abortion rights, who consider personhood to begin when the baby is capable of living outside the protection of the mother's body, Pinker counters that this depends on the condition of the infant and the willingness of the parents to accept the risks inherent in a premature birth. In paragraph 19, Pinker also rejects the position that all life deserves to be preserved. If this were practiced, Pinker reasons, then "delousing a child is akin to mass murder." Pinker's stance forces us to reexamine how we define a "person" and how we can determine at what point the right to live unharmed begins.

We can briefly summarize Pinker's warrants and backing as follows:

Warrant 1	Biology is destiny. We are at the mercy of our neurological programming, which has been handed down from our evolutionary ancestors.
Backing	Examples of women who grieve for the newborns they killed; references to Melissa Drexler and Amy Grossberg, who killed their newborn infants.
Warrant 2	If human behavior is controlled by deeply ingrained biological forces, then women can't be held legally responsible for following their natural impulses.
Backing	Examples of lenient criminal treatment of women who commit neonaticide; examples of less severe penalties for women who kill newborns, as opposed to those given for the murder of older children or adults.

Warrant 3	A newborn infant is not a full person. Neonates do not yet possess those human qualities that bestow on them the right to life.
Backing	A description of a newborn infant's physical helplessness; a definition of a "full person" according to some moral philosophers; a comparison of the intellectual and moral awareness of a newborn infant with that of a mouse.

Qualifiers

Throughout his essay, Pinker is careful to use *qualifiers* that limit and clarify his claim. There are many examples of these; we will point out a few that appear early in the essay along with our emphasis and comments:

Paragraph 4	"But it's *hard* [difficult but not impossible] to maintain that neonaticide is an illness when we learn that it has been practiced and accepted in *most* [but not all] cultures throughout history. And that neonaticidal women do not *commonly* [typical but not in all cases] show signs of psychopathology."
Paragraph 5	"But normal human motives are *not always* [happens some of the time] moral, and neonaticide *does not have to be* [but it could be] a product of malfunctioning neural circuitry or a dysfunctional upbringing."

By using qualifiers, Pinker demonstrates his awareness that his claim may not always be true under all circumstances and accounts for the differing experiences of his audience.

As we stated at the beginning of this chapter, to construct a persuasive argument, you must pay careful attention to the logical structure you are building. As the Toulmin method illustrates, unless your claim is supported by a firm foundation (your warrants) and well buttressed by convincing grounds and backing, your structure will not withstand the rebuttals that will test its strength.

Pinker's view on neonaticide is disturbing, to say the least. For his essay to be persuasive, the reader must be willing to accept each of his warrants and the backing he uses to support them. Four days after Pinker's essay appeared in the *New York Times,* the following article was published in the *Washington Post.* As you read the article, notice how author Michael Kelley, a senior writer at the *National Journal,* attacks Pinker's claim by questioning each of his warrants and their backing. Calling Pinker's premise one of the "most thoroughly dishonest constructs anyone has ever attempted to pass off as science," Kelley also levels severe criticism at one of Pinker's sources, Michael Tooley. Kelley comments that Pinker's citation of Tooley's radical views, even though he may not directly agree with them, makes him "guilty by association." Kelley's accusation demonstrates why you should choose your sources carefully. Your audience will associate your views with the company they keep.

Arguing for Infanticide

Michael Kelley

1   Of all the arguments advanced against the legalization of abortion, the one that always struck me as the most questionable is the most consequential: that the widespread acceptance of abortion would lead to a profound moral shift in our culture, a great devaluing of human life. This seemed to me dubious on general principle: Projections of this sort almost always turn out to be wrong because they fail to grasp that, in matters of human behavior, there is not really any such thing as a trendline. People change to meet new realities and thereby change reality.

2   Thus, for the environmental hysterics of the 1970s, the nuclear freezers of the 1980s and the Perovian budget doomsayers of the 1990s, the end that was nigh never came. So, with abortions, why should a tolerance for ending human life under one, very limited, set of conditions necessarily lead to an acceptance of ending human life under other, broader terms?

3   This time, it seems, the pessimists were right. On Sunday, Nov. 2, an article in the *New York Times,* the closest thing we have to the voice of the intellectual establishment, came out for killing babies. I am afraid that I am sensationalizing only slightly. The article by Steven Pinker in the *Times Magazine* did not go quite so far as to openly recommend the murder of infants, and printing the article did not constitute the *Times'* endorsement of the idea. But close enough, close enough.

4   What Pinker, a professor of psychology at the Massachusetts Institute of Technology, wrote and what the *Times* treated as a legitimate argument, was a thoroughly sympathetic treatment of this modest proposal: Mothers who kill their newborn infants should not be judged as harshly as people who take human life in its later stages because newborn infants are not persons in the full sense of the word, and therefore do not enjoy a right to life. Who says that life begins at birth?

5   "To a biologist, birth is as arbitrary a milestone as any other," Pinker breezily writes. "No, the right to life must come, the moral philosophers say, from morally significant traits that we humans happen to possess. One such trait is having a unique sequence of experiences that defines us as individuals and connects us to other people. Other traits include an ability to reflect upon ourselves as a continuous locus of consciousness, to form and savor plans for the future, to dread death and to express the choice not to die. And there's the rub: our immature neonates don't possess these traits any more than mice do."

6   Pinker notes that "several moral philosophers have concluded that neonates are not persons, and thus neonaticide should not be classified as murder," and he suggests his acceptance of this view, arguing that "the facts don't make it easy" to legitimately outlaw the killing of infants.

7   Pinker's casually authoritative mention of "the facts" is important, because Pinker is no mere ranter from the crackpot fringe but a scientist. He is, in fact, a respected explicator of the entirely mainstream and currently hot theory of evolutionary psychology, and the author of *How the Mind Works,* a widely read and widely celebrated book on the subject.

8   How the mind works, says Pinker, is that people are more or less hard-wired to behave as they do by the cumulative effects of the human experience. First cousins to the old Marxist economic determinists, the evolutionary psychologists are behavioral determinists. They believe in a sort of Popeye's theory of human behavior: I do what I do because I yam what I yam because I wuz what I wuz.

9   This view is radical; it seeks to supplant both traditional Judeo-Christian morality and liberal humanism with a new "scientific" philosophy that denies the idea that all humans are possessed of a quality that sets them apart from the lower species, and that this quality gives humans the capacity and responsibility to choose freely between right and wrong. And it is monstrous. And, judging from the writings of Pinker and his fellow determinists on the subject of infanticide, it may be the most thoroughly dishonest construct anyone has ever attempted to pass off as science.

10   Pinker's argument was a euphemized one. The more blunt argument is made by Michael Tooley, a philosophy professor at the University of Colorado, whom Pinker quotes. In this 1972 essay "Abortion and Infanticide," Tooley makes what he calls "an extremely plausible answer" to the question: "What makes it morally permissible to destroy a baby, but wrong to kill an adult?" Simple enough: Personhood does not begin at birth. Rather, "an organism possesses a serious right to life only if it possesses the concept of a self as a continuing subject of experiences and other mental states, and believes that it is itself such a continuing entity."

11   Some would permit the killing of infants "up to the time an organism learned how to use certain expressions," but Tooley finds this cumbersome and would simply establish "some period of time, such as a week after birth, as the interval during which infanticide will be permitted."

12   And Tooley does not bother with Pinker's pretense that what is under discussion here is only a rare act of desperation, the killing of an unwanted child by a frightened, troubled mother. No, no, no. If it is moral to kill a baby for one, it is moral for all. Indeed, the systematic, professionalized use of infanticide would be a great benefit to humanity. "Most people would prefer to raise children who do not suffer from gross deformities or from severe physical, emotional, or intellectual handicaps," writes eugenicist Tooley. "If it could be shown that there is no moral objection to infanticide the happiness of society could be significantly and justifiably increased."

13   To defend such an unnatural idea, the determinists argue that infanticide is in fact natural: In Pinker's words, "it has been practiced and accepted in most cultures throughout history." This surprising claim is critical to the argument that the act of a mother killing a child is a programmed response to signals that the child might not fare well in life (because of poverty, illegitimacy or other factors). And it is a lie.

14   In fact, although millions of mothers give birth every year under the sort of adverse conditions that Pinker says trigger the "natural" urge to kill the baby, infanticide is extremely rare in all modern societies, and is universally treated as a greatly aberrant act, the very definition of a moral horror. The only cultures that Pinker can point to in which infanticide is widely "practiced and accepted" are those that are outside the mores of Western civilization: ancient cultures and the remnants of ancient cultures today, tribal hunter-gatherer societies.

15   And so goes the entire argument, a great chain of dishonesty, palpable untruth piled upon palpable untruth. "A new mother," asserts Pinker, "will first coolly assess the infant and her situation and only in the next few days begin to see it as a unique and wonderful individual." Yes, that was my wife all over: cool as a cucumber as she assessed whether to keep her first-born child or toss him out the window. As George Orwell said once of another vast lie, "You have to be an intellectual to believe such nonsense. No ordinary man could be such a fool."

QUESTIONS FOR ANALYSIS AND DISCUSSION

1. Briefly outline the basic Toulmin components of Kelley's argument: What is his claim? What grounds does he use to support it? Then find and identify Kelley's warrants and the backing he provides to demonstrate their reliability.

2. To what aspects of Pinker's claim and warrants does Kelley object? On what grounds does he object?

3. Pinker limits his discussion of neonaticide to the behavior of "depressed new mothers" (paragraph 9). Does Kelley ignore this distinction in his response to Pinker? How does Kelley shift the discussion from Pinker's "anguished girls" (paragraph 23) to "millions of mothers" (paragraph 14 in Kelley)? Do you think this is a fair interpretation of Pinker's intent?

4. Kelley begins his essay with a reference to the legalization of abortion. On what basis does he suggest a link between the "widespread acceptance of abortion" and Pinker's theories about neonaticide?

5. In paragraph 3 of his essay, Kelley states that Pinker "did not go quite so far as to openly recommend the murder of infants." Discuss the implications of Kelley's use of the qualifiers *quite* and *openly*. What do you think he intends to imply about Pinker's objectives?

6. In paragraph 10, what does Kelley mean by describing Pinker's argument as "euphemized"? What connection does Kelley make between Pinker's views and the theories expressed by Michael Tooley in his 1972 essay? Does your analysis of Pinker's claim and warrants lead you to believe that Pinker endorses Tooley's theories, as Kelley asserts?

7. In your journal, discuss your own response to Kelley's essay. Which reasons do you find particularly persuasive? With which reasons do you disagree, and why?

8. In paragraph 9, Kelley criticizes Pinker's attempt to take a "scientific" approach to a serious moral issue by suggesting that humans lack "the capacity and responsibility to choose freely between right and wrong." In your journal, consider how Pinker might respond to that statement. Would he agree with Kelley's interpretation of his ideas? How would Pinker suggest that society should deal with the problem of neonaticide?

SAMPLE STUDENT ARGUMENT FOR ANALYSIS

The previous two essays focused on parental love becoming grossly dysfunctional as the possible result of tragic neurological wiring. What follows is a paper about the effects of parental love on children of divorce. Given the fact that half of all children will see their parents' marriage terminate by the time they turn 18, divorce has become an American way of life. While society may shake its collective head at such a statistic, lamenting the loss of the traditional family, not all children of divorce see it as a problem. In the following essay, Lowell Putnam explores the effect of his parents' divorce on his development, arguing that divorce should not be a taboo topic and that children of broken homes are not always damaged.

Putnam wrote this essay when he was a college freshman. When he is not living on campus, he splits his time between his mother's home in New York and his father's home in Massachusetts.

Read through Putnam's essay and make notes in your journal. Notice whether and how its parts work together—and, if possible, where some of the parts may need to be reworked. Then respond to the questions that follow.

Putnam 1

Lowell Putnam
Professor Ramos
English 201
5 March 2010

Did I Miss Something?

1   The subject of divorce turns heads in our society. It is responsible for bitten tongues, lowered voices, and an almost pious reverence saved only for life-threatening illness or uncontrolled catastrophe. Having grown up in a "broken home," I am always shocked to be treated as a victim of some social disease. When a class assignment required that I write an essay concerning my feelings about or my personal experiences with divorce, my first reaction was complete surprise. An essay on aspects of my life affected by divorce seems completely superfluous because I cannot differentiate between the "normal" part of my youth and the supposed angst and confusion that apparently come with all divorces. The separation of my parents over sixteen years ago (when I was three years old) has either saturated every last pore of my developmental epidermis to a point where I cannot sense it or it has not affected me at all. Eugene Ehrlich's *Highly Selective Dictionary for the Extraordinarily Literate* (1997) defines divorce as a "breach"; however, I cannot sense any schism in my

Putnam 2

life resulting from the event to which other people seem to attribute so much importance. My parents' divorce is a ubiquitous part of who I am, and the only "breach" that could arrive from my present familial arrangement would be to tear me away from what I consider my normal living conditions.

Though there is no doubt in my mind that many unfortunate people have had their lives torn apart by the divorce of their parents, I do not feel any real sense of regret for my situation. In my opinion, the paramount role of a parent is to love his or her child. Providing food, shelter, education, and video games are of course other necessary elements of successful child rearing, but these secondary concerns stem from the most fundamental ideal of parenting, which is love. A loving parent will be a successful one even if he or she cannot afford to furnish his or her child with the best clothes or the most sophisticated gourmet delicacies. With love as the driving force in a parent's mind, he or she will almost invariably make the correct decisions. When my mother and father found that they were no longer in love with each other after nine years of marriage, their love for me forced them to take the precipitous step to separate. The safest environment for me was to be with one happy parent at a time, instead of two miserable ones all the time. The sacrifice that they both made to relinquish control over me for half the year was at least as painful for them as it was for me (probably even more so), but in the end I was not deprived of a parent's love, but merely of one parent's presence for a few weeks at a time. My father and mother's love for me has not dwindled even slightly over the past fifteen years, and I can hardly imagine a more well-adjusted and contented family.

As I reread the first section of this essay, I realize that it is perhaps too optimistic and cheerful regarding my life as a child of divorced parents. In all truthfulness, there have been some decidedly negative ramifications stemming from our family separation. My first memory is actually of a fight between my mother and father. I vaguely remember standing in the end of the upstairs hallway of our Philadelphia house when I was about three years old, and seeing shadows moving back and forth in the light coming from under the door of my father's study, accompanied by raised voices. It would be naïve of me to say that I have not been at all affected by divorce, since it has permeated my most primal and basic memories; however, I am grateful that I can only recall one such incident, instead of having parental conflicts become so quotidian that they leave no mark whatsoever on my mind. Also, I find that having to divide my time equally between both parents leads to alienation from either side of my family. Invariably, at every holiday occasion, there is one half of my family (either my mother's side or my father's) that has to explain that "Lowell is with his [mother/father] this year," while aunts, cousins, and grandparents collectively arch eyebrows or avert eyes. Again, though, I should not be hasty to lament my distance from loved ones, since there are many families with "normal" marriages where the children never even meet their cousins, let alone get to spend every other Thanksgiving with them. Though divorce has certainly thrown some proverbial monkey wrenches into some proverbial gears, in general my otherwise strong familial ties have overshadowed any minor blemishes.

4   Perhaps one of the most important reasons for my absence of "trauma" (for lack of a better word) stemming from my parents' divorce is that I am by no means alone in my trials and tribulations. The foreboding statistic that sixty percent of marriages end in divorce is no myth to me, indeed many of my friends come from similar situations. The argument could be made that "birds of a feather flock together" and that my friends and I form a tight support network for each other, but I strongly doubt that any of us need or look for that kind of buttress. The fact of the matter is that divorce happens a lot in today's society, and as a result our culture has evolved to accommodate these new family arrangements, making the overall conditions more hospitable for me and my broken brothers and shattered sisters.

5   I am well aware that divorce can often lead to issues of abandonment and familial proximity among children of separated parents, but in my case I see very little evidence to support the claim that my parents should have stayed married "for the sake of the child." In many ways, my life is enriched by the division of my time with my father and my time with my mother. I get to live in New York City for half of the year, and in a small suburb of Boston for the other half. I have friends who envy me, since I get "the best of both worlds." I never get double-teamed by parents during arguments, and I cherish my time with each one more since it only lasts half the year.

6   In my opinion, there is no such thing as a perfect life or a "normal" life, and any small blips on our karmic radar screen have to be dealt with

Putnam 3

appropriately but without any trepidation or self-pity. Do I miss my father when I live with my mother (and vice versa)? Of course I do. However, I know young boys and girls who have lost parents to illness or accidental injury, so my pitiable position is relative. As I look back on the last nineteen years from the relative independence of college, I can safely say that my childhood has not been at all marred by having two different houses to call home.

QUESTIONS FOR ANALYSIS AND DISCUSSION

1. Identify Putnam's claim. Where does he state it in his essay? From your experience, do you agree with him? Do you agree that people discuss divorce "in an almost pious reverence saved only for life-threatening illness"?

2. On what grounds does Putnam base his claim? Find specific evidence he presents to support his claim. Do you find it convincing and supportive?

3. Do you agree with Putnam's definition of what makes a good parent?

4. Putnam has several warrants, some of them stated explicitly and some implied. In paragraph 2, he states: "A loving parent will be a successful one even if he or she cannot afford to furnish his or her child with the best clothes or the most sophisticated gourmet delicacies." Do you agree with his warrant? On what commonly shared values or beliefs does he base this warrant? Are there any aspects of his warrant with which you disagree? What backing does Putnam provide to support his warrant? Is it sufficient?

5. What other warrants underlie Putnam's claim? In a small peer group, identify several layers of warrants and discuss whether these need additional backing to be convincing.

6. Notice the qualifier Putnam uses in paragraph 3 when he says, "In all truthfulness, there have been *some* decidedly negative ramifications stemming from our family separation" (emphasis added). What limitations does this qualifying statement put on his argument? Does this limitation weaken his argument at all?

7. Does Putnam acknowledge and address anticipated rebuttals to his argument? Can you locate any in his essay? What rebuttals can you make in response to his argument?

8. If you are a child of divorced parents, write about the experience as it affected your emotional and psychological outlook. How did it impact

your life growing up, and how did it affect your adult view of marriage? Answer the same questions if your parents remained married, considering in your response how your life may have been different if your parents had divorced while you were young.

9. In your peer group, discuss the effects of divorce on children. Further develop Putnam's idea that it is just another way of life. Compare notes with classmates to assemble a complete list. Based on this list, develop your own argument about the effects of divorce on children.

Using Visual Arguments: Thinking Like an Illustrator

Ours is a visual world. From the first cave paintings of prehistoric France to the complicated photomosaic posters that adorn dormitory walls today, we are inspired, compelled, and persuaded by visual stimuli. Everywhere we look images vie for our attention—magazine ads, T-shirt logos, movie billboards, artwork, traffic signs, political cartoons, statues, and storefront windows. Glanced at only briefly, visuals communicate information and ideas. They project commonly held values, ideals, and fantasies. They relay opinion, inspire reaction, and influence emotion. And because competition for our attention today is so great and the time available for communication is so scarce, images must compete to make an impression or risk being lost in a blur of visual information.

Because the goal of a calculated visual is to persuade, coax, intimidate, or otherwise subliminally influence its viewer, it is important that its audience can discern the strategies or technique it employs. In other words, to be a literate reader of visuals, one must be a literate reader of arguments.

Consider the instant messages projected by brand names, company logos, or even the American flag. Such images may influence us consciously and unconsciously. Some visual images, such as advertisements, may target our emotions, while others, such as graphics, may appeal to our intellect. Just as we approach writing with the tools of critical analysis, we should carefully consider the many ways visuals influence us.

Common Forms of Visual Arguments

Visual arguments come in many different forms and use many different media. Artists, photographers, advertisers, cartoonists, and designers approach their work with the same intentions that authors of written material do—they want to share a point of view, present an idea, inspire, or evoke a reaction. Think back to when you had your high school yearbook photo taken. The photographer didn't simply sit you down and start snapping pictures. More likely, the photographer told you how to sit, tilt your head, and where to gaze. You selected your clothing for the picture carefully and probably spent extra time on your hair that day. Lighting, shadow, and setting were also thoughtfully considered. You and your photographer crafted an image of how you wanted the world to see you—an image of importance because it would be forever recorded in your yearbook, as well as distributed to family and friends as the remembrance of a milestone in your life. In effect, you were creating a visual argument.

While there are many different kinds of visual arguments, the most common ones take the form of artwork, advertisements, editorial cartoons, and news photos. These visuals often do not rely on an image alone to tell their story, although it is certainly possible for a thoughtfully designed visual to do so. More often, however, advertisements are accompanied by ad copy, editorial cartoons feature comments or statements, and news photos are placed near the stories they enhance.

Ancillary visuals—that is, tables, graphs, and charts—have great potential for enhancing written arguments and influencing the audience. They provide snapshots of information and provide factual support to written information. We will discuss these types of visuals, and how you can use them to enhance your own written arguments, later in this chapter. But first, let us examine some powerful visual images and the ways they capture our attention, impact our sensibilities, and evoke our responses.

Analyzing Visual Arguments

As critical readers of written arguments, we do not take the author simply at face value. We consider the author's purpose and intent, audience, style, tone, and supporting evidence. We must apply these same analytical tools to "read" visual arguments effectively. As with written language, understanding the persuasive power of "visual language" requires a close examination and interpretation of the premise, claims, details, supporting evidence, and stylistic touches embedded in any visual piece. We should ask ourselves the following four questions when examining visual arguments:

■ Who is the target *audience?*
■ What are the *claims* made in the images?
■ What shared history or cultural *assumptions*—or warrants—does the image make?
■ What is the supporting *evidence?*

Like works of art, visuals often employ color, shape, line, texture, depth, and point of view to create their effect. Therefore, to understand how visuals work and to analyze the way visuals persuade, we must also ask questions about specific aspects of form and design. For example, some questions to ask about print images such as those in newspaper and magazine ads include:

■ What in the frame catches your attention immediately?
■ What is the central image? What is the background image? foreground images? What are the surrounding images? What is significant in the placement of these images? their relationship to one another?
■ What verbal information is included? How is it made prominent? How does it relate to the other graphics or images?
■ What specific details (people, objects, locale) are emphasized? Which are exaggerated or idealized?
■ What is the effect of color and lighting?
■ What emotional effect is created by the images—pleasure? longing? anxiety? nostalgia?
■ Do the graphics and images make you want to know more about the subject or product?

■ What special significance might objects in the image have?
■ Is there any symbolism embedded in the images?

Considering these questions helps us to survey a visual argument critically and enables us to formulate reasoned assessments of its message and intent. In the next pages of this chapter, we will analyze in greater detail some visual arguments presented in art, advertising, editorial cartoons, and photographs. Part Two of this book continues the investigation of visual arguments as they connect to the topics of each chapter.

Art

The French artist Georges Braque (1882–1963) once said, "In art, there can be no effect without twisting the truth." While not all artists would agree with him, Braque, who with Pablo Picasso originated the cubist style, "saw" things from a different perspective than the rest of us, and he expressed his vision in his paintings. All art is an interpretation of what the artist sees. It is filtered through the eyes of the artist and influenced by his or her own perceptions.

Throughout history, artists have applied their craft to advance religious, social, and political visual arguments. Portraits of kings and queens present how the monarchs wanted their people to see them, with symbolic tools of power such as scepters, crowns, and rich vestments. Art in churches and cathedrals was used as a means of visual instruction for people who could not read. Much of modern art reveals impressions, feelings, and emotions without remaining faithful to the actual thing depicted. While entire books are written about the meaning and function of art, let's examine how one particular artist, Pablo Picasso (1881–1973), created a visual argument.

Pablo Picasso's *Guernica*

Pablo Picasso, with fellow artist Georges Braque, invented a style of painting known as **cubism.** Cubism is based on the idea that the eye observes things from continually changing viewpoints, as fragments of a whole. Cubism aims to represent the essential reality of forms from multiple perspectives and angles. Thus, cubist paintings don't show reality as we see it. Rather, they depict pieces of people, places, and things in an unstable field of vision.

Picasso's painting *Guernica* (Figure 8.1, page 207) represents the essence of cubism. During the Spanish Civil War, the German air force bombed the town of Guernica, the cultural center of the Basque region in northern Spain and a Loyalist stronghold. In only a few minutes on April 26, 1937, hundreds of men, women, and children were massacred in the deadly air strike. Two months later, Picasso expressed his outrage at the attack in a mural he titled simply, *Guernica.*

The mural is Picasso's statement about the horror and devastation of war. The painting is dynamic and full of action, yet its figures seem flat and static. It is balanced while still presenting distorted images and impressions. It is ordered while still evoking a sense of chaos and panic. To better understand Picasso's "statement," let's apply some of the questions about visual arguments described earlier in the chapter to this painting.

Figure 8.1 *Pablo Picasso, Guernica, 1937*

Who Is Picasso's Target Audience?

Knowing the history of the painting can help us understand whom Picasso was trying to reach. In January 1937, Picasso was commissioned to paint a mural for the 1937 *Exposition Internationale des Arts et Techniques dans la Vie Moderne,* an art exhibition to open in France in May of that same year. Although he had never been a political person, the atrocity of Guernica in April compelled him to express his anger and appeal to the world.

Before the mural went on display, some politicians tried to replace it with a less "offensive" piece of art. When the picture was unveiled at the opening of the expo, it was received poorly. One critic described it as "the work of a madman." Picasso had hoped that his work would shock people. He wanted the outside world to care about what happened at Guernica. However, Picasso may have misjudged his first audience. In 1937, Europe was on the brink of world war. Many people were in denial that the war could touch them and preferred to ignore the possibility that it was imminent. It was this audience who first viewed *Guernica*—an audience that didn't want to see a mural about war, an audience that was trying to avoid the inevitable. Years later, the mural would become one of the most critically acclaimed works of art of the twentieth century.

What Claims Is Picasso Making in the Images?

Picasso's painting comprises many images that make up an entire scene. It depicts simultaneously events that happened over a period of time. The overall claim is that war itself is horrible. The smaller claims address the injustice of Guernica more directly. A mother wails in grief over her dead infant, a reminder that the bombing of Guernica was a massacre of innocents. Picasso also chose to paint his mural in black and white, giving it the aura of a newspaper, especially in the body of the horse. He could be saying, "This is news" or "This is a current event that you should think about."

It should be mentioned that Picasso created many versions of the images in the mural, carefully considering their position, placement, and expression, sometimes drawing eight or nine versions of a single subject. He thoughtfully considered how the images would convey his message before he painted them in the mural.

What Shared History or Cultural Assumptions Does Picasso Make?

The assumptions in any argument are the principles or beliefs that the audience takes for granted. These assumptions implicitly connect the claim to the evidence. By naming his mural *Guernica*, Picasso knew that people would make an immediate connection between the chaos on the wall and the events of April 26, 1937. He also assumed that the people viewing the painting would be upset by it. In addition, there are symbols in the painting that would have been recognized by people at the time—such as the figure of the bull in the upper-left-hand corner of the mural, a long-time symbol for Spain.

What Is Picasso's Supporting Evidence?

Although Picasso was illustrating a real event, cubism allowed him to paint "truth" rather than "reality." If Picasso was trying to depict the horror of Guernica, and by extension, the terror and chaos of war, all the components of his mural serve as supporting evidence. The wailing figures, panicked faces, the darkness contrasted by jumbled images of light all project the horror of war. Even the horse looks terrified. Overall, *Guernica* captures the emotional cacophony of war. Picasso wasn't just trying to say, "War is hell." He was also trying to impress upon his audience that such atrocities should never happen again. In essence, Picasso was making an appeal for peace by showing its opposite, the carnage of war.

QUESTIONS FOR ANALYSIS AND DISCUSSION ————————

Referring to the more specific questions regarding visual arguments discussed earlier in the chapter, apply them to Picasso's painting.

1. What images in the painting catch your attention, and why?
2. What is the central image? Is there a central image? What appears in the foreground? What is significant about the placement of the images? How do they relate to one another?
3. What verbal information, if any, is included, and why? (Remember that Picasso did title his painting *Guernica*. What might have happened if he had named it something more abstract?)
4. What specific details are emphasized? What is exaggerated or idealized?
5. What is the effect of color and light?
6. Does the image make you want to know more?
7. What symbolism is embedded in the image?

Norman Rockwell's *Freedom of Speech*

Picasso's mural was designed to be displayed in a large hall at the World Exposition and later, presumably, in a museum. Other artists had less grand aspirations for their work. Norman Rockwell (1894–1978) was an artist who featured most of his work on the covers of magazines, most notably the *Saturday Evening Post,* a publication he considered "the greatest show window in America." In 47 years, Rockwell contributed 321 paintings to the magazine and became an American icon.

On January 6, 1941, President Franklin Delano Roosevelt addressed Congress, delivering his famous "Four Freedoms" speech. Against the background of the Nazi domination of Europe and the Japanese oppression of China, Roosevelt described the four essential human freedoms—freedom of speech, freedom of worship, freedom from want, and freedom from fear. Viewing these freedoms as the fundamental basis on which our society was formed, Roosevelt called upon Americans to uphold these liberties at all costs. Two years later, Rockwell, inspired by Roosevelt's speech, created his famous series of paintings on these "Four Freedoms," reproduced in four consecutive issues of the *Saturday Evening Post.* So popular were the images that they were used by the U.S. government to sell war bonds, to inspire public support for the war effort, and to remind people of the ideals for which they were fighting. The paintings serve as an example of how art can sometimes extend into advertising.

Let's take a closer look at one of the four paintings, *Freedom of Speech* (Figure 8.2 below). When the war department adopted the painting for the war bond effort, it added two slogans to the image. The command "Save Freedom of Speech" was printed at the top of the painting in large, capital letters and, in even larger typeface, "Buy War Bonds" was printed at the bottom. As we analyze this painting, we will also make references to its later use as part of the effort to sell war bonds.

Figure 8.2   *Norman Rockwell,* Freedom of Speech, *1943*

Before he took a brush to his canvas, Rockwell consciously or unconsciously asked himself some of the same questions writers do when they stare at a blank piece of paper while preparing to create a written argument. After determining that he would use the American small-town vehicle of democracy, the town meeting, as the means to express the theme of freedom of speech, he then painted his "argument."

Who Is Rockwell's Audience?

The *Saturday Evening Post* was widely read in America in the 1930s and 1940s. Rockwell would have wanted his work to appeal to a wide audience, readers of the magazine. If we examine the people in the painting—presumably based on Rockwell's Arlington, Vermont, friends and neighbors—we can deduce the kind of audience the artist was hoping to touch: small-town citizens from a middle-income, working-class environment. Like the language of an argument written for a "general audience," the figures represent what Rockwell considered all-American townsfolk.

The venue is a meetinghouse or town hall because people are sitting on benches. The figures represent a generational cross-section of men and women, from the elderly white-haired man to the left of the central standing figure to the young woman behind him. Style of dress reinforces the notion of class diversity, from the standing man in work clothes to the two men dressed in white shirts, ties, and suit jackets. The formality of the seated figures also opens audience identity to life beyond a small, rural community. That is, some of the men's formal attire and the woman in a stylish hat broaden the depiction to include white-collar urban America. While diversity in age and class is suggested, diversity of race is not. There are no Asians, African Americans, or other nonwhites in the scene. This exclusion might be a reflection of the times and, perhaps, the popular notion of what constituted small-town America 70 years ago. While such exclusion would be unacceptable today, it should be noted that in the years following this painting's completion, Rockwell used his considerable talent and fame to champion the civil rights struggle.

What Is Rockwell's Claim?

When the government adopted Rockwell's painting for their World War II effort campaign to sell war bonds, they added the caption: "Save Freedom of Speech. Buy War Bonds." When we consider the poster as an advertising piece, this essentially becomes the poster's claim. And we know the artist's intention, to illustrate the theme of freedom of speech. Rockwell's challenge was in how he makes his claim—how he dramatizes it on canvas. Just as a writer uses words to persuade, the artist makes his claim in symbolic details of the brush.

It has been said that Norman Rockwell's paintings appeal to a dreamy-eyed American nostalgia and at the same time project a world where the simple acts of common folk express high American ideals. In this painting, we have one of the sacred liberties dramatized by a working-class man raised to the figure of a political spokesperson in the assembly of others. Clearly expressing his opinion as freely as anybody else, he becomes both the illustration and defender of the democratic principles of freedom and equality.

What Are Rockwell's Assumptions?

As with written arguments, the success of a visual argument depends on whether the audience accepts the assumptions (the values, legal or moral principles, commonsense knowledge, or shared beliefs) projected in the image. One assumption underlying Rockwell's illustration is that freedom of speech is desirable for Americans regardless of gender, class, or position in society. We know this instantly from the facial expressions and body language of the figures in the canvas. For example, the face of the man standing seems more prominent because it is painted against a dark blank background and is brighter than any others, immediately capturing our attention. His face tilts upward with a look of pride, lit as if by the inspiration of the ideals he represents—freedom of expression. One might even see suggestions of divine inspiration on his face as it rises in the light and against the night-blackened window in the background. The lighting and man's posture are reminiscent of religious paintings of past centuries. Additionally, the man's body is angular and rough, while his facial characteristics strongly resemble those of a young Abraham Lincoln—which suggests a subtle fusion of the patriotic with the divine. The implied message is that freedom of speech is a divine right.

As for the surrounding audience, we take special note of the two men looking up at the speaker. The older man appears impressed and looks on with a warm smile of approval, while the other man on the right gazes up expectantly. In fact, the entire audience supports the standing man with reasonable, friendly, and respectful gazes. The speaker is "Everyman." And he has the support and respect of his community. Rockwell's audience, subscribers of the *Saturday Evening Post,* saw themselves in this image—an image that mirrored the values of honest, decent, middle America.

What Is Rockwell's Supporting Evidence?

The key supporting image in Rockwell's painting is the sharp contrast between the standing man and those sitting around him. Not only is he the only one on his feet, but he is the only working-class person clearly depicted. He stands out from the others in the room; and it is significant that they look up to him—a dramatic illustration of what it means to give the common man his say. Were the scene reversed—with the central figure formally dressed and those looking up approvingly attired in work clothes—we would have a completely different message: that is, a representative of the upper class perhaps "explaining" higher concepts to a less-educated people. The message would be all wrong. In the painting, class barriers are transcended as the "common man" has risen to speak his mind with a face full of conviction, while upper-class people look on in support. That's the American ideal in action.

Because this is a painting instead of a newspaper photograph, every detail is selected purposely and, thus, is open to interpretation. One such detail is the fold of papers sticking out of the man's jacket pocket. What might those papers represent? And what's the point of such a detail? What associations might we make with it? There are words printed on the paper, but we cannot read them, so we're left to speculate. The only other paper in the painting is in the hand of the man on the right. The words "report" and "town" are visible. So, we might conclude that the speaker's pocket contains the same pamphlet, perhaps a summary report of the evening's agenda or possibly a resolution to be voted on. Whatever the documentation, the man clearly doesn't need it because his remarks transcend whatever is on that paper. And here lies more evidence of Rockwell's claim and celebration of the unaided articulation of one man's views out of many—the essence of freedom of speech.

QUESTIONS FOR ANALYSIS AND DISCUSSION

Referring to the more specific questions regarding visual arguments discussed earlier in the chapter, apply them to Rockwell's painting.

1. What images in the painting catch your attention, and why?
2. What is the central image? Is there a central image? What appears in the foreground? What is significant about the placement of the images? How do they relate to one another?
3. What verbal information, if any, is included, and why?
4. What specific details are emphasized? What is exaggerated or idealized?
5. What is the effect of color and light?
6. Does the image make you want to know more?
7. What symbolism is embedded in the image?

Advertisements

Norman Rockwell sought to embody a concept through his art; and, as a result, his painting tries to prompt reflection and self-awareness. In other words, his visuals serve to open the mind to a new discovery or idea. Advertising also selects and crafts visual images. However, advertising has a different objective. Its goal is not to stimulate expansive and enlightened thought but to direct the viewer to a single basic response: buy this product!

Images have clout, and none are so obvious or so craftily designed as those from the world of advertising. Advertising images are everywhere—television, newspapers, the Internet, magazines, the sides of buses, and on highway billboards. Each year, companies collectively spend more than $150 billion on print ads and television commercials (more than the gross national product of many countries). Advertisements comprise at least a quarter of each television hour and form the bulk of most newspapers and magazines. Tapping into our most basic emotions, their appeal goes right to the quick of our fantasies: happiness, material wealth, eternal youth, social acceptance, sexual fulfillment, and power.

Yet, most of us are so accustomed to the onslaught of such images that we see them without looking and hear them without listening. But if we stopped to examine how the images work, we might be amazed at their powerful and complex psychological force. And we might be surprised at how much effort goes into the crafting of such images—an effort solely intended to make us spend our money.

Like a written argument, every print ad or commercial has an *audience, claims, assumptions,* and *evidence.* Sometimes these elements are obvious; sometimes they are understated; sometimes they are implied. They may boast testimonials by average folk or celebrities, or cite hard scientific evidence. And sometimes they simply manipulate our desire to be happy or socially accepted. But common to every ad and commercial, no matter what the medium, is the *claim* that you should buy this product.

Print ads are potentially complex mixtures of images, graphics, and text. So in analyzing an ad, you should be aware of the use of photography, the placement of those images, and the use of text, company logos, and other graphics such as illustrations, drawings, sidebar boxes, and so on. You should also keep in mind that every aspect of the image has been thought about and carefully designed. Let's take a look at how a recent magazine ad for Toyota uses some of these elements including social appeal, the use of color and light, and setting to convince us to buy the Toyota Prius hybrid car.

Toyota Prius Ad

When analyzing a print ad, we should try to determine what first captures our attention. In the Toyota Prius ad (Figure 8.3 on page 214), it is the bold, white outline of a car. The instant suggestion is a compact vehicle with a simple and streamlined design. The outline format barely intrudes upon our view of the beach scene; and, ironically, we're not even shown the actual vehicle the ad is selling. Second, we note a smiling, ethnically diverse couple. The man and woman are not in contact with one another but with the outline of the vehicle, suggesting that in their relationship they share positive interest in the car outline they are leaning on. Their attire is sporty and casual; and their smiles are relaxed and content. We wonder: Are they potential buyers? Did they design the car? Are they simply feeling good about what the car represents? But the small print at the bottom identifies them as "Toyota Associates," perhaps meaning that they had something to do with the design or production of the Prius.

The third component we notice is the beach itself. The soft lighting signals approaching dusk; the sand, sand dunes, sea, and sky are quiet, pristine, and undisturbed. We see a simple and unblemished image of nature. The fourth aspect we note is the text. The slogan, "WE SEE BEYOND CARS" is rendered in a large font, bold print; the lower expository text is in a smaller font; and the last segment of the ad identifying the couple is smaller still. The last item our eye moves to is in the upper right hand corner: Toyota and the url: toyota.com/beyondcars.

One of the most striking aspects of this ad is how it doesn't look like any other car ad. We are accustomed to images that show the actual vehicles—images that highlight particular features that manufacturers want consumers to associate with their cars: power, speed, ruggedness, luxury, handling, durability, et cetera. This ad defies those traditional approaches. Instead, we see a clean-cut twosome—who may or may not be romantically involved—leaning against the outline of a car we cannot see, though we know from the text it is a Prius. The message is that the Prius is an idea as much as it is a car. And driving this zero-emissions vehicle isn't just about transportation; it's about being part of a movement that will preserve the environment. The pristine environment, which the Prius will protect, is what shines through in this ad. In short, the Prius is desirable because it is barely there.

Figure 8.3

Who is the Audience for the Ad?

The ad attracts viewers not unlike the young couple in the ad—young to middle aged men and women who are technologically savvy, educated, and concerned over the environment. In fact, the ad assumes that protection of the environment takes precedence over the luxury of a polluting, powerful, gas-guzzling vehicle. The appeal is to individuals seeking alternatives to the typically over engineered powerhouse machines. In its understated approach, the ad also assumes that viewers appreciate nuance and subtlety. In fact, the ad does not talk about the car, but rather about Toyota's mission to protect the environment. In so doing, viewers are invited to explore the relationship between the visuals and the text.

What Is the Claim?

Because advertisers are vying for our attention, they must project their claim as efficiently as possible in order to discourage us from turning the page. The stated or implied claim of all advertising is that the product will make life better for us. Of course, most ads aren't so bold in their claims. But the promise is there by inference. The claim of this ad is that if you want to save the environment from the fallout of fossil-fuel consumption, you should buy a Prius. Further, by purchasing one, you become part of a community of responsible, "with-it" and technologically savvy people.

Lastly, the ad claims in its slogan, "WE SEE BEYOND CARS." Combined with the minimalist outline of the Prius and the undisturbed beauty of the beach, that slogan suggests that there is something beyond cars that you the consumer are really interested in: preserving the beauty and purity of nature. Beyond advertising a car, the ad makes the claim that you can be part of a transcendent movement, the green movement, simply by purchasing a Prius and helping make the world a better place. The ad claims that Toyota is devoted to protecting the environment, in fact, announcing that it spends $23 million per day on research. Such a claim re-brands Toyota not just as a manufacturer of cars but as a key player in the preservation of the environment.

What Is the Evidence?

The evidence for the desirability of the Toyota Prius is in the visuals and the text. If one goes to the website toyota.com/beyondcars, one sees a minimalist visual in the same style as this ad which presents evidence about Toyota's presence in the U.S. car market, its research funding and Toyota car production, and sales.

What Are the Assumptions?

The creators of this ad made several assumptions about us, the audience: (1) that we are familiar with the traditional car ads that showcase their vehicles; (2) that a significant segment of the car-buying public is environmentally conscious and looking for ways to save it; (3) that a company associated with protecting the environment via hybrid cars is admirable; and (4) that the audience cares less about a vehicle's power, glamour, or speed and more about the environmental impact of the vehicle. In short, the ad assumes people are as interested in supporting a cause as they are in buying a car.

Sample Ads for Analysis

Apply the principles of critical analysis described in the above section on advertising, as well as the elements of form and design discussed earlier in the chapter, to the ads that appear in the following pages.

Cats everywhere are having a hard time smelling their litter boxes.

Figure 8.4

Fresh Step Cat Litter

QUESTIONS FOR ANALYSIS AND DISCUSSION ――――――――

1. What first caught your eye in this ad? In what order do you look at other elements in the ad? Do you think the advertiser intends you to look at each component of the ad in a particular order? Why?
2. What is the visual joke in this ad? Consider the cat's posture, body language, facial expression, and relationship to the setting. What do the furniture, wall decorations, and other decorative touches say about the occupant? Do you find the ad visually pleasing? (Consider the size and placement of the cat, the background, and graphics.)
3. Who might be the target audience for this ad? Consider gender, age group, socioeconomic level, lifestyle, and self-image. Defend your answers using specifics in the ad.
4. There is a minimal amount of text here. How does the wording relate to the visuals? With reference to the copy, what is the implied argument in the copy? Explain the claim in the text. What are the warrants?

Figure 8.5

Victoria's Dirty Secret

QUESTIONS FOR ANALYSIS AND DISCUSSION ───────────

1. In what ways does the model look like the typical Victoria's Secret model? Be specific. In what ways does this model differ? Consider her attire, the wings, hair styling, expression, body posture, shoes, and so on. If you see any differences, how would you explain them? How do the similarities and/or differences contribute to the ad's criticism of the catalogue production of Victoria's Secret?
2. Consider the chain saw. What is the effect of having the model holding a sketched chain saw instead of a real one? And what do you make of the style of the drawing? Why not have a more realistic drawing than this roughly drawn one?
3. After reading the text of the ad, consider some of the characteristics of its argument. What is the basic claim? Locate specific evidence. Are opposing points of view presented? Where specifically?
4. Is this ad a proposal or a position argument? Explain your answer.
5. Visual arguments should inspire or provoke a reaction. On a scale of one to ten, how persuasive is this ad? Are you inspired to take action—specifically to contact Leslie H. Wexner, CEO of Victoria's Secret's parent company? Does it inspire you to get involved with ForestEthics' campaign?
6. Consider the small photograph insert. What is depicted, and how well does it illustrate the argument being made in the ad? How does it relate to the image of the model? Explain in detail.

Editorial or Political Cartoons

Editorial cartoons have been a part of American life for over a century. They are a mainstay feature on the editorial pages in most newspapers—those pages reserved for columnists, contributing editors, and illustrators to present their views in words and pen and ink. As in the nineteenth century when they first started to appear, such editorial cartoons are political in nature, holding up political and social issues for public scrutiny and sometimes ridicule.

A stand-alone editorial cartoon—as opposed to a strip of multiple frames—is a powerful and terse form of communication that combines pen-and-ink drawings with dialogue balloons and captions. They're not just visual jokes, but visual humor that comments on social/political issues while drawing on viewers' experience and knowledge.

The editorial cartoon is the story of a moment in the flow of familiar current events. And the key words here are *moment* and *familiar.* Although a cartoon captures a split instant in time, it also infers what came before and, perhaps, what may happen next—either in the next moment or in some indefinite future. And usually the cartoon depicts a specific moment in time. One of the most famous cartoons of the last 50 years is the late Bill Mauldin's Pulitzer Prize-winning drawing of the figure of Abraham Lincoln with his head in his hands. It appeared the morning after the assassination of President John Kennedy in 1963. There was no caption nor was there a need for one. The image represented the profound grief of a nation that had lost its leader to an assassin's bullet. But to capture the enormity of the event, Mauldin brilliantly chose to represent a woeful America by using the figure of Abraham Lincoln as depicted in the sculpture of the Lincoln Memorial in Washington, D.C. In so doing, the message implied that so profound was the loss that it even reduced to tears the marble figure of a man considered to be our greatest president, himself assassinated a century before.

For a cartoon to be effective, it must make the issue clear at a glance and it must establish where it stands on the argument. In the Mauldin illustration, we instantly recognize Lincoln and identify with the emotions. We need not be told the circumstances, since by the time the cartoon appeared the next day, all the world knew the horrible news that the president had been assassinated. To convey less obvious issues and figures at a glance, cartoonists resort to images that are instantly recognizable, that we don't have to work hard to grasp. Locales are determined by giveaway props: An airplane out the window suggests an airport; a cactus and cattle skull, a desert; an overstuffed armchair and TV, the standard living room. Likewise, human emotions are instantly conveyed: pleasure is a huge toothy grin; fury is steam blowing out of a figure's ears; love is two figures making goo-goo eyes with floating hearts overhead. People themselves may have exaggerated features to emphasize a point or emotion.

In his essay "What Is a Cartoon?" Mort Gerberg says that editorial cartoons rely on such visual clichés to convey their messages instantly. That is, they employ stock figures for their representation—images instantly recognizable from cultural stereotypes like the fat-cat tycoon, the mobster thug, and the sexy female movie star. And these come to us in familiar outfits and props that give away their identities and profession. The cartoon judge has a black robe and gavel; the prisoner wears striped overalls and a ball and chain; the physician dons a smock and holds a stethoscope; the doomsayer is a scrawny long-haired guy carrying a sign saying, "The end is near." These are visual clichés known by the culture at large, and we instantly recognize them.

The visual cliché may be what catches our eye in the editorial cartoon, but the message lies in what the cartoonist does with it. As Gerberg observes, "The message is in twisting it, in turning the cliché around."

Mike Luckovich's "Let's Be Responsible" Cartoon

Consider Mike Luckovich's cartoon (from the *Atlanta Journal-Constitution*) in Figure 8.6 that addresses the issue of texting while driving. The visual cliché is a group of friends gathering in a very ordinary bar. We know that from the familiar props: the ubiquitous signage identifying the setting as a bar, the single dangling light fixture, bottles of alcohol, draft pulls, and the broad back of the bartender. Even the patrons are familiar figures—four casually dressed, slightly unkempt, individuals who look neither prosperous nor polished but slightly down on their luck. Note the dark-haired young man wears a T-shirt with a cartoon figure on it; another male sports unconventionally messy hair and the suggestion of beads

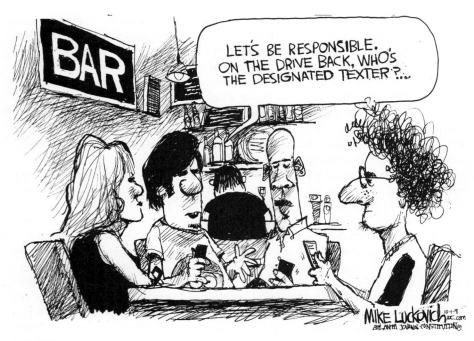

Figure 8.6

around his neck. The woman has over-styled blond hair, and the bald man wears a plain white shirt. The twist, of course, is that instead of clasping a martini or a beer, the patrons of this bar are all regarding their cell phones. There is not a drink on the table, (though we can assume that they have had or will be having considerable alcohol since they are concerned about who will be driving.) Maybe not.

The issue, of course, is the debate about driving while texting. The cartoon addresses the numerous deadly accidents caused by drivers who were texting rather than paying attention to the road, thus causing accidents which fill the news. A public debate still rages about outlawing texting while driving, fueled by the increased number of text messages being sent as well as the number of resulting accidents. (In June 2008, 75 billion text messages were sent. A year later, 135.2 billion text messages were sent.) According to a recent *New York Times*/CBS news poll (NYTimes.com/polls), nearly all Americans say sending a text message while driving should be illegal; and half of all Americans say texting behind the wheel should be punished at least as harshly as drunk driving. This concern is reflected in some legislation: it is now illegal in at least 15 states to text while driving, and the federal government is exerting pressure to ban it in all states.

The cartoon's joke is in the twist—the gap between the familiar and the unexpected. The familiar is the bar scene; the unexpected is the fact that the patrons are not holding alcoholic drinks but texting devices. What is important is a sober texter not a sober driver. Thus, the caption: "Let's be responsible. On the drive back, who's the designated texter?"

What Is the Cartoon's Claim?

The claim in this cartoon is that driving while texting is as dangerous and possibly more dangerous than driving while drinking. This claim is implicit in the satirical image of the bar patrons holding their cell phones and concentrating on texting. And it is implicit in the comment, "Let's be responsible. On the drive back, who's the designated texter?"

What Are the Cartoon's Assumptions?

This cartoon makes the assumption that people are preoccupied with texting and that they recognize that texting while driving is irresponsible and dangerous. It also presumes that readers are aware of the spate of serious accidents caused by "texters" and that they equate such behavior with drunk driving. Furthermore, the cartoon assumes familiarity with the campaign to designate a sober driver if other passengers are drinking. Part of the humor of the cartoon is based on the substitution of texting devices for alcohol.

What Is the Cartoon's Evidence?

The cartoon presents the ironic and humorous notion that its bar patrons are not even thinking about drinks. None are present. Instead, they are preoccupied with text messaging. This is the vice they go to the bar to indulge. They are so consumed with texting, that they want to be certain they can continue on the drive home. The implication is that they will not be able to restrain themselves from texting and must appoint a "designated texter" so texting will not be interrupted.

QUESTIONS FOR ANALYSIS AND DISCUSSION

Apply the principles of critical analysis described in the above section on editorial cartoons, as well as the elements of form and design discussed earlier in the chapter, to the cartoons. First take a look at Figure 8.7, Cartoon by Pat Bagley.

1. What is the claim or claims embodied in the visual elements of this political cartoon? What constitutes the evidence of the claim or claims? Cite the specific pieces of evidence.
2. Consider the audience for this cartoon. What groups of citizens would be most likely to have a strong reaction? Does the cartoon suggest a solution to the problems depicted? Are the problems interrelated?
3. What is the tone of the cartoon? Would you describe it as comical? satirical? facetious? overstated? amusing? disturbing?
4. This cartoon originally appeared on the editorial page in the *Salt Lake City Tribune*. Is the cartoon particular to the Salt Lake City area? Why or why not? What could you change in the piece so that it applied to a different city or area?
5. What is the grill-like tray on the top of the cars? And what is the bumper extension jutting off each car? How do they fit into the ad? What is the significance of the insignia on the vehicle on the lower right corner that says "SUV2020"?

" BACK IN AUGHT-FIVE WE HAD TO CHOOSE BETWEEN HIGHWAYS AND EDUCATION..."

Figure 8.7   *Cartoon by Pat Bagley*

6. What might "back in aught-five we had to choose" most likely refer to?
7. Based on the cartoonist's "argument," what do you think he is advocating? Is he for or against highway improvement? for or against education? Can you tell? Does it matter?

QUESTIONS FOR ANALYSIS AND DISCUSSION ───────────

Refer to Figure 8.8, cartoon by Daryl Cagle.

1. What is happening in this cartoon? Whom does the first kid "hate"? Does the cartoon make more sense when we know that it appeared shortly after September 11, 2001? Why or why not?
2. Consider the comment made by the middle kid in the cartoon, who agrees at first, but then asks a clarifying question. Is this significant? Why doesn't the first kid ask the same thing?
3. What is the cartoonist's claim in this cartoon? What evidence does he provide? Explain.
4. Although this cartoon was drawn in the context of the events following September 11, 2001, would it have been equally effective ten years ago? ten years into the future? Would the previous cartoon be as timeless? Explain.

Figure 8.8 *Cartoon by Daryl Cagle*

News Photographs

Although editorial cartoons can stand on their own, they are frequently featured on editorial pages in newspapers that include commentary on the topic they depict. Photographs are another vehicle used to augment commentary in newspapers, journals, and magazines. Indeed, sometimes the photograph *tells* the story better than words ever could, because it has the ability to touch our deepest emotions instantly.

At first glance, you may think that photos are simply snapshots of an event or moment. But most photographs presented in leading newspapers and journals are the result of effort and planning. Photojournalists are constantly making editorial decisions when they take a picture. They think about where to take the photo, the right moment, whom to include, the angle, the lighting, the depth of field, and the ISO selected. They consider the subject matter and how it might affect an audience. In some cases, they think about why they are taking the picture and what argument they want to present on film. Some of the most compelling photographs in history come from photojournalists capturing one moment. These photos are not posed, but they still tell a story. Some famous photos include the shot of a sailor kissing a nurse in

New York City's Times Square when victory was declared at the end of World War II. Or, who can forget the Pulitzer Prize-winning photo of firefighter Chris Fields carrying the lifeless body of 1-year-old Baylee Almon from the wreckage of the federal office building after the Oklahoma City bombing? While we might not recall the names of the people involved, the image itself remains stamped on our memory.

As a unit, the news story and the photo work together to tell a story. The best photos often tell a story without using any words. But knowing the context in which the photo was taken is important as well. At the very least, the date and location establish the circumstances. Consider Figure 8.9, a photograph of the aftermath of a home foreclosure, taken by Larry Downing in Waco, Texas, for Reuters. A young girl jumps rope on the sidewalk next to her family's belongings after she, her parents, and her four brothers and sisters received a court order of eviction that was carried out by McLennan County Deputy Constables. The photograph, one of the Reuters news photo Images of the Year 2009, speaks to the human toll of home foreclosure, especially on families with young children. Anyone who has read a newspaper or watched a newscast last year knows the high number of foreclosures that came with the weakening real estate market and a declining economy. According to the United States Foreclosure Report, by the third quarter of 2009 1 in every 136 homes was in some stage of foreclosure. And the emotional toll is heavy. Losing one's home can result in chronic anxiety, depression, and feelings of

Figure 8.9

failure—all sources of strain on personal and family relationships. This photograph captures some of the painful consequences of foreclosure on both a social and emotional level. The image also powerfully conveys the injustice of the process that leaves a family's worldly possessions on the sidewalk, including the children. At the same time, while capturing the pain and humiliation of dispossession, central is the innocence of a child who can jump rope during this cataclysmic event. One wonders if her jump-roping is a product of her youthful innocence or a desperate distraction from what is happening to her and her family.

Who Is the Target Audience?

This photograph was selected by the Reuters News Photo Service as one of the best Images of the Year 2009 because it was newsworthy, powerful, and artful. The photo targets a general audience likely to be concerned with social and economic issues and open to an exploration of the human consequences of such. The cost of foreclosure is not just the loss of a home but the loss of childhood innocence as well.

What Is the Purpose of the Image?

The image captures a moment in time—one that the photographer felt was important to underscore. It shows a family's experience of foreclosure: their possessions suddenly mere rubble on the sidewalk; their small but cozy home no longer a shelter; the constables on the far left, overseeing this eviction; and, most importantly, the youngest victim, a young girl jumping rope in front of her former home. The purpose of the photograph is to document the human toll when a home is foreclosed.

What Are the Claims Made in the Image?

This photograph puts flesh on a statistic from the rash of home foreclosures in the U.S. in the past few years. It dramatizes something of the human toll. Given this economic context, the viewer can draw a number of claims from the image. Foremost is that the home offers a family security and shelter. Rich or poor, being a home-owner is part of the American Dream. Another claim is that foreclosure turns one's valued possessions into rubble. The jumble of chairs, mattresses, and stuffed plastic bags looks like stuff to be discarded. Almost washed out are three men at the far left in the photograph, most probably the officials conducting the eviction. The claim here might be that they are the heartless enforcers of a foreclosure. Most importantly, the viewer notes the young girl jump roping. She is the heart of the photograph. And what are the claims here? To some viewers the young girl might be the embodiment of youthful innocence. The claim could also be that she is too young to be fully aware of what is happening and can rebound with resilience. On the other hand, one could see the child jump roping as a desperate distraction. The claim, thus, would be that this event will rob this child of all that childhood should be about: security, family, and certainty.

What Assumptions Does the Image Make?

The photographer assumes that most people will find this image arresting. Given the context, a crisis in housing, it is assumed that the photograph is emotionally charged.

QUESTIONS FOR ANALYSIS AND DISCUSSION

Consider the photograph in Figure 8.10 taken by *Boston Globe* photojournalist Suzanne Kreiter. It shows two panhandlers on a Boston street. The photograph accompanied an article, "A Street to Call Home," which reports on how some homeless people panhandle on the very spot where they live.

Figure 8.10

1. This photograph accompanied an article about homelessness in an urban area of the Northeast. What assumptions about the audience does the photographer make?
2. What details in the photograph convey homelessness to the viewer? Consider objects, location, and background.
3. A close examination of the two main figures in this photograph makes a strong statement about their character. Consider their position, posture, relationship to one another, the direction of their gazes, the facial expressions, and their clothing, and describe the character of these individuals.
4. Would you describe these people as heroic? downtrodden? defiant? helpless victims? noble survivors? Explain why.
5. What argument about homelessness is embedded in this photograph? In other words, what is the claim?
6. Does the background of the photograph detract from or add to the meaning of the photograph?
7. How do you expect to see the homeless depicted? Is this expectation based on stereotype? Does this image of the homeless reinforce or contradict the stereotypical view of the homeless? Explain your answer. Does this photograph change your idea of urban poverty? Why or why not?
8. Do you see any similarities in style or content between this photograph and Norman Rockwell's "Freedom of Speech"?

Ancillary Graphics: Tables, Charts, and Graphs

Art, advertisements, editorial cartoons, and news photos all present interesting visual ways to persuade, and knowing how they do this improves your critical thinking and analytical skills. Ancillary graphics, however, such as tables, charts, and graphs, are some visual tools you can use in your own persuasive essays. In Chapter 6, we discussed how numerical data and statistics are very persuasive in bolstering an argument. But a simple table, chart, or graph can convey information at a glance while conveying trends that support your argument. In fact, such visuals are preferable to long, complicated paragraphs that confuse the reader and may detract from your argument.

Ancillary graphics usually take the form of tables, charts, graphs (including line, bar, and pie graphs), and illustrations such as maps and line drawings (of a piece of equipment, for example).

Numerical Tables

There are many ways of representing statistical data. As you know from courses you've taken in math or chemistry, the simplest presentation of numerical data is the table. Tables are useful in demonstrating relationships among data. They present numerical information arranged in rows or columns so that data elements may be referenced and compared. Tables also facilitate the interpretation of data without the expense of several paragraphs of description.

Suppose you are writing a paper in which you argue that part-time faculty at your institution teach more hours, but are underpaid and undersupported when it comes to benefits. Your research reveals that most part-time faculty receive less than $4,000 per course, and nearly one-third earn $3,000 or less per course—which is little more than the minimum wage. You also discover that the treatment of part-timers at your own school reflects a national trend—faced with rising enrollments and skyrocketing costs, colleges and universities have come to rely more on part-time instructors. Moreover, while they may carry heavier teaching loads, these part-time faculty do not receive the same benefits as professors. Your claim is that such lack of support is not only unfair to the instructors but also that it compromises the nature of higher education since low compensation drives instructors to take on other jobs to meet the cost of living.

Presenting this information in a table will allow you to demonstrate your point while saving space for your discussion. The tables below provide the results of a survey conducted by the Coalition on the Academic Work Force (CAW), describing how history faculty are facing this situation.

As the title indicates, the table reproduced in Figure 8.11 shows the percentage of history courses taught by full- and part-time faculty. The table intends to help readers understand how much institutions have come to depend on part-time instructors, especially graduate teaching assistants and part-time nontenure-track teachers—people who are paid the least and often denied the benefits enjoyed by full-time faculty. The horizontal rows break down faculty types into five discrete categories—from "Full-Time Tenure Track" at the top to "Graduate Teaching Assistants" at the bottom. The three vertical columns tabulate the percentages according to categories: "Intro Courses," "Other Courses," and "All Courses," which is the median—the calculated halfway point between the other two categories.

Reading from left to right along the first row, we see that 49 percent of the introductory history courses and 72 percent of the "other courses" were taught by full-time tenure-track faculty. This compares with 41 percent of the introductory courses taught

Percentage of History Courses Taught, by Faculty Type

	Intro Courses	Other Courses	All Courses
Full-Time Tenure Track	49%	72%	59%
Full-Time Nontenure Track	9%	5%	7%
Part-Time Tenure Track	1%	1%	1%
Part-Time Nontenure Track	23%	15%	19%
Graduate Teaching Assistants	17%	8%	13%
Percentage of All Courses Taught	55%	45%	
Number of Courses Taught	5,825	4,759	10,584

Source: AHA Surveys.

Figure 8.11

by part-timers (part-time tenure track [1%] + part-time nontenure-track faculty [23%] + graduate teaching assistants [17%]). The last column, which represents the median percentage of intro and other courses, tells us that part-timers taught 33 percent or a third of all history courses. That is a compelling figure when tabulated for comparison to full-time faculty.

The second table (Figure 8.12) presents the reported benefits for nontenure-track and part-time faculty. Here nine categories of benefits are tabulated according to three categories of faculty. (Presumably nearly 100 percent of history departments provide full-time tenure-track faculty the kinds of support and benefits listed.) The first line shows the comparative institutional support for travel to professional meetings for the three categories of instructors: 76.9 percent for full-time nontenure track, 46.4 for part-time faculty paid a fraction of full-time salary, and 15.2 for part-time faculty paid by the course.

The fifth line down tabulates the copaid health plan for the three categories of faculty. As we can see at a glance, 72 percent of the institutions with full-time nontenure-track faculty and 63 percent of the departments with part-time faculty paid a fraction of full-time salaries provide some kind of health plan copaid by the school and faculty

History Departments, Benefits

	% for Full-Time Nontenure-Track Faculty	% for Part-Time Faculty (Paid by semester)	% for Part-Time Faculty (Paid by course)
Support Travel to Prof. Mtgs.	76.9	46.4	15.2
Support Attendance at Prof. Mtgs.	41.0	28.6	22.9
Provide Regular Salary Increases	68.4	53.6	28.1
Access to Research Grants	52.1	39.3	13.3
Health Plan Paid by Both	72.17	62.96	12.99
Health Plan Paid by School	32.17	22.22	2.26
Health Plan Paid by Employee	1.74	7.41	3.95
Retirement Plan	73.91	55.56	10.17
Life Insurance	76.52	44.44	5.65

Source: AHA Surveys.

Figure 8.12

member. This compares with just 13 percent of institutions providing such a benefit to part-time faculty paid on a per-course basis. Similarly, 32 percent of the institutions with full-time nontenure-track faculty provided a health plan paid for by the school, as compared to 2.26 percent of those with faculty paid by the course. Reading across the other benefits categories reveals how much more generous institutions were to full-time nontenure-track faculty than to part-timers—including retirement plans and insurance.

As the above paragraphs demonstrate, explaining all this information in the body of your text can be complicated and confusing. And when you are trying to prepare a compelling argument, simplicity of style and clarity of text are essential. Using tables helps you clearly depict data while you move forward with your discussion.

Line Graphs

Line graphs show the relationship between two or more sets of numerical data by plotting points in relation to two axes. The vertical axis is usually used to represent amounts, and the horizontal axis normally represents increments of time, although this is not always the case. Line graphs are probably easier for most people to read than tables, and they are especially useful when depicting trends or changes over time. Consider the graph in Figure 8.13 below.

This graph plots the comparative increase and decrease of full- and part-time faculty over a 30-year period (based on data from American Historical Association [AHA] surveys). The vertical or y-axis represents the percentage of part-time faculty, and the horizontal or x-axis represents the time starting from 1980. There are two lines on the graph: The upper line represents the decreasing

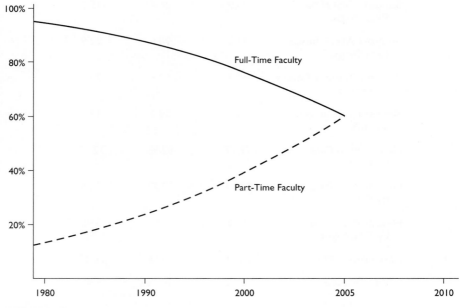

Figure 8.13

percentage of full-time history faculty of the colleges and universities surveyed, while the lower line represents the increase in part-time history faculty over the same 30-year period. The declining slope of the upper line instantly captures the decreasing dependence on full-time faculty, whereas the rising slope of the lower line illustrates the increasing dependence on part-time hires. Because the data are plotted on the same graph, we understand how the two are interrelated.

We also notice that neither line is straight but slightly curving. The upper line (full-time faculty) curves downward, while the lower line (part-time faculty) curves upward. Around the year 2005, these lines cross just below the 50th percentile level on the *y*-axis—that is, more than half the college history courses surveyed are currently being taught by part-timers. Also, if we extrapolate both lines toward the right along the curves they are defining, we will eventually arrive at some hypothetical future date when 100 percent of all history courses are taught by part-time faculty and none by full-timers. While we presume that most colleges and universities would not allow this to happen, the trend suggests just how the increased dependence on part-timers is changing the nature of higher education, as fewer courses are taught by full-time faculty. The graphs indeed make a persuasive argument.

Bar Graphs

Bar graphs are often used to compare parts and enable readers to grasp complex data and the relationships among variables at a glance. A bar graph uses horizontal or vertical bars and is commonly used to show either quantities of the same item at different times, quantities of different items at the same time, or quantities of the different parts of an item that make up the whole. They are usually differentiated by contrasting colors, shades, or textures, with a legend explaining what these colors, shades, or textures mean.

The bar graph in Figure 8.14 shows the increase of part-time and adjunct faculty in history departments over a 29-year period as broken down by type of employment and gender (based on data from the AHA survey of the historical profession and unpublished data from AHA departmental surveys). As indicated, the graph demonstrates a dramatic increase in that time period. In 1980, only 4.3 percent of male and 2.0 percent of female history faculty were part-time—a total of 6.3 percent. Nearly three decades later, part-time male and female faculty increased to over 46 percent. This number could be even larger if graduate teaching assistants were included. As this graph shows, bar graphs take comparative amounts of data and transform them into instant no-nonsense images.

Pie Charts

Pie charts present data as wedge-shaped sections of a circle or "pie." The total amount of all the pieces of the pie must equal 100 percent. They are an efficient way of demonstrating the relative proportion of the whole something occupies—an instant way to visualize "percentages" without thinking in numbers. But when using pie charts, it is best to include six or fewer slices. If more pieces than that are used, the chart becomes messy and its impact is muted. Figure 8.15 dramatically demonstrates the portion of all history courses in the CAW survey that were taught by part-time faculty, including graduate students.

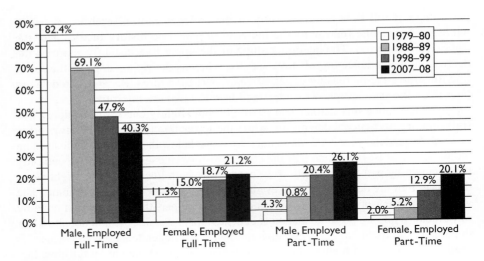

Figure 8.14

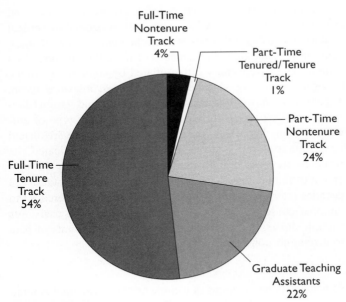

Figure 8.15

This pie chart clearly reveals that the combined wedges of graduate teaching as-sistants and part-time instructors form a substantial portion of the pie. In fact, they comprise almost half of the teaching population. This image quickly and powerfully demonstrates the point of your argument that part-time faculty make up a dispropor-tionately large part of history faculty while receiving a disproportionately small percentage of the benefits. The chart allows readers to visualize the information as they read it. In the student sample in Chapter 9, Shannon O'Neill includes a pie chart along with an editorial cartoon to bolster her written argument, "Literature Hacked and Torn Apart: Censorship in Public Schools." (See page 279)

Used together, these visuals can play an invaluable role in bolstering a written argument on behalf of part-time faculty. Instead of blinding readers with reams of raw data, these visuals organize confusing numbers, and at-a-glance bring their significance to life. Comparative benefits and changing dependencies are transformed into memorable and easy-to-understand tables, graphs, and charts.

Tips for Using Ancillary Graphics

While understanding the types of ancillary graphics at your disposal is important, it is also important to know how to use them properly. Here are a few guidelines to consider when using graphics in your persuasive essays:

- Include only the data you need to demonstrate your point.
- Make a reference to the chart or graphic in the body of your text.
- Try to keep the graphic on the same page as your discussion.
- Present only one type of information in each graph or chart.
- Label everything in your graph and provide legends where appropriate.
- Assign a figure number to each graphic for easy reference.
- Don't crowd your text too closely around the graphic.
- Remember to document the sources used to create the graphics.

As you begin to incorporate visuals into your own papers, consider the discussion provided earlier in this chapter regarding visual arguments. Consider why you wish to use the graphic and what you want it to do. Think about your audience's needs.

SAMPLE STUDENT ARGUMENT FOR ANALYSIS

Lee Innes, a first-year business major, was interested in the subject of women in sports—an enormous topic that he needed to narrow down. He began by asking why male athletes dominate the world of sports. What the impact of sex-role stereotyping is on women's athletics? What is Title IX and what is its impact on college athletics? Is scholarship money unfairly distributed to male athletes? In what major sports do women excel? In what major sports do women receive the most attention or the highest salaries or the most product endorsement fees? Why is it that tennis, volleyball, and soccer are among the sports in which women receive the most attention? Why does a sport like women's beach volleyball attract a large and enthusiastic audience?

Although each question presented an interesting issue to explore, he decided to narrow the focus to one that he could cover in a paper of reasonable length. While anticipating the 2008 Summer Olympics in Beijing, he thought back on the 2004 summer games in Greece, an event he had followed closely. He recalled feeling conflicted as he watched the women's beach volleyball. The athletic skill and strength of the women was dazzling. But their athletic feats attracted less attention than their scant bikinis. Reflecting on this, Lee realized he had a narrowly defined a specific topic: women's volleyball uniforms. His essay would consider the controversial issue of women as sexual spectacles in the Olympics—in particular, if the selection of their uniforms was a case of sexism in sport. He arrived at a *working* claim that both limited the range of his topic and very clearly expressed his point of view about it:

> Women in all sports, including Olympic beach volleyball, should be judged and promoted on their skill as athletes not on how they look in bikinis.

This claim helped him concentrate his research on those areas pertinent to his ideas. In addition to referencing expert views from magazines, newspapers, and websites. Lee bolstered his claim—and argument—by including a photo of a woman in Olympic uniform and a comparative schematic of men's versus women's uniforms. The visuals clearly enhanced his written argument.

Innes 1

Lee Innes
Professor Khoury
Writing 122
19 February, 2010

1   A Double Standard of Olympic Proportions

As the London Olympics of 2012 loom on the horizon, I find myself considering the pressing issues facing this international event. After losing our bid to host these games in 2012, how will we perform? Will America prove to be an athletic force? Will performance-enhancing drugs taint the games again? Will the French judges ever favor anyone but the French? And will the women's volleyball team still sport skimpy bikini uniforms?

2   Admittedly, the last question may carry less weight than the others, but as a stereotypical red-blooded heterosexual male, I certainly appreciated the aesthetic value of the volleyball competition in 2008 in Beijing. However, the display—and it indeed seemed to be just that—troubled me on a more visceral level. If I had been reading a popular magazine targeting young males, *Maxim* or *FHM* for example, ogling young women in bikinis would have felt fine. But this was the Olympics, and these women were representing my country—the United States—in an athletic competition.

3   So to be honest, as both an athlete and an American, I cringed each time one of the women paused to adjust her "uniform." How could these women concentrate on winning Olympic gold with the constant threat of a wedgie on international television? Just what were these women thinking when they picked this uniform, I wondered? How could I take their sporting event seriously when it was so obvious that they didn't take *themselves*

Innes 2

seriously? And how could they objectify themselves in this way as they represented not only U.S. athletes, but in many ways, female athletes in particular?

4   When I shared this observation with a friend who played college volleyball herself, I was surprised to learn that not only did the women of the U.S. Volleyball Team *not* pick those uniforms; they were *forced* to wear them by the Olympic committee. At the time, I was shocked—both by the idea that an official sports organization would require such a uniform, and by the fact that women had not reacted with more outrage.

5   In 1998, the International Volleyball Federation (FIVB), based in Switzerland, decided volleyball uniforms should be standardized. It was this organization that chose the bikini uniform worn by the Olympic athletes. Interestingly, there was only one woman on the committee when they designed and implemented the uniform. Kristine Drakich, in a 1997 interview with the Canadian Association for the Advancement of Women and Sport and Physical Activity, commented that she was the only female athlete representative for the International Volleyball Federation's Beach Volleyball World Council at that time. The council, she observed, was "an intimidating place for anybody . . . this is a place with about 50 members, all men, except for my position" (Robertson). One can surmise that a predominantly male committee was responsible for voting in favor of adopting the bikini uniform for women for beach volleyball competition. (It makes one wonder if Hugh Heffner sat in on the meetings.)

6   Perhaps more at issue and culturally significant is that the men's beach volleyball uniform was nowhere near as revealing. The men's uniform featured a tank top and lose fitting shorts. The women's uniform, in addition to the bikini top, sports a brief with a waistline that falls below the belly button. And the women's uniform bottoms must be two and a half inches wide on the sides, providing very little coverage, even for the toned glutes of these women. That's only *five* inches wide.

7   Surprisingly, the women's uniform provoked little public outcry, and not for lack of publicity. Jeanne Moos reported on the decision in a *CNN Online* article: "Women's volleyball uniforms will be standardized in order to banish t-shirts and shorts." Moos expressed her own viewpoint bluntly, "Beach volleyball has now joined go-go girl dancing as perhaps the only two professions where a bikini is the required uniform." Yet the announcement of the FIVB's decision created little more than a ripple of controversy. Even men

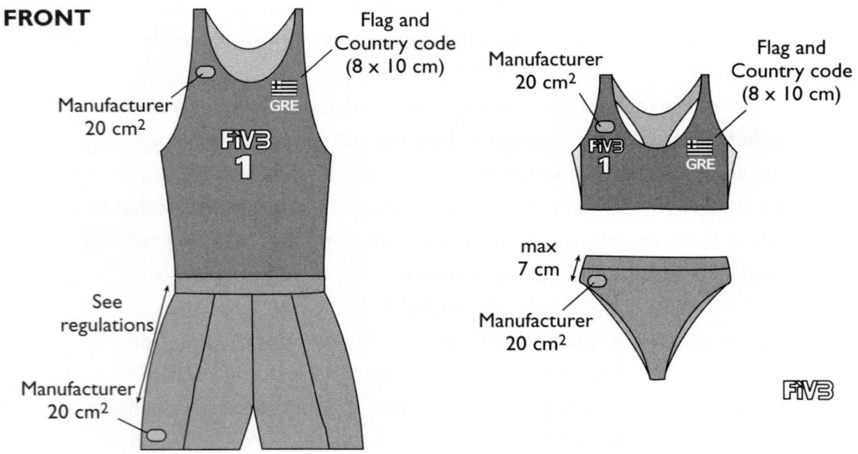

Innes 3

Figure 1 Men's Volleyball uniform is shown on the left, and women's volleyball uniform on the right.

noticed the inequality. Blogger Sean P. Aune observed that photos of beach volleyball players were "little more than soft-porn." "There is no doubt these women work just as hard as any other athletes to get where they are, and all you ever see or hear about them is just these blasted outfits. How many people know that Misty May-Treanor and Kerri Walsh are on a run of nearly 100 consecutive wins as a team? Does that matter? Oh who cares, slap some more butt shots up there!" Aune also noted that the country of origin of each player is written across their rear ends. Something I hadn't noticed before.

Opponents of the uniform seemed to become more vocal as the extensive television coverage of the Olympic beach volleyball matches brought the issue to the public eye. Jeneé Osterheldt reported in the August 20, 2004, *Kansas City Star* that the required uniform was upsetting some sports officials and players. "[Female] players can't cover up, even if they want to. . . . Donna Lopiano, executive director of the Women's Sports Foundation, [says] 'It's like telling a swimmer she has to wear a bikini instead of a high-performance suit, when the material has been shown to increase speed. Elasticized attire on leg muscles, especially larger muscles like the thigh, has been proven to reduce fatigue. If you are looking for performance enhancement, you wouldn't choose bikini bottoms'" (Osterheldt).

Innes   4

9   But Lopiano's statement addressed what seems to be an irrelevant detail to the IFVB board. Official commentary on the "performance enhancement" of the uniforms is absent from the literature. It would appear that performance has little, if anything, to do with the decision at all. The uniforms, it seems, were designed not for functionality but for marketing purposes. In a *Business Week* article addressing the "comeback" of beach volleyball as a legitimate sport, Leonard Armato, the marketing man responsible for getting volleyball on NBC as an athletic event, was quoted admitting, "[Beach volleyball is] an incredibly sexy sport. We're not embarrassed that the women [wear] bikinis (Khermouch)."

10   Based on ticket sales for beach volleyball, it seems like the IFVB had the right idea.

11   Even when the IFVB rendered its initial decision in 1999, few players complained, and even those who did seemed to lack spirit. "I'm kind of bummed—I like my tights," said the sport's perhaps most famous player, Gabrielle Reece, to a CNN reporter at the time. Reece, who was known for wearing black Lycra tights rather than a bikini suit while playing, added "You take one step, that bathing suit goes straight up. You're always yanking and fiddling" (Moos).

Figure 2   Player giving hand signal that she will block on both sides.

12   "Bummed" doesn't exactly express the feminist fury one might expect. If the Williams sisters of tennis fame have taught us anything, women like to choose what to wear, and they will often select uniforms that are both performance enhancing and flattering. If they choose to be sexy, that's one thing. But to be ordered to wear a sexy uniform with no alternatives, one would expect more protests than were reported in media outlets. It also seems like female viewers aren't all that upset—they seem to accept this as a part of a male-dominated sports culture. *Fanhouse* reporter Stephanie Stradley observed that "King Kaufman at *Salon* wondered [in an online essay] why women wear bikinis and the men wear shirts, [well] duh, so men will watch."

13   All of which then leads me to my next question: If the women aren't complaining, is there anything wrong here? As we approach the next summer Olympiad, is it permissible for me to enjoy both the view, so to speak, as well as the competition? It would appear to be the case. Michael Noble commented in his article "Can't Wait for the Next Olympixxx" in the Canadian newspaper *Townie*,

> Of course there is a sexual element to all sports, male and female, and there always has been. Tight pants, skirts, shorts and bathing suits can be found throughout the Olympic lineup. In proper and respectful sports though, admiring the bodies within these suits is kept on a "wink-wink, nudge-nudge" level. They know what you're looking at, but they don't make new rules to accentuate it.
>
> Volleyball has taken a different route. Instead of a nudge and a wink, it's a point and a yell—"Hey everyone, take a look at this ass!" Clearly women's sports are changing. At one time, female athletes were all portrayed as manly "butches." Today they're shown as suped-up sex machines. You've come a long way, baby.

14   However, one could also argue that such media attention helps out both the sport and the athletes. Since their victory in Athens seven years ago, Kerri Walsh and Misty May have enjoyed tremendous popularity. One could argue that their cute bikinis certainly didn't hurt their careers. Donning bikinis long before their foray into Olympic glory, the pair was in a Visa ad during the 2004 Super Bowl, playing beach volleyball in the snow and ice. Their likenesses have been displayed on McDonald's wrappers and boxes. And after their Olympic win, they were featured on the front page of practically every sports section of every newspaper in the country. Even the *Wall Street Journal* ran a photo.

15   Reflection on the issue at hand—is it fair that a group of men have mandated what most female athletes seem to agree is a less than ideal uniform—seems to have no satisfactory answer. A look at the uniforms in the *2009 Beach Volleyball Handbook* leads one to presume that little will change in London. Despite the lack of vocal protest, I am still left with the gnawing feeling that something is amiss. Perhaps Andrea Lewis, a writer for the Progressive Media Project, summarizes it best: "The games are a great showcase for athletic talents of both genders, but it's still an Olympian task for women to be treated equally."

Works Cited

Aune, Sean P. "Olympic Beach Volley Ball Uniforms. SeanPAune.com, 13 Aug. 2008. Web. 2 Feb. 2010.

Hruby, Patrick. "A Day at the Beach." *Washington Times* 20 Aug. 2004. Web. 6 Feb. 2010.

Khermouch, Gerry. "Son of a Beach Volleyball." *Business Week* 20 Apr. 2002. Print.

Lewis, Andrea. "Women Athletes Shined at Olympic Games." *Progressive Media Project,* 30 Aug. 2004. Web. 5 Feb. 2010.

Moos, Jeanne. "Bikini Blues–Beach Volleyball Makes the Swimsuit Standard." *CNN Online.* CNN, 13 Jan. 1999. Web. 5 Feb. 2010.

Moore, David Leon. "Beach Volleyball's Dynamic Duo." *USATODAY.com.* USA Today, 13 Aug. 2004. Web. 8 Feb. 2010.

Osterheldt, Jeneé. "Olympic Athletes Prance Chic to Cheek." *Kansas City Star* 20 Aug. 2004, late ed.: A1. Print.

Robertson, Sheila. "Insight Into an Activist." ACTION Canadian Association for the Advancement of Women and Sport and Physical Activity. CAAWS, n.d. Web. 4 Feb. 2010.

Stradley Stephanie. "In Beach Volleyball, Why Do Men Wear Shirts and Women Wear Bikinis?" *Olympics Fanhouse.* AOL, 14 Aug. 2008. Web. 7 Feb. 2010.

QUESTIONS FOR ANALYSIS AND DISCUSSION

1. Do you agree with Lee Innes's working claim here? What are your thoughts about the role of male and female athletic attire? about the use of attire to promote or popularize a sporting event? In your journal, respond to Innes's ideas by exploring your own views on the media's promotion of women athletes and whether or not the promotion is based on talent or appearance.

2. Consider the effectiveness of the author's use of the visuals—the photograph of the female player's bikini and the comparative uniform schematics for men and women. Do the illustrations bolster Innes's argument? Do the visuals convince you of an inequity if not sexual exploitation in uniform guidelines? Explain your answers.

3. Even if you didn't watch the 2008 Olympic women's beach volleyball competition or don't follow the sport, do you think that most fans are concerned with what Innes and others see as sexual exploitation? Do you think that the media will ever respond to Innes's concern? Why or why not?

4. What do you make of the fact that few female athletes complained that they had to wear bikinis? Does that weaken Innes's argument? Or do you see that lack of concern as legitimate disinterest? Or as suggested by the article, do you think that the lack of complaints suggests more deeply rooted gender issues in our culture?

5. In the last paragraph, Innes wonders if there's really a problem in what female athletes wear. What specific counterarguments to his position does he cite? In spite of these, why is he still left with a "gnawing sense that something isn't right here"? Do you agree? Are you also convinced as Andrea Lewis claims that rendering equal treatment for woman athletes is "an Olympian task"?

6. In your journal, write an entry as if done by a member of the Women's Olympic Volleyball Team after the first day of competition. In it, explore how she felt about her uniform.

Researching Arguments: Thinking Like an Investigator

Most arguments derive their success from the evidence they contain, so good argumentative writers learn to find evidence in many sources and present the best evidence to support their claims. In the academic world, much of that evidence is gathered through *research,* either conducted in a lab or field or through examination of the previously published work of other investigators and scholars. The research paper you may be asked to write challenges you to learn how more experienced writers find and present evidence that meets the standards of the academic community.

In the previous chapters, we've stressed the importance of finding evidence that will impress readers of your argument's merits. To review, researched evidence plays an important role in convincing readers of the following:

■ Expert, unbiased authorities agree with your position in whole or in part, adding to your credibility.

■ Your position or proposal is based on facts, statistics, and real-life examples, not mere personal opinion.

■ You understand different viewpoints about your subject as well as your own.

■ Your sources of information are verifiable because researched evidence is always accompanied by documentation.

A good analogy to use, once again, is that of the lawyer presenting a case to a jury. When you write a researched argument, you're making a case to a group of people who will make a decision about a subject. Not only do you present your arguments in the case but also you call on witnesses to offer evidence and expert opinion, which you then interpret and clarify for the jury. In a researched argument, your sources are your witnesses.

Writing an argumentative research paper isn't different from writing any other kind of argument, except in scale. An argument research paper is not a different species from the essays you have been writing; but it is usually longer than nonresearched papers; and the formal presentation (including documentation) must be addressed in more detail.

Sources of Information

There are two basic kinds of research sources, and depending partly on the type of issue you've picked to research, one may prove more helpful than the other. The first is *primary sources,* which include firsthand accounts of events (interviews, diaries, court records, letters, manuscripts). The second is *secondary sources,* which interpret, comment on, critique, explain, or evaluate events or primary sources. Secondary sources include most reference works and any books or articles that expand on primary sources. Depending on whether you choose a local or a more global issue to write about, you may decide to focus more on primary or more on secondary sources; but in most research, you'll want to consider both.

Primary Sources

If you choose a topic of local concern, your chief challenge will be finding enough research material. Very current controversies or issues won't yet have books written about them, so you may have to rely more heavily on electronic databases, which you can access through a computer, or interviews and other primary research methods to find information. If you choose a local issue to argue, consider the following questions.

■ Which experts on campus or in the community might you interview for the pros and cons of the debated issue? an administrator at your college? a professor? the town manager? Think of at least two local experts who could provide an overview of the issue from different perspectives.

■ What local resources—such as a local newspaper, radio station, TV station, or political group—are available for gathering print or broadcast information? If one of your topics is a campus issue, for example, the student newspaper, student committees or groups, university online discussion groups, or the student government body might be places to search for information.

Once you determine the several possible sources of information, your next step is to set up interviews or make arrangements to read or view related materials. Most students find that experts are eager to talk about local issues and are willing to be interviewed. However, you'll need plenty of time to gather background information, phone for interviews, prepare questions, and write up your notes afterward. If you're depending on primary research for the bulk of your information, get started as soon as the paper is assigned.

Preparing for Interviews

A few common courtesies apply when preparing for interviews. First, be ready to discuss the purpose of your interview when setting up an appointment. Second, go into the interview with a list of questions that shows you have already thought about the issue. Be on time and have a notebook and pen or recorder, especially if you decide to quote people directly. But first ask their permission to do so.

Conducting Interviews

Be prepared to jot down only key words or ideas during the interview, reserving time afterward to take more detailed notes. Keep the interview on track by asking focused questions if the interviewee wanders while responding. When leaving, ask if it would be okay to call should you have follow-up questions.

Writing Up Interviews

As soon as possible after the interview, review your notes (or recording) and flesh out the details of the conversation. Think about what you learned. How does the information you gathered relate to your main topic or question? Did you learn anything that surprised or intrigued you? What questions remain? Record the date of your interview; you will need to document your source when you write the paper.

Preparing Interview Questions

Consider the following guidelines as you prepare questions for an interview:

- Find out as much information as you can about the issue and about the expert's stand on the issue before the interview. Then you won't waste interview time on generating details you could have found in the newspaper or on the local TV news.
- Ask open-ended questions that allow the authority to respond freely, rather than questions requiring only yes or no answers.
- Prepare more questions than you think you need and rank them in order of priority according to your purpose. Using the most important points as a guide, sequence the list in a logical progression.

Secondary Sources

Many primary sources—published interviews, public documents, results of experiments, and first-person accounts of historical events, for example—are available in your library, which is also a vast repository of secondary source material. If your topic is regional, national, or international in scope, you'll want to consider both of these kinds of sources. For example, if your topic is proposed changes to the Social Security system, you might find information in the *Congressional Record* on committee deliberations, a primary source, and also read articles on the op-ed page of the *New York Times* for interpretive commentary, a secondary source.

A Search Strategy

Because the sheer amount of information in the library can be daunting, plan how you will find information before you start your search. Always consult a reference librarian if you get stuck in planning your search or if you can't find the information you need.

Preview: A Search Strategy

- Choose your topic.
- Get an overview of your topic.
- Compile a working bibliography.
- Locate sources.
- Evaluate sources.
- Take notes.

Choosing Your Topic

Your argument journal may remind you of potential topics, and Chapter 3 covered how to develop a topic. But what if you still can't think of one? You might try browsing through two print sources that contain information on current issues:

Facts on File (1940 to the present). A weekly digest of current news.

Editorials on File (1970 to the present). Selected editorials from U.S. and Canadian newspapers reprinted in their entirety.

Or go online to the *Political Junkie* website, which will provide you with ideas from the latest news stories in national and regional newspapers and magazines, columnists' viewpoints on current issues, up-to-the-minute reports on public figures, and links to the websites of numerous political and social organizations. You can access this site at http://www.politicaljunkie.com. Also, think about which subjects you find interesting from the essays in Part Two of this book. These four sources should give you a wealth of ideas to draw on.

Getting an Overview of Your Topic

If you don't know a lot about your topic, encyclopedias can give you general background information. Just as important, encyclopedia articles often end with bibliographies on their subjects—bibliographies prepared by experts in the field. Using such bibliographies can save you hours in the library.

Your library no doubt houses in print generalized and specialized encyclopedias. Your library also should allow you access to online general and specialized encyclopedia databases related to your topic. What follows are a few of the dozens of major online encyclopedias that you may find helpful:

> ***Some General and Specialized Online Encyclopedias***
> *Academic American Encyclopedia*
> *New Encyclopedia Britannica*
> *Cambridge Histories Outline*
> *Encyclopedia of Life Sciences*
> *Gale Encyclopedia of Medicine*
> *International Encyclopedia of Social and Behavioral Sciences*
> *Oxford Art Online*
> *Oxford Encyclopedia of American Literature*
> *Oxford Encyclopedia of British Literature*
> *Oxford Music Online*

This is just a brief listing of the many encyclopedias available in areas that range widely. It is worth discussing the value of online encyclopedias, such as the ever popular *Wikipedia* (en.wikipedia.org). *Wikipedia* has been described as a sort of "collective brain" of information that is provided by anyone who wants to share knowledge about a subject. Hundreds of thousands of people have contributed to *Wikipedia* entries, and thousands more have edited and amended them. *Wikipedia*'s strengths include its currency, the vast quantity of information available, and the fact that entries may be amended and challenged. Within seconds of breaking news, *Wikipedia*'s entries will reflect new information, provided someone wishes to add it. Many entries will feature source material at the end of the page. Review these sources with the same critical eye that you evaluate the *Wikipedia* entry. While the information on *Wikipedia* is expected to be correct, it is not guaranteed; and be aware that there is no central editorial authority who confirms the accuracy of the entries. Likewise, source material may sometimes be questionable. Our recommendation is to use *Wikipedia* as a resource, but not the *only* resource in your research arsenal. Note any challenges or disputes to the entry (which will appear in a block above the entry), and use the information only if you feel confident that the information is accurate.

Compiling a Working Bibliography

Because you don't know at the beginning of your search which sources will prove most relevant to your narrowed topic, keep track of every source you consult. Record complete publication information about each source in your notebook, on index cards, or on printouts of online sources. The list that follows describes the information you'll need for particular kinds of sources.

For a Book

- Authors' and/or editors' names
- Full title, including subtitle
- Place of publication (city, state, country)
- Date of publication (from the copyright page)
- Name of publisher
- Volume or edition numbers
- Library call number

For an Article

- Authors' names
- Title and subtitle of article
- Title of periodical (magazine, journal, newspaper)
- Volume number and issue number, if any
- Date of the issue
- All page numbers on which the article appears
- Library location

For an Electronic Source

- Authors' names, if given
- Title of material accessed
- Name of periodical (if applicable)
- Volume and issue numbers (if applicable)
- Date of material, if given
- Page numbers or numbers of paragraphs (if indicated)
- Title of the database
- Publication medium (e.g., CD-ROM, diskette, microfiche, online)
- Name of the vendor, if relevant

■ Electronic publication date
■ Date of your access to the material
■ Path specification for online media (e.g., FTP information; directory; file name). APA also asks for DOI (digital object identifier), instead of a URL.

Note that for electronic sources, which come in many different formats, you should record all the information that would allow another researcher to retrieve the documents you used. This will vary from source to source, but it's important to give as much information as you can.

Your instructor may ask you to prepare an *annotated bibliography,* in which you briefly summarize the main ideas in each source and note its potential usefulness. You will also want to evaluate each source for accuracy, currency, or bias.

Sample Entries for an Annotated Bibliography

Shannon O'Neill, a journalism major, decided to write her argument essay on book banning in the public schools. Here are some sample entries from her annotated bibliography. (Shannon O'Neill's paper can be found on pages 279–285 in the Documentation Guide.)

Barnhisel, Greg, ed. *Media and Messages: Strategies and Readings in Public Rhetoric.* **New York: Longman, 2005.** This book contains many useful essays, editorials, and articles examining contemporary issues in the media and presents a balanced view of a large variety of topics. Barnhisel draws useful summaries and conclusions based on information in each chapter. The book is unbiased because it presents criticisms from all angles. In my paper, I used an article and an editorial because they give interesting perspectives on censorship of the written word; one focused on student newspapers; the other criticized censorship as the result of "politically correctness." Both pieces oppose censorship. While the text as a whole is balanced, there aren't any useful pieces advocating for censorship of the written word; rather, they focused on censorship of the visual media or Internet.

"Challenging a Book in Your School." *Gateways to a Better Education.* **1998. 5 Oct. 2009** http://www.gtbe.org. This website is for a national organization that promotes the spread of Christian values. While it does not advocate censorship or removal of specific works, it encourages parents to challenge their children's curriculum and take an active part in deciding what should or should not be taught in public schools—all with a Christian agenda. This site is clearly biased, but it is an important and useful source for the presentation of the religious argument for book censorship.

"Challenged and Banned Books." **American Library Association. 2009. 5 Oct. 2009** http://www.ala.org/ala/oif/bannedbooksweek/challengedbanned/challenged banned.htm#web. This organization's website is extremely useful because it gives background information on the banning and censoring of books and lists recently and frequently banned books and authors. It also gives statistics on reasons for challenges, which I used for a pie chart. The site could be considered biased, though, because it encourages the idea of free speech and discourages censorship based on the premise of the First Amendment. It also encourages people to read banned books and coined Banned Book Week, which celebrates books that have been banned or challenged.

A working bibliography (as opposed to an annotated bibliography) would include the complete publication information for each source, but not the evaluation of its usefulness to the paper.

Locating Sources

Your college library offers a range of methods and materials for finding the precise information you need. Here is a brief guide to locating periodicals, books, and electronic sources.

Finding Periodicals

Instead of going to the periodicals room and leafing page by page through magazines, journals, and newspapers for information pertinent to your topic, use periodical indexes to locate articles you need. Your library will have these indexes available in print, CD-ROM, or online databases. The form you choose will depend on what is available and how current your information must be. When deciding whether to use the printed or electronic versions, carefully note the dates of the material the indexes reference. For example, you cannot use the CD-ROM version of *The Readers' Guide to Periodical Literature* to find a source from 1979. However, for a more current source (from 1983 to the present), use the CD-ROM version since it provides abstracts of articles. They will allow you to decide whether locating the full article is worth your time and effort. Here is a list of some of the periodical indexes often available in college libraries. If your library does not have these indexes, ask the reference librarian about the best way to find periodical articles in your library.

Periodical Indexes

General

Readers' Guide to Periodical Literature. 1915 to present. Print. Indexes popular journals and magazines and some reviews of movies, plays, books, and television.

Readers' Guide Abstracts. 1983 to present. Same content as *Readers' Guide* but with abstracts.

Newspaper Abstracts. 1985 to present. Abstracts of articles in national and regional newspapers.

New York Times. 1851 to present. Extensive coverage of national and international news.

Periodical Abstracts. 1986 to present. Abstracts and full-text articles from more than 950 general periodicals.

ABI/Inform. August 1971 to present. About eight hundred thousand citations to articles in 1,400 periodicals. Good source for business-related topics. Complete text of articles from five hundred publications since 1991.

LexisNexis Universe. Full-text access to newspapers, magazines, directories, legal and financial publications, and medical journals.

Specialized

Applied Science and Technology Index/Applied Science and Technology Abstracts. 1913 to present. Covers all areas of science and technology.

Art Index/Art Abstracts. 1929 to present. Wide coverage of art and allied fields.

Business Periodicals Index. 1958 to present. Covers all areas of business.

Education Index/Education Abstracts. 1929 to present; June 1983 to present. Covers elementary, secondary, and higher education.

PAIS International in Print/PAIS Database (formerly *Public Affairs Information Service Bulletin*). 1915 to present. Excellent index to journals, books, and reports in economics, social conditions, government, and law.

Ethnic Newswatch. 1990 to present. Indexes news publications by various ethnic groups. Includes full texts of most articles.

Social Sciences Index (*International Index* 1907–1965; *Social Sciences and Humanities* 1965–1974; *Social Sciences Index* 1974 to present). 1907 to present. Indexes scholarly journals in political science, sociology, psychology, and related fields.

Humanities Index. (See *Social Sciences Index* entry for name changes.) 1907 to present. Covers scholarly journals in literature, history, philosophy, folklore, and other fields in the humanities.

America: History and Life. 1964 to present. Index and abstracts to articles in more than 2,000 journals. Covers the histories and cultures of the United States and Canada from prehistory to the present.

SPORT Discus. 1975 to present. Covers sports, physical education, physical fitness, and sports medicine.

Social Issues Researcher (SIRS). Full-text articles from newspapers, journals, and government publications related to the social sciences.

Congressional Universe. Offers a legislative perspective on congressional bills, hearings, public laws, and information on members of Congress.

Sociofile. 1974 to present. Coverage includes family and socialization, culture, social differentiation, social problems, and social psychology.

Essay and General Literature Index. 1900 to present. Indexes essays and chapters in collected works. Emphasis is on social sciences and humanities.

Finding Books

Your library catalogue—whether in print (card), electronic, or microform format—indexes the books your library holds. Books are listed in three basic ways: by author, title, and general subject. If the catalogue is electronic, you can also use keyword searches to locate books. On a computer terminal, you type in a word related to your topic, and the catalogue lists all the sources that include that word.

To make keyword searching more efficient, you can often combine two or more search terms. For example, if you know that you want information on "violence" and can narrow that to "violence and music not rap music," the catalogue will give you a much shorter list of sources than if you had typed only "violence," a very broad topic. This is called Boolean searching, and the typical ways you can combine terms are to use "and" to combine search terms; "or" to substitute search terms (e.g., "violent crime" or "assault"); and "not" to exclude terms. For example, suppose you are looking for information on cigarette smoking by teenagers. In a Boolean search, you could use the search phrase: "teenager or youth and smoking not marijuana."

If you are searching by subject rather than author or title, it's useful to know that libraries organize subject headings according to the *Library of Congress Subject Headings (LCSH)*. These are large red books, usually located near the library's catalogue. You will save time and be more successful if you look up your subject in the *LCSH*. For example, if you search the catalogue using the term "movies," you won't find a single source. If you look up "movies" in the *LCSH*, it will tell you that the subject heading is "motion pictures." Type in "motion pictures," and you'll find the sources you need.

Listed below are other useful sources of information.

Biographies

There are so many different biographical sources it is difficult to know which one has the information you need. The following titles will save you a lot of time:

Biography and Genealogy Master Index. (Spans from B.C. to the present.) Index to more than one million biographical sources.

Biographical Index. 1947 to present. International and all occupations. Guide to sources in books, periodicals, letters, diaries, etc.

Contemporary Authors. 1962 to present. Contains biographical information about authors and lists of their works.

Almanacs

World Almanac and Book of Facts. 1968 to present. Facts about government, business, society, etc. International in scope.

Statistical Abstract of the United States. 1879 to present. Published by the U.S. Bureau of the Census. Good source for statistics about all aspects of the United States including economics, education, society, and politics.

Statistical Masterfile. 1984 to present. State and national government statistics and private and international.

Reviews, Editorials

Book Review Digest. 1905 to present. Index to book reviews with excerpts from the reviews.

Book Review Index. 1965 to present. Indexes to more books than the above but doesn't have excerpts from reviews.

Bibliographies

Look for bibliographies in journal articles, books, encyclopedia articles, biographical sources, etc.

Finding Internet Sources

The Internet offers countless possibilities for research using government documents, newspapers and electronic journals, websites, business publications, and much more.

You may have access to the Internet through campus computer labs, your own computer, or your handheld device.

To make your search easier and more efficient, you can rely on several of the powerful search engine databases available for exploring the Internet. Search engine databases are built by computer robot programs called "spiders" that "crawl" the web. Each of the search engines we've listed below uses keyword searches to find material on your topic. These words can specify your topic, supply the title of a book or article about your topic, name a person associated with your topic, and so on. It's important to try out a number of keyword combinations when you are searching for resources. For instance, if your topic is assisted suicide, you might also search under "euthanasia" and "physician-assisted suicide." By adding additional terms such as "terminal illness," "legalization," and "patient's rights," you may be able to both narrow your search and find material filed under different topic headings that are related to your subject. And you'll get a more accurate response if you use quotation marks around key search phrases.

Here is a list of the more popular search engines. You'll find them useful for locating information on the Internet:

Google   http://www.google.com
This search engine is the first line for searching and the most popular. It will give you a lot of options, including blog posts, wiki pages, group discussion threads, and various document formats such as PDFs. Keywords can be used for subject searches or to find a phrase that appears in the sources. You may also supply the name of a person or a title to prompt your search. It will search for each of your keywords separately or as a unit. You can also limit or expand the time parameters of your search from the current date to up to two years. A word of caution: Information found on *Google* may not always be appropriate or credible, and advertisers pay to appear higher up in the search results. Thus, you may receive some recommendations that have little or nothing to do with your search. (See section below on evaluating sources.)

Yahoo!   http://www.yahoo.com
Yahoo! works just like *Google*. It will also expand your search by linking you to two other search engines if you request them.

Exalead.com   http://www.exalead.com/search
Although not as useful for academic research as are *Google* and *Yahoo!* this search engine provides thumbnail preview pages.

About.com   http://www.about.com
Although not as useful for academic research as are *Google, Dogpile*, and *Yahoo!* this search engine connects users to a network of experts or "guides" who offer practical solutions to common problems spanning a wide field of topics.

In addition to the traditional search engines, there are others that conduct "meta searches"; that is, they allow you to leverage the power of many popular search engines at the same time. Combined, these engines cover more of the Internet than a single search engine can cover. Here is a list of some of the most popular and powerful meta-search engines:

Dogpile   http://www.dogpile.com
This is a popular meta-search engine that combines the power of several other major search engines including *Google, Yahoo! Search, Bing, Ask.com,* and *LookSmart.* It displays results from each different search engine.

Ixquick.com   http://ixquick.com
This meta-search engine ranks results based on the number of "top 10" rankings a site receives from the various search engines.

Zworks.com   http://zworks.com
Like *Ixquick,* when you use *Zworks* you are searching many popular search engines at the same time. Combined, these engines cover more databases on the Internet than any one search engine covers.

Wikipedia   http://wikipedia.org
Wikipedia is an online multilingual encyclopedia (see description on page 246). It is not a search engine, but it can provide you with both information and links to more information. *Wikipedia* covers a vast range of topics with articles that are useful and current and that offer links to related pages and additional information. Because entries are created by anyone who registers and are constantly being revised, material is subject to error and misinformation.

When you are using any search engine, be sure to check the instructions so you can use it as effectively as possible. Also, don't rely on only one search engine. Use several to give yourself access to the broadest range of materials.

Three additional websites that may help you if you are searching for information related to government, politics, legislation, or statistics are the following:

Library of Congress   http://www.loc.gov
This website provides information about the U.S. Congress and the legislative process. It will search for past legislative bills by topic, bill number, or title; allow you to read the *Congressional Record* from the current and past years' Congresses; find committee reports by topic or committee name; and provide full-text access to current bills under consideration in the House of Representatives and the Senate.

U.S. Census Bureau   http://www.census.gov
You can find facts, figures, and statistics derived from the last census at this site. There is also some information about world population.

White House   http://www.whitehouse.gov
At this site, you can find current and past White House press briefings and news releases, as well as a full range of statistics and information produced by federal agencies for public use.

Remember that the Internet is constantly changing, so no book will be completely up to date on how to access its information. Check to see if your college has workshops or courses on using the Internet—it's an important research tool, and it's worth your time to learn how to navigate in cyberspace.

Evaluating Sources

The first examination of your sources is a preliminary assessment to help you decide whether the material is *relevant* and *reliable* for your purposes.

Print Sources

You can often sense a print source's relevance by skimming its preface, introduction, table of contents, conclusion, and index (for books) or abstract and headings (for articles) to see whether your topic appears and how often. Many students mark their bibliography cards with numbers (1 = most relevant, 2 = somewhat relevant, 3 = not very relevant) to help them remember which sources they most want to examine. If a source contains no relevant material, mark the bibliography card "unusable" but don't discard it; if you refine your topic or claim later, you may want to go back to that source.

The reliability of a printed source is judged in a number of ways:

■ Check the date: Is it recent or timely for your topic?

■ Look at the citations: Is the author's evidence recent or timely?

■ Is the author an expert in the field? To find out, use the biographical sources listed earlier in this chapter or find book reviews in the reference section.

■ Where does the author work? A source's credentials may influence your readers. You may also find out what biases the author may have; for example, if the author is the founder of Scientists Against Animal Research, you'll have a good idea about his or her personal beliefs on that subject.

Electronic Sources

Using Internet material presents special challenges in determining the value of a source. Unlike most printed journal and newspaper articles and books, online materials are not necessarily reviewed by editors or professional colleagues to determine whether facts are correct and conclusions reliable. Anyone with the technical skills can develop a website and post opinions for the world to read. So it's difficult to determine whether such information is worth using. But here are a few suggestions that will help you determine if a source is credible:

■ **Domain address** Each Internet host computer is assigned a domain indicating the type of organization that created the site. This domain indicator appears at the end of the address. Most sites will be labeled one of the following:

edu for an educational site
gov for a government site
com for a commercial site
org for an organizational site

While we can't vouch for the quality of all the material at these different domains, it is more likely that sites affiliated with an educational institution or a government office will provide information that has been carefully researched and prepared. Although commercial and organizational sites may also provide valid information, it is important to check carefully for bias or misinformation that might be made available to further the interests of the business or organization.

■ **Author of the site** Try to identity the author or authors of the material published at the site. Is the author a professional or an authority in a field relevant to the topic? The director of a public health clinic may have opinions worth considering on the medical use of marijuana; he may or may not have the same level of credibility in a discussion about punishment for juvenile criminals.

■ **Identity of the organization** If the site is maintained by an organization, find out what interests the organization represents. Who created the organization? A government-appointed committee investigating public support of family planning will have a very different agenda from a committee organized by private interest groups. While both groups may be scrupulously honest in their presentation of the facts, each may interpret those facts with a particular bias. Your awareness of their "slant" will help you decide how to use the information. The reference section of most libraries can provide directories of associations and organizations.

■ **Date of posting** Check the date when the site was posted. Has the site been updated recently? If not, is the material still current and relevant?

■ **Quality of references** Are sources provided to support the information posted on the site? Most credible sites will document their facts, research studies, and statistics. Many articles and essays will be followed by a bibliography. It's always a good idea to double-check these references to determine whether the information is accurate. The absence of any references to support statements of fact and statistics may indicate that the site is unreliable.

■ **Quality of material** Look for indications that the material has been written or assembled by an educated, well-informed individual who offers a balanced and thoughtful perspective on the issue. Is the written text free of obvious grammatical mistakes, spelling errors, problems with sentence structure, and so on? Does the author indicate awareness and respect for other views even while disagreeing with them? Is the coverage of material thorough and well supported? Although poorly written websites can indicate low reliability, don't be fooled by slick, attractive presentations. You need to investigate beneath the surface to determine whether the content of the site meets academic standards of fairness and thoroughness.

■ **Intended use** Consider how you will use the material at the site. If you are looking for reliable statistics and factual information, then checking the author's credentials and the status of the organization or company will be important to maintaining your own credibility. However, sometimes personal examples and experiences of individuals who are not professionally qualified may still be of value. For example, a student writing a paper on Alzheimer's disease came across a site in which an Alzheimer's patient kept a diary of the progression of her illness. Even though she was not qualified to give expert medical opinion on the disease itself, her diary provided a unique insight into the feelings and perceptions of someone experiencing the loss of her intellectual capabilities. In her paper, the student writer was able to incorporate some of this compelling personal testimony.

Let's see how this advice works in practice. Shannon O'Neill decided to do an Internet search to find background information for her argument essay on book banning in the public schools. (Sample entries from her annotated bibliography appear earlier in this chapter.) Using several search engines and a keyword search, Shannon had no trouble finding a large number of sites concerned with this subject. However, before relying on the information at the sites, Shannon had to determine which sites were reliable. To do this, she examined several features of each site, as recommended above.

The first site Shannon found was *The Online Books Page: Banned Books Online* at http://onlinebooks.library.upenn.edu/banned-books.html. Using the criteria from the list we've provided, Shannon made the following evaluation of the site (see Figure 9.1):

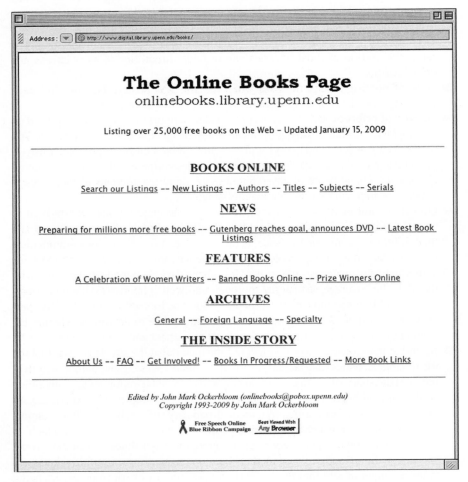

Figure 9.1

■ **Domain address** As Shannon noted, the domain address identified the website as being based at the University of Pennsylvania, a well-known and reputable school.

■ **Author of the site** At the end of the site, the author identified himself by name. Using the home page link "About Us" under "The Inside Story" (see Figure 9.1), Shannon found information about the author who identified himself as a computer scientist who works in a library at the University of Pennsylvania and who received a PhD in computer science at Carnegie Mellon University. But since this description didn't indicate any special expertise on the subject of banned books, Shannon returned to the home page and clicked on the link "Banned Books."

■ **Identity of the organization** That link provided on the home page allowed Shannon to gather more information about *The Online Books Page* and its author. Shannon found a number of links that provided her with considerable information on banned books including classics by Geoffrey Chaucer and John Milton. Another link specified the criteria used to determine which books were placed on the banned book list. Still other links provided further background information about the goals of the site and its association with the Library of Congress. This information and the support of well-known and credible organizations and projects made Shannon feel confident about the value of this site.

■ **Date of posting** Shannon noted that the material on the website was current, having last been updated in the very month in which she was doing her research. The site itself contained information about both recent attempts to limit public library Internet access and historical accounts of book banning.

■ **Quality of references** The author provided frequent references to other websites on banned books, as well as to printed books on censorship. Checking through the Internet and the college library, Shannon confirmed that these references were used reliably and even decided to incorporate some of them into her research.

■ **Quality of material** Shannon found the text well written and the entire site organized and thorough. To evaluate whether the author's perspective was balanced, Shannon checked to see if books from the full range of the political spectrum were included in the list. She discovered that the list included a group of diverse books, from the Bible to the Qur'an to works of nineteenth-century poetry to contemporary books that had been criminalized under "hate speech" laws in other countries. Although it was clear to Shannon that the author of the site did not approve of book banning, this bias did not seem to distort the information he provided.

■ **Intended use** Shannon was interested in finding out the titles of books that were banned, those responsible for the banning, and the reasons behind the decisions. She found *The Online Books Page* very useful. Shannon was particularly impressed by its range of titles. The site's list covered classic and historical works, as well as more modern ones. The explanations that accompanied each listing briefly explained the circumstances surrounding the book's censorship and provided specific dates and information about it.

After carefully evaluating *The Online Books Page: Banned Books Online,* Shannon concluded that it was a reliable source that might supply her with valuable information for her argument essay.

Shannon found three other websites that were also concerned with the issue of banned books. However, after using the criteria outlined above to evaluate the three, Shannon decided not to use them. Here are some of the reasons why:

■ **Domain address** Two of the sites had addresses that indicated that they had no association with any educational institution, government, business, or organization; the websites were developed by individuals for their own personal use. Shannon decided that the materials on these sites were more likely to reflect personal opinion than careful research. The third site was maintained by an organization that Shannon decided to investigate further.

■ **Author of the site** By using the links provided in each site, Shannon discovered that one author was a student writing a paper for an Internet course; another was an individual who supplied some personal information about his life (as well as family photographs) but nothing that indicated expertise on book banning; and the third was identified as a news editor for a newspaper published in California. Shannon needed more information before she could conclude that any of these authors was a reliable source.

■ **Identity of the organization** Only the site authored by the newspaper editor indicated an association with an organization. Using links in the site, Shannon found that he was affiliated with a religious group that strongly advocated the elimination of different races and religions in American life. After reading several articles on the group's website, Shannon concluded that the material contained strong political and racial bias that made her question the reliability of the newspaper editor.

■ **Date of posting** None of the sites had been updated within the past year. Although Shannon was interested in both historical and current information on book banning, she was concerned that the authors had made no attempts to keep the information in the sites current and timely.

■ **Quality of references** Only one site contained a list of related readings, and none of the sites used references to support statements of fact or opinion.

■ **Quality of material** Shannon immediately noticed the poor writing quality of the student paper. It was filled with misspellings and grammatical errors and was poorly organized. The second site demonstrated better quality writing, but the author did not develop or support his ideas sufficiently. For instance, he based much of his claim on an "informal survey" without specifying the details of how the survey was conducted. The site authored by the newspaper editor did not reflect respect for other viewpoints or any attempt to present a balanced perspective on the issue of book banning.

■ **Intended use** Shannon wanted to be sure that the information she used in her argument essay was accurate. The absence of information about two of the authors and the political affiliations of the third caused her to doubt that any of these sites could be relied on for accuracy.

As Shannon discovered, the Internet can offer a wide array of source material to research, but it does take additional effort to determine which sources will meet the standards required for academic research. If you remember to think like an investigator and examine your findings carefully, you'll discover reliable and valuable information and ideas for your argument essays.

Taking Notes

There are as many different styles of note taking as there are writers. Some people like to use index cards, recording one idea on each card. This is useful because you can easily shift cards around as you change your outline; you don't have to recopy material as often. Other students take notes in a journal or on sheets of paper so they can make notes or copy bibliographic references in the margins. If you decide to use note cards, we offer two words of advice: First, mark every note card in some way to identify the source. You might want to use the author's name, an abbreviation of the title, or a numbering system tying your note cards and bibliography together. Don't neglect this or you'll find yourself desperately searching for a reference at 2 a.m. on the day your paper is due, with no way to track it down. Second, on each note card indicate whether it's a summary, paraphrase, or direct quote; some people use different colored cards, pens, or highlighters to distinguish the three kinds of notes. Other people use the initials *S, P,* and *Q* to mark the cards. This designation proves useful when deciding how and when to *document* your sources (see the Documentation Guide).

Most research notes fall into one of three categories: summary, paraphrase, and quotation.

You may also make use of online note-taking. The Internet offers several sites that help students to take, manage, and store their notes and documents—including images and audio data—securely online. Most of these services offer easy systems for organizing notes according to categories just as you would with index cards or file folders as well as search engines for finding old notes. You can also create as many folders as you like, while assigning as many notes as desired to each folder. Because these services are Web applications rather than desktop programs, you can access material from any computer.

Some of these services require a fee; one is NoodleTools http://www.noodletools .com which offers students innovative software that searches, accesses, records, and organizes information using online note cards. It also formats your bibliography in MLA or APA style. (NoodleTools is included in Pearson Longman's MyCompLab. If this book was packaged with an access code to MyCompLab, you will have free access to NoodleTools.) In spite of the fee, NoodleTools is an excellent resource that might be worth the money for all the conveniences offered. Other online services are free, such as mynoteit.com, *Google Docs*, WordPress.com, and Yahoo! Notepad, which is accessible upon opening a free e-mail account with Yahoo!

A word of caution: You can lose track of sources if the particular research link goes down. To avoid such pitfalls, always make copies of your information on CDs, discs, and/or data sticks. You should also make hard copies and print notes with particularly important information.

Summary

Summary is most useful for recording an author's main idea without the background or supporting evidence. To summarize accurately, condense an extended idea into a sentence or more in your own words. Your goal is to record the *essence* of the idea as accurately as possible in your own words.

Here's Shannon's summary of a passage from one of her sources:

Original

In Mark Twain's lifetime, his books *Tom Sawyer* and *Huckleberry Finn* were excluded from the juvenile sections of the Brooklyn Public Library (among other libraries), and banned from the library in Concord, MA, home of Henry Thoreau. In recent years, some high schools have dropped *Huckleberry Finn* from their reading lists, or have been sued by parents who want the book dropped. In Tempe, Arizona, a parent's lawsuit attempted to get the local high school to remove the book from a required reading list and *went as far as a federal appeals court* in 1998. (The court's *decision in the case*, which affirmed Tempe High's right to teach the book, has some interesting comments about education and racial tensions.) The Tempe suit, and recent others, were concerned with the use of the word "nigger," a word that also got *Uncle Tom's Cabin* challenged in Waukegan, Illinois. (From Ockerbloom, John Mark. *The Online Books Page: Banned Books Online.* http://digital.library.upenn.edu/books/banned-books.html.)

Shannon's Summary

Mark Twain's *Huckleberry Finn* is one of the most infamously banned books, as some say it promotes racism by using the "n" word. In 1998, parents in Arizona filed a lawsuit attempting to remove the book from a high school reading list, and the suit went all the way to the federal appeals court. The court's decision returned the book to the reading list.

For more on writing summaries, see Chapter 2.

Paraphrase

Paraphrasing is useful when you want to preserve an author's line of reasoning or specific ideas but don't want or need to use the original words. When you paraphrase, you restate the original as accurately as possible using your own words and sentence structure.

Here is an excerpt from another source that Shannon used in her paper:

Original

Textbook publishers are sensitive to the often right-wing committees and boards of education that purchase books for large states like Texas and California, and will also delete references to evolution or the scientifically hypothesized age of the Earth. (From Barnhisel, Greg, ed. *Media and Messages: Strategies and Readings in Public Rhetoric*, p. 422.)

Shannon's Paraphrase

When they prepare their book lists, publishers put their business at risk if they forget that states with large, expensive, book-consuming school systems—Texas, for example—often have unyielding opinions about a number of sensitive topics. Evolution, for example, is not discussed in some of the science textbooks students use in school—an inappropriate move that denies students exposure to an important scientific theory.

Quotation

Direct quotation should be used only when the author's words are particularly memorable or succinct, or when the author presents factual or numerical evidence that can't be easily paraphrased. You must copy the author's *exact* wording, spelling, capitalization, and punctuation *as you find it* (even if it contains an obvious mistake). Proofread every direct quotation at least twice; it's easier than you think to leave something out, change a verb tense, or add a word or two. If you want to add words for grammatical completeness or clarity, put them in square brackets such as these [ ]. If you want to eliminate words, mark the omission with three spaced periods, called *ellipsis points* (if the omission comes at the end of a sentence, the ellipsis is typed with four spaced periods). If you find a source you are certain to quote from, it might be worthwhile to photocopy it to avoid errors when rewriting the words.

Here is an example of the effective use of quotation, based on another of Shannon's sources:

Original

Congress shall make no law respecting an establishment of religion, or prohibiting the free exercise thereof; or abridging the freedom of speech, or of the press; or the right of the people peaceably to assemble, and to petition the Government for a redress of grievances. ("About the First Amendment." *First Amendment Center.* http://www.firstamendmentcenter.org/about.aspx?item=about_firstamd.)

Shannon's Effective Use of Quotation

According to the First Amendment, citizens of the United States are guaranteed the right to freedom of speech, which also includes the freedoms of thought and expression: "Congress shall make no law respecting an establishment of religion, or prohibiting the free exercise thereof; or abridging the freedom of speech, or of the press [. . .]."

Drafting Your Paper

Sometimes the sheer size of a researched argument paper can be intimidating. As a result, some writers suffer from "writer's block" at the outset. Here are strategies for starting your draft.

1. **Write a five-minute summary.** Write a quick, one- or two-paragraph description of what your final paper will say—that is, a thumbnail sketch of the paper to clarify in your own mind how it will come together. The summary doesn't have to be formal; some people don't even use complete sentences. Almost always, these summaries dispel writer's block and get your creativity flowing.

2. **Divide the paper into sections.** Dividing the paper into sections makes the task of writing a long paper more manageable. Most writers divide a paper, as we did in Chapter 5, into beginning, middle, and end, and further subdivide the middle.

3. **First, draft the sections you're confident about.** Drafting first the sections you feel most confident about builds momentum for drafting other parts of the paper. As reported by many students, this strategy might also lead you to alter the slant or emphasis of the final paper, thereby resulting in a better outcome.

4. **Use a simple code to indicate sources.** Using a simple code to indicate sources will save you a great deal of time in revising your paper. As you write your draft, you may not want to interrupt the flow of your ideas to copy quotations or summaries from note cards; instead, you can insert into your draft the author's or source's name and a quick reference to the content so that you'll know on a later draft what you intended to include. Here's an example of how Shannon used coded references in her first draft:

> Attempts to ban books in public schools is on the rise. [People, Attacks 6] John Steinbeck's *Of Mice and Men* is a frequent target of protest for parents. [Mitchell, NYT B17]

Here you can see Shannon's code at work as she refers to notes from a report published by People for the American Way and an article from page B17 of the *New York Times.* Later, she will have to incorporate these sources into her first draft and provide parenthetical citations; for the time being, she simply lists in shorthand the evidence to support her general statements.

Incorporating Your Research

Because the effort made in finding sources and taking notes is so time-consuming, some writers think that their work will be "wasted" if they don't somehow cram all the notes they've taken into their final papers. Unfortunately, the results of such cramming often look less like a paper and more like note cards stapled together with an occasional sentence wedged between to provide transitions. Every successful writer ends up gathering more research data than is needed for a paper. But it's better to have a lot of material to choose from than not enough to make a persuasive case. The five tests at the end of Chapter 6 (sufficiency, detail, relevance, avoidance of excess, and appropriateness) should help you determine which notes to incorporate into the final draft. Here, too, the flexibility of having one note per card may help because you can shuffle and change the sequence of sources to see which order of presentation will have the most impact on your readers. If you are working on a computer, you may mark and move blocks of text around as you judge the arrangement of your evidence. The first arrangement may not always be the best, so allow yourself some flexibility.

When incorporating sources into your paper, you don't want the "seams" to show between your own writing and the summaries, paraphrases, and quotations from your sources. So it's worth the effort to write sentences and phrases that smoothly introduce sources into the text. Consider two examples:

Awkward   The Anaheim school board decided to ban *Beloved,* and this was "not an example of censorship, but an isolated incident."

Revised   The school board in the Anaheim, California, school system stated that their decision to ban *Beloved* was "not an example of censorship, but an isolated incident."

Remember that while *you,* the writer, may understand how a particular source supports your points, your *readers* may miss the connections unless you provide them. Again we fall back on the analogy of making a case to a jury: A good attorney not only presents a witness's testimony but also helps the jury understand what that testimony means.

Attribution

Many students fail to understand the importance of introducing their sources when incorporating them into a paper. This introduction is called **attribution,** and it is an important part of the process of documentation. Attribution shows your readers that your evidence comes from identifiable, reliable sources. When the attribution contains the name of a book or the author's professional affiliation or other credentials, it also suggests to your readers how reliable the source may be. For instance, if you present a statistic on divorce and attribute it to the book *How to Pick Up Women,* your readers are less likely to respect that statistic than if it came from the U.S. Census Bureau. Likewise, if you cite evidence that eating rutabagas prevents colon cancer, your readers will treat the evidence differently if it comes from an unbiased researcher at the Mayo Clinic rather than from one at the American Rutabaga Institute. In neither case is the evidence less likely to be true, but the attribution in both cases makes the difference in plausibility.

Many students have only one phrase in their repertoires for attribution: "According to. . . ." This works, but it is not very informative. By choosing a more connotative argumentative verb, as you do when you state a position or proposal, you can signal to your readers the source's attitude toward the statement. For instance, consider this sentence:

Senator Smith _____ that the change is needed.

Using the list of attribution verbs below, look at how selecting a verb can determine the way your audience regards Smith's position (not all these verbs will work in this sentence structure).

If you're not sure of the connotations of any of these verbs, or you're not sure that the sentence you created works with a particular choice, consult an unabridged diction-

Attribution Verbs

Source Is Neutral

comments	observes	says
describes	points out	sees
explains	records	thinks
illustrates	reports	writes
notes		

Source Implies or Suggests but Doesn't Actually Say

analyzes	asks	assesses
concludes	considers	finds
predicts	proposes	reveals
shows	speculates	suggests
supposes	infers	implies

Source Argues

alleges	claims	contends
defends	disagrees	holds
insists	maintains	argues

Source Agrees with Someone/Something Else

admits	agrees	concedes
concurs	grants	allows

Source Is Uneasy or Disagrees

belittles	bemoans	complains
condemns	deplores	deprecates
derides	laments	warns

ary or your instructor. Clumsy attribution can distract readers in the same way typos and grammatical errors can; so you want to make your attributions as smooth as possible. (For placement of a bibliographic reference after attributed material, see the next section on documentation.)

Revising and Editing Your Paper

After you have worked your source material into a draft, it's time to look at your writing skeptically, as your readers will. Start by testing all the parts of your argument. This may not be easy to do because you've been living with this topic for some time and may have lost your objectivity and ability to see the gaps. (If you're working in writing groups, ask another member to read your paper and offer you some feedback on it.) Then change, delete, add, or reorganize material to make your case more effectively.

To help you revise your argument, we recommend making an outline of the draft *as you've written it*—not as you intended to write it. This will serve as an X-ray of the paper, helping you detect any holes or imbalances. Moreover, it will show you the actual order in which points are presented so that you can consider reorganizing or changing your argumentative strategy. The strategies explained in Chapters 6 and 7 for assessing evidence and considering claims ought to help you at this stage; apply them as stringently to your own writing as you would to an essay you're reading.

If you made notes in your journal about connections you wanted to make in your final paper, now is the time to include those connections if, in fact, they still fit. You might also consider other kinds of evidence to include. Can you think of personal experiences—yours or others'—to support the evidence of your outside authorities? Have you found facts and statistics to buttress the opinions you present? What are your readers' criteria for judging an issue? Have you presented claims that meet those criteria and phrased them in that manner? It's also time to make sure that all transitions between points are included and are accurate. For instance, if you switch points around, make sure that the point you call "second" is actually the second, not the third or fourth. Also, check that you've included documentation for all your sources and that you have bibliographic note cards or other records of documentation information to prepare the notes in your final copy. Then polish your prose so that your sentences are smooth, your paragraphs are complete, and your grammar and punctuation are precise. Many students let down their efforts when they sense their papers are nearing completion; as a result, their final grades suffer. The revising and editing stage requires sharp attention. Don't undercut all your hard research efforts by presenting your argument in anything but its best form.

Preparing and Proofreading Your Final Manuscript

Once you have polished the draft to your satisfaction, it is time to attend to the presentation of your paper. Flawless presentation is important in research, not only because of the appreciation it will win from your instructor and readers, but also because it will reinforce your credibility with your readers. A sloppy paper with typographical or grammatical errors, missing documentation, or illegible print makes your readers think that your argument might be sloppy as well. A well-prepared paper suggests to your readers that you have taken care to ensure that everything is correct—not only the presentation, but the content as well. This good impression may make readers more inclined to accept your arguments.

Most instructors expect research papers to be neatly and legibly typed with clear titles, double spacing, standard margins (1-inch) and type sizes (10- or 12-point), and minimal handwritten corrections. Your last name and the page number should appear in the upper-right-hand corner of every page after the title page. For English courses, the standard guide to manuscript format is the *MLA Handbook for*

Writers of Research Papers, 7th edition. MLA requirements are spelled out in most college composition handbooks and illustrated in Shannon's final paper (see the Documentation Guide). Before you submit your paper, proofread it carefully for typographical errors, misspellings, omitted words, and other minor errors. If possible, let several hours elapse before your final proofreading so you can see what you've actually typed instead of what you *think* you typed.

Plagiarism

Plagiarism is a crime in the academic community. The scholarly world operates by exchanging information and acknowledging its sources. If you fail to acknowledge your sources or let it appear that someone else's work is your own, you are sabotaging the exchange of scholarly information. You're blocking the channels. And plagiarism has very serious consequences: It can earn you a failing grade on an assignment or for a course, a suspension or even expulsion from school, and/or a permanent notation on the transcript that future employers and graduate schools will see.

Plagiarism falls into two categories: intentional and accidental. Intentional plagiarism includes copying a phrase, a sentence, or a longer passage from a source and passing it off as your own; summarizing or paraphrasing someone else's ideas without acknowledgment; and buying or borrowing a paper written by someone else and submitting it as your own. Accidental plagiarism includes forgetting to place quotation marks around someone else's words and not acknowledging a source because you were ignorant of the need to document it. Carelessness and ignorance are not defenses against plagiarism.

Many questions about plagiarism involve the tricky subject of *common knowledge*—that is, standard information in a field of study as well as commonsense observations and proverbial wisdom. Standard information includes the major facts in a discipline—for example, the chemical formula for water is H_2O or the Seneca Falls Convention for Women's Rights took place in 1848. If most of your sources accept such a fact without acknowledgment, you can assume it is common knowledge to readers in that field. However, if you're dealing with lesser-known facts (the numbers of soldiers at the Battle of Hastings), interpretations of those facts (assessments of the importance of the Seneca Falls meeting), or a specialist's observation (a scholar's analysis of Susan B. Anthony's rhetoric), you'll need to provide documentation.

Commonsense information, such as the notions that politicians are concerned with getting votes and that icy roads make driving dangerous, need not be documented. Proverbs and clichés don't need documentation either, although proverbs taken from recognized poems or literary works do. (Thus, "A stitch in time" needs no documentation, but "To be or not to be" should carry a reference to *Hamlet.*)

Here are four simple rules to help you avoid plagiarism:

1. *Take your research notes carefully.* Write down (or print out) a full bibliographical reference for each source (the forms appear in the Documentation Guide). Also, note whether you are quoting, paraphrasing, or summarizing what you find in your source (see earlier discussion in this chapter). If your notes are clear and

thorough, you'll never have to worry about which words and ideas are yours and which come from your sources.

2. *Always introduce your source carefully so that your audience knows to whom they're listening.* Proper attribution is a signal to your readers that you're switching from your own work to someone else's. It also is a signal to you to check that a source is represented accurately (with no exaggeration) and that a bibliographic citation appears in your list of Works Cited or References.

3. *When in doubt, document.* While it is possible to overdocument, it is not an intellectual crime to do so. Rather, it reveals a lack of self-confidence in your own argument or your determination to prove to your instructor and readers that you've seen every source ever published on your subject. However, overdocumenting is a less serious academic sin than plagiarizing!

4. *Enter the documentation right after the use of the source; it doesn't "carry over" between paragraphs or pages.* It is tempting, especially when using one source for an extended period, to leave all the documentation until the end of a large passage of text (which might be several paragraphs or several pages in length). But even if you weave attribution skillfully throughout the whole passage, the convention in academics is that you document a source in each paragraph in which you use it. If another source intervenes, it is twice as important that the main source be documented on every use. So if you use the same article in four successive paragraphs, each of those paragraphs must have some parenthetical source reference. With skillful attribution, the parenthetical reference can be reduced to a simple page number, which won't interrupt the flow of your text.

To understand how plagiarism works, let's look at some of the ways writers might handle, or mishandle, this passage from Dennis Baron's article "English in a Multicultural Society," which appeared in the Spring 1991 issue of *Social Policy.* Here's the original passage from page 8:

> The notion of a national language sometimes wears the disguise of inclusion: we must all speak English to participate meaningfully in the democratic process. Sometimes it argues unity: we must speak one language to understand one another and share both culture and country. Those who insist on English often equate bilingualism with lack of patriotism. Their intention to legislate official English often masks racism and certainly fails to appreciate cultural difference; it is a thinly veiled measure to disenfranchise anyone not like "us."

Plagiarized Use
Supporters of U.S. English argue we must all speak one language to understand one another and share both culture and country. But Dennis Baron argues that "[t]heir intention to legislate official English often masks racism and certainly fails to appreciate cultural difference" (8). English-only legislation really intends to exclude anyone who is not like "us."

This is plagiarism because the writer has copied Baron's words in the first sentence and paraphrased them in the last, but made it appear as though only the middle sentence was actually taken from Baron's article.

Plagiarized Use

Calls for a national language sometimes wear the disguise of inclusion, according to linguist Dennis Baron. When U.S. English argues that we must all speak English to participate meaningfully in the democratic process, or that we must speak one language to understand one another and share both culture and country, Baron says they are masking racism and failing to appreciate cultural difference (8).

Here the plagiarism comes in presenting Baron's actual words without quotation marks, so it looks as if the writer is paraphrasing rather than quoting. Even with the attribution and the citation of the source, this paragraph is still an example of plagiarism because the direct quotations appear as the writer's paraphrase.

Acceptable Use

Linguist Dennis Baron argues that supporters of official English legislation use the reasons of inclusion, unity, and patriotism to justify these laws, but that their efforts may hide racist and culturally intolerant positions. Baron says that sometimes English-only laws are "thinly veiled measure[s] to disenfranchise anyone not like 'us'" (8).

Here the source is properly handled. The writer paraphrases most of the original text in the first sentence, then skillfully incorporates a direct quotation in the second (note the use of square brackets to make the noun agree in number with the verb, and the conversion of double quotation marks from the original into single quotation marks in the quote). The attribution clearly says that both points are taken from Baron, but the quotation marks show where Baron's own words, rather than the writer's, are used.

Documentation Guide:

MLA and APA Styles

The two most common systems of documentation used in colleges and universities are the Modern Language Association (MLA) style, used widely in the humanities, and the American Psychological Association (APA) style, used widely in the social sciences. We will explain them in detail in this chapter. (Some of your courses may also require you to use the Council of Science Editors, or CSE, style; *The Chicago Manual of Style*, which you might know as Turabian style; or a journalistic style guide such as *The Associated Press Style Book*.) Your instructor will tell you which rules to follow.

Where Does the Documentation Go?

Both MLA and APA styles call for parenthetical citations within the paper and a source list at the end of the paper. In both styles, you use a brief reference or attribution to your source in parentheses within the body of the paper and a full bibliographical citation in a list of Works Cited (MLA) or References (APA). (These are the equivalents of what you probably called a "Bibliography" in high school.) Documenting your sources, if performed properly, will help you avoid plagiarism. The shape that citations take in the two systems, however, is a little different, so make sure you observe the forms carefully.

Documentation Style

Let's look at how both systems handle documentation for some of the most commonly used information sources. Suppose you want to quote from Matt Bai's article "The New Boss," which appeared in the January 30, 2005, issue of the *New York Times Magazine*. Here's how it would appear in your list of sources or bibliography:

MLA Bai, Matt. "The New Boss." *The New York Times Magazine* 30 Jan. 2005: 38+. Print.

APA Bai, M. (2005, January 30). The new boss. *The New York Times Magazine*, pp. 38–45, 62, 68, 71.

As you can see, each style orders information differently.

Likewise, both styles use a parenthetical reference in the paper to show where the evidence comes from, but again they do it differently.

MLA One author talks about giving "added value" to employers, some of whom have come to view him, warily, as a partner (Bai 42).

If the author's name appears in your attribution, only the page number needs to go in the parentheses:

MLA Matt Bai talks about giving "added value" to employers, some of whom have come to view him, warily, as a partner (42).

Both references tell your readers that they can find this source in your Works Cited list, alphabetized by the last name *Bai*. If you had more than one reference to Bai in your Works Cited list, then you would add a shortened form of the title in the parentheses so readers would know to which Bai article you were referring (Bai, "New Boss" 42).

The APA style references for the same situations would be

APA One author talks about giving "added value" to employers, some of whom have come to view him, warily, as a partner (Bai, 2005, p. 42).

or

APA Bai (2005) talks about giving "added value" to employers, some of whom have come to view him, warily, as a partner (p. 42).

When you use more than one work by an author in your paper, APA style distinguishes them by date of publication. For example, if you cited two Bai articles from 2005, the earlier one would be designated 2005a, and the second as 2005b.

Using parenthetical citations for electronic sources can be much trickier because such sources typically have no page numbers. If your source uses paragraph numbers, provide the paragraph number preceded by *par.* or *para.* If you need to include the author's name or a brief title, place a comma after the name or title. If another type of designation is used in the source to delineate its parts (such as *screens* or *Part II*), write out the word used for that part:

MLA Between 2000 and 2004, the message delivered by political advertisements changed dramatically (Edwards, par. 15).

APA Between 2000 and 2004, the message delivered by political advertisements changed dramatically (Edwards, 2005, para. 15).

If your source has no numbering, no page or paragraph numbers should appear in your parenthetical reference unless your instructor indicates that you should do otherwise. Some instructors ask students to number the paragraphs of electronic sources to make references easier to locate.

A Brief Guide to MLA and APA Styles

The handbooks for MLA and APA documentation are available in most college libraries. If you don't find the information you need in this brief guide, look for these books or websites:

MLA *MLA Handbook for Writers of Research Papers.* 7th ed. New York: MLA, 2009. Print.

The website of the Modern Language Association is http://www.mla.org.

APA *Publication Manual of the American Psychological Association* (6th ed.). (2009). Washington, DC: American Psychological Association.

The American Psychological Association does not provide a guide to documentation on its website; however, the Purdue University Online Writing Lab provides a useful guide to APA documentation: http://owl.english.purdue.edu/handouts/research/r_apa.html.

Books

MLA Author. *Title.* Edition. City of Publication: Publisher, Year. Medium of Publication.

APA Author. (Year of Publication). *Title.* City of Publication, State: Publisher.

One Author

MLA Krakauer, Jon. *Where Men Win Glory: The Odyssey of Pat Tillman.* New York: Random, 2009. Print.

APA Krakauer, J. (2009) *Where men win glory: The odyssey of Pat Tillman.* New York, NY: Random House.

MLA uses the author's full first name plus middle initial, whereas APA uses the initial of the first name (unless more initials are needed to distinguish among people with the same initials). APA capitalizes only first words and proper nouns in titles and subtitles; MLA capitalizes all words except prepositions, conjunctions, and articles. MLA lists only the city; APA lists the city but also includes the state. MLA shortens certain publishers' names, whereas APA just drops unnecessary words such as *Co., Inc.,* and *Publishers.* Lastly, MLA includes the medium of the publication consulted, which is "Print" in this case.

Two or More Authors

MLA Reinhart, Carmen M., and Kenneth S. Rogoff. *This Time Is Different: Eight Centuries of Financial Folly.* Princeton: Princeton UP, 2009. Print.

APA Reinhart, C. M., & Rogoff, K. S. (2009). *This time is different: Eight centuries of financial folly.* Princeton, NJ: Princeton University Press.

In MLA style, only the first author's name is given in inverted form. In APA style, the ampersand (&) is used to join authors' names. The ampersand is also used in parenthetical references in text, for example "(Reinhart & Rogoff, 2009, p. 63)," but not in attributions, for example, "According to Pyles and Algeo." In MLA style, for works with more than three authors you may replace all but the first author's name by the abbreviation *et al.* In APA style, list the names of up to six authors, and use the abbreviation *et al.* to indicate the remaining authors.

More Than One Book by an Author

MLA   Gladwell, Malcolm. *Outliers.* New York: Little, 2008. Print.

---. *What the Dog Saw and Other Adventures.* New York: Little, 2009. Print.

In MLA style, if you cite more than one work by a particular author, the individual works are listed in alphabetical order. For the second and any additional entries, type three hyphens and a period instead of the author's name; then skip a space and type the title in italics.

In APA style, when you cite more than one work by an author, the author's name is repeated for each work. The order of the entries is based on the publication dates of the titles, with the earliest-published given first, instead of alphabetical order. If two works by one author are published in the same year, alphabetization is done by title and the letters *a, b,* etc., are placed immediately after the year.

Book with an Editor

MLA   Haynes, Kenneth, ed. *Geoffrey Hill: Collected Critical Writings.* New York: Oxford UP, 2008. Print.

APA   Haynes, K. (Ed.). (2008). *Geoffrey Hill: Collected critical writings.* New York, NY: Oxford University Press.

Essay in a Collection or Anthology

MLA   Fisher, M. F. K. "Gare de Lyon." *Americans in Paris: A Literary Anthology.* Ed. Adam Gopnik. New York: Library of America, 2004. 581-91. Print.

APA   Fisher, M. F. K. (2004). Gare de Lyon. In A. Gopnik (Ed.), *Americans in Paris: A literary anthology* (pp. 581–591). New York, NY: Library of America.

Book in a Later Edition

MLA   Janaro, Richard, and Thelma Altshuler. *The Art of Being Human.* 9th ed. New York: Longman, 2009.

APA   Janaro, R., & Altshuler, T. (2009). *The art of being human* (9th ed). New York, NY: Longman.

Multivolume Work

MLA   Doyle, Arthur Conan. *The New Annotated Sherlock Holmes*. Ed. Leslie S. Klinger. 2 vols. New York: Norton, 2004. Print.

APA   Doyle, A. C. (2004). *The new annotated Sherlock Holmes* (L. S. Klinger, Ed.). (Vols. 1–2). New York, NY: Norton.

Book with a Group or Corporate Author

MLA   American Medical Association. *Handbook of First Aid and Emergency Care*. New York, Random, 2009. Print.

APA   American Medical Association. (2009). *Handbook of first aid and emergency care*. New York, NY: Random House.

Begin the entry with the corporate or group name alphabetized by the first letter of the main word (not including *a, an,* or *the*).

Article from a Reference Work

MLA   Bragg, Michael B. "Aircraft Deicing." *The McGraw-Hill Concise Encyclopedia of Science and Technology*. 6th ed. 2009. Print.

APA   Bragg, M. (2009). Aircraft deicing. In *The McGraw-Hill concise encyclopedia of science and technology* (Vol. 1, pp. 339–342). New York, NY: McGraw-Hill.

If the reference book is widely available (such as a major encyclopedia or bibliography), a short bibliographic form as shown here is acceptable in MLA; APA recommends including more information rather than less. For a less widely known reference book, MLA recommends using the form for a book, multiple-authored book, or series, depending on what the book is.

Editor's Preparation of a Previous Work

MLA   Lovecraft, H. P. *Tales*. Ed. Peter Straub. New York: Library of America, 2005. Print.

APA   Lovecraft, H. P. (2005). *Tales* (P. Straub, Ed.). New York, NY: Library of America.

Translated Work

MLA   Pamuk, Orhan. *The Museum of Innocence*. Trans. Maureen Freely. New York: Knopf, 2009. Print.

APA   Pamuk, O. (2009). *The museum of innocence* (M. Freely, Trans.). New York, NY: Alfred A. Knopf. (Original work published 2008)

In APA style, the date of the translation is placed after the author's name. The date of the original publication of the work appears in parentheses at the end of the citation. This text would be cited in a paper as (Pamuk, 2008/2009).

Anonymous Work

MLA   *The Chicago Manual of Style: The Essential Guide for Writers, Editors, and Publishers*. 16th ed. Chicago: U of Chicago P, 2010. Print.

APA   *The Chicago manual of style: The essential guide for writers, editors, and publishers* (16th ed.). (2010). Chicago, IL: University of Chicago Press.

Periodicals

MLA format and APA format for articles in journals, periodicals, magazines, newspapers, and so on, are similar to the formats for books. One of the few differences concerns the volume number of each issue. Volume numbers for magazines or journals found in a library or acquired by subscription (these usually appear six times a year or less frequently) should be included in your entry. If a journal appears monthly or more frequently, or can be acquired on newsstands, you can usually omit the volume number. If the journal has continuous pagination (i.e., if the January issue ends on page 88 and the February issue begins on page 89), you don't need to include the month or season of the issue in your citation. If the journal starts over with page 1 in each issue, then you must include the month or season in your citation.

Magazines and newspapers (unlike scholarly journals) often carry articles on discontinuous pages (e.g., pages 35–37 and then 114–115). MLA permits the use of the form "35+" instead of giving all the pages on which such articles appear. With APA style, all page numbers must be noted.

MLA   Author. "Article Title." *Journal or Magazine Title* volume number (Date): inclusive pages. Medium of publication.

APA   Author. (Date). Article title. *Journal or Magazine Title, volume number,* inclusive pages.

Scholarly Journal

MLA   Spandler, Helen, and Tim Calton. "Psychosis and Human Rights: Conflicts in Mental Health Policy and Practice." *Social Policy and Society* 8. (2009), 245-256. Print.

APA   Spandler, H., & Calton, T. (2009). Psychosis and human rights: Conflicts in mental health policy and practice. *Social Policy and Society, 8*(1), 245–256.

Magazine Article

MLA   Wallace, Amy. "An Epidemic of Fear." *Wired* Nov. 2009: 128+. Print.

APA   Wallace, A. (2009, November). An epidemic of fear. *Wired,* 128–135, 166, 168, 170.

This is the form for a magazine that appears monthly. For a magazine that appears bimonthly or weekly, provide the complete date.

MLA   Mahr, Krista. "A Tough Catch." *Time* 16 Nov. 2009: 38-43. Print.

APA   Mahr, K. (2009, November 16). A tough catch. *Time,* 38–43.

Review

MLA   Vaill, Amanda. "Brooklyn Bohemians." Rev. of *February House*, by Sherill Tippins. *New York Times Book Review* 6 Feb. 2005: 8. Print.

APA   Vaill, A. (2005, February 6). Brooklyn bohemians [Review of the book *February house*, by S. Tippins]. *The New York Times Book Review*, p. 8.

When newspapers designate sections with identifying letters (e.g., *A*, *B*), that information is included in the reference. With MLA style, "4+" indicates that the review begins on page 4 and continues on other nonadjacent pages in the newspaper. APA includes initial articles such as "The" in a newspaper title; MLA omits them. If the reviewer's name does not appear, begin with "Rev. of *Title*" in the MLA system or "[Review of the book *Title*]" in the APA system. If the reviewer's name does not appear but the review has a title, begin with the title of the review in both systems.

Newspaper Article

MLA   Begley, Sharon. "Reversing Partial Blindness." *Wall Street Journal* 1 Feb. 2005: D1. Print.

APA   Begley, S. (2005, February 1). Reversing partial blindness. *The Wall Street Journal*, p. D1.

Newspaper Editorial

MLA   Judge, Michael. "Epitaph on a Tyrant." Editorial. *Wall Street Journal* 7 Feb. 2005: A19. Print.

APA   Judge, M. (2005, February 7). Epitaph on a tyrant [Editorial]. *The Wall Street Journal*, p. A19.

Letter to the Editor of a Magazine or Newspaper

MLA   Rafferty, Heather A. Letter. "The Other 'CIA.'" *Weekly Standard* 7 Feb. 2005: 5. Print.

APA   Rafferty, H. (2005, February 7). The other "CIA" [Letter to the editor]. *The Weekly Standard*, p. 5.

If the newspaper or magazine doesn't give a title to the letter, for MLA style use the word *Letter* followed by a period after the author's name. Do not underline the word or enclose it in quotation marks. For APA style, skip that information and use the rest of the citation form.

Internet Sources
Web Page

MLA   Redford, Robert. "Common Sense for the Clean Energy and Climate Debate." *OnEarth*. Natural Resources Defense Council, 11 Nov. 2009. Web. 12 Nov. 2009.

APA   Redford, R. (2009, November 11). Common sense for the clean energy and climate debate. Retrieved from http://www.onearth.org/node/1603

For MLA, begin with the name of the individual who created the website. Follow with the title of the work in quotation marks (if you are citing a smaller work within a larger site), then the title of the entire website in italics. Then write the name of the organization associated with the site, if available; the date of publication, if available; the medium of publication, which is the "Web" in this case, and the date of access.

MLA does not require a URL in the citation. However, if your source is difficult to locate, you can provide the complete URL in angle brackets after the date of access. If the URL is long, you can break it onto the next line after a single or double slash.

For APA, begin with the last name of the author followed by initials and period. Follow with the date of publication or latest update. Use "(n.d.)" if no date is available. If there is no author, begin with the title of the site, and then the date of publication or update. Close with the electronic address, whether it is the URL or DOI (digital object identifier).

Online Magazine Article

MLA   Upbin, Bruce, and Dan Bigman. "The Carbon Question." *Forbes Magazine*. Forbes.com, 15 Oct. 2009. Web. 12 Nov. 2009.

APA   Upbin, B., & Bigman, D. (2009, October 15). The carbon question. *Forbes Magazine*. Retrieved from *http://www.forbes.com/forbes/2009/1102/opinions-steve-forbes-climate-change-lets-get-real.html*

MLA gives the date of access for electronic sources, and this date of access appears right after *Web*. APA provides the date of publication and lists this date after the author.

Online Article in Electronic Journal

MLA   Knypstra, Syste. "Teaching statistics in an Activity Encouraging Format." *Journal of Statistics Education*, 17.2 (2009): n. pag. Web. 23 Oct. 2009.

APA   Knypstra, S. (2009). Teaching statistics in an activity encouraging format. *Journal of Statistics Education, 17*(2). Retrieved from www.amstat.org/publications/jse/v17n2/knypstra.html

Online Article Retrieved from a Database

MLA   Thompson, Ayanna. "Introduction: Shakespeare, Race, and Performance." *Shakespeare Bulletin* 27.3 (2009): 359-61. *Project Muse*. Web. 7 Nov. 2009.

APA   Thompson, A. Introduction: Shakespeare, race, and performance. *Shakespeare Bulletin, 27*(3), 359–361. doi: 10.1353/shb.0.0109

To document material from a database in MLA, italicize the database service, indicate the medium of publication, i.e., Web, and the date of access. For APA, provide the DOI (digital object identifier) if available. Otherwise, you can list the database after *Retrieved from*.

Online Book

MLA Bacon, Jono. *The Art of Community: Building the New Age of Participation.* Sebastopol: O'Reilly, 2009. *Art of Community.* Web. 4 Nov. 2009.

APA Bacon, J. (2009). *The art of community: Building the new age of participation.* Retrieved from http://www.artofcommunityonline.org/get/

CD-ROM

MLA "Electrometer." *The McGraw-Hill Encyclopedia of Science and Technology.* 9th ed. CD-ROM. New York: McGraw, 2002.

APA Electrometer. (2002). In *The McGraw-Hill encyclopedia of science and technology (9th ed.).* [CD-ROM]. New York, NY: McGraw-Hill.

E-Mail

MLA Mendez, Michael R. "Re: Solar power." E-mail to Edgar V. Atamian. 13 Sept. 2009.

In APA, electronic correspondence via e-mail typically does not appear in the reference list. It is cited only in an in-text reference: (M. Mendez, personal communication, September 13, 2009).

Miscellaneous Sources

Film, Filmstrip, Slide Program, Videotape, DVD

MLA Nair, Mira. *Amelia.* Perf. Hilary Swank, Richard Gere, and Ewan McGregor. Fox Searchlight Pictures, 2009. Film.

APA Forster, M. (Director). (2004). *Finding neverland* [Motion picture]. United States: Miramax.

To cite a filmstrip, slide program, videotape, or DVD in MLA style, include the name of the medium after the distributor and year of release. If you are citing the work as a whole rather than the work of one of the creative artists involved in the project, start with the title instead. For instance:

MLA *Harry Potter and the Half-Blood Prince.* Dir. David Yates. Warner Bros., 2009. DVD.

APA Heyman, D. (Producer), & Yates, D. (Director). (2009). *Harry Potter and the half-blood prince* [Motion picture]. United States: Warner Bros.

Television or Radio Program

MLA Burns, Ken, dir. *The National Parks: America's Best Idea.* PBS. KCTS, Seattle. 28 Sept. 2-Oct. 2009. Television.

APA Burns, K., and Duncan, D. (Producers). (2009) *The National Parks: America's Best Idea.* [Television series]. Seattle: KCTS.

In MLA, include the network as well as the call letters and city of the local station, if available. Then, add the broadcast date and medium of reception. For a radio broadcast, substitute *Radio*.

In APA, list the producer for an entire television series. To cite an individual episode in a series, list the writer and director instead, and substitute "Television series episode."

Interview

MLA   Pennington, Linda Beth. Personal interview. 20 Apr. 2003.

In APA, personal communications including interviews do not appear in the reference list. They are cited only in an in-text reference: (L. Pennington, personal interview, April 20, 2009).

The APA doesn't offer forms for "nonrecoverable" materials such as personal letters, e-mail messages, lectures, and speeches, and these sources are not included in reference listings. However, in college writing assignments, most instructors will ask you to include them. You may, therefore, have to design a hybrid citation form based on the standard forms. Remember that the APA encourages you to provide more, rather than less, information in your citations. The MLA has forms for almost any kind of communication, even nonrecoverable ones. Consult the *MLA Handbook for Writers of Research Papers,* 7th edition, to find additional forms.

SAMPLE RESEARCH PAPERS

Following are two sample student research papers, the first in MLA format and the second in APA format. As you read them, notice the margins and other format requirements of the two styles, such as the use of running heads, the placement of titles, and the different citation forms. We have added marginal annotations to highlight special features and to demonstrate the structural elements of the arguments.

As these research papers demonstrate, the researched argument is different from the other arguments you've written only in quantity and format, not in quality. You must still make a claim and find evidence to support it, tailor your presentation to your readers, and use a logical structure that considers the various sides of an issue. As you progress in your academic life and, later, in your professional life, you will find that variations on the researched argument can become successful senior projects, theses, sales proposals, journal articles, grant proposals, and even books—so mastering the skills of argumentative writing will serve you well.

Shannon O'Neill
Professor Martinez
English 111
13 November 2009

Literature Hacked and Torn Apart:
Censorship in Public Schools

During the 2008 Summer Olympic Games in Beijing, international journalists covering the event found their access to certain Web sites restricted by the Chinese government—something that the country's citizens deal with every day. But even in America, where we wouldn't dream of a government that told us what sites we could not browse, an industry of censorship is lurking in the fine print: the banning of books in public schools.

According to the First Amendment, citizens of the United States are guaranteed the right to freedom of speech, which also includes the freedom of expression: "Congress shall make no law respecting an establishment of religion, or prohibiting the free exercise thereof; or abridging the freedom of speech, or of the press . . . ." Although rooted in the Constitution, these rights are considered inconvenient by some who would censor the voices of others in order to promote a private agenda.

Greg Barnhisel of Duquesne University observes that book banning is nothing new. Since the advent of the printing press, "society has bemoaned how information or entertainment corrupts the youth and coarsens the intellectual atmosphere." He says that in the early 1800s, "parents fretted about the craze for rebellious Romantic writers like Byron and Goethe that resulted in a rash of faddish suicides of young men imitating the melancholy heroes of literature" (465).

Two centuries later, parents are still the loudest advocates for book censorship. Taking the authority of schools into their own hands, they arrogantly assert that what they think is best for *their* children to read is what is best for *all* children. According to the American Library Association's (ALA) Web site, 10,220 challenges to books were reported between 1990 and 2008. They estimate, however, that for every challenge that is reported, four or five are not. Seventy percent of those challenges were to literature in schools or school libraries, and parents were the initiators fifty-seven percent of the time. The reasons for the challenges ranged from homosexuality to a religious viewpoint.

Gateways to a Better Education, a national organization devoted to promoting Christian values in public schools, envisions them as "learning

1" margin on each side and bottom

Heading appears on first page.

Double-space between title and first line and throughout

Introduces general topic and position

Ellipsis indicates words omitted from quotation

Use of authority

Narrows topic to book banning

Gives sense of history

Identifies opposition and cites statistics

1"

1"

1/2"

1"

1/2"

Last name and page number at right-hand corner of each page

communities enriched by the appropriate and lawful expression of Christian values and ideas." Their Web site continues, "We are making the case that implementing our vision is culturally appropriate, academically legitimate, legally permitted, and morally imperative. ("Our Mission")" But their case is "imperative" only if you share their vision of using the classroom to advocate Christian beliefs. If unchecked, such efforts can blur the separation of church and state, imposing religious ideals on students and parents who may not share those beliefs.

Cites specific opposition group and its position

Claim

In an article on the group's Web site, Gateways spokesperson Eric Buehrer asserts that parents and teachers have the moral obligation to censor the material presented to students: "There are many educators who believe that when parents question something being taught in the classroom, it's meddling. When parents ask to have something removed . . . it's censorship! But, is it? To hear certain groups tell it, you'd conclude that Hitler is alive and well and lurking in the wings of Hooterville High School." While Beuhrer does not advocate the banning of a specific book in his article, he supports and encourages parents who wish to challenge books on a local level.

Quotes opposition

Reasons support author's claim

Denying students access to literature that does not support one individual's religious or moral beliefs is detrimental to the learning process. By questioning the authority of schools, parents are questioning the art of learning itself. Books should be selected based on established academic principles and not on the fulfillment of religious or moral agendas. Censors have criticized many classic, exemplary literary works. John Mark Ockerbloom of "*The Online Books Page*" reports that Mark Twain's *Adventures of Huckleberry Finn*, an infamously banned book, is controversial because it contains the "n" word. In 1998, parents in Arizona filed a lawsuit attempting to remove the book from a high school reading list, and the suit went all the way to the federal appeals court. The court's decision returned the book to the reading list.

Specific evidence

Acknowledges possible objections

Sometimes, in their zeal to protect young readers from offense, even well-intended people miss the point. Literature is created in a context, reflecting the fears and prejudices of the time. Twain did not intend to ridicule African Americans. To the contrary, his work reflected the dialect and prejudice of the book's period. Reading the book, we join Huck Finn on a moral journey that leads him to question and finally reject the accepted—and hypocritical—social institutions of his time. Today we consider the "n" word brutal and insulting, but without it, the book would be less effective in helping us understand our sad history of racism and tolerance for slavery. Excising the word to avoid offense is an odd sort of denial, a way to pretend that people of the time spoke respectfully to those whom they

Specific evidence

O'Neill 3

brutalized. When we remove the word, we are reaching back in time and altering the record of what people said.

Responds to objections

The human body is often the target of challenges and bans. Robert Lipsyte's novel *One Fat Summer,* about an overweight boy who gains self-confidence, was removed from a seventh-grade class in New York because one parent complained about its mention of adolescent sexuality. The teachers in the district, however, praised the book for addressing the difficulties of growing up, and claimed that students enjoyed reading it (Vinciguerra). In fighting to have the book removed, the critic confronted reality and ignored it, asserting in effect that adolescents are unaware of sex—a preposterous notion. Where students benefited from the book's lessons, others peeked beneath the covers and saw something dangerous.

Acknowl-
edges
specific
objections

Responds to
objections

Similarly, *It's Perfectly Normal,* by Robie H. Harris, has made the ALA's top ten list of most frequently challenged books three times since 2003, topping the list once. The association's Web site gives "homosexuality, nudity, sex education, religious viewpoint, abortion, and being unsuited to age group" as the reasons. The message sent by parents who criticize this book is that what their kids are going through during puberty is *not* normal, but is shameful and embarrassing.

Specific
evidence

My Sisters Keeper, by Jodi Picoult, in which a young girl sues her parents over the right to control her own body when they want her to donate an organ to her dying sister, was banned in 2008 in a Michigan school district ("Book Is Banned"). Perhaps parents were threatened by the novel's strong-willed protagonist. Clearly the message being sent is that anything that has to do with our bodies is off limits and inappropriate.

Also under attack are books that have encouraged kids to read—J. K. Rowling's *Harry Potter* series. Number two on the ALA's list of the most frequently challenged books of 2003, the series has also climbed the ladder of success. The fifth in the series, *Harry Potter and the Order of the Phoenix,* had the largest first printing of any work of fiction—8.5 million copies (Rutten). The ALA states that the series has been challenged because of "Satanism."

Specific
evidence

An article on the Christian Web site "*Surf-in-the-Spirit*" cites the Bible and claims that the Harry Potter series persuades children to enjoy the "ungodly practice" of magic. The author asserts that the books promote Satan's goals, which are to "destroy [our children's] lives and condemn their souls. He will surely succeed if parents fall into the trap of believing that these books 'are only a story' and are just innocent evil. . . . This is the worst kind of evil, because it has deceived so many . . . into accepting it" (Smith). People

Acknowl-
edges
opposition
with direct
quotation

O'Neill 4

Parenthetical
reference
have the right to believe that wizardry is Satan's work, but banning the popular series is yet another way of imposing personal beliefs on those who may have a different opinion about magic.

Response to
opposition

Acknowl-
edges other
sources of
censorship
liberals
Conservatives are not alone in promoting censorship; liberals share the affliction. The art of deciding what is politically correct has become its own industry. The English language has been hacked and torn apart in the effort to promote equality, but the result is a disconnection from reality. It seems like nothing is acceptable enough for literature, since both political spectrums endure a conflicting battle.

In her essay "Cut on the Bias," education scholar Diane Ravitch says that the educational publishing industry adheres to specific guidelines that prevent the exposure of controversial words or topics, notably those involving gender, race, religion, or sex. Ravitch compiled a list of over five hundred words that have been banned by publishers, including "landlord," "senior citizen," "yacht," and "actress" (428). "Founding Fathers" is avoided because it is

Use of
authority
supposedly sexist, and a story about animals living in a rotted tree trunk was criticized because it could be offensive to people who live in low-income apartments (Barnhisel 422). It cannot be denied that the country's Founding Fathers were men; the sad fact is that during the establishment of the United States, women were not *considered* capable of running a revolution. Ravitch correctly asserts that the enforcement of politically correct—but

Supports claim
with editorial
cartoon

Fig.1.   "This is acceptable!" cartoon. From Mike Cramer, 26 July 1993.
Illinois Issues. edu. Illinois Issues. 26 July 1993. Web. 6 Feb. 2005.

O'Neill 5

historically inaccurate—language promotes denial and ignorance: "Bowdlerization is not only dishonest, it leads to the dumbing down of language and ideas. And . . . I'm convinced: The widespread censorship of language and ideas in education caused by the demands of advocacy groups will not end unless it is regularly exposed to public review and ridicule" (429).

But for some, censoring books is not enough; they want to destroy them. In 2004, officials at a high school in New York ripped certain pages, deemed inappropriate because of sexuality, from tenth-grade students' copies of Susan Kaysen's *Girl, Interrupted* (Staino). The destruction of books is insulting to anyone who has any respect for literature. In Wisconsin in 2009, a fight between a town library and a group of locals ensued over eighty-two "sexually explicit" books in the young-adult section. When the library refused to move the books in question to the adult section, four disgruntled men filed a suit, asked for financial damages, and called for a novel about a homosexual teenager to be publicly burned because it was "explicitly vulgar, racial and anti-Christian" and it "damaged" their "mental and emotional well-being" (Hanna).

Students at a high school in Florida came close to being denied access to literature that would not only teach them about life in Afghanistan and the impact of war, but also about redemption and forgiveness (Denis). *The Kite Runner*, a highly acclaimed novel by Khaled Hosseini, made the ALA's top ten list of most frequently challenged books of 2008. Their Web site explains that the blame was placed on having "offensive language" and being "sexually explicit" and "unsuited to age group." That year, a parent from the Florida school questioned the novel's appropriateness, but the school board voted to keep the book in the curriculum ("Board Rejects" 2). A sophomore from the school said of the book, "This is . . . the real word. This is what goes on in other countries and it really opens your eyes . . ." (Denis).

Appallingly, students' writing is subject to censorship as well. Jill Rosen explains in her article "High School Confidential" that:

> Yanked newspaper stories, disappointed student journalists and resolute administrators are an unfortunately common part of the high-school expe- rience. Censorship occurs so consistently, so ubiquitously that it's almost clichéd, no more eyebrow-raising than the cafeteria serving mystery meat or a nerd getting books smacked out of his arms in the hallway. (498)

Rosen claims that school administrators can do this because of the Supreme Court's 1988 decision in *Hazelwood School District vs. Kuhlmeier*.

Marginal annotations:

Specific evidence

Quotes authority

Claim with evidence

Specific evidence

Long quotation (more than four lines); left margin indented 1 inch (10 spaces double-space)

Before that case, "papers operated under the premise that a student's right to free speech should only be limited in cases where it could disrupt school or invade the rights of others" (498).

Barnhisel states that censorship is an especially complicated issue in a country as diverse as the United States: "For every George W. Bush fighting for 'family values'. . . there is a Madonna . . . seeking to expand the bounds of what's permissible." He says that standards are "handled by thousands of different people and groups with thousands of different agendas and values and hundreds of ways of enforcing their desires" (471).

If we ban everything that might offend anyone, what is left to write? Books that discuss diversity, our bodies, and the struggles of minorities expose children to life's truths. Senseless and gratuitous violence is woven into television shows, video games, and movies to enhance their popularity, but literature chosen by educators with the intention of making students think is at the center of a crossfire.

Censorship denies reality and creates false worlds in which certain words or actions do not exist. U.S Supreme Court Justice Louis D. Brandeis put it perfectly that "Fear of serious injury alone cannot justify oppression of free speech. . . . Men feared witches and burnt women. It is the function of speech to free men from the bondage of irrational fears" ("Schools and Censorship").

Should parents be concerned about what their children are reading? Of course. The issue is not about parental supervision; it is about efforts to censor reading material to advance a narrow and not necessarily shared agenda. If unchecked, we could find ourselves in a time when it's acceptable for books, like "witches," to be burned.

Margin notes:

Cites authority to support claim

Cites authority to support claim

Cites evidence to support claim

O'Neill 7

Works Cited

ALA.org. American Library Association, 2009. Web. 5 Oct. 2009.

Barnhisel, Greg, ed. *Media and Messages: Strategies and Readings in Public Rhetoric.* New York: Longman, 2005. Print.

"Board Rejects Book Ban." *Brechner Report* 33.4 (2009): 2. Web. 14 Oct. 2009.

"Book Is Banned by Clawson School District." *WXYZ.com.* Scripps TV Station Group, 18 Dec. 2008. Web. 10 Oct. 2009.

Buchanan, Brian J., ed. "About the First Amendment." *Firstamendment center.org.* First Amendment Center, n.d. Web. 12 Oct. 2009.

Buehrer, Eric. "Challenging a Book in Your School." *Gtbe.org.* Gateways to a Better Education, 1998. Web. 5 Oct. 2009.

Denis, Alex. "Parent's Complaint May Get Novel Banned in Schools." *WJHG.com.* Gray Television, 17 Nov. 2008. Web. 8 Oct. 2009.

Hanna, Jason. "Library Fight Riles Up City, Leads to Book-Burning Demand." *CNN.com.* Cable News Network, 22 July 2009. Web. 8 Oct. 2009.

Ockerbloom, John Mark, ed. "Banned Books Online." *The Online Books Page.* U Pennsylvania, 2009. Web. 10 Oct. 2009.

"Our Mission." *Gtbe.org.* Gateways to a Better Education, 2006. Web. 6 Oct. 2009.

Ravitch, Diane. Cut on the Bias." Barnhisel. 428-429.

Rosen, Jill. "High School Confidential." Barnhisel. 496-503.

Rutten, Tim. "It's All Hillary and Harry." *Los Angeles Times.* Los Angeles Times, 18 June 2003. Web. 6 Oct. 2009.

"Schools and Censorship: Banned Books." *Pfaw.org.* People for the American Way, n.d. Web. 11 Oct. 2009.

Smith, Kathy A. "Harry Potter: Seduction into the Dark World of the Occult, Part One." *Surf-in-the-Spirit.* Fill the Void Ministries, 2000. Web. 6 Oct. 2009.

Staino, Rocco. "NY High School Interrupts 'Girl, Interrupted.'" *School Library Journal.* Reed Business Information, 12 Dec. 2008. Web. 8 Oct. 2009.

Twain, Mark. *Adventures of Huckleberry Finn.* Ed. Susan K. Harris. Boston: Houghton Mifflin, 2000. Print.

Vinciguerra, Thomas. "A 1977 Novel Comes under Scrutiny." *New York Times* 8 June 1997, LI ed., sec. 1:3:8. Print.

List is alphabetical by author's last name. Use title if no author. Double-space throughout

Title of books, journals, and newspapers are underlined

Websites are constantly updated. Include date of access.

Website with individual author

‡ 1/2"

Running head: TAPPED OUT   1

Abbreviated
title and
number appear
on each page,
including the
title page.

Tapped Out: Bottled Water's Detrimental Side
Dan Hoskins
Roger Williams University
Professor Goodfellow
ENG 102
November 20, 2009

If your
instructor
requires an
abstract of your
paper, locate it
on the second
page of your
paper.

TAPPED OUT   2

Tapped Out: Bottled Water's Detrimental Side

Less than a generation ago, getting a drink of water was as simple as turning on the kitchen faucet. Over the last two decades, however, bottled water has emerged as a healthier and environmentally friendly alternative. Whether this perception is accurate is a matter currently being scrutinized. But it can be argued that bottled water is not, in fact, more pure than tap water. Furthermore, the disposal of the bottles poses a threat to the environment. Therefore steps should be taken to discourage the use of bottled water.

The rise in the use of bottled water can be attributed to a national health movement that began in the late 1970s. The bottled water conglomerate Nestle Waters claims on its Web site that bottled water products emerged in the late 1970s as "the refreshing alternative to sugary drinks" (Nestle-Waters NA, 2009).

Federal and state legislation passed in the late 1970s and 1980s to ensure the purity of public water sources reflected a growing sense that tap water was polluted and unsafe. In *H2O: The Guide to Quality Bottled Water,* Arthur von Wiesenberger (1988) cites acts such as the Resource Conservation and Recovery Act of 1976 and California's Safe Drinking Water and Toxic Enforcement Act of 1986 as significant initiatives aimed at cleaning up public water supplies. While these acts did contribute to the protection of public water, Wiesenberger claims that they also created the impression that tap water was inherently unsafe, thus paving the way for bottled water as a healthy alternative.

Since the passage of such legislation, bottled water consumption has risen. According to *The Washington Post,* bottled water has replaced juice as America's third most popular drink of choice behind soda and milk (Mui, 2009). Now a staple of the American household, bottled water has over the last 20 years become a multibillion dollar industry, as shown in Figure 1 (Fiberwater, 2009).

This industry has grown primarily on the idea that bottled water is safer and healthier than tap water. The difference in price between bottled water and tap water implies a gap in quality: if it cost more, it must be better, right? Generally, bottled water sells for about one to four dollars per gallon. By comparison, tap water costs 0.003 dollars per gallon (San Francisco Public Utility Commission, 2004). Also suggestive of superiority are marketing images of refreshing streams or picturesque mountain ranges, promoting images of natural wholesomeness and environmental friendliness. In spite of such images, bottled water companies stretch the truth.

Double-space between title and first line and throughout paper.

States proposal

1" margins

Quotes authority

Author is not cited in text, so name and date appear in parentheses

Cites supporting evidence with price comparision

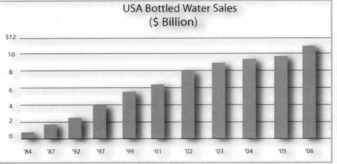

TAPPED OUT   3

Figure 1. Bottled water: The brightest star in the beverage universe. Adapted from Fiberwater.com (2009, October 25).

Includes graph of statistical data as supporting evidence

Governmental agencies regulate both tap and bottled water. The Environmental Protection Agency (EPA) (as well as state and local governments) controls tap water consumption, while the Food and Drug Administration (FDA) handles the safety of bottled water. But it is clear that the EPA, which controls tap water, is a stronger regulatory body than the FDA, which, unfortunately, is limited to inspecting only products that are sold over state borders. Since bottled water conglomerates have distilleries in different states, many a bottled water can slip through the cracks of inspection. Tap water, on the other hand, has no such luxury and thus is held to higher standards than bottled water (San Francisco Public Utility Commission, 2004).

Use of authority as support

Obviously, a difference in inspectors does not necessarily mean that bottled water is contaminated. However, the Web site *Food and Water Watch* (2009) cites a Natural Resources Defense Council investigation of bottled waters that found many to contain bacteria not allowed under the safety guidelines of most United States legislatures. The article, "Bottled Water: Illusions of Purity," states that the investigation tested "more than 1,000 bottles of water of 103 brands" to find that "nearly one in five brands contained, in at least one sample, more bacteria than allowed under microbiological-purity guidelines adopted by some states, the industry, and the European Union" (Food and Water Watch, 2009).

Use of authority as support

In case contaminants in the water are not bad enough, there's the second part of the *bottled* water equation: the bottle. Bottle plastics often

TAPPED OUT   4

contain harmful chemicals, such as phthalates, that can contaminate the
contents. According to "Bottled Water: Illusions of Purity," when heated,
"Phthalates can cause reproductive difficulties, liver problems and increased
risk of cancer" (Food and Water Watch, 2009).

> Use of authority as support

Another false charge is that tap water contains dangerous levels of
lead. Most often cited as the source is the piping through which the water
travels. However, frequent EPA field testing shows that the lead content in tap
water is not potentially harmful. Bottled water, on the other hand, it has been
shown, can carry harmful compounds such as phthalate in both its water and
the bottle carrying it.

> Presents other position
> Refutes other position

Even more damaging than bottled water's effects on the human body
are the cumulative effects on the environment by the production and disposal
of billions of water bottles. In "Message in a Bottle: What a Waste," M. F.
Epstein notes the large number of discarded water bottles littering Boston's
Charles River. He writes that while picking up trash along the river, "the 112
bottles that I picked up are a minute portion of the 3 billion plastic bottles of
water that Americans buy and discard annually" (Epstein, 2009).

> Cites supporting evidence with statistics

If this one section of Boston can have such an epidemic of bottle
littering, one can only imagine the impact on a global scale. While bottled water
does use recyclable plastic, the San Francisco Public Utility Commission points
out that "not all of the containers are recycled and a portion inevitably end up
in the land fill" (2004).

The improper disposal of bottles is one detrimental effect on the
environment. Another is the bottle's actual production. While the plastic used is
of high quality and can be recycled, an article on the Web site
lighterfootsteps.com, "Five Reasons Not to Drink Bottled Water," claims that the
1.5 million tons of plastic used for bottled water each year "requires up to 47
million gallons of oil per year to produce" (Baskind, 2008). Many brands, such
as Fiji, claim their water comes from an exotic location where the water is
natural and untouched by human hands. While this claim may be a promotional
gimmick, the actual transport of bottled water over thousands of miles from
those exotic locations, if a reality, is detrimental in itself. A great deal of carbon
dioxide and other greenhouse gasses are released in the process.

> Reasons supporting proposal

A number of solutions exist for stopping the rising tide of bottled
water and its impact on our health and the environment. The simplest and
most obvious, of course, is to stop buying bottled water. On an individual level,

TAPPED OUT   5

we each can make a difference by refraining from purchasing the product and by helping to recycle and pick up discarded bottles when we see them.

Proposes solution to problem

Reusable aluminum containers, which allow for portable water without the threat of waste, can be purchased at most retailers. If consumers still feel threatened by the rumors surrounding tap water, these aluminum containers can be refilled with water from a household filter. Currently, there are many different types of filters on the market, some of which can be attached to a sink faucet. Aluminum containers and household filters create the same benefits of bottled water—portability and pureness—without the littering.

Acknowledges weakness of proposol

Of course, this personal boycott may only have minor results. But there are larger solutions that can stop bottled water use on a national level. Many Web sites and environmental advocates suggest federal legislation aimed at limiting the sale of bottled water. Short of a national ban, which is highly improbable, the only governmental option to discourage consumption is to legislate a sales tax on bottles.

Implementation of proposol

But how do we address the other problems posed by bottled water—the litter of plastic bottles and carbon emissions? To accomplish these, something larger than expanded FDA regulations would be needed. In conjunction with a sales tax on bottled water there should be a national campaign against bottled water similar to campaigns against tobacco use.

Cites other solutions to problem

Since a number of Web sites, books, and newspaper articles are already discrediting America's dependency on bottled water, this process may have already begun informally. Furthermore, there is at least one film, *Tapped,* that speaks out against the use of bottled water. Some Web sites have propagated a "No Bottled Water Pledge" with signers pledging themselves to end the use of bottled water.

Cites authorities

Is there hope for significant change? Is a campaign against bottled water enough to make Americans forgo the convenience and overcome the notion that tap water is unhealthy? Recent reports suggest there is. While an article in *The Washington Post* suggests decreased sales of bottled water is a result of the current economic recession, other articles note this trend is caused by a backlash against bottled water itself. Robinson-Jacobs (2008) suggests that one of the reasons bottled water sales are suffering is because "Environmentalists are making inroads in their efforts to get consumers back to the tap."

Cites solution to problem

Bottled water sales originally grew out of fears about tap water and an inclination to become healthier. If these motivations to become healthier drove Americans away from the tap, they can certainly drive them back there. Most Americans who drink bottled water are unaware of the negative consequences. But as this message is distributed, bottled water sales are more than likely going to decrease. As such, it is important to do our part by spreading the word that bottled water is not good for our health or our environment.

One Web site, fakeplasticfish.com, goes so far to suggest that readers write to President Obama asking him to set an example as our nation's leader and stop his consumption of bottled water. The Web site has even dug up some rather unglamorous shots of him drinking bottled water at a press conference (Terry, 2009). An Obama-supported boycott on bottled water could be quite effective in diminishing bottled water sales.

Cites solution to problem

However, whether you are the president of the United States or just a lowly undergraduate student like myself, you too can aid in the fight against bottled water. Remember that tap water, while dirt cheap, is not necessarily dirty. Keeping these ideas in mind, small steps can be taken to help protect our health.

Conclusion

References

Baskind, C. (2008, May 11). Five reasons not to drink bottled water. *Lighter Footsteps.* Retrieved from http://lighterfootstep.com/ 2008/05/five-reasons-not-to-drink-bottled-water/

Robinson-Jacobs, K. (2008, October 31). Bottled water sales growth slow to trickle. *Dallas Morning News.* Retrieved from http:// www.dallasnews.com/

Epstein, M. F. (2009, October 7). Message in a bottle: What a waste. *The Boston Globe.* Retrieved from http://www.boston.com

Fiberwater. (2009, October 25). Bottled water: The brightest star in the beverage universe. Retrieved from http://www. fiberwater.com/industry_bwi.php

Begin first line of each citation at left margin.

Indent all subsequent lines five spaces from left margin.

TAPPED OUT   8

Food and Water Watch. (2009, October 24). Bottled water: Illusions
        of purity. Retrieved from http://www.foodandwaterwatch.
        org/water/bottled/bottled-water-illusions-of-purity

Mui, Y. Q. (2009, August 13). Bottled water boom appears tapped
        out. *Washington Post*. Retrieved from http://www.
        washingtonpost.com

Nestle-Waters NA. (2009, October 25). *History of bottled water*.
        Retrieved from http://www.nestle-
        watersna.com/popup.aspx?w=600&h=400&f=/NR/rdonlyres/E
        40D0A10-2D3F-415A-A8E4-7503B9DBBF27/693/timeline.swf

San Francisco Public Utility Commission. (2004, April). Bottled water
        vs. tap water: Making a healthy choice. Retrieved from http://
        www.dph.sf.ca.us/phes/water/FactSheets/bottled_water.pdf

Terry, B. (2009, July 9). Bottled water problem: It's not just the bottle.
        Fake Plastic Fish. Retrieved from http://fakeplasticfish.com/
        2009/07/bottled-water-problem-its-not-just/

Wiesenberger, A. von. (1988). *H2O: The guide to quality bottled
        water*. Santa Barbara, CA: Woodbridge Press.

Capitalize
the first
letter of
titles and
subtitles.

Credits

Image Credits

Page 207: Pablo Picasso/Museo Nacional Centro de Arte Reina Sofia, Madrid, Spain/Art Resource. © 2009 Estate of Pablo Picasso/Artists Rights Society (ARS), New York; Page 210: Printed by permission of the Norman Rockwell Family Agency. Copyright © 1943, the Norman Rockwell Family Entities; Page 215: Courtesy Toyota Motors North America, Dentsu America; Page 217: "FRESH STEP" is a registered trademark of The Clorox Pet Products Company. Used with Permission. © The Clorox Pet Products Company. Reprinted with permission; Page 219: Courtesy of ForestEthics/Half-Full; Page 222: By permission of Mike Luckovich and Creators Syndicate, Inc.; Page 224: Courtesy of Pat Bagley; Page 225: Daryl Cagle, MSNBC.com/Cagle Cartoons; Page 226: Larry Downing/Reuters/Landov; Page 228: Suzanne Kreiter/Boston Globe/Landov; Page 239: David Bunting; Page 282: Courtesy of Mike Cramer

Text Credits

Arthur Allen. "Prayer in Prison: Prison: Religion as Rehabilitation." Reprinted with permission by the author.

Stephanie Bower. "What's the Rush? Speed and Mediocrity in Local TV News." Reprinted with permission by the author.

Danise Cavallaro. "Smoking: Offended by the Numbers." Reprinted with permission by the author.

Amanda Collins. "Bring East Bridgewater Elementary into the World." Reprinted with permission by the author.

Joel Epstein. "Parental Notification: Fact or Fiction?" from *Prevention File*, Vol. 14, No. 2. Reprinted with permission of the publisher.

Jerry Fensterman. "I See Why Others Choose to Die," from *The Boston Globe*, January 31, 2006. Reprinted with permission by the author's widow, Lisa Bevilaqua.

Sean Flynn. "Is Anything Private Anymore?" from *Parade Magazine*, September 16, 2007. © 2007 Sean Flynn. All rights reserved.

Dan Hoskins. "Tapped Out: Bottled Water's Detrimental Side." Reprinted with permission by the author.

Lee Innes. "A Double Standard of Olympic Proportion." Reprinted with permission by the author.

Derrick Jackson. Let's Ban All Flavors of Cigarettes," from *The Boston Globe*, September 30, 2009.

Michael Lewis. "The Case Against Tipping," from the *New York Times*, Tipping" September 23, 1997. Reprinted with permission from the author.

Shannon O'Neil. "Literature Hacked and Torn Apart: Censorship in Public Schools." Reprinted with permission by the author.

Stephen Pinker. "Why They Kill Their Newborns," from *The New York Times Sunday Magazine*, November 2, 1997. Reprinted with permission by the author.

S. Fred Singer. "The Great Global Warming Swindle," from *The San Francisco Examiner*, May 22, 2007. Reprinted with permission by the author.

Henry Wechsler. "Binge Drinking Must Be Stopped," from *The Boston Globe*, October 2, 1997. Reprinted with permission by the author.

Index

Page numbers followed by an f refer to figures.